An Introduction to Sociology

Feminist perspectives

SECOND EDITION

- Pamela Abbott
- Claire Wallace

ROUTLEDGE

First published 1997
by Routledge
11 New Fetter Lane, London EC4P 4EE

Simultaneously published in the USA and
Canada
by Routledge
29 West 35th Street, New York, NY 10001

Transferred to Digital Printing 2003

Typeset in Times and Futura by Keystroke,
Jacaranda Lodge, Wolverhampton
Printed in Great Britain by
Biddles Short Run Books, King's Lynn

*British Library Cataloguing in Publication
Data*
A catalogue record for this book is
available from the British Library

*Library of Congress Cataloging in
Publication Data*
Abbott, Pamela.
    An introduction to sociology:
    feminist perspectives/
    Pamela Abbott and Claire Wallace.
    — 2nd ed.
        p.   cm.
    Includes bibliographical references and
index.
    1. Sociology–Philosophy.
    2. Sociology–Methodology.
    3. Feminist theory.
    I. Wallace, Claire.
II. Title.
HM24.A215 1996
301'.01—dc20   95–49777

ISBN 0–415–12292–9

Contents

Tables

Preface

Five years after the first edition of *An Introduction to Sociology: Feminist Perspectives* we are writing the second edition. During this time the debates within feminism and within sociology have moved on. Debates about postmodernism, about sexuality, about 'race', about the body and about culture have begun to dominate the feminist agenda, displacing to some extent more traditionally sociological preoccupations with work, family and stratification. The original text embodied the argument that an appreciation of society from a women's perspective leads to a recasting of traditional sociological distinctions between, for example, work and the family or between crime and sexuality. Now the blossoming of Gender/Women's Studies within higher education has led to a recasting of former boundaries between disciplines as well as within them. Much of the material in the first edition remains relevant, but we have brought the statistical data up to date and included material on new debates and issues.

One important debate which has developed since we wrote the first edition is that some writers, influenced by postmodernist perspectives, have challenged the view that a unitary category 'woman' exists at all. Our own position is that while there are important differences in women's experience, there are also important commonalities; while acknowledging the contributions postmodernist scholars have made to the study of gender, we nevertheless argue that sociology as a critical discipline can help to elucidate women's position and that feminist sociology still has an important contribution to make – one that is by no means universally recognised.

Some of the criticisms we made of malestream sociology have now in the main been taken on board by sociologists, but feminist arguments still tend to be ignored or marginalised in many areas. Although feminism has had more of an impact in sociology than in many other disciplines, it is still the case that the reconceptualisation of the discipline which we argue that accepting the feminist critique entails has not taken place in many texts and research projects. Despite the proliferation of feminist studies over the last twenty years in sociology, their impact has been uneven. Our book still stands as the one feminist commentary and corrective to the other introductory textbooks in sociology.

The first edition of the textbook was written from a British perspective – we were British sociologists who had spent our working lives in Britain and were reporting British research. However, the textbook has been used in many countries of the world and translated into Chinese and Korean. Moreover, the mood within British sociology over the last five years has been towards becoming less ethnocentric. To take account of the wider readership and the shift in British thought we have therefore introduced a more comparative perspective. This is by necessity centred on European and Anglo-Saxon material, however, because of the lack of easily accessible materials from elsewhere in the world: the text should therefore be read as one about women's position in core capitalist counties, with a particular focus on Britain.

This book, intended for students and the general reader interested in understanding the feminist contribution to sociology, provides an introduction to feminist perspectives in sociology that stands on its own or can be used in conjunction with more conventional introductory textbooks. For those readers who want to incorporate feminist perspectives into their sociological understanding we suggest reading the appropriate chapter in this book after reading the corresponding chapter of a conventional textbook. The chapters in this book do not have to be read in the order in which they are written. We would suggest that you read Chapters 1 and 2 first. After that, you can follow your own interests or read the relevant chapters in line with the sequencing of the syllabus that you are following.

We are not presenting this as a 'true' account of social reality, nor do we see ourselves as neutral scientists merely recounting the work of sociologists and feminists. Sociology textbooks have been criticised for being biased and leaving out key areas of sociological concern (see Marsland, 1988, and correspondence in *Network*, the newsletter of the British Sociological Association – particularly issues dated October 1987 and June and July 1988). Indeed, we are ourselves critical of sociology textbooks because of the ways in which they have marginalised feminist knowledge. We write this book as two feminists who argue that malestream research has ignored, distorted and marginalised women and that feminists are concerned to reconceptualise the production of knowledge. All knowledge is partial and provisional, and this applies as much to feminist as to malestream knowledge. However, feminist knowledge takes account of the experiences of women as women. It starts from the position that in modern Britain women are subordinated and that it is necessary to explain this subordination in order that women can be liberated. We take this as a truth, as the starting point, not something that needs to be proved. Feminism is not one theoretical perspective within sociology, but a political movement concerned with furthering the cause of women's liberation. However, feminist knowledge has made an important contribution to sociology and has challenged the basic theoretical assumptions of malestream work, arguing that sociological theories, methods and explanations need to be reconceptualised. It is with these arguments that we are concerned in this book.

Feminism is not a unified movement. While all feminists are agreed that women are subordinated and that it is necessary to develop strategies to liberate them, there are fundamental disagreements about the causes of that oppression and the strategies for achieving liberation. There are even disagreements about what the feminist project is about and indeed, what women are! There is a large number of feminisms. In this book we have tried to describe some of the main theories of relevance to sociology, but this inevitably means that some – such as psychoanalysis, which has made a great contribution to the understanding of women's experience – have been left out.

This problem of distinguishing between different feminist perspectives is not just an academic one, but a personal one. We have to try to identify *ourselves* as well. In the last edition we described ourselves as marxist feminists who had evolved into socialist feminists – feminists who saw class and gender as carrying equal weight. This affected our interpretation of material used in the book. We have since then been influenced by the post-structuralist and postmodernist debates criticising modernity and associated theories – including those of Marxism and socialism. Our position would now be a rather more eclectic one; while still seeing the need to take a critical perspective on society, on sociology and on the 'woman question', we are inclined to work more from a diversity of theoretical perspectives, arguing that all of them contribute to our understanding of what is going on. It is understanding rather than purity of theory that is of crucial importance. This book is therefore centrally a contribution to documenting how feminist sociology can enable us the better to understand our social lives.

It is important that you, the reader, be aware of our position. We do not feel that it is possible for us to detach ourselves from our theoretical perspectives and become neutral reporters of other feminists' arguments and research findings. This is of course what we are *trying* to do – but it is important that you are aware that we are not neutral, nor is it possible for anyone to be neutral. This lack of neutrality is especially important for you, the reader, to keep in mind when we are evaluating the adequacy of other women's work.

We hope you will enjoy reading this book and learn much from it. We have learned much from writing it and enjoyed the process of production. Feminism and sociology are not academic subjects that are just to be learned, but ways of coming to understand the society in which we live and our position in it. We hope that this book will stimulate you to look at the world afresh and come to new insights.

Acknowledgements

We should like to acknowledge the help that Roger Sapsford has given us at every stage of the production of both editions. We should also like to thank our students at various universities, who inspired us to write this book and helped with the discussion of its ideas. We alone, of course, remain responsible for the contents.

Chapter one

Introduction: Feminist critiques of malestream sociology, and the way forward

Setting the agenda

Sociology remains a male-dominated discipline, and this has fundamental implications for its theories, methods, research and teaching. Despite some thirty years' criticism of the discipline for its malestream orientation and bias, much remains the same (Stanley and Wise 1993). While the majority of students taking the subject are women, a majority of lecturers are male. Women are less often found in the senior posts in the discipline, and women are taught 'malestream' sociology – that is, they are inducted into knowledge that plays a key role in justifying the inferior structural position of (the majority of) women in modern British society. Ann Oakley suggested in 1974 that

> male orientation may so colour the organisation of sociology as a discipline that the invisibility of women is a structured male view, rather than a superficial flaw. The male focus, incorporated into the definitions of subject areas, reduces women to a side issue from the start.
>
> (Oakley, 1974b, p. 4)

However, there has been some progress. Sociologists can no longer afford to ignore women and gender divisions, and there is discussion about the changes needed for the malestream bias to be overcome. There has been a steady flow of books published by women writing from feminist perspectives in sociology, and most academic social science publishers have a Feminist, Gender or Women's Studies list. However, much sociological research continues to focus on men and boys and to ignore women and girls or to incorporate women but without modifying the theories that justified their subordinate status. There is still a tendency, albeit a declining one, to generalise from male samples to the whole population, for textbooks to 'add women on' as an appendix – an extra topic or chapter – rather than fully incorporating research findings on women in each substantive area, and for feminist perspectives to be seen as an addendum deserving at most one or two lectures or something that can safely be left for women to teach as an option course. The very success of this textbook indicates that there has been a demand for an alternative perspective. It is now the case that in Britain and the USA few courses in sociology could be designed without at least some recognition of feminist perspectives, while journal articles and research designs are routinely required by their reviewers to problematise gender, or to include a gender perspective. Indeed, in the Anglo–American cultures feminist perspectives are more developed and more influential in sociology than in most other social science disciplines. Sociology nevertheless remains a male-dominated discipline, and in many other parts of the world a gender perspective is marginalised, missing or (as in the former Communist countries) treated with outright hostility.

Within Western sociology we can identify a number of malestream responses/defences to feminist sociology – at one extreme ghettoisation, and at the other, colonisation and theft.

By ghettoisation we mean the marginalisation of feminist sociology as something the female lecturers can do or that can be taught on Women's Studies courses. While gender divisions may be accepted as important, gender is added on as another variable along with class and race; the serious challenge posed by feminists to malestream theories is ignored or distanced. In the main, men do not teach on these courses – possibly because they are not seen as prestigious or likely to lead to promotion (Richardson and Robinson, 1994).

At the other extreme we find colonisation and theft – the development of male studies and the argument that men need to study men in a way analogous to the way in which women have argued the need to study women (see, e.g., Brod, 1987; Hearn and Morgan, 1990; Seidler, 1989). Seidler (1994), for example, has argued that issues of gender and masculinity are now central to social theory. Dianne Richardson and Victoria Robinson (1994) suggest that the development of male studies may actually enable men to avoid taking seriously the key issues about masculinity that feminists have highlighted. They point out that men's studies is mainly concerned with masculine subjectivity rather than with research that would provide a greater understanding of how men gain, maintain and use power to subordinate women. Indeed, men's studies is conceived as concerned with liberating men (Seidler, 1994). As Jalna Hanmer has suggested,

> To conceive of the study of men to be about liberating men is to have little interest in any area of social analysis that seriously critiques men as men, as part of the problem, not just to women and each other but to society and our continuation as a species.
>
> (Hanmer, 1990, p. 29)

The other move has been to rename Women's Studies or to develop new courses entitled 'Gender Studies'. Indeed, some publishers have changed the name of their list from Women's Studies to Gender Studies (Richardson and Robinson, 1994). Similarly some courses have been retitled Gender Studies rather than Women's Studies. In some (many) cases this has not changed the content of courses – the concern has been to recognise that feminist research and theorising are not just on women and for women but must include an analysis of women in relationship to men, and that if women are to be liberated men must change. However, in others the change involves the notion that it is as important to study men as women, and fails to recognise the ways in which malestream disciplines, including sociology, have been implicated in the subordination of women. As Richardson and Robinson point out, the move towards gender studies 'represents a de-radicalisation of women's studies, taking the heat off patriarchy' (1994, p. 25). The danger is that the key insights and challenges to malestream sociology made by feminists will be diluted. The key issue for feminists is not that gender divides – that differences between men and women need to be taken seriously – but that the subordination and exploitation of women (albeit recognising differences and divisions *between* women) need to be explained and overcome. In other words, an awareness needs to be maintained that the subjectivity of women has to be understood in a structural relationship with men – a relationship of subordination and exploitation.

The feminist challenge to malestream sociology is one that requires a radical rethinking of the content and methodology of the whole enterprise, one that recognises the need to see society from the position of women as well as from the standpoint of men – to see the world as fundamentally gendered. Indeed, it is the feminist challenge to sociology that has been instrumental in triggering the now almost taken-for-granted understanding that there is a variety of standpoints – gendered, racialised, disabled, sexualised, aged – that need to be recognised; we need not only to deconstruct 'human' into men and women, but also to deconstruct these categories themselves.

Thus many of the criticisms we have made above apply as much, if not more, to questions of ethnicity. Sociology is a discipline that has been and is dominated by white males who are middle-class by destination if not by origin. Women have come into the discipline and challenged the blinkered view of malestream sociology, but they too have tended to be white. Racialised women have criticised many white feminist sociologists for their one-sided view; racialised people are even more under-represented in the discipline than white women. Acutely aware of this, we have attempted to incorporate material on racialisation and ethnic divisions and to explore theories which have tried to analyse these processes. Other forms of diversity have also emerged as important – differences based upon age, upon disability, upon sexuality. These other forms of social division – of oppression and disadvantage – have emerged partly as a result of the space created by a feminist politics. In Chapter 3 we explore accounts of these differences and how to explain them.

In this book we examine the contribution that feminists have made and are making to sociology. We are concerned with helping the reader to understand the society in which we live, and for this reason we concentrate mainly on modern Britain. We have not aimed to provide an exhaustive overview of all the contribution of female sociologists to the theories and methodologies of sociology, nor a summary of all empirical research findings. Rather, we have selected material that enables us to demonstrate the contribution that feminism has made. As soon as we take the feminist criticisms of malestream sociology seriously we realise that we need to ask new, different questions and that in order to answer them we need to develop new tools, new concepts and new theories. This is because malestream sociology has in the main seen women's roles as natural and therefore not investigated or problematised them; sociology's tools, concepts and theories have been developed to investigate the public world of men and are inadequate for investigating the world that women inhabit and the relationships between men and women. Questions such as 'Why don't men care for children?', 'Why do men and not women have leisure?', become key issues to be researched and explained. Concepts such as social class are seen to be inadequate as theorised in malestream research (see Chapter 3), and the methods used in malestream research are seen to be inadequate for investigating women's lives (see Chapter 11).

Britain is increasingly integrated into Europe and more European material is becoming available. We have therefore tried to include comparative material where possible, including some comparison between Eastern and Western Europe. Although some issues – such as women's oppression within the family – are as important in other parts of the world as in Britain, they are often treated differently. Hence, although domestic violence is usually a consequence of women failing to fulfil their wifely duties, just what these wifely duties are can vary considerably throughout the world. In some countries women may be attacked because their families failed to supply them with the full dowry, whereas in other countries women are attacked for failing to cook or clean or manage the housekeeping budget adequately. Many of the issues are the same. In Eastern Europe women were not liberated by their entry into the working world, although Western feminists had seen this as the road to independence. However, in order to understand why women are disadvantaged in the work force under both Communism and capitalism we need to use feminist perspectives.

We have mainly referred to British research and British statistics in the book, since Britain can be seen as a case study for understanding women's position in late modern society. Readers in other parts of the world will need to read the text with this understanding in mind.

The sociological imagination

Sociology is about understanding the relationship between our own experiences and the social structures we inhabit. However, in the 1960s and 1970s women began to express the feeling that sociology did not relate to their experiences, because it examined the world only from the perspective of men. Indeed, existing theories and explanations could be challenged, they argued, if the perspective of women was also taken into account. The realisation of this failure of sociology to speak to the experiences of women, and its consequent failure to theorise comprehensively, led feminists to examine more closely why this was the case – why sociology, despite its claims to neutrality, had a malestream bias. Dorothy Smith (1979) argued that this was because women's concerns and experiences were not seen as authentic, but subjective, while men's were seen as the basis for the production of true knowledge. Consequently, sociological knowledge portrayed women as men saw them, not as they saw themselves. Sociology also played a key role in maintaining women's subordinate and exploited position. While sociology claimed to put forward a detached and impartial view of reality, in fact it put forward a view from the perspective of men.

It has been argued that women are relegated by political theory, by sociology and within other disciplines to a more 'natural' role, one tied to their biology and to nature, while men are seen as more part of the cultural life of society – cultured man/natural woman. French feminists have argued that women constitute the 'Other' against which culture, society, men and so on are constructed. Thus women are gendered but men are not. Men are seen as part of universal rationality – those who analyse and understand the world from a scientific perspective – and women are the ones who need explaining or 'bringing in'. Arguments for the special perspective and understanding of women often reinforce this point of view. Women are seen as subject to a special perspective which is rooted in the unique experiences of their bodies, of motherhood and menstruation, which are different from that of men. Some feminists have therefore argued that differences between men and women are rooted in the biological differences of bodily development, while others argue that differences between men and women are a cultural construction. We would prefer to argue that gendering is a process whereby jobs, activities and people are 'sexualised' just as they can become 'racialised'; biological differences are used *post hoc* to justify subordination and exploitation and are not the *basis* of the original differentiation. This is not a fixed process but is culturally and socially variable, so that to be understood it needs to be subjected to sociological analysis.

Feminist critiques of conventional sociology

Feminists have made a number of criticisms of sociology:

1 that sociology has been mainly concerned with research on men and by implication with theories for men;
2 that research findings based on all-male samples are generalised to the whole of the population;
3 that areas and issues of concern to women are frequently overlooked or seen as unimportant;
4 that when women are included in research they are presented in a distorted and sexist way;
5 that sex and gender are seldom seen as important explanatory variables;
6 that when sex and gender are included as variables they are just added on, ignoring the fact that the explanatory theories used are ones which have justified the subordination and exploitation of women.

In summary, sociology has been seen as at best sex-blind and at worst sexist. That is, there is at best no recognition that women's structural position and consequent experiences are not the same as men's and that sex is therefore an important explanatory variable; and at worst women's experiences are deliberately ignored or distorted. Furthermore, the ways in which men dominate and subordinate women are either ignored or seen as natural.

Ann Oakley (1982) has suggested that there are three explanations for this sexism in sociology:

1   that sociology has been biased from its origin;
2   that sociology is predominantly a male profession; and
3   that the 'ideology of gender' results in the world being constructed in particular ways and in assumptions being made about how we explain differences between men and women.

It is evident that these three factors are interrelated. Sexist assumptions were built into sociology from its origins and these still underlie sociological theory and research. Sociology as a discipline developed in the nineteenth century, and sociologists were concerned with understanding political and economic changes (including liberal theory, with its emphasis on the individual), capitalism and the consequent class relationships that developed, and the impact they had on people's lives. These changes included the growth of factory production, new class divisions and relationships, the growth of a politically conscious (male) working class and the extension of political participation to more of the adult (male) population. A central aspect of this process for women was the increased separation of home from work, the separation of production from consumption and reproduction, and the development of an ideology that 'a woman's place is in the home'. Women became increasingly associated with the domestic (private) sphere of the home and domestic relationships, and men with the public sphere of politics and the market-place.

Sociologists concentrated on the public sphere of government and the work-place and ignored the private sphere of the home and domestic relationships. This was at least in part because the division of labour between the public sphere (men) and the private sphere (women), was seen as natural – that is, as having a biological basis. The biologist Charles Darwin indicated that

> The chief distinction in the intellectual powers of the two sexes is shown by man attaining to a higher eminence, in whatever he takes up, than woman can attain – whether requiring deep thought, reason, or imagination, or . . . the use of the senses and the hands.
>
> (Darwin, 1871)

This meant that there was no reason for sociology to explain gender divisions; it accepted biology as explanation and therefore had no need to consider gender as an explanatory variable or to theorise the subordination and domination of women. Women were consequently 'hidden' from the sociological gaze, both theoretically and empirically.

Sociology has ignored not just women, but the whole private sphere of domestic relationships; areas of interest to women have not been theorised and researched. Furthermore, sociology has failed to develop analytical tools that can be used to understand the public and the private sphere and the changing relationships between the two. While men have been seen as inhabiting both spheres and indeed as mediating between the two, women have been seen as inhabiting the private sphere, even when they have paid employment outside the home. Consequently, explanations for men's attitudes and behaviour are generally based on their position in the public world (social class), while women's are explained by reference to their role in the private sphere as wives and mothers and by their biology. Men are frequently said to influence the behaviour of their wives, while women are rarely seen as influencing their husbands (see Chapters 3 and 10).

Feminists have argued that theories and research that ignore the experiences of over half the population and the private sphere of domestic relationships are not just inadequate, but sexist. What is needed is a sociology that investigates and theorises these areas and treats the sex/gender system as important along with class, ethnicity, 'race', disability and age. While sociologists have characterised as inadequate or wrong the theories that account, for example, for class divisions, crime, educational success or failure, on the basis of biological differences, they have continued to accept them for explaining women's role in the domestic sphere. Feminists challenge this.

The feminist challenge has meant that, at least in Anglo-Saxon sociology, women's perspective is seen as more important now than it was in the past. We can identify some areas of sociology where feminist perspectives have not been recognised, some areas where there has been some impact and some areas which have been reconstructed.

1 *Areas of sociology where feminist perspectives have not in the main been incorporated*: social class and stratification, the sociology of transformation in East–Central Europe, nationalism, social theory.

2 *Areas of sociology where feminist perspectives have made a significant impact*: the sociology of health and illness, the sociology of the family, the sociology of the professions, the sociology of work, the sociology of education, the sociology of crime and deviance, the sociology of age and the life course.

3 *Areas of sociology which have been constructed anew or totally reconstructed from feminist perspectives*: sexuality and the body, identity and difference, visual and cultural sociology, the sociology of community care.

Ideologies of masculinity and femininity

Malestream sociological theories underpin and justify the subordination and exploitation of women by men, while claiming to be 'factual'. Feminists argue that malestream theories in fact fail to meet the criteria for being accepted as adequate and valid knowledge because they are both objectionable and mistaken. They in fact serve as an ideological justification for the subordinate position of women.

By 'ideology' we mean a pattern of ideas (common-sense knowledge) – both factual and evaluative – which purports to explain and legitimate the social structure and culture of a social group or society and which serves to justify social actions which are in accordance with that pattern of ideas. Ideology also shapes our everyday feelings, thoughts and actions. However, the knowledge provided by an ideology is partial or selective and sometimes provides contradictory descriptions and explanations of the social world. Ideologies, especially dominant ones, also serve to construct certain aspects of the social world as natural and universal and therefore unquestionable and unchangeable. Aspects of the social world that are created as natural and universal by an ideology are thereby protected from the charge of being socially produced. There is a number of ideologies of masculinity and femininity which do not necessarily present consistent accounts but cohere together to form a 'dominant ideology'. A dominant ideology is more easily able to present its ideas as natural and universal because it is produced and reproduced by those in a position of power. The exclusion of women from positions of power and from the production of knowledge has, feminists argue, meant that male ideology has been able to present itself as universal knowledge. However, feminists have challenged and continue to challenge male (patriarchal) ideologies – that is, ideas that support male supremacy – arguing that they are partial and distorting, but because men are in the positions of power they are able to marginalise feminist knowledge.

Ideology as we are using the term, then, is seen as made up of a set of common-sense beliefs, practical knowledge – that is, it forms the basis for action. For example, familial ideologies present the nuclear family – of mother, father and dependent children living as a household, with the man as economic provider and the woman as carer in the domestic sphere – as a natural (biologically based) and universal institution. Alternative styles of living are represented as deviations because they try to change that which is inevitable. However, ideologies conceal the fact that they are socially constructed and benefit some groups more than others. The nuclear family, with a gendered division of labour, has served the interests of men as well as capitalist development (see Chapters 2, 6 and 8).

However, ideologies have changed and continue to do so, and they can be opposed by subordinate social groups. Feminists challenge and oppose patriarchal ideologies by demonstrating their partial and distorted view of the world. Feminists then seek to replace inadequate patriarchal ideologies by more adequate, more comprehensive knowledge. Patriarchal ideologies have the effect of disguising the actuality of male power. Men defined themselves as powerful because of their ability to master nature – to be dominant. Women, because of their biological role in reproduction, are defined as being closer to nature than men, thus justifying their domination by men. Male ideology confirms and reinforces men's dominant status by devaluing women's work and reproductive functions while at the same time presenting male work as of cultural importance and as necessary. Masculinity (man) is equated with the public sphere; to be a man is to be a person who does important things outside the domestic sphere – who does man's work.

In some countries of Eastern and Central Europe, all women were compelled to work in the public sphere in the same way as men. However, this did not 'liberate' them in the way that Marxists and socialists assumed that it would, because of the patriarchal division of labour which continued in the home and the patriarchal assumptions which pervaded the workplace and public life (see Chapter 10). Therefore it is not simply a question of changing laws and putting women in the same position as men which can change their situation. What is needed is an understanding of the structures of power and the way in which the sex/gender system forms part of it. This means an understanding of the private as well as the public sphere from a feminist perspective.

Feminists have challenged the notion that biology is destiny. They have argued that biological differences between men and women do not explain their social roles and that these need to be understood as socially constructed or in need of sociological explanation. While there may be anatomical differences between boys and girls, what is important is the way these are per-ceived, the way boys and girls are socialised into what is seen as appropriate gender behaviour, and what behaviour is valued. That is, parents, teachers and society in general both treat boys and girls differently and have different expectations as to how they should behave. The expected behaviour of boys and girls is both encouraged and reinforced by the adults with whom they come into contact and the institutions of which they are members. Thus television programmes and school reading schemes both show appropriate role models. Boys and girls who do not conform to the appropriate role model are both chastised and ridiculed by adults and by their peers. Boys who display what are seen as feminine traits are referred to as 'wimps', and girls who behave in masculine ways as 'tomboys'. While some girls may actually welcome being referred to as tomboys, boys dislike being called cissies, which is seen as a term of derision; boys and young men act to avoid any notion that they have what may be seen as female traits (see, e.g., Willis, 1977).

However, historical and anthropological research suggests that what is seen as an appropriate role for men and women is specific to particular societies, or social strata within societies, at particular times (Oakley, 1972). Different societies have different images of what is appropriate behaviour for males and females, and these have also differed over time in our own society. There are important differences in the way in which gender roles are defined even within any given society either at different points in history or between social and ethnic groups. Female sexuality, for example, can be seen as a source of untrammelled libido at one point in time or by one social group and as completely missing in other social groups or at other points in time. In the nineteenth century in Britain and the USA, for example, white women were seen as having no sexual desires at all, while Black women were seen as uncontrollably promiscuous. While working-class women were required to work long hours in paid employment, middle-class women were excluded from paid employment on the grounds of their 'biological weakness'. Explanations based on biological differences or biological factors are therefore inadequate. It is necessary for sociology to develop theories that are adequate both for explaining gender divisions and for taking account of gender differences.

Sex has been seen as separate from gender: while 'sex' refers to the biological differences between males and females, 'gender' is used as a way of understanding the cultural and social construction of roles appropriate to men and women. However, post-structuralist and postmodernist perspectives within feminism questioned the sex/gender distinction. They have argued instead that, just as 'gender' is a social construct, so is 'sex' – in other words, that sex is used as a justification for the subordination of a group, rather than providing any basis for social differentiation.

Postmodernist feminists also emphasise the differences between women, and resist dividing the world into simplistic categories from which interests are supposed to derive. Thus simple divisions between 'black' and 'white' or 'male' and 'female' are not sufficient – we need, they argue, to take into account the complex cross-cutting divisions based upon a variety of identities and divisions. This means, however, as Susan Bordo (1990) argues, that an endless process of fragmentation starts to take place from which any viewpoint is impossible.

A sociology for women: the way forward

Feminists are not agreed on what is required to fill the gaps in existing theory and research in sociology. We would suggest that there have been three broad responses:

1   integration;
2   separatism; and
3   reconceptualisation.

We will deal with each of these in turn.

Integration

This position sees the main problem as being the sexist bias in malestream sociology. The task is seen as being to remove this bias by reforming existing ideas and practices in sociology, to bring women in and thereby to fill in the existing gaps in our knowledge. The way forward is to carry out research that incorporates women in samples and to reform existing theories by removing sexism.

The major problem with this approach is that women are likely to continue to be marginalised. They will become merely an addition to the syllabus and lip service will be paid to incorporating women in research samples. Moreover, it leaves the basis of the discipline untouched, fails to challenge the assumption that the discipline is scientific, and does not take into account feminist criteria of what counts as knowledge. For example, this approach would leave unchallenged malestream assumptions about the division between the public and the domestic, about the primacy of paid work, about class being the fundamental division in society, and so on. Possibly most serious of all, it fails to recognise that gender is not just a variable of differentiation, but that men subordinate and exploit women and that sociology as a discipline has played a role in justifying that exploitation of women by men.

Separatism

This position argues that what is needed is a sociology *for* women *by* women. Feminists should not be concerned with trying to change the biases of existing sociology, but with developing a sociology knowledge which is specifically by and about women. Explicit recognition is given to the fact that the world is always seen from a particular position or site and that women's perceptions are different from men's. Furthermore, gender is seen as the primary division in society; all women share a common position because they are both exploited and dominated by men. Feminist scholarship should be concerned with developing theories and carrying out research on women that is of benefit to women.

The problem of this approach is that it perpetuates the marginality of women. Malestream sociology can get on with the 'real' theorising and research and continue to ignore women and feminist perspectives. Furthermore, feminist knowledge would not benefit from potentially valuable inputs from conventional sociology. Finally, by ignoring men, important aspects of women's social reality would be ignored, including the ways in which men exploit, dominate and subordinate women in the public and the private spheres. Any analysis of women's oppression must analyse the role played in this by men.

Reconceptualisation

This position recognises the need for sociological research by women and for women, the notion that women have a different point of view from men and that it is essential that there be a sociology constructed from the position of women. It recognises that it is necessary for women to carry out research on men and boys as well as women and girls and acknowledges that malestream sociological theories and research findings can have an impact on feminist sociology as well as *vice versa*.

However, it rejects the view that all that is needed is to integrate feminist sociology into existing sociological theory and research findings – that is, as it were, to fill in the gaps in our knowledge and to tinker with the edges of existing theories. Instead it is seen as necessary to reconceptualise sociological theories – a total rethinking, rather than partial reform, is necessary. This is both because existing theories are sexist beyond reform by mere tinkering, and because feminist research actually challenges assumptions and generalisations made from malestream research. What is needed is a total and radical reformulation of sociology so that it is able to incorporate women adequately.

The major problem is that many malestream sociologists are resistant to the view that there is a need for a reconceptualisation. Nevertheless, this is the position that we (the authors) accept, and while we recognise that this is an uphill struggle we think that it is a necessary one if we are to achieve an adequate sociology.

Conclusions

In this chapter we have concluded that there is a need for a sociology from the perspective of women. We have argued that malestream sociological theories and practices are inadequate because they have either ignored or marginalised women or else accepted biological explanations as adequate for explaining gender divisions and women's social behaviour. We have suggested that biological reductionism is insufficient because it assumes that biological differences between the sexes can explain gender divisions. The latter, we have argued, are socially constructed and cannot be explained by references to biological sex differences. Furthermore, we argue that jobs or activities are sexualised as part of a social process which needs to be explored.

We have argued that it is necessary for there to be a sociology from the position of women and that if this is to become an integral part of sociology then sociology itself needs to be reconceptualised. 'Filling in the gaps' by carrying out research on women and tinkering with existing theories is not sufficient. Looking at the world through the female prism means that we need to rethink sociology and to challenge existing theories and research findings as at best inadequate and at worst wrong. In the rest of this book we demonstrate this, by not only explaining what feminist sociologists have found out but demonstrating how this requires a rethinking of existing sociological theories.

Finally, we want to point out that we have subtitled this book 'feminist perspectives', not '*the* feminist perspective' or 'a feminist perspective'. This is because there are a number of feminist perspectives, not just one. In sociology there are a number of competing perspectives – marxist, weberian, symbolic interactionist, ethnomethodological, structural functionalist and post-modernist, to name those most frequently encountered. Feminist sociologists are also divided among these schools; what they have in common is a commitment to looking at the world through the female prism. We go on to examine the main feminist perspectives in the next chapter.

SUMMARY

What is needed is a sociology, both theoretical and in practice, that recognises:

1   the importance of gender as well as class, 'race', age, sexuality, disability and other forms of differentiation as explanatory variables;

2   that the world needs to be seen through the female as well as the male prism;

3   that the public and domestic spheres are not separate worlds, but areas of mutual influence, and that the relationship between the two changes and needs explaining; and

4   that the existing tools and theories of sociology need to be refurbished.

FURTHER READING

Oakley, A. (1986) *Taking it Like a Woman*, London: Flamingo.
Stanley, L. and Wise, S. (1993) *Breaking Out Again*, London: Routledge.
Walby, S. (1990) *Theorising Patriarchy*, Oxford: Blackwell.

Chapter two

Feminist theory and sociology

Feminist sociology

A feminist sociology is one that is *for* women, not just or necessarily *about* women, and one that challenges and confronts the male supremacy which institutionalises women's inequality. The defining characteristic of feminism is the view that women's subordination must be questioned and challenged. This involves a critical examination of the present and past situation of women. It involves challenging the dominant patriarchal ideologies that seek to justify women's subordination as natural, universal and therefore inevitable, as well as knowledge that is put forward as universal and demonstrating that this 'knowledge' views the world from the perspective of men. What is necessary is a view of the world from the position(s) of women, who have been excluded from the production of knowledge. Such a view will provide more adequate knowledge because it will seek to explain what patriarchal knowledge does not recognise as existing – the subordination and exploitation of women by men.

Feminism starts from the view that women are oppressed and that for many this oppression is primary. Women's freedom of action is limited by the power of men – because men possess more economic, cultural and social resources than women. This is not to ignore the fact that there are differences between

17

women and indeed that the differences themselves involve subordination and exploitation. Nor is it to suggest that differences are additive; we recognise, for example, that race and gender articulate to produce a unique subjectivity for Black women. Nonetheless we would point out that the traditional emphasis in sociology on the state, economy and other public institutions as the main sources of oppression ignore power and oppression in 'private' institutions such as the family and in personal relationships in both the public and the private sphere. Feminists have argued that the personal is political – that is, that it is active agents who 'do the oppressing' and that it is necessary to give credence to women's concrete experiences of oppression – ones occurring in personal, everyday encounters – as well as those at the collective and institutional level. Men and women, oppressors and oppressed, confront one another in their everyday lives – they are not just role-players acting out a prepared script. Human actors in specific social contexts can and do oppose each other; men do exercise power and women do experience pain and humiliation. However, the power of men over women is collective; society's sexist assumptions advantage all men – patriarchal ideologies support and sanction the power of men over women. Feminist sociologists, then, are concerned to examine the relationship between individuals and the social structure, between women's everyday experiences and the structure of the society in which they live, between men's power in interpersonal relationships and the ways in which that power is institutionalised in Western industrial society.

Feminist perspectives and sociology

In order to understand why sociology needs feminism it is necessary to understand what sociology is trying to do as a discipline. It is concerned with providing understandings of the social, to enable us to understand the social world we inherit and our position within it. Sociological theory needs to be reformulated to take cognizance of the position of women. Feminist theory has pre-eminently been concerned with enabling women (and men) to understand the subordination and exploitation of women. Without taking account of the criticisms that feminists have made of traditional sociological theory and reformulating these theories to take account of feminist theorisation, sociology will continue to produce distorted accounts of the social world which are complicit in the subordination of women.

As feminists and sociologists we want a reformulated sociology. However, one of the areas of sociology that has been most resistant to change has been theory. Before we consider feminist theories and the ways they enable us to think about the social world, we want to consider what sociological theory *is* and what it means 'to think sociologically'.

Theory is the basis of sociology. Theories determine the ways in which we make sense of the world – the questions we ask and the range of answers that are permitted. As John Scott (1995, p. xii) has pointed out, 'Theory is fundamental to the whole sociological enterprise; it defines its central concepts and it. Sociology is a theoretical enterprise' – it is about making sense of the world in which we live – yet, as we pointed out in Chapter 1, it is not just that the discipline has ignored gender divisions, but rather that it has been complicit in justifying the subordination and exploitation of women. Theory is also the area that has been slowest to change – to take seriously the feminist critique.

While empirical sociology has by and large recognised at least the need to include gender as a variable, theorists tend to remain silent on gender. Giddens (1993), for example, has a brief section in his theory chapter on feminist criticisms of malestream theory, but no reference to feminist theory as such or even to the ways in which feminists have modified malestream theories – for example, marxist feminism. John Scott (1995), while stressing that theory is central to the sociological enterprise, has no reference to feminist theory or indeed to any feminist criticisms of malestream theory (with the exception of those raised by Mary Wollstonecraft, a liberal feminist at the turn of the nineteenth-century). The omission not only marginalises and devalues the contribution that female sociologists have made to sociological theory but perpetuates the myth that theory is 'difficult' and something that only men can do – also reinforcing the view that theory is an account of the ideas of great men rather than the attempt to construct frameworks that enable us to understand and make sense of the world in which we live. Furthermore, it demonstrates that male sociological theorists have not recognised the need to reformulate theory to take account of the critique made by feminist sociologists. It is in the area of theory, then, that we can see the greatest resistance within sociology to the challenge made by feminists to the phallocentrism of the discipline. What is even more noteworthy, however, is the ways in which many of the criticisms that feminists have made of sociology as a discipline have been taken up by male sociologists – especially those who take postmodernist positions and those developing 'male studies' – and expounded as if men were the originators of them (see, e.g., Hekman, 1990; Smart, 1995). However, we remain committed as feminists to sociology – to the development of a reformulated sociology that is able adequately to theorise the social world, for women as well as for men.

An invitation to feminist sociology

Both of us, when we first started sociology, did not really understand what we were supposed to be learning, but we also found that what we were doing was not just interesting but exciting. We were being asked to look at, make sense of and ask questions about the society in which we lived, in ways that had never occurred to us, and we found the tentative answers put forward by sociologists challenging – they made us think about society and social relations in new ways and provided a much clearer and much more interesting set of answers than we had come across before. We were being invited to grasp what the North American sociologist Charles Wright Mills (1954) has called 'the sociological imagination'. It was not easy to come to understand how to think sociologically, and indeed we are still learning, but we certainly came to a new perspective, a new way of thinking and, equally importantly, we came to want to ask 'new' questions about what was going on.

We are going to introduce you to what sociology is, to what it means to 'think sociologically', and specifically to 'thinking feminist sociology'. In Chapter 11 we shall look at questions related to the status of feminist sociological knowledge, but the focus of this chapter is the plurality of feminist perspectives – frameworks for understanding and making sense of social relations in modern societies, which is the subject matter of sociology.

Sociology is of interest to us all because it is about subjects that concern us all in our everyday lives: crime, families, work, employment, education, race relations, class, gender, political behaviour and so on. These are issues of general concern, the frequent topics of newspaper articles and news broadcasts, the subjects of novels and plays. Sociologists, including feminist sociologists, explore these issues and try to provide answers to the kinds of questions we commonly ask – for example: why people commit crimes, why some working-class people vote Conservative, why so many people are divorced. We also ask these questions in relationship to our own lives: why did I 'fail' in the education system? why did my son commit suicide? why did I become unemployed? why didn't I get the job? why am I poor? However, the questions feminist sociologists ask often take a different slant: why do so few women commit crime, why do women experience poverty on divorce, why are so few women involved in politics? When we answer these questions we do not just look at 'the facts'; the 'facts' can only tell us that something is the case, not *why* it is the case. When we try to say why, we are going beyond the facts; we are trying to explain them. Doing this, we are using theories. In explaining to ourselves what is going on in our lives we often use 'common-sense' theories; we justify our answers by saying that 'it stands to reason', or 'it is common sense', or 'everyone knows that'. We do not ask ourselves what our theory is and where it comes from, nor do we try to refute our own conclusions. Common-sense theories frequently 'blame the victim' – divorced women are living in poverty because they would rather live on state benefits than take a job, girls 'fail' in school because they are less intelligent than boys, women look after children because they are naturally good at it, unmarried teenage girls get pregnant in order to get a council house, children are psychologically disturbed because their mothers work. Sociologists share these common-sense views – they are members of society – but they try to go beyond them, to construct theories which provide a greater understanding and are not based on taken-for-granted assumptions and values.

The insights of sociology

As feminist sociologists we do not want to reject sociology and the insight with which it provides us; what we want is to develop a feminist sociology. What defines sociology is not *what* it studies but *how*: the sociological perspective is a distinctive way of looking at social institutions and social relations. It is concerned with the patterned regularities in social life and rejects the view that these can be explained adequately by reference to the biology or psychology of individuals. This is not to say that biological or psychological explanations are wrong, but that on their own they are insufficient. It is not possible, sociologists argue, to understand the social purely by reference to characteristics that are presumed to be inherent in the individual, nor by reference to the psychological qualities of individuals. Yet this is how we often explain things to ourselves. It is 'natural' to grow up and fall in love and marry one's lover, for example; it is 'natural' for teenagers to be rebellious, women who are beaten by their husbands want to be beaten, intelligent children do well at school, and so on. Sociologists challenge these as explanations and argue that they are inadequate because they do not take into account the ways in which the structures of society and our social interactions with others influence and shape us. Sociologists point out that we need to question these taken-for-granted explanations and then construct more adequate explanations – theories that help us to understand and make sense of what is going on, to ask what is really going on here, to be sceptical and to have a questioning mind. What is necessary is to develop feminist sociological perspectives that enable women to become fully integrated into sociological understanding.

One way of questioning our common sense is to ask ourselves if things have always been as they are and if they are the same in all countries. If we take the example of growing up, falling in love and getting married, we can see how historical and cross-cultural research can lead us to question this as a natural process. It has not always been seen as 'natural' in our own society for young people to grow up, fall in love and get married, nor is it seen as natural in all societies today. In some societies marriages are arranged by parents or other relatives and people are expected to 'fall in love' after they are married. This does not mean that the feelings young people have for the people they marry in Britain are not 'real', but it does lead us to ask questions about the relationships between these feelings, the ways in which we make sense of them and the relationship between this and marriage that are not answered by 'it is natural'.

Sociology transforms our understanding of self and society – the individual is not subsumed under the collective, but sociology reveals how varieties of individual growth and development and the formation of different types of processes are dependent on forms of social organisation and culture. The sociological perspective is rooted in the fact that we live in societies and within historical periods, and it raises questions about the social organisation of our lives and provides provisional understanding. Feminist sociologists have pointed out, however, that malestream theories are inadequate because they do not provide this understanding from the position of women.

Once sociology has achieved one kind of understanding, one form of explanation of the social world, it can question it and begin to reformulate it, to ferret out, from the problems with the existing image of reality that is provided, new ways of understanding and explanation. Sociological understanding is always provisional and partial – if we had complete understanding we would have no more need for sociology. In the same way, if we knew the truth about the natural world we would have no more need for biology or physics or chemistry. We would suggest that while many substantive areas in sociology have recognised the need to take feminist critiques seriously, there has not been the same awareness of a need to reformulate sociological theory in the same way. Indeed, this has been the area where the response that 'the women can teach that' has been clearest. Feminist theory has been seen as of the middle range – as concerned with explaining the specific position of women. We would argue that it is much more than this, even if the position of women has been a central concern. Once the feminist critique of conventional sociology is taken seriously, and feminist theories are actually given careful consideration, it becomes evident that sociological theory as a whole needs to be reformulated.

Charles Wright Mills, in his book *The Sociological Imagination* (1954), provides one of the best accounts of what it is to grasp the sociological imagination, the relationship between biography and history, and to recognise the inadequacy of individualistic explanations. The sociological imagination should enable us to grasp that personal troubles are frequently social ills, that what we perceive as social problems can only be understood and explained fully when we examine social, political and economic factors – when we look for social explanations. One example feminist sociologists have used is the gendered labour market – the systematic way in which women are in jobs that have a lower status and lower remuneration than men, with some jobs labelled as 'for men' and others as 'for women'. Feminists have argued that this cannot be explained by reference to the characteristics of individual women; we have to consider *structured* inequalities in society, government policies, and so on.

Sociology, then, is about understanding the relationship between our own experiences and the social structures we inhabit. This creates a tension between agency – the extent to which we act on the world – and structure, the extent to which our actions are determined by the structures. Students are often resistant to sociology because they feel that it denies that they and other people have 'free will' – that it takes away from people the responsibility for their actions and suggests that we are all puppets. Sociology is not the only subject in danger of reductionism and determinism: biological and psychological explanations can be equally reductionist. Biology and psychology tend to blame the 'victim's' biology (genetic make-up) or psychological constitution; sociologists tend to shift the blame to outside the individual, to external factors outside, impinging in (as indeed do some psychological perspectives – behaviourism, for instance). Thus there is a tension between making social statements and giving due allowance to individual variation in human behaviour. To grasp the full complexity of individual social behaviour and to discover the underlying patterns of similarity which may link them together requires a theory which can explain how the moral imperatives of 'society' are translated into the norms and standards which form the guidelines for people's lives. We are socially determined and yet determining; we are acted on and yet we act. This tension between agency and structure is one of the issues that distinguishes different sociological and indeed feminist positions; some give more weight to structures, emphasising the social, and others give more weight to agency, stressing the ways in which we act on the world and in the process change it.

The historical context of sociology

To understand fully the sociological imagination and the contemporary theoretical debates in sociology and feminism it is necessary to understand the historical development of sociology as a discipline. Although men and women have always asked questions about and tried to understand and explain society and social relations, sociology as a distinct discipline developed in the nineteenth century. It arose in a distinct historical, intellectual and social context, at a particular period in the development of European societies, with the development of what is referred to as 'modernity'. The changes that took place in European societies during the course of the nineteenth century, and which have subsequently become global, resulted in the social transformation of those societies. Three specific developments are crucial: the scientific revolution which started in the sixteenth century, Enlightenment thought of the eighteenth century culminating in the French Revolution, and the industrial revolution which started in the late eighteenth century in England. Sociology is seen as a reaction to each of these developments.

The scientific revolution made possible the understanding and control of the natural world. Nineteenth-century sociologists thought that the methodology of the natural sciences would make it possible to understand and control the social world. Enlightenment thought led to the dominance of ideas of progress and of liberty and individualism. Sociologists took on the idea of progress but reacted against the emphasis on individualism, stressing the importance of the collectivity and the inter-relationship and interdependence of members of society. The industrial revolution – the development and growth of industrial capitalism – resulted in dramatic social and economic changes – urbanisation, new class relationships, paid employment, the economic dependence of women and children, and so on. The foundations of modern societies are capitalism, industrialism, surveillance and militarism. These modern societies reject religious thought as the guarantor of truth and replace it with rationality, reason and science. The scientific method – the experiment – is seen as the guarantor of truth. Sociologists wanted to understand and explain these changes. In doing so they also suggested ways in which societies could be reformed.

Some sociologists and feminists argue that the late twentieth century has witnessed a further transformation, into a 'postmodern' society, and that new theories, postmodern theories, are necessary to make sense of what is happening. The postmodern condition is seen as arising from a variety of social and cultural changes that are taking place at the end of the twentieth century – rapid technological change, shifting political concerns and the rise of new social movements – including feminism. Postmodernism rejects the ideas of the Enlightenment – of progress, of scientific truth and the possibility of universal totalising theories – theories such as Marxism which would claim to explain everything and to have the *sole* explanation. It argues that there are no grand narratives, no notions of progress and no single history – there are different histories and different foci of knowledge. Many different and equally authoritative voices and orientations are possible in the postmodern pluralistic world. Postmodernism therefore questions the foundationalism and absolutism of modernism – it challenges both positivistic and humanistic approaches to social science. Postmodernism rejects the declaration of difference between natural and social sciences – even humanism did not challenge the status of scientific knowledge but argued that social-science knowledge was equally as good as scientific knowledge but different.

Feminists, too, have questioned many of the epistemological foundations of Western thought and argued that modernist knowledge, in the name of objectivity and truth, has subordinated and subjugated women. It could be argued that feminism and postmodernism are natural allies – and there is a growing number of feminists who identify themselves as postmodernist. However, others have indicated that total relativism and the abandonment of theory are as problematic for feminism as for sociology. Postmodernism, in their perception, challenges the very enterprise of both sociology and feminism – which is not just understanding what is going on but changing the social world, achieving progress by acting on the world.

Theory and theorising

As has already been suggested, we are all theorists, and we all theorise about society. Everybody takes part in social thought, everybody thinks, everybody has ideas – not just experts and intellectuals. We all analyse and interpret in order to make sense of what is going on. Theories are how we all try to explain how society works. What is the difference, then, between our everyday, common-sense theories and sociological ones? Stuart Hall (1982) suggests that:

> In social science we tend to call an explanation a theory if it is open-ended, open to new evidence, capable of modification and improvement, and clear about the way its concepts are formed.
>
> (p. 43)

However, he goes on to suggest that:

> there is no absolute distinction in social science between science (knowledge based on disinterested explanation) and ideology (knowledge which reflects particular interests). Marxism is both a theory and an ideology. It tries to explain how society works, but also provides a guide for action.
>
> (p. 43)

Feminist theories are also concerned with explaining and with providing guides for action.

All sociologists think theoretically, and sociological theories (and feminist ones) can be distinguished from our common-sense, everyday understandings and explanations in the following ways:

1   social theory attempts to be more systematic about explanations and
     ideas;
2   it attempts to provide adequate explanations – that is, it tries to take
     account of all the 'facts', to be coherent in itself; and
3   it is open to refutation.

A theoretical perspective, or world view, is a framework that provides
the tools for theorising – that is, the tools for explaining and making sense of
what is going on. A theoretical perspective helps us to ask questions, directs
us to the information that needs to be collected and suggests how to interpret/
explain that information. Sociology is always theoretical; sociologists work
within theoretical perspectives. From a narrow scientific view, a theory is a set
of properties that describes a set of observations. Theories summarise and
organise what we know about the world. A theoretical perspective, however,

1   provides us with the concepts to use in our analysis and accounts of our
     observations of social life – e.g. social class, patriarchy, isolated nuclear
     family;
2   suggests the types of question we should be asking and draws our
     attention to certain kinds of events rather than others – e.g. feminist
     sociologists ask the question 'Why do women do housework?';
3   provides us with ways of answering questions in the form of orienting
     assumptions and guides to observation – e.g. feminist sociologists
     assume that the gendered division of labour is something that needs to
     be explained;
4   helps us to interpret what we observe – theory structures the process
     of perception – e.g. feminist sociologists explain the gendered division
     of labour as the outcome of patriarchal processes;
5   involves value judgements about what social scientific knowledge is for
     and how it is to be applied to social life.

Thus sociological (and feminist) theories provide answers to 'how' and
'why' questions but they do not necessarily agree on the answers to these
questions. Just as we can disagree on how something is to be explained in our
day-to-day lives, so sociologists (and feminists) disagree when they are
explaining the same thing. This is because 'facts do not speak for themselves';
they have to be explained, and it is theory that enables us to understand them.
For example, the examination results of boys and girls are different at 16+:

> In 1986/87 girls were more likely than boys to have gained a higher-
> grade 'O' level result (GCSE grades 1–3; SCE grades 1–3, CSE grade 1)
> in English, biology, French, history and/or creative arts. Only a tiny

number of boys gained passes in commercial or domestic studies. In physics, when 22 per cent of boys achieved a higher-grade pass, only 9 per cent of girls did so. Boys are more likely than girls to take and pass mathematical, scientific and technological subjects, and girls are more likely to take and pass the arts and domestic subjects.

(*Social Trends* quoted in Abbott and Wallace, 1990, p. 51)

This is an account of the statistical data – you can check its accuracy by looking up the statistics in a copy of *Social Trends*, a compilation of statistics collected by the Government and published annually. However, to know that there is a difference in the subjects studied for and passed at 16+ years by boys and girls does not tell us how or why. We have to interpret, make sense of the facts – and to do so we need a theory that enables us to make sense of what we have observed. (See Chapter 4 for the ways in which feminists have explained the differential educational achievement of girls and boys.)

Furthermore, what the facts are is not always self-evident. For example, what counts as educational success or failure? what counts as crime? This might seem self-evident at first, but on closer examination we realise that it is not. For example, is 'crime' all behaviour that breaks the law, or is it only that behaviour which is labelled as 'criminal' – and, if so, by whom? Even when the facts are straightforward, no amount of observation and data-gathering will explain them. For example, in Britain statistics on birth are probably almost totally reliable. It is very difficult not to register the birth of a baby. However, no amount of collecting and dissecting birth statistics will lead to an explanation of fluctuations in the birth rate. Description alone will explain neither the fluctuation nor how it relates to other events and processes – e.g. the economic situation, the proportion of the population marrying, the infant mortality rate. (Indeed, which other events I think fluctuations in the birth rate might be related to will be influenced by my theoretical perspective – even if this is just common sense.)

Sociologists (and feminists), then, develop theories which enable them to make sense of the social. Theories make sense of the facts – they interpret them for us. In sociology, theories are used to provide arguments about how society should be viewed and how the 'facts' should be apprehended and ordered. Facts alone cannot resolve theoretical disputes, because theories are explanations of the facts. Even when there is agreement as to what the facts are, they can be used to support different theories; two theories may be incompatible with each other and yet agree on what the available facts are. For example, radical feminists and dual-systems feminists agree that women are subordinated and exploited by men in contemporary Britain. However, while radical feminists explain this as the result of a system of patriarchy and the ways in which men use their biological strength and sexuality to control women, dual-systems feminists see it as the outcome of the articulation of capitalist and patriarchal ideologies.

Theories, then, direct us to what evidence to look for and then enable us to make sense of the facts that we have collected. This does not mean that facts and factual knowledge are not important for sociological knowledge. It is important that sociological and feminist theories are open to refutation – facts can refute our theories – and that theories take the facts fully into account. There is a complex relationship between fact and theory and dis- agreement over what is to count as a fact, as valid evidence or information. There are three types of evidence, and feminist sociologists need to be aware of them:

1   evidence that is more or less 'factual' – that is, is easily checked and difficult to dispute (e.g. birth statistics);
2   evidence which appears factual but contains implicit background assumptions (e.g. employment statistics, statistics on assaults on wives);
3   general and abstract theoretical statements (e.g. that women are naturally maternal). These statements are open to refutation by evidence, however. It is in principle possible to collect evidence which demonstrates that women are *not* naturally maternal.

Sociological and feminist theories are 'under-determined' by the facts, and they consist of statements of the three types described above as evidence. Theories guide us as to what counts as evidence. When we describe the relationship between two events as causal we are making a theoretical statement, not a factual one – we are explaining and interpreting, not describing.

Sociological and feminist theories are attempts to explain social life, and they comprise sets of logically connected ideas that can describe and explain social reality and be validated/refuted by evidence from social reality. There are, however, four clearly different theoretical positions on the nature of social reality:

1   the positivist approach;
2   the idealist approach;
3   the realist approach; and
4   the post-structuralist approach.

Each of these approaches answers the questions (1) 'What is the nature of social reality?' and (2) 'How can we best obtain knowledge of it?'

The positivist approach sees a continuity between the natural and the social sciences, with society existing as an analytic reality. Social structures and social processes are seen as comparable to those of the natural world and can be studied by the same methods as are used in the natural sciences. The sociologist's task is to collect empirical evidence – social facts – and on the basis of this to explain and predict the social world. Sociologists construct theories that comprise general statements about relationships existing in the social world.

In contrast, the idealist approach sees social life as the product of human consciousness – of the meaning that human beings give to their conduct. The sociologist's task is to explain the ideas, beliefs and motives of social actors – to interpret the meaning of social events. Sociology's subject matter is the meaning of social-historical reality. This approach rejects the view that the methods of the natural sciences are appropriate for sociologists.

The realist approach argues that there is a social reality, but that it is not immediately apprehensible. The task of the sociologist is to uncover the structure in the social world – the reality that underlies and explains particular events. Sociology is seen as an empirically based, rational and objective discipline, but realists make a distinction between explanation and prediction and see the primary object as explanation. Realist sociologists explain why something happens by showing how and by what means it occurs.

The post-structuralist approach argues that there are only interpretations – 'readings' – of texts, that there is an indeterminacy and heterogeneity of actual meanings and meaning-productions. Like the idealist approach it rejects the ideals of objectivity and neutral judgement and argues that the ideas are the creation of social beings rather than the (more or less adequate) representations of material reality. However, the postmodernists reject the Cartesian body – that which locates the knower in time and space and therefore situates and relativises perception and thought, and which needs to be transcended in order to achieve objective knowledge. Whereas modernists argue that the body can be transcended – objective knowledge can be obtained, in principle at least – and that scientists' knowledge is thereby objective as opposed to the everyday subjective knowledge of 'lay people', for post-modernists there can be no escape from human perspectives and subjectivity cannot be transcended even in principle. Furthermore, given the multiplicity of subjective positions and the ways human beings make and continuously remake the world, there are endless 'points of view' on things.

Sociologists (and feminists), then, disagree about what valid sociological knowledge is, and about how that knowledge can best be obtained. Thus sociology and feminism are characterised by fierce and open debates about intractable and important questions. Students have been introduced to socio-logical theory via a 'schools of thought' approach, each perspective being seen as internally coherent and as rejecting the validity of the other approaches. However, there has been a move more recently in sociology to accept that all theories, all understandings, all explanations are provisional and partial, and perhaps that they provide different versions of 'truth'. While some accounts may be seen as more authoritative than others, this judgement is itself based on the world view of the judge. This is also the case with feminist theories.

Sociologists and feminists are not priesthoods of scholars, removed from the concerns of the ordinary people, but rather part of that social reality – and if they were not, they could not make sense of it. Think what it would be like to understand what was going on at a hockey match if you did not know the rules of the game and the social context within which it took place. You would have to use some kind of theory to make sense of what was going on. For example, someone from ancient Rome might try to explain it in terms of gladiatorial contests, and someone from Africa in terms of religious ceremony.

Sociologists and feminists do need a framework that enables them to make sense of the social world, to make it meaningful and intelligible. There is no one sociological or feminist framework, but a set of inter-related theories all providing provisional and partial accounts. Some of them provide competing explanations, but others provide understanding of different aspects of social reality and social processes and enable us to develop our understanding of what is 'really' going on.

Feminist theory

The major criticism that feminists have made of sociological theory is that it is inadequate because it does not take account of women – it is unable to explain, make sense of, what is going on in the social world from the perception of women. We would argue that sociologists must take this challenge seriously and take account of feminist theory.

Feminism, like sociology, is a theory – a world view. However, it is not a unified one; feminists do not agree on the ways in which we can explain women's subordination or on how women can be emancipated. There is a large number of feminisms, and any attempt to classify feminist theories is fraught with problems. Any system of classification is arbitrary and incomplete: arbitrary because we force women into a category, one with which they may not themselves identify, and describe a given position as if it were totally unified rather than representing a range of ideas that show some broad agreement. It is incomplete because our categories do not incorporate all feminisms. We have tried to provide a classification that does cover the range of feminist theories that have made important contributions to British sociology, in order better to understand the differences between them. In doing this, however, we wish to emphasise that our aim is to demonstrate what such theories can contribute to sociology, rather than an analysis of theory itself. Some theories are useful for explaining some things, but not others. We are not therefore stressing the primacy of any one theoretical perspective although we try to show the strengths and weaknesses of each. The epistemological foundations of different feminist positions are explored more fully in Chapter 11.

We have identified seven feminist perspectives: liberal/reformist, marxist, radical, dual-systems, postmodernist/post-structuralist, materialist and Black feminist. All these perspectives address the question of what constitutes the oppression of women, and all suggest strategies for overcoming it. All argue that women are oppressed in Western industrial societies but they differ in their explanations of the 'cause' of the oppression and their suggested strategies for overcoming it. Liberal feminism is concerned to uncover the immediate forms of discrimination against women in Western societies and to fight for legal and other reforms to overcome them. Marxist feminists argue that the major reason for women's oppression is the exclusion of women from public production and that women's struggle for emancipation is an integral part of the fight of the proletariat (working class) to overthrow capitalism. Radical feminists see male control of women (patriarchy) as the main problem and argue that women must fight to free themselves from this control. Materialist feminists argue that women as a social class are exploited and sub-ordinated by men as a class. Dual-systems feminists argue that women's oppression is both an aspect of capitalism and of patriarchal relations. An end to capitalism, they argue, will not lead automatically to the emancipation of woman – women also need to fight to free themselves from control by men. Postmodernist/post-structuralist theories argue that the ideas which are the foundation of social divisions can be explored only through texts or language. The challenge is to construct a discourse from a woman's point of view. They also argue that rationality, and therefore sociology, is a product of a masculine attempt to objectify and control the world. The solution is to reject rationality as a form of explanation. Black feminists argue that a feminist perspective needs to take into account the differential situation for racialised women as well as racialised men, and therefore their solution is to fight for liberation for Black people as well as women.

Feminist theories differ, then, in the ways they explain the subordination of women, and the different theories mean that feminists working in different perspectives tend to be interested in different aspects of women's lives, to ask different questions and to come to different conclusions. This will become evident as you read this book, when we look at specific aspects of women's lives.

Liberal/reformist feminist theory

Historically, liberal feminism has been concerned to argue for equal rights for women – for women to have the same citizenship rights as men. Equal Rights feminists have fought against laws and practices that give rights to men and not women, or which are designed to 'protect' women. Recognising that mere formal equality is insufficient, they have also advocated the passing of laws to outlaw discrimination against women and to give women rights in the workplace such as maternity leave and pay.

Women, they argue, are human beings; they have the same inalienable natural rights as men. A woman's sex is irrelevant to her rights; women are capable of full rationality and therefore are entitled to full human rights. However, in Western industrial societies women are discriminated against on the basis of sex; that is, certain restrictions are placed on women as a group without regard to their own individual wishes, interests, abilities and needs. Women are denied equal rights with men, and as a group are not allowed some freedoms that men as a group are permitted to enjoy. Furthermore, while men are judged on merit as individuals, women tend to be judged on their accomplishments as females – that is, they are denied the same right as men to pursue their own interests.

In sociology, liberal/reformist feminists have been concerned to demonstrate that the observable differences between the sexes are not innate but a result of socialisation and 'sex-role conditioning'. The ways in which boys and girls are treated differently, from about the moment of birth, arguably discourage women from developing their full potential as human beings. Feminist researchers have carried out research to demonstrate that women are discriminated against and treated differently from men, and argue that this explains women's subordinate position in society. To liberate women it is necessary to demonstrate that men and women are equal in potential, that women are fully human, that the differences between men and women in Western society are due to the different ways in which boys and girls are socialised and the different social expectations they face, together with discriminatory legislation.

However, sociological research from a reformist position does not explore women's experiences, nor challenge the use of concepts and tools developed to explore society from the standpoint of men. Nor does it adequately challenge malestream views of what the major issues are to be researched. It argues for the incorporation of women in research samples and for women to carry out research, but leaves intact the foundations of existing theoretical perspectives. However, research from this perspective has demonstrated the ways in which women are denied equal opportunities and are discriminated against, and has challenged the view that the sexual division of labour is adequately explained by biological sex differences.

Radical feminism

Radical feminists argue that women's oppression is primary and fundamental. Patriarchy, an elaborate system of male domination which pervades all aspects of culture and social life, is seen as trans-historical. All women are oppressed irrespective of historical, cultural, class or racial differences. The family is seen as a key instrument of the oppression of women, through sexual slavery and forced motherhood – through male control of women's bodies. Radical feminists do not, on the whole, deny biological differences between men and women, but they challenge the meanings given to them. Women's oppression is seen as rooted either in women's biological capacity for motherhood or in the innate, biologically determined aggression of the male, as manifested in rape.

The central tenet of radical/revolutionary feminists is that gender inequalities are the outcome of an autonomous system of patriarchy and that gender inequalities are the primary form of social inequality. They argue that there has always been a sexual division of labour underpinning and reinforcing a system of male domination. Patriarchy is a universal system in which men dominate women. Radical feminism is primarily a revolutionary movement for the emancipation of women. Its exponents argue that no area of society is free from male definition, and consequently every aspect of women's lives currently accepted as 'natural' has to be questioned and new ways of doing things found. Theory, they argue, is not a separate area of activity, carried out by an elite, but is an integral aspect of feminist practice. Theory arises out of practice and is continually measured against experience and continually reformulated. The revolution, for radical feminists, begins here and now, by women taking positive action to change their lives and to remove oppression.

Radical and revolutionary feminism is not a unified area. There are three major issues within it:

1   the relationship between feminist politics and personal sexual conduct – a key question being whether women can continue to live with men, or whether separation is essential;
2   whether sex differences are biologically or socially constructed;
3   the political strategy that should be adopted – withdrawal or revolution.

Radical feminists do, however, reject the view that women's subordination is anything to do with their biological inferiority. They reject the idea that the victim (woman) is to blame. Those who do argue for a biological explanation argue that *male* biology is to blame: men are naturally aggressive and use their aggression to control women (as, for example, in rape). Mary Daly, in *Gyn/Ecology: the metaethics of radical feminism* (1978), documents the horrors of the ways in which men have used aggression to control women. She cites Indian suttee, Chinese foot binding, African genital mutilation, European witch hunts and American gynaecology as examples of ways in which men have abused women and used violence to control them (and continue to do so). These feminists encourage women to create a new identity for themselves founded on 'true' femaleness, based in the biological nature of women which has been distorted by patriarchy. Women are encouraged to celebrate a new female creativity, based on sisterhood and self-identification. They reject androgyny because they argue that the most valuable qualities are those that are specific to women. Also, because men dominate women even in the most intimate of relationships, women must live separately from men. The ideal, they argue, is for women to live freed from patriarchy, which divides and mutilates them.

For radical feminists the subordination of women is the central concern, and their theories seek to uncover and eliminate the subordination of women by men. Men, it is argued, systematically dominate women in every sphere of life, and all relationships between men and women are institutionalised relationships of power and therefore an appropriate subject for political analysis. Thus radical feminists are concerned to reveal how male power is exercised and reinforced in all spheres of life, including 'personal' relationships such as child-rearing, housework and marriage and in all kinds of sexual practices including rape, prostitution, sexual harassment and sexual intercourse.

Women's subordination is seen to be universal and primary, as not having changed significantly over time or place. Men, it is maintained, benefit from women's subordination. The relationship between the sexes is thus political, and any permanent and far-reaching change will necessitate the transformation of sexual relationships – the elimination of male domination of women.

Radical feminists argue that women's culture, women's knowledge and women's subjective understanding have all been denied by men. What is taken as truth and is seen to be valued has been defined by men. Male science has been used to legitimate the ideologies that define women as inferior, and women's role to be that of domestic labourers. Sociology is seen as part of this male-defined, distorting male culture. Radical feminists, then, do not want to participate in sociology – to bring women in – but to transform the way knowledge is produced so that women's subjective understandings are revalued. Much radical feminist research has been concerned with analysing male violence towards women and the ways in which this is hidden, marginalised or blamed on the women by malestream social science and patriarchal values. Radical feminists have also been concerned to uncover her-story, to recover for women their history and their cultural heritage and to reveal the ways in which women's knowledge has been devalued both historically and in other societies.

Radical feminism has uncovered the ways in which even the most intimate and personal relationships are political – that is, are power relationships. Also they have documented the universality of patriarchal relationships. However, they have failed to explain adequately the ways in which women are subordinated and exploited by men. They fail to take sufficient account of the different forms that patriarchal relationships have taken in different societies. They also tend to discount the differences that exist in the experiences of women from different social classes. Radical feminist biological explanations, while very different from those developed by malestream theorists, are equally reductionist and fail to take account of ideology and culture. Also they give the opportunity for sociobiological theories to be developed as a counter to the feminist ones – ones that argue that women's role as presently constituted is naturally determined. However, not all radical feminists accept biological theories, arguing that they are developed to justify the subordination of women and that it is necessary to challenge the argument that there are two biologically determined sexes.

Marxist feminism

Marxist feminism has developed out of the attempts by women to develop marxist theory so that it provides an adequate explanation for the subordination and exploitation of women in capitalist societies. Marxist feminists recognise that Marxism is inadequate as it stands and needs to be developed in order to explain adequately why women are excluded from the public sphere and are the main unpaid workers in the domestic sphere. They have also had to deal with the 'fact' that women did not become subordinated under capitalism but were subordinated already, and with the strong suspicion that the overthrow of the capitalist mode of production would not result in the emancipation of women. However, while they recognise that the struggle between the sexes is not reducible to the class struggle, they give primacy to the latter. For marxist feminists the defining feature of contemporary society is capitalism, within which women are subject to a special form of oppression which is mainly the effect of their exclusion from wage labour and of their role in the domestic sphere reproducing the relations of production. That is, women's unpaid work in caring for the labour force and raising the next generation of workers benefits capitalism and is essential to its continuation. The main beneficiary of women's unpaid labour is capitalism, although individual men also benefit to some extent.

A major problem that marxist feminists confront is that Marx himself was not concerned with the position of women in capitalist society. Marx rejected notions of morality, justice and equal rights as bourgeois ideas. He was concerned not with reform, but with developing a scientific account of the exploitation of the working class under capitalism with a view to overthrowing that system.

The concepts Marx uses appear to be neutral, but they are in fact sex-blind; he fails to recognise that women are subject to a special form of oppression within capitalist societies and does not analyse gender differences and gender ideologies. Although he uses abstract categories such as 'labour power', his specific analyses suggest that he assumed a male waged labour force. He also adopted a naturalistic approach to the family, maintaining that women should provide care in the domestic sphere. The paid labour of women and children was seen by Marx as a threat to male workers – women and children, he argued, were used by capitalists to reduce the costs of production. Cheap female labour was or could be used to replace more expensive male labour. (Marx did not challenge the practice of paying women less than men.) This analysis ignores the fact that women have always made a contribution to the economic survival of the household and does not challenge the view that men should be paid more for their labour than women – presumably because men should be paid a family wage.

Marxist feminists want to retain the marxist analysis of capitalist societies, integrating into it an explanation for the subordination of women. A starting point for the development of an adequate marxist feminist theory has been the work of Engels, Marx's collaborator. In his analysis of the re-lationship between the origins of the family and the development of capitalism (1884), Engels argues that the bourgeois nuclear family was formed because of the needs of the capitalist system, and specifically because men wanted to pass on their property to their legitimate heirs. Engels argues that this meant that men needed to control women in marriage so that they knew who their heirs were. Women's subordinate position was/is a form of oppression that serves the interests of capitalism. All women are oppressed, whether they are married to bourgeois or proletarian men.

Marxist feminists have adapted this line to develop a theory which attempts to provide an adequate account of the subordination of women as well as forms of class exploitation and which overcomes the theoretical marginalisation of women in conventional marxist theory. They seek to analyse and explain the relationships between the subordination of women and other aspects of the organisation of the capitalist mode of production. The attempt to marry feminism with Marxism has been difficult, but marxist feminists have argued that it is essential to recognise that the oppression of women is inextricably linked with the capitalist order. Given this and given Marxism's sex-blindness, it is necessary to reformulate it so that it provides an adequate explanation for the subordination of women, and of ethnic minorities and other exploited groups in such societies as well. Such a theory, it is argued, will enable us to develop strategies that result in the emancipation of subordinated groups – something that the overthrow of the capitalist system would not automatically achieve by itself.

One of the most fully developed marxist feminist accounts is Michelle Barrett's in *Women's Oppression Today* (1980). She sets out to construct a marxist analysis of the relationship between women's oppression and class exploitation in capitalist society that rejects the view that women's exploitation can be explained either by the biological difference between men and women or by reference to the 'needs' of the capitalist system, or by dominant ideas (ideologies) which posit that women are inferior to men, that women's role is as a wife and mother, or the like. She argues against approaches such as Domestic Labour Theory, which begin from the premiss that women's oppression is an integral part of the capitalist system, by maintaining that it cannot be demonstrated that privatised (family) reproduction using the unpaid domestic labour of women *is* the cheapest way of reproducing labour power. Also, it does not explain why it is women who work in the domestic sphere and not men.

The need is to understand women's social position as exploited by capital and their dependent and powerless relationship with husbands and fathers. Patriarchal relationships need to be incorporated into class analysis; that is, it is necessary to recognise that men have privileges as men and wield power over women even within the working class. Barrett rejects the view that class and gender hierarchies are two separate systems (a point of contrast with the dual-systems feminists discussed below) and argues that what is necessary is to revise and develop marxist theory so that gender relations are placed at the centre of its analysis.

The key to women's oppression, she suggests, is the 'family/household' system, a complex which includes a social structure and a given ideology – familialism. The household is made up of a number of people, usually biologically and legally related, who live together and share domestic arrangements. Familial ideology defines the nuclear family as 'naturally' based and universal, and specifies a 'natural' division of labour such that the man is seen as the provider of economic resources and the woman as the carer and provider of unpaid domestic labour. This family/household system is not an inevitable aspect of capitalist society but has come to form a historically constituted element of class relations. It was not inevitable, but emerged through a historical process in which an ideology that maintained that a woman's natural role is as a domestic labourer – that is, as a wife and mother – became incorporated into capitalist relations of production. This ideology came in part from pre-capitalist views of a woman's place, but mainly developed because it fitted the way in which bourgeois family relations had become established with the emergence of industrial capitalism. This ideology, Barrett argues, became accepted by the organised working class in the early nineteenth century. The family/household system became established in the mid-nineteenth century as a result of an alliance of craft unions and capitalists, both arguing that women should be excluded from the labour force and that men should earn a family wage. Thus the male fight for a family wage and protective legislation passed by the state eliminated the low-waged competition from women in the labour market and forced women into the domestic sphere. (See Chapters 4 and 6.)

While the family/household system was in the short-term interests of men, it was not in their long-term interests because it split the working class so that working-class men and women came to have different interests. It was in the long-term interests of capital because it divided the working class and women came to provide a pool of lowly paid workers who could be used as a flexible, disposable extra work force. Women's oppression did not have a material basis in the period in which it was formed but has now come to acquire one. It has come to form an essential element in the relations of production, in the sexual division of labour in paid work and between wage labour and domestic labour. The oppression of women is necessary for the reproduction of the capitalist mode of production in its present form.

The major problem with marxist feminist theory is that it fails to place sufficient emphasis on the ways in which men oppress women and the ways in which men benefit from their unpaid domestic labour. While marxist feminists have recognised that it is necessary to allow the importance of patriarchal relationships and how these are intertwined with capitalism, they see them as unchanging and fail to recognise that there is no necessary and inevitable congruence between the interests of patriarchy and the interests of capital. Barrett, for example, fails to explain why it is in capital's interests to exclude cheap female labour, given its concern to maximise profit. Marxist feminism tends to reduce explanations to the categories of marxist theory. It fails to take account of patriarchal relationships in societies other than capitalist ones, nor fully to consider the specific location of Black or Third World women. It also tends to be abstract and far removed from the everyday experiences of women in their relationships with men.

Materialist feminism

All feminists agree that women's oppression is primary. However, some feminists argue that women have shared interests because they are all exploited and oppressed by men. Women, then, are said to form a class that is in conflict with another class, men. The materialist feminist position has mainly been developed by the French feminist Christine Delphy (1977, 1981,

1984). Delphy argues that while sociologists have regarded occupational class inequalities as primary, their own research demonstrates that sexual inequality is primary and more fundamental than occupational inequality. Thus women's oppression cannot be regarded as secondary to, and therefore less important than, class oppression. Delphy argues that women (or at least wives) form a class that is exploited by men (husbands):

> While the wage-labourer sells his labour power, the married woman gives hers away; exclusivity and non-payment are intimately connected. To supply unpaid labour within the framework of a universal and personal relationship (marriage) constructs primarily a relationship of slavery.
>
> (Delphy, 1977, p. 15)

Women, then, according to materialist feminists, form a class in opposition to men. Women are exploited by men and therefore all women share common interests in opposition to those of men. Patriarchal structures are fundamental to our form of social organisation, and therefore it follows that the main axis of differentiation in our society must be gender. While housewives may differ in their standard of living because their husbands are in different social classes, they share a common class position because they are exploited by another class (husbands) – their domestic labour is expropriated (taken away from them, in the same way that the goods produced by male manual workers are taken away from them).

Materialist feminists such as Christine Delphy, Monique Wittig (1979) and Colette Guillaumin (1995) have argued that to give birth is not a biological process, a natural given, but a social-historical construction of 'forced production'. They argue that it is birth that is planned and women are socially programmed (socialised) to give birth. Women are forced to behave in ways that are seen as natural, and this has resulted in the creation of two discrete biological sexes, but this division falsifies the reality of human variation – the wide variety of sexual characteristics – because an over-gendered society has evolved. Society is structured around the belief that there are two polar opposite sexes, male and female.

Biological theories of sex differences are social constructs which, they argue, serve the interests of the socially dominant group. Women are a class in themselves because the category 'woman' (as well as the category 'man') is a political and economic one, not an eternal, biological category. What is necessary is to eliminate the sex distinction itself. Wittig (1979) argues that

> Our fight aims to suppress men as a class not through a genocidal but a political struggle. Once the class 'men' disappears, women as a class will disappear as well, for there are no slaves without masters.
>
> (Wittig, 1979, p. 72)

Because some women are appropriated and constructed as female, all females become appropriated and designated by their female genitalia as women. Women thereby come to form a sex–class – not a class based on biological sex, but one where 'sex' operates as a signifier, acting to identify a group constituted in the context of a social relationship of appropriation. 'Sex', however, articulates with other social relations to produce a multiplicity of positions and overlapping categories of women.

Dual-systems feminism

'Socialist' or 'dual-systems' feminists argue that what is necessary is a dual analysis that articulates marxist class theory with the feminist theory of patriarchy: a theory that takes account of what unites all women – oppression by men – as well as the class divisions between them. While marxist feminist theory continues to give primacy to class analysis, dual-systems feminists take as their question the relationship of women to the economic system as well as the relationship of men to women. The key question for dual-systems feminists is the cause of male exploitation and domination of women. Hartmann (1978) points out that the categories of Marxism are sex-blind and that patriarchal oppression preceded capitalism and will undoubtedly succeed it as well. In order to understand the subordination of women in capitalist societies, she suggests, it is necessary to articulate marxist with patriarchal perspectives – that is, to show the specific form that female exploitation takes in capitalist societies.

This position, then, attempts to develop an analysis that recognises two systems: the economic, and the sex–gender. Patriarchy is seen as trans-historical – that is, men exercise power over women in all societies. However, an adequate feminist theory, dual-systems feminists argue, has to recognise that patriarchy takes a specific form in capitalist societies. Capitalism and patriarchy are seen as two separate systems. The aim is to develop a theory of capitalist patriarchy that makes possible an understanding of the ways in which the capitalist system is structured by male domination.

In contemporary societies all human beings belong to a social class and a specific gender. Dual systems feminists argue that gender, class, race, age and nationality all shape women's oppression, but they are not committed to any one of these oppressions as any more fundamental than any other. The specific forms of women's subordination in capitalist society are seen as specific to that particular socio-economic system. Women's lack of freedom is a result of the ways in which women are controlled in the public and domestic spheres, and women's emancipation will come about only when the sexual division of labour is broken down in all spheres: the abolition of social relationships that construct people as workers and capitalists and as women and men.

Marxist theory presents the world from the position of the proletariat (working class); what is necessary, dual-systems feminists argue, is to develop a world view from the position of women. Traditional marxist theory ignores women's labour outside the market (domestic labour) and the gender-defined character of women's work within the market, and therefore obscures the systematic domination of women by men. Women, however, are controlled both by the ruling class and by men; male capitalists determine the conditions under which women sell their labour, and male workers receive monetary and other advantages from the fact that women's waged labour is remunerated at a lower rate than men's and that women perform unpaid domestic labour. Also, men's sexual desires are taken as primary in the definition of women as sexual objects.

To understand women's oppression fully it is necessary to examine the sexual division of labour in the domestic sphere as well as in the labour market, and the relationship between the two. Women's reproductive labour limits their access to wage labour, but the limited range of wage labour available to women is what drives many of them into marriage. The ideology of marriage and motherhood as women's primary role serves to conceal this. The public/private distinction not only benefits capital but also men. The exclusion of women from the public sphere benefits men as well as capitalists, while women's unpaid domestic labour also benefits both men and capitalists.

Sylvia Walby (1988b), emphasising the need for a dual analysis, argues that patriarchy is never the only mode of production but is always articulated with another mode. She also points out the need to analyse variations in the forms of patriarchy. She argues that in capitalist society the key sets of patriarchal relations are to be found in domestic work, paid work, the state, and in male violence and sexuality. Social relations in domestic work constitute the patriarchal mode of production, and this, she argues, is of particular significance in the determination of gender relations. However, when patriarchy is articulated with the capitalist mode of production, patriarchal relations in paid work are of central importance to the maintenance of the system. The form that patriarchy takes under capitalism is different from the form that it takes in other socio-economic systems. Patriarchy predates capitalism, but it takes new forms with capitalist development. There was a well developed sexual division of labour in feudal and proto-industrial England. In agricultural work in pre-industrial England men had to leave the home to work, and poor women worked in the fields. With industrialisation men went out to work and poor women continued to work for others than their families, though gradually women were excluded from much paid work. The confining of women to the home is not unique to capitalist society; in most Islamic societies – industrial and pre-industrial – women are confined to the home, and upper-class women did not work in pre-industrial or industrial Britain.

However, the development of industrial capitalism did lead to changes. Women were excluded from certain types of paid work, especially skilled work, and lost certain legal rights they had previously held over property. Men also made gains: men had control over credit, and some men but no women had access to political arenas including Parliament. Men developed many new bases of power in the public sphere from which women were barred, and domestic ideologies became more dominant. The form that women's subordination takes in capitalist society is not an outcome of the logic of capitalism or patriarchy, but the result of a shift in the resources of male power consequent upon the development of capitalism. Men were in a position to develop new power bases as the domestic economy contracted and was replaced by capitalist production.

Walby also argues that the form of patriarchy changes. Since the rise of capitalism there has been a move from private patriarchy to public patriarchy because of the capitalist demand for labour and because of feminist political activity. However, the interests of patriarchy and of capital are not necessarily the same; the main basis of tension between the two lies in the exploitation of women's labour. It is in capital's interests, she argues, to recruit and exploit cheap female labour, labour which is cheaper than men's because of patriarchal structures. This is resisted by patriarchy, which seeks to maintain the exploitation of women in the household. In the nineteenth century, when men struggled to exclude women from competition for jobs, there was a strong cross-class patriarchal alliance. However, this cross-class alliance is weakened when it is in the interest of employers (capitalists) to recruit women, and then there is conflict between capitalism and patriarchy, as during World War One. An alternative strategy is for capital to recruit women to jobs defined as women's jobs – jobs which pay less than men's and have a lower status. When this happens patriarchy fights to ensure that women are recruited only for women's work. Walby argues that the power of capital prevents the exclusionary strategy working in the long term and that segregation as an alternative develops at least in part because of the feminist movement – women demanding the right to have paid employment. Consequently, in Britain there has been a move from private patriarchy where women were kept in the house to a public form where women are controlled by men in all spheres.

Black feminist perspectives

While marxist and dual-systems feminists have argued that it is necessary to analyse and explain class, gender and racial subordination, Black feminists have been critical of the lack of centrality given to issues of ethnic difference, racialisation and racism in feminist theory and research. They point out that racial ideologies see it as natural and inevitable that one group of people are superior to another group based upon factors such as skin colour, language, cultural patterns, diet and so on (Anthias and Yuval Davis, 1993). It is not just that racialised groups are different, but that they have been racialised – they have been constituted as inferior, subordinated groups:

> ... racism is a specific form of exclusion. Racist discourse posits an essential biological determination to culture, but its referent may be any group that has been 'socially' constructed as having a different 'origin', whether biological or historical. It can be 'Jewish', 'black', 'foreign', 'migrant' ... any group that has been located as a basis of exclusion.
> (Floya Anthias and Nira Yuval Davis, in MacDowell and Pringle, 1992, p. 110)

Black feminists have argued, then, that the universal theories of white feminists do not make sense of/provide theoretical explanations for the unique experiences and structural location of Black women. They have suggested that the argument that they can do so is a process of colonisation. Black women are 'the Other' within feminist theories in much the same way as women are 'Other' in malestream theories. They point out, for example, that the relationship between white women and white men is not the same as that between Black Women and Black men. They do not deny that Black men oppress Black women in patriarchal ways but, as Joseph (1981) argues,

> Capitalism and patriarchy simply do not offer to share with Black males the seat of power in their regal solidarity ... there is more solidarity between white males and females than there is between white males and Black males.
>
> (p. 101)

(See also hooks, 1982; Carby, 1982.)

The need to recognise that the experience of Black women is different from that of white women, therefore, is central to the arguments of Black feminists. However, the factors are not additive – it is essential to understand the ways in which sexualisation and racialisation *articulate*. As Patricia Hill Collins (1990) has indicated, it is necessary to recognise that racialised women have a unique standpoint – they share with white women a history of patriarchal oppression and with Black men a history of racialisation. Their standpoint is racialised as well as sexualised. This is not, she argues, to suggest that Black women's knowledge represents a more accurate view of oppression than that of other subordinate groups, but that it is a *different* perspective – a standpoint evolved in real material conditions (see Chapter 11).

Hill Collins has also pointed to the ways in which Black women have to 'pass' in their daily lives. To do this she uses the metaphor of a 'mask' to describe the experience of being constrained to hide feelings and thoughts that may not be 'there' but which may be thought to be so by white women and/or Black men. Thus Black feminists feel constrained to pass on the one hand as 'real' feminists with white feminists, and on the other as Black with Black men.

The Southall Black Sisters have pointed out that Black women had to struggle against a tradition and a culture which precludes women from having autonomy over their own lives, and they indicate that white women should be prepared to struggle with them:

> Why is it if a white woman is killed as the result of domestic violence it is an issue for all feminists, if a black woman is killed it is an issue for black women only. It is as feminists, not as white women, that we ask you to participate in this action. Until you see the struggles of black women against oppression as your struggle there can be no basis of solidarity between black and white women.
>
> (in a speech at a socialist feminist conference in 1995, quoted by Pearson, 1992, p. 268)

The Sisters argue that there is a danger that Black women will be dissuaded from promoting the interests of women in the name of union against racism. They point to the shared experience of oppression of Black and white women, with the rise of fundamentalism in a number of countries – for example, the banning of abortion in the USA, dowry deaths in India, arranged marriages, and separate schools for Muslim girls (which they regard as a strategy for keeping Muslim girls out of mainstream education and thereby restricting their life chances).

A central point, then, is to recognise that racialised women are not different, but racialised – they are subordinated and exploited as Black women. It is necessary to understand that there are very real differences between those women who are both sexualised and racialised and those who are just appropriated as women. Feminist theories must be able to take account of and make sense of these differences. In the process it is essential to recognise, as Guillaumin (1995) has pointed out, that

> women, blacks and other dominated social groups are not categories existing of and by themselves ... they are constituted in the context of social relations of domination and dependence.
>
> (p. 17)

The process of sexualisation and racialisation ... functions so as to allocate humans within specific social categories and positions.

(p. 19)

In Britain the domination of white people over racialised groups can be traced to the historical legacy of colonialism which continues to legitimise the exploitation of Black, Asian and other racialised people and to sustain institutional as well as individualised discrimination. Black people are portrayed as 'aliens' who bring 'problems' and who cannot or will not be integrated into British society. In sociology Black women have been stereotyped, or the common-sense stereotypes of Black women have not been challenged. Asian women are seen as passive and as being controlled within patriarchal family systems. Afro-Caribbean women are seen as dominating and running matriarchal family structures. This analysis is empty of class reference, yet Black immigrants are situated most often in low-paid, low-status jobs. Despite the development of a Black and Asian middle class, they nevertheless suffer discrimination and prejudice. Feminist sociologists tend to have ignored the specific problems experienced by Black and Asian women living in contemporary Britain in their research, and theories have paid only lip service to incorporating racial oppression into analysis of gender oppression.

Although in Britain skin colour is used as an important marker of ethnic and racial difference, it is not the only form of ethnic boundary. Skin colour can be used to create an alien 'Other' in British society which is then blamed for various problems such as crime and unemployment, but other boundaries of ethnic difference can be constructed too – ones based upon language or family names, or religion, for example – and these can be more important in other parts of Europe, as the current war in former Yugoslavia illustrates (Anthias and Yuval Davis, 1993). Thus people or actions or jobs can become 'racialised' just as they can become sexualised and this is then the legitimation for treating those people differently or worse than other groups, or for paying those workers less than other workers.

Postmodern feminism

Postmodern feminists argue that it is not simply that we live in a postmodern world – the postmodern condition – but that postmodernism is itself a style or a way of theorising. Postmodern theory abandons explanatory goals and argues that there is no power outside discourse (Baudrillard, 1988). There can no longer be any attempt to describe, analyse or explain reality in an objective or scientific way. The boundary between theory and entertainment has broken down – theory has no superiority over common-sense thinking. Theorising in the modern world is play – playing with fragments, with pieces and making superficial generalisations.

Central to postmodern theory is the recognition of difference – race, sex, age – and deconstruction – 'a multiply divided subject in a multiply divided society'. By rejecting the idea of an essential core constituting the person, postmodernism shifts attention away from the subject as a manifestation of her 'essence' to 'the subject in process' – never unitary and never complete. Thus postmodern feminists reject both the humanist (modern) idea that the subject exists, as it were, in a state of nature – that there is 'a doer behind the deed' – and the existentialist theory that we are purely constituted by actions. Instead, postmodern theories argue that there *is* a doer behind the deed, but that the doer is variably constructed in and through the deed. 'Things' have a prediscursive existence, but they acquire a social and historical meaning only in discourse.

Postmodern feminists, therefore, reject the naturalism of biology. Sex differences, they argue, do not exist before being brought into consciousness through language. There is no natural pre-linguistic existence, a reality outside our understanding of it. Modern feminist theories argued that sex differences existed in a real world – that they had an objective existence independent of our understanding of them. Postmodernists argue that sex differences do not 'really' exist – they have no natural pre-linguistic reality.

Postmodern feminists reject, then, the idea of substituting feminist theories for malestream ones, because they reject the possibility of true knowledge and argue that there is a multiplicity of truths. They argue instead for the need to deconstruct truth claims and analyse the power effects that decisions as to truth entail – to recognise that knowledge is a part of power. It is necessary to focus on knowledge as opposed to truth, not only because there is no Truth, but because there is no reality 'out there' that can be the arbiter between competing truth claims. There is no one truth, no privileged knowledge or producers of knowledge. All knowledge is historically and culturally specific, the product of particular discourses. The discourses that create knowledge also create power – the power that constitutes subjects and objects and the mechanisms whereby subjects are subjugated. The power of the discourse depends on the extent to which its truth claims are successful – the extent to which the knowledge it produces is accepted as true.

The emphasis in postmodernist theory, then, is on heterogeneity, multiplicity and marginality and on the production of knowledge as opposed to truth – on the existence of multiple realities. There is a rejection of general/universal theory and an emphasis on the analysis of the local and the specific.

Postmodern theory, it is argued, rejects the possibility of sociology and indeed, for many, of feminism. It rejects the emancipatory project of the

Enlightenment and thereby it rejects the project of liberation. Difference, it is suggested, is a way of *not* having to think about oppression and subordination. It makes it possible to ignore the centrality and reality of male power – of the ways men oppress and subordinate women by, for example, sexual harassment, date rape, domestic violence and so on.

The adequacy of feminist theories

Feminist theory and research have contributed to our understanding of the subordination of women. All feminists are concerned to develop theories that enable women to understand their situation and to enable them to work towards liberating themselves. Feminists are not united and have developed a number of different theories that seek to uncover the causes of women's subordination and develop strategies for emancipating women.

The key questions become: what are the criteria of adequacy for a feminist theory, and which (if any) of the existing theories satisfy these criteria? All theory, including feminist theory, is simultaneously political and scientific. Feminist scholars have a common political interest in ending women's oppression and see their work as contributing to a comprehensive understanding of women's subordination. Feminist theory has to be politically adequate as well as scientifically adequate. A political theory puts forward values that are seen as morally desirable and acts as a guide to conduct. A scientific theory should be self-consistent, well supported by the available evidence, comprehensive in accounting for all the data, and have explanatory power. However, the competing feminist theories disagree as to what is to count as evidence, what needs explaining and which explanations are illuminating.

Liberal/reformist feminists tend to take a positivistic position, arguing for unbiased and impartial research. Theories and research developed within this perspective are seen as more adequate because they overcome the biases of malestream positivistic research by incorporating women so that gender-fair knowledge is produced.

Radical feminists are critical of malestream or patriarchal forms of knowledge. They argue that men as the dominant group or class impose their own distorted view of reality. Women's subjective understandings must be researched if they are to free themselves from the constraints of the distorting patriarchal knowledge. The ways in which women's knowledge can be revealed is by 'consciousness-raising', by small groups of women getting together and sharing their experiences. They argue that when women discuss their lives they will become aware of the ways in which they are oppressed by men. Shared experiences will make possible the constant development of the understanding of women's situation and ways to change it. The collective knowledge that is developed is guided by the special interests and values of women. The aim is to produce practical knowledge, and theory development is guided by practical interests and informed by the experiences of all women. It is argued that all women should be included in the production of knowledge, that it is impossible to separate the observer from the observed and the knower from the known.

Marxist and dual-systems feminists have developed a marxist realist epistemology to justify the way that their knowledge is produced (see Chapter 11). For traditional marxists knowledge is seen as socially constructed: knowledge production is one aspect of human productivity and consequently the basic categories of knowledge are always shaped by the human purposes and values on which they are based. Empirical knowledge is never value-free because the conceptual frameworks which are used to make sense of our lives and our place in them are shaped and limited by the interests and values of the society in which we live. In capitalist society the interests and values of the most powerful class – the bourgeoisie – shape and limit knowledge production, and the knowledge (ideologies) produced as truth tends to obscure or to justify the oppression of the proletariat. It is only in a classless society that it will be possible to produce undistorted knowledge.

However, in capitalist society it is evident that despite the dominance of ruling-class ideology, reality is perceived very differently by different groups. The different understandings of reality depend on group positions within society. A different view of reality is produced from the standpoint of the bourgeoisie than from the standpoint of the proletariat. The marxists argue that the view of the proletariat is more adequate because as the subordinate class it has a wider vision, because it includes the perspective of the subordinate class which is ignored in middle-class knowledge. Marxist theory, it is argued, is the most adequate, because it has the most comprehensive picture of the world – it reflects the interests and values of the working class, which it is argued are those of the totality of humans.

Marxist and dual-systems feminists have developed this epistemology to argue for women's standpoint as the basis for adequate knowledge. The special position of women gives them a special epistemological standpoint and therefore enables them to produce a less distorted view of the world than those available to capitalist or proletarian men. The adequacy of a feminist theory is tested by the extent to which it presents the world from the standpoint of women. The class position of the bourgeoisie prevents them from understanding the suffering of the oppressed; the position of men in the sex–gender system prevents them understanding the position of women. Women's standpoint is able to produce a less biased and more comprehensive view of reality than is provided by bourgeois science or male-dominated left alternatives.

To reveal the standpoint of women it is necessary to go beyond appearances to the essence of things: to go beyond the appearance of the naturalness of women's place and women's work to reveal the relations of subordination and domination of the sex–gender system. Feminist knowledge and feminist consciousness are not abstract or divorced from experience, but come from practice, from working on and changing the world – from revealing that women's subordination is not natural and inevitable but socially constructed and ideologically justified. This involves struggle because the ruling class and men want to preserve the *status quo* and prevent the development of women's knowledge and the emancipation of women. Women's knowledge transcends masculinist knowledge in the same way that proletarian knowledge transcends ruling-class knowledge. Hilary Rose (1976) illustrates this by reference to time. Time, she points out, has been a major issue between workers and the ruling class, but women's time has been ignored; the time that women spend on domestic labour has been naturalised – women are said to do it for love. However, women are aware of the hard, long hours that they work performing domestic labour, and this has led women to search for explanations for the unequal sexual division of labour, for why women do the unpaid domestic labour and for ways of transforming the situation. Marxist feminists have argued that this can be explained by capitalist class relations – the relationship between women and the capitalist system. Dual-systems feminists, however, argue that this is inadequate because it does not take account of patriarchal relationships and that it is necessary to understand how the two systems work together – patriarchy and capitalism – that man as well as capitalism benefits from women's unpaid domestic labour.

Postmodern and post-structuralist feminist theory rejects the view that feminist knowledge is in any way more adequate than other forms of knowledge. There is, they argue, no way of arbitrating between competing truth claims.

We would argue that the competing feminist theories ask different questions and thereby provide different understandings of what is going on. Rather than argue that one is more adequate than the others, we would suggest that the findings from empirical research guided by the different theories will all contribute to our understanding of the social and help us make sense of what is going on; each adds another piece to the patchwork.

Conclusions

In this chapter we have argued that malestream sociology has failed to develop theories that can make sense of the social world for women. Furthermore, there has been a resistance to taking account of the critique of malestream theory that has been developed by feminist sociologists. We have indicated that feminists have developed a number of theoretical perspectives that provide a basis both for making sense of what is going on in the social world and for political action – for challenging and changing patriarchy. These provide the basis for developing a sociology for women, one that provides an understanding of the social world that speaks to the experiences of women – a 'sociological imagination' for women.

SUMMARY

1   Sociology as a discipline is concerned with enabling us to understand the social world we inhabit and our position within it – to grasp the sociological imagination.

2   Feminist sociologists wish to reformulate sociology so that it provides a sociological imagination for women as well as men, something that malestream sociology has failed to do adequately.

3   Sociology is concerned to develop theories – frameworks that help us ask questions, direct us to the information that needs to be collected and suggests how to interpret/explain this information in order to provide answers to 'how' and 'why' questions.

4   Sociologists disagree both on what it is that is being explained and on how it can be explained. There are four theoretical positions on social reality – the positivist, the idealist, the realist and the poststructuralist.

5   Feminist theory is concerned with explaining and making sense of the social for women. There are a number of feminist theories, which differ in the ways in which they explain and on the strategies they indicate for women to become emancipated. Seven feminist perspectives were considered above – liberal/reformist, marxist, radical, dual systems, post-modern/poststructuralist, materialist and Black feminist perspectives.

FURTHER READING

Jaggar, A. (1983) *Feminist Politics and Human Nature*, Brighton: Wheatsheaf.

Tuana, N. and Tong, R. (eds) (1995) *Feminism and Philosophy*, Oxford: Westview.

Chapter three

Women and stratification

In all societies there are differences between people in terms of the amount of power and wealth which they command. The basis of stratification – the division of people according to a hierarchical system – varies from society to society. In very simple societies the divisions may be based on age and gender, older people having more power and prestige than younger ones and men more than women. In contemporary industrial societies such as Britain, sociologists argue, primary stratification is based on social class.

> Capitalist industrial societies are still stratified, and theories of social class still provide us with essential insights into the manner in which established inequalities in wealth and power associated with production and markets, access to educational and organisational resources and so on have systematically served to perpetuate these inequalities over time.
>
> (Crompton, 1993, p. 266)

However, class processes are not the only factors contributing to the reproduction and maintenance of social inequalities. As we have seen in Chapter 2, feminists argue that the sex–gender system also provides a primary form of stratification, with men having more power and prestige than women. Racial differences are likewise a primary basis of stratification, with Black people in Britain having less power and prestige than white people. (We are using 'Black' here in a political sense, to refer to non-white people – see p. 70.) Age is also a form of stratification, with young people and elderly ones having less power than those in the middle age groups (see Chapter 5). The division between the West (the advanced industrial societies) and the Rest, to use a distinction made by Stuart Hall (1992), also involves a relationship of exploitation and subordination and forms a principle of stratification.

In this chapter we will discuss the debates surrounding the exclusion of women from class research and the practice of determining a woman's class by the occupation of the (male) head of household. We shall also look briefly at sociological theories of racial subordination and Black feminist criticisms of white feminists for ignoring the racialised concerns of Black women. Finally, we shall examine the exploitation of women outside the West by Western countries, including Britain.

It is important to recognise that while all societies are divided along the fault-line of gender and all women are victims of inequality, women are not a unified and homogeneous group. They share a gender identity but are differentiated by age, sexual preference, race, class and geopolitical status. White, Western, middle-class varieties of feminist theory and practice are increasingly coming to be challenged as ignoring the experiences of other women. Postmodernist feminists have highlighted the dangers of inaccurate and inappropriate generalisation, stressing the importance of acknowledging the many voices of women (Barrett and Phillips, 1992). While it is important to recognise the different interests of women differently situated in terms of class, race, age and so on, other feminists (e.g. Doyal, 1995) have warned of the danger that in rejecting general categories we may lose sight of the *communalities* between women. Lesley Doyal points out, for example, that the body imposes real constraints on women's lives and that 'this is evidenced by the fact that the fight for bodily self-determination has been a central feature of feminist politics across very different cultures' (p. 7).

Malestream theories of social class

In all complex societies there is an unequal distribution of material and symbolic resources, resulting in economic and social inequality. Inequalities in modern industrial societies are generally seen as based on social class – inequalities associated with production, distribution and exchange. In Western sociology two main theories of social class dominate: those based on marxist theory, and those based on weberian theory. They are often referred to as neo-marxist and neo-weberian, to indicate that the basic theories of Marx and Weber have been developed to enable an explanation for and an understanding of class divisions and relationships in modern Western society. These theories are jointly referred to as *European* theories of class and see classes as distinct groups, each class comprising individuals with shared economic and social interests which are different from and may be in conflict with those in other classes. Members of a household are said to share a common class position, and generally the male head of household's class position determines that of all the members of his household.

Neo-weberian theories of social class

Weberian theories of social class are based on the view that class position is determined by the job market. Occupations that share a similar market position – that is, ones in which employees have comparable conditions of employment – are said to be in the same social class. Weber argued that members of a social class would seek both to protect their advantages *vis à vis* other groups and to try to enhance their share of rewards and resources. A group would exclude subordinate groups from securing its advantages by closure of opportunities to those below it, which it defines as inferior and ineligible. Subordinate groups try to break through this closure and to bite into the advantages of higher groups. Parkin (1979) and Murphy (1984) have argued that Weber's view of social stratification, and especially the concepts of market position and social closure, can be used to provide an adequate explanation of gender inequalities. Men, it is argued, have used strategies of social closure to exclude women from those occupations with the highest rewards and status.

Neo-marxist theories

In marxist theory social class is determined by relationship to the means of production – that is, basically, whether one controls capital or has merely labour to 'sell'. Those who share a common relationship to the means of production – owners, labourers – share the same class position. Marx argued that members of the same class would come to realise that they shared common interests and that these were in opposition to those of other social classes. The resulting class conflict would lead to the overthrow of the existing mode of production and its replacement by a new one. Marx argued that eventually there would be a classless society where no group exploited any other group.

According to Marx there are two main classes in capitalist society, the bourgeoisie and the proletariat. The former are the owners of the means of production and exploit the labour of the latter, who have to sell their labour on the market and at market-determined rates in order to subsist. Exploitation comes about because capitalists pay workers less than the true value of their labour and thus make a profit. The price of goods on the market (the exchange value) is made up of two elements, according to Marx: the costs of the raw materials, and the cost of labour. However the worker is only paid for some of his labour – that amount he can demand as a wage; the remainder is kept by the capitalist as profit. Thus a worker produces surplus value. However, only use value is produced when the product is consumed by the producer (as, for example, when a housewife provides a meal for a family, knits a cardigan for a child or grows vegetables for the table).

This distinction is important when we consider the position of women. Women's labour in the home produces use value, not surplus value, because the goods that women produce are consumed rather than sold on the market in the same way as the products that factory workers make are sold. Given that class position is determined by relation to the means of production and that the basis for class identification is the production of surplus value, then women with no direct relationship to paid labour cannot have a class position other than via an association with someone in paid employment. It is evident that classes for Marx were predominantly made up of men and that women were seen as marginal. Further, Marx saw class exploitation as the key issue and other forms of exploitation such as gender and race as secondary or derivative.

Feminist criticisms

Feminists have challenged the conventional view that stratification theory should only be about explaining class (economic) inequalities, and have suggested that it should be equally (or more) concerned with gender inequalities. Radical feminists have argued that sexual oppression is primary, while marxist and socialist feminists suggest that gender, class and racial inequalities have a mutual influence and cannot be analysed in isolation from each other (although marxist feminists tend to give primacy to economic class) – see Chapter 2.

The malestream response to such criticisms has tended to be defensive: either to argue that stratification theory is not concerned with explaining gender inequalities, or that existing theories are adequate. However, neither of these responses is adequate, because explaining the location of women in the stratification hierarchy is essential (as we will show) to understanding that of men. This is a major theme of feminist sociology and is developed throughout this book.

The class system in Britain

Rosemary Crompton (1993) has pointed out that there is a number of different ways in which the concept 'class' is used, both by sociologists and in everyday discourse. She indicates four ways in which the term has been and is used:

1   to refer to groups, ranked in a hierarchy, which are formally unequal and have legally defined rights;
2   to refer to groups ranked according to social standing or prestige;
3   to refer to structural inequalities – to the unequal resourcing of groups – which are the outcomes of competition for social resources in capitalist market societies; and
4   to refer to actual or potential social forces competing for control over scarce resources.

Sociologists make use of social class in virtually all their research; a person's social class is regarded as a summary variable which tells us about attitudes and values, standards of living, levels of education and so on. Sociological research has shown that social class is an important determinant of life chances in terms of education, health and so on (see Chapters 4 and 7). While there is a variety of social class scales used by sociologists and others, probably the best known are the Registrar General's and the Hope–Goldthorpe scales. Broadly, sociologists identify three social classes – upper, middle and working. The upper class forms a very small proportion of the population – about 10 per cent – and has received little sociological attention. It comprises the landed aristocracy and those who live on income derived from the ownership of land, business, property, etc. – what marxists refer to as the bourgeoisie. Top civil servants, the heads of the armed forces and members of the government may also be classified as upper class. The middle class comprises professional and managerial workers – for example, teachers, doctors, university lecturers, the clergy, factory managers, clerks, civil servants and so on. The working class is made up of service personnel and manual workers – e.g. waitresses, cooks, car mechanics, bricklayers, dustmen and so on.

The division between manual and non-manual workers was seen as an important class divide by Weber, who saw the skills that individuals brought to the market as the key determinant of the rewards they received for their work. Those with scarce skills could command higher pay and superior conditions of work. However, with universal schooling and the routinisation of clerical work (see Chapter 8) the significance of the manual/non-manual divide has been eroded as the pay and work conditions of (male) routine non-manual workers have declined relatively to those of skilled manual workers.

The Registrar General's scale (the government-devised scale) divides the population into six social classes based on the occupation of the head of household:

I   higher professional or managerial;
II   lower professional or managerial;
IIIN supervisory and lower/routine non-manual;
IIIM skilled manual;
IV   semi-skilled manual; and
V   unskilled manual.

The Hope–Goldthorpe scale, specifically developed for the Oxford Mobility Study (see, e.g., Goldthorpe *et al.*, 1980), is similarly hierarchical, except that in the middle range classes III–V are seen as distinct but of equivalent standing. The seven classes of the scale are:

I   higher professional and managerial, and large proprietors;
II   lower professional and managerial;
III   routine non-manual;
IV   small proprietors and the self-employed (petty bourgeoisie);
V   foremen and technicians;
VI   skilled manual workers; and
VII   semi-skilled and unskilled manual workers.

As Heath (1980) has pointed out, there is general agreement among the various classifications as to who is at the top and who is at the bottom, but some disagreement about the ordering in the middle.

As the basis of classification is occupation, those who do not have paid employment cannot easily be classified. For men the difficulty of classifying the non-employed is overcome by allocation to class of former employment or by declaring a special class position/category for the unemployed/retired. However, these solutions are not considered for married women because they are assumed to share their husbands' class, being their husbands' dependants and therefore sharing their class position and interests. For this reason, even if women do have paid employment it is often not thought to determine their class position.

Women in class theory

Feminists have challenged the practice by which many women (the majority) are said to have a derived class position, determined by the occupational experiences of the man with whom they live. Ann and Robin Oakley (1979) have pointed out that the instructions generally given to survey interviewers are such that if a man is living in the household it will be his occupation that determines the household's class. This is not just a coding device: it amounts to a theoretical statement that women's experiences, loyalties and social action are determined by the occupational position of the man with whom they live, and not by their own experiences. Acker (1973) suggests that there are five shortcomings to the conventional approach:

1   the assumption that the family is the rational unit of analysis, with complete class equivalence within it;
2   that the social position of the family is determined by the occupation of the head of the household;
3   that the male is necessarily the head of the household;
4   that women not living with a man nonetheless determine their own class;
5   the assumption that inequalities between men and women are inherent and inevitable.

Feminists argue not just that the classification of women by the class of male heads of household is sexist, but that the basic assumptions on which this position rests are false. Sheila Allen (1982) points out that a wife does not acquire her husband's education on marriage, nor does she automatically acquire a socially or politically powerful background (which can often be lost on divorce or widowhood). Feminists have gone on to demonstrate that the incorporation of women in research on social class necessitates at the very least a modification of existing theories and conclusions, if not a complete rethinking of them (see Crompton and Mann, 1986; Abbott and Sapsford, 1987a). Elizabeth Garnsey (1978) argues that taking the family as the only relevant unit of analysis obscures the inequalities between women and men within it (see Chapter 6) and also the different market and work situations which they face outside it (see Chapter 8). Women are at the bottom within each occupational class, and this pervasive inequality needs to be seen as central to the study of social stratification. The participation of women in the labour market affects the nature of that market for men. Women are concentrated in low-paid, low-status jobs, and this affects the range of jobs available for men. The sex-typing of jobs as 'female' has resulted, historically, in them losing status and economic reward – as in the case of clerical work – or being created as lowly paid, low status jobs – as, for example, speech therapy in Britain (Crompton and Sanderson, 1990). It is just not the case, as David Lockwood (for example) has argued, that 'it is the position of an occupation within some hierarchy of authority that is decisive for its status and not the sex of the person who happens to be in it' (1986, p. 21). The ways in which female wage labour and domestic labour are combined and interact with each other and with the capitalist system also have complex consequences for class structure and class consciousness.

Michele Stanworth (1984) argues that assimilating a woman's class position to that of her husband is not justified by the evidence, and that doing so closes off some of the most interesting issues in class analysis. She points out that John Goldthorpe (e.g. 1983), who argues for the conventional approach, rests his case on three key assertions: that husbands are more involved in the labour process than wives (being more likely to have full-time, continuous employment), that wives' patterns of employment can largely be explained by the class position of husbands, and that contemporary marriages are largely homogeneous with respect to class (i.e. that husbands and wives have the same class of occupation when both are in paid employment). She demonstrates that Goldthorpe's own evidence does not support two of these claims and that none of them has the logical consequences which he implies. It is true that most women do take time out from the labour market at some point, but Jean Martin and Ceridwyn Roberts (1984), for example, demonstrate that they nonetheless show a substantial and life-long commitment to paid employment. That women's labour-market participation is dependent on husband's class receives little support even from Goldthorpe's own data (the Oxford Mobility Survey), and the timing of a woman's withdrawal from the labour market seems to be less affected by husband's occupational class than by the class of her own job. Finally, if female routine non-manual workers are to be reclassified as working class, as Goldthorpe suggests, in an attempt to 'solve' the problem of cross-class marriages, this does indeed abolish one kind of cross-class marriage – but only at the expense of creating another kind, where a routine non-manual woman (now classified as working class) is married to a non-manual man. In addition Anthony Heath (1980 – see also Heath and Britten, 1984) demonstrates that cross-class marriages are in fact qualitatively and quantitatively different from other households on most criteria associated with social class.

Abbott and Sapsford (1987a) argue that their analysis of the data on the female respondents in the Open University *People in Society* survey demonstrates that women do have a subjective class identification and that this is no better predicted from husband's or head of household's occupation than from own occupation and/or personal and 'premarital' attributes such as class of origin (determined by father's occupation) and educational level. Women's overall social imagery, whether they saw society as conflictual or harmonious and divided or homogeneous, was again no better predicted by head of household's class than by a woman's own attributes. They conclude that the view that a woman's class sentiments are solely and necessarily determined by the occupation of the man with whom she lives is not sustainable.

On the basis of the research to date it is evident that there is a need for women to be included in social class research. It is equally evident that women's class placement should be determined by their own occupations, or that the household's class position should be determined by reference to the occupation of both husband and wife. In sociological research generally, however, the most common approach is still to use husband's occupation to determine the social class of wives.

Women and social mobility

Social mobility is a central process in modern society. From its study we learn both about people's life chances and about the underlying structures of our society. When we compare the social circumstances of a person's early life with the social and occupational position that he or she currently holds, we can see how that person has 'got on in life'. When we examine career paths through education, first job and subsequent employment, we discover routes, blockages, successes and failures which are patterned and systematic. They therefore need to be understood as shared experiences, and also as the outcome of social processes as well as of individual talents and achievements. Social mobility combines the study of paid employment, labour markets and occupational change with the analysis of structured inequalities and social class. Not only is it a central topic in sociology as a discipline; it is also a topic that lies at the heart of our experience of our own lives.

Feminist sociologists have drawn attention to the invisibility of women in most sociological studies of social mobility. On the other hand it would be wrong to claim that we know nothing about female mobility. There *has* been research into the social mobility of women, but much of it has not been published or received the attention it arguably deserves. The apparent absence of women from British mobility analyses until quite recently can mainly be attributed to their absence from the main published reports of three of the most extensive empirical studies of social mobility – Glass, 1954; Goldthorpe *et al.*, 1980; Payne, 1987a,b. (The exception is Marshall *et al.*, 1988.) However, the Scottish Mobility Study (Payne, 1987a,b) did collect information on the wives of the male sample (Chapman, 1990a,b), and the Irish Mobility Study collected data on both men and women (see, e.g., Miller and Hayes, 1990). Pamela Abbott and Roger Sapsford (1987a) have produced information from the Open University's *People in Society* survey. John Goldthorpe and Clive Payne (1986) have extracted relevant data from the British Election Survey, and Dale *et al.* (1983) have analysed short-term shifts and female classification using the General Household Survey and the Labour Force Survey. Most comprehensively of all, Gordon Marshall and his colleagues (1988) drew a random sample of men and women for the Essex Class Project. The UK Office of Population Censuses and Surveys has also carried out a very comprehensive study of women's intergenerational mobility – see Martin and Roberts (1984) and Dex (1987).

The problem is that this growing body of work has not yet been taken up by sociologists in general, who have been influenced by the fact that most of the large empirical studies have focused mainly on men. Reports of these studies are often written in a way that suggests that their findings from male samples can be generalised to the whole population. Alternatively, the impression is given that patterns of female social mobility are of no importance or interest.

Reasons for the exclusion of women from mobility studies

The conventional view justifies the non-inclusion of women in mobility studies in two ways:

1   Mobility is about movement between social classes, and as social class is based on the occupation of the head of household, most women have only a derived class position – i.e. their class is determined by the occupation of their male partners or fathers. If women have no independent class position, they cannot be mobile between classes, and there is no need to study the movement of women.

2   Women do not have the same occupational career patterns as men and it is therefore difficult, if not impossible, to measure their mobility patterns. For example, John Goldthorpe (1983, 1984) has claimed that

   (a)   women have a low economic participation rate and therefore tend to have no measuring points (jobs) for the calculation of class mobility;

   (b)   the apparent rise in participation rate is largely due to part-time employment, and therefore women's employment is less salient than men's permanent and full-time employment;

   (c)   there are relatively few cross-class marriages (that is, men married to women in the same social class as themselves), so for most women taking husband's class would do no disservice to the real position; and

   (d)   whether a woman works at all is largely dependent on her husband's class position.

Empirical research, however, throws doubt on these claims. The majority of women are fully committed to the labour market and work there for most of their employable lives (Martin and Roberts, 1984). Patterns of female mobility are broadly similar, whether women work full or part time (Abbott and Sapsford, 1987a). Nearly half of all marriages where both partners have paid employment cross classes – i.e. husbands and wives are in different classes (Payne *et al.*, 1981; Marshall *et al.*, 1988). Nor do empirical data support the contention that wives' employment is conditioned by their husbands' class (see Stanworth, 1984; Abbott and Sapsford, 1987a; Payne and Abbott, 1990a).

Measuring social mobility

Sociologists are interested in two types of social mobility – *inter*generational and *intra*generational. Intergenerational mobility measures the movement up or down the class structure of a son or daughter, compared with his or her parents. Generally, in the major mobility studies, a son's occupation at the time of the survey has been compared with that of his father when the son was 14 years old (before the beginning of the son's working life). When women have been incorporated in studies, again their occupational class has been compared with that of their fathers. (The Irish Mobility Study did collect data on mothers' occupations, but most studies have not done so because married women were much less likely to be economically active in the past.) Intragenerational mobility measures the movement of an individual up or down the occupational class structure during their own lifetimes.

Male mobility studies

A number of major conclusions have been reached as a result of the analysis of male mobility. It has been demonstrated that there is a high rate of social mobility and that upward mobility outweighs downward mobility. The major reason for the relatively high rate of (male) upward mobility is said to be change in occupational structure – a decline in manual jobs and an increase in white-collar, professional and managerial jobs. Because of differential fertility – the middle classes produce insufficient children (sons) to replace themselves – there is a need for net upward mobility. While the majority of men in manual occupations are the sons of manual workers, those in white-collar, professional and managerial occupations have fathers from across the occupational class structure. Nevertheless, middle-class fathers generally have sons in middle-class occupations. It is argued, therefore, that high rates of social mobility in Britain are not so much the result of an open society – a society open to talent – but to changes in the occupational structure (see, e.g., Goldthorpe *et al.*, 1980).

In terms of intragenerational mobility, it has been suggested that it is still possible for men to be upwardly mobile as a result of advancement at work, as opposed to the gaining of credentials (again, see Goldthorpe *et al.*, 1980). Geoff Payne (1987a,b) has suggested that the possibilities of upward social mobility while in employment in the absence of credentials vary by occupational sector – it is more likely to occur in the old heavy industries (e.g. mining, metal work) but unlikely in the service sector (e.g. teaching, health services, public sector white-collar employment, banking, insurance).

Female social mobility

Analysis of female social mobility suggests that patterns of intergenerational and intragenerational social mobility are very different from those of men. This is perhaps not surprising, given that the female occupational distribution is very different from that of males (see Chapter 8). There is vertical and horizontal segregation of the labour market by gender. Women are much more likely to be found in service occupations (teacher, nurse, librarian) than in 'professions' (doctor, lawyer, chartered accountant), and there are concentrations of women in routine office work and shop work. Also of interest is the segment within a class filled by women as opposed to men. From labour market studies we know that women are more likely than men to occupy the lower-status positions within occupations – to be teachers rather than school heads, lecturers rather than professors – and that women's work is less likely to be classified as skilled in the manual sector.

There is also some evidence that women are less likely than men to be seen as promotable, and that they are recruited on the specific understanding that they will not seek promotion. The Essex Survey (Marshall *et al.*, 1988) provides information on this by examining the market and work situations of men and women in each Hope–Goldthorpe category. Table 3.1 shows the average gross annual pay, percentage seeing themselves as on a career ladder, and average scale scores for autonomy, decision-making and supervision. These data clearly indicate that men score higher than women on virtually every item within each class. Especially important is the clear difference between men and women in routine non-manual work (where women predominate, Class III). The data indicate clearly that men in this type of employment, on average, earn considerably more than women and are much more likely to be on a career ladder.

Labour market segmentation is a crucial factor in understanding female intergenerational mobility, and this has been demonstrated in all the major

TABLE 3.1 Market and work situation of men and women in full-time employment

Social class/ gender		Mean wages (£000)	Career (% affirmative)	Autonomy (mean score)	Decision-making (mean score)	Supervision (mean score)
I	M	14.1	80	5.1	3.7	4.5
	F	9.4	77	4.7	2.2	3.0
II	M	11.0	75	4.4	2.4	3.1
	F	7.0	72	3.8	1.5	2.5
III	M	7.2	60	3.5	0.7	0.4
	F	4.9	43	2.7	0.4	0.4
V	M	8.6	72	3.0	1.6	3.3
	F	3.6	56	3.5	1.3	2.8
VI	M	7.0	36	1.9	0.4	0.2
	F	4.4	35	1.7	0.3	0.1
VII	M	6.6	26	1.9	0.2	0.2
	F	4.6	11	1.4	0.0	0.0

Source: Marshall *et al.*, 1988, Table 4.9.

Notes:
Class IV (self-employed) has been omitted from the table. 'Full time' is defined as working 30+ hours per week. The mean scores refer to composites of questionnaire items and can score from 0 (low) to 6 (high).

studies (see Abbott and Sapsford, 1987a, for a review). The occupational categories and classes that daughters enter are likely to be different from those entered by sons, meaning that the intergenerational social mobility of daughters and sons is likely to be different. This can be illustrated using data from the Essex Mobility Study (Marshall *et al.*, 1988). Table 3.2 shows that the limited availability of service positions for women creates a downflow of the daughters of service-class men into Hope–Goldthorpe Class III (office/sales work). Sons are, first, less likely to be downwardly mobile, and second, more likely, if they are mobile, to move into manual work. The sons of men in manual occupations are more likely to be upwardly mobile than their daughters, and much more likely to enter professional or managerial occupations. The upwardly mobile daughters of men in manual occupations are most likely to end up in Hope–Goldthorpe Class III (see Table 3.3). Compared with men, when women do experience downward mobility into the working class, it is more likely to be to semi- or unskilled manual work than to the skilled manual class.

Thus the distributions between and within occupational classes are not just different; the terms 'upwards' and 'downwards' cover different types of movement for women than for men. Brothers and sisters are likely to

TABLE 3.2 Current class and class of origin, percentaged by current class

| | Current class | | | | | | |
	I	II	III	IV	V	VI	VII
	Males						
Class of origin	%	%	%	%	%	%	%
I	14.1	13.8	15.8	4.1	3.0	4.6	2.1
II	12.0	19.3	5.3	8.2	1.5	6.4	3.4
III	8.7	6.4	0.0	2.7	4.5	9.2	1.4
IV	14.1	12.8	13.2	35.6	13.6	9.2	9.0
V	17.4	19.3	13.2	11.0	22.7	13.8	21.4
VI	13.0	16.5	34.2	12.3	30.3	29.4	24.1
VII	20.7	11.9	18.4	26.0	24.2	27.5	38.6
	Females						
Class of origin	%	%	%	%	%	%	%
I	20.0	8.9	8.6	4.3	0.0	0.0	2.1
II	20.1	13.3	5.6	0.0	0.0	0.0	3.2
III	5.0	10.0	5.6	4.3	0.0	4.8	3.2
IV	25.0	15.6	10.5	21.7	13.3	4.8	11.7
V	0.0	24.4	21.0	21.7	6.7	23.8	13.8
VI	20.0	18.9	30.2	13.0	40.0	42.9	24.5
VII	10.0	8.9	18.5	34.8	40.0	23.8	41.5

Source: Marshall *et al.*, 1988, Table 4.7.

experience different chances of mobility despite sharing a father. These points can be made strongly from the full mobility tables of the Essex Mobility Study (Marshall *et al.*, 1988). Of men in Class I (see Table 3.2), 26 per cent came from Class I or II origins, 40 per cent from Class III–V, and 34 per cent from Classes VI or VII (which are manual occupations). The comparable figures for women are 40 per cent from Classes I and II, 30 per cent from Classes III–V, and 30 per cent from Classes VI or VII. Looking specifically at the highest class, we can see that 14 per cent of the men in it come from Class I origins, and 20 per cent of women (Table 3.2), but that almost 28 per cent of men with Class I fathers finished up in Class I, but only 14 per cent of such women (Table 3.3). What emerges, therefore, is not so much the relative power of Class I fathers to transmit their status as the relative dearth of occupational places in Class I which are open to women, meaning that entering this class is a far less realistic possibility for women than for men. Women's

TABLE 3.3 Current class and class of origin, percentaged by class of origin

		Current class						
		I	*II*	*III*	*IV*	*V*	*VI*	*VII*
Class of origin/gender		%	%	%	%	%	%	%
I	M	27.7	31.9	12.8	6.4	4.3	10.6	6.4
	F	13.8	27.6	48.3	3.4	0.0	0.0	6.9
II	M	20.8	39.6	3.8	11.3	1.9	13.2	9.4
	F	14.3	42.9	32.1	0.0	0.0	0.0	10.7
III	M	25.0	21.9	0.0	6.3	9.4	31.3	6.3
	F	4.2	37.5	37.5	4.2	0.0	4.2	12.5
IV	M	14.4	15.6	5.6	28.9	10.0	11.1	14.4
	F	9.1	25.5	30.9	9.1	3.6	1.8	20.0
V	M	14.4	18.9	4.5	7.2	13.5	13.5	27.9
	F	0.0	27.5	42.5	6.3	1.3	6.3	16.3
VI	M	8.0	12.4	9.5	6.6	14.6	23.4	25.5
	F	3.6	15.3	44.1	2.7	5.4	8.1	20.7
VII	M	11.9	8.1	4.4	11.9	10.0	18.8	35.0
	F	2.0	8.2	30.6	8.2	6.1	5.1	39.8

Source: Marshall *et al.*, 1988, Table 4.8.

mobility from Class I origins is partly into Class II but more into Class III, where there are vastly more opportunities for women than for men. A few women of Class II origins finish up in Class I, but the vast majority remain in Class II or fall to Class III. Long-range social mobility is also more common among men than women: 21 per cent of men from working-class origins are in Class I or II occupations, but only 15 per cent of women. Whatever their origins, women are much more likely than men to finish up in Class III. Men are also more likely than women to be upwardly mobile into self-employment (Class IV) or supervisory positions (Class V). If women are mobile into the 'service class' (Classes I and II), they are more likely to finish up in Class II than Class I. Within the working class (Classes VI and VII), men are far more likely than women to achieve the higher of the two classes.

Conclusions

In the above analysis we have concentrated on examining female inter-generational mobility compared with that of men. Empirical findings also suggest, not surprisingly, that patterns of female intragenerational mobility are different from those of men (see Abbott and Sapsford, 1987a; Marshall *et al.*, 1988; Payne and Abbott, 1990a). This demonstrates that we cannot generalise from the findings of research on men to the nature of the social structure for men *and* women. Furthermore, it leads us to question the major conclusions drawn from the findings of research on male-only samples.

Three major mobility studies (Glass, 1954; Goldthorpe *et al.*, 1980; Payne, 1987a,b) were concerned to test the openness of British society – how much social fluidity there is in the class structure. To leave out women is to miss important aspects of this question. The changes in the occupational structure of advanced capitalist societies in recent times have been in the expansion of white-collar occupations. There has also been an expansion in the proportion of jobs done by women and in the proportion of women engaged in paid work. However, women come in at the bottom of job categories and, particularly, as routine non-manual workers, 'driving' men further up the social scale. Both men and women are potential candidates for the mobility opportunities generated by the changes in demand for labour. However, women have exhibited a different pattern of mobility from men's. Seventy-five per cent of professional and managerial jobs are 'male jobs'. Women are allocated to other classes, by structural processes which owe little to ability, natural right or the success of capitalism.

However, while women have all this in common, they are also divided by class (see Goldthorpe and Payne, 1986; Abbott and Sapsford, 1987a). Women are not equally likely to end up in the same class of job irrespective of class origins; there is a tendency to gravitate towards routine non-manual work, but women in professional and managerial jobs are highly likely to have come from a similar background – this holds particularly for the highest class of occupations – and women in manual jobs are likely to have come from a working-class background. Gender inequalities do not abolish the need to look at class inequalities; they exist, and they are demonstrably important.

Measuring women's social class

The research we have discussed so far uses the existing class scales, measuring women's social class as if the scales used for classifying men's occupations can equally be used for women. However, some women – for example, full-time housewives – are currently without paid employment outside the home. Others may be in paid employment but not at a level compatible with their qualifications or with the place they could achieve in the labour market if free from domestic responsibilities. Even the apparently simple case of single women is not so simple in practice because labour-market segregation means that women tend to be clustered in particular occupations (see Chapter 8), which are themselves clustered into relatively restricted ranges of the occupational scales which have been developed with men's jobs in mind. This makes fine discrimination difficult and tends to suggest that women are more homogeneous with respect to occupational class than women's own views and experiences would suggest. For example, on some scales an airline stewardess and a waitress end up in the same social class, as do a shop assistant and a personal secretary.

Four basic positions have been taken on how to cope with these problems:

1   to retain the household (family) as the unit of analysis, but to take women's occupational position and/or other characteristics into account when determining its class position;
2   to locate women in the class system on the basis of their own paid employment, without reference to the remainder of the household, but to develop more adequate measures of social class;
3   to attempt to develop a measure of 'consumption class' for families which will take account of the influence of all family members on lifestyle, and to look in parallel at an occupation-based measure of *individuals'* market position, one which more adequately distinguishes between women's occupations than the conventional scales; or
4   to locate women in the class system by taking into account both their paid employment (if any) and their role in unpaid domestic labour.

The position that the household should remain the unit of analysis, but taking account of women's employment in assigning it a class, has resulted in two distinct 'solutions'. One, the 'dominance principle' (Haugh, 1973; Erikson, 1984; Goldthorpe and Payne, 1986), would in practice make very little difference to conventional practice. It involves taking as the class of the household the occupational class of whichever partner has the highest class of occupation, provided that this person works full-time and is fully committed to the labour market. In practice, then, husband's class will determine the class of most households, but in a (non-trivial but relatively small) minority of 'deviant' households the class would be taken from the wife's occupation. The other solution is to compute a joint social class for the household as a whole by combining the classes of husband and wife, if the wife is economically active (Britten and Heath, 1983; Heath and Britten, 1984; Pahl and Wallace, 1985). A variant which goes further by giving some weight to personal characteristics of full-time housewives would combine a number of possible indicators – education, housing tenure – with occupational levels (Osborne and Morris, 1979).

If we are to look at women's social (occupational) mobility then it is necessary to classify them on the basis of their own occupations. If women are classified by their own occupations, market and class inequalities are available as topics of investigation for both men and women in a way that they are not if we aggregate men and women together into a household class. Doubts have been raised, however, about the adequacy of existing class scales for this purpose, because of the concentration of women in certain occupational groups that are much more rarely filled by men. A number of attempts has been made to develop an alternative social class scale that more adequately reflects the class position of women. In some cases the scales have been developed for use on both men and women, and in others for women only. For a review of the alternative scales that have been developed, see Pamela Abbott and Roger Sapsford (1987a).

Conclusions: social class

There is increasing empirical evidence to suggest that women's social class position cannot be ignored or treated as derivative from the social class position of husbands or fathers; not only does this fail to explain their social and political behaviour, but it often leads to mistaken conclusions about the social mobility of men and the structure of British society for both genders. For example, the social mobility of men and the openness of the occupational structure to upward mobility cannot be fully understood without taking the mobility and occupational distribution of women into account. Women's preparedness to 'have a job' rather than following a career is certainly important in explaining male mobility; few 'dual career' families actually have two partners following careers – more often the male has a career and the woman fits her work in to the demands of that career (Crompton and Sanderson, 1986). Janet Finch (1983a) has demonstrated the importance of a wife's unpaid labour for many men in enabling them to follow their occupations, and Tony Chapman (1984) has suggested that most upward mobility depends on the wife being able to take on the 'higher' lifestyle.

The study of women's social class convinces us at least of the importance of studying family members in their own right and not making common-sense assumptions about shared family norms and interests or shared experience of the social world. It may be, contingently, that there are considerable shared interests and a considerable amount of shared experience. It may be that class is a more important principle of stratification than gender in our society. That this is the case must be demonstrated, however, not taken for granted in the untheorised way which has been typical of malestream sociologists, and for this we need adequate tools and unblinkered theories so that women can be fully incorporated in sociological research. Crompton (1993) concludes that

In certain situations – for example, in the labour market and employment contexts – a woman's 'own' occupational class situation is probably the most appropriate measure to use. In respect of other factors – such as, for example, voting behaviour and social attitudes – there is a considerable body of evidence to the effect that 'household class' might be a more useful indicator. To use a simple example, a low-level female clerical worker married to a bricklayer is considerably more likely to vote Labour than a woman in a similar job who is married to an insurance manager. Both women, however, would on an individual basis be in Goldthorpe's 'Intermediate' class.

(pp. 96–7)

This conclusion is borne out by recent analysis of class identification and voting intentions of married women in the 1991 British Social Justice Survey and the 1987 and 1992 British General Election Surveys, which indicated that women's voting intentions correlated more strongly with their husbands' occupation than with their own (Marshall *et al.*, 1995). A similar conclusion was reached using cross-national data for other advanced capitalist societies, but data for the former communist countries suggested that women's voting intentions correlated more highly with their own employment class than that of their husbands (Marshall *et al.*, 1995). However, it is important to recognise that both partners in a marriage are contributing to the economic and social status of the household and are likely to bring attitudes and values into the relationship (see Leiulfsrud and Woodward, 1987). It is perhaps not surprising that men's and women's class identifications and actions relate to the interests of their household. It is also the case that domestic partnerships open up opportunities for individuals and that changes in female employment opportunities may be modifying the extent of class inequalities. Peter Townsend and his colleagues (1987), for example, have shown that income rather than class is a major determinant of health status – two-income working-class households are likely to have better health than one-income working-class households. Norman Bonney (1988) has shown that high-earning women tend to have high-earning partners and that the female partners of professional and managerial male employees have higher earnings than other employed females. This finding indicates an accentuation of class divisions between households – a trend that could not even be detected if data were not collected on both men and women.

SUMMARY

1   The study of social class has been a key issue in sociology, and women have traditionally been excluded from it on the grounds that they are not continuously in the labour market and that their social class is determined by their husbands' jobs. Recently some have argued that this tradition should be continued.

2   Feminists have argued that this treatment of women in class theory is not only sexist but leads to a distortion of our understanding of social class, particularly in matters such as social mobility, the openness of society and the question of class identification.

3   Feminists have offered a number of alternative ways of working. Some have attempted to incorporate an understanding of women into existing social class schemas. Others have tried to develop new forms of classification which take both men and women into account. Finally, others have argued that men's classifications are totally inadequate for accounting for women's social class and have developed classifications based upon women's occupations alone.

Racialised women in Britain

In this section we want to examine the situation and life experiences of women who have come to Britain as migrants, from Third World countries, and their daughters. We refer to them as 'Black women' because of the problems associated with other possible terms. The term 'coloured' has distasteful connotations because of its use in South Africa. 'Ethnic minority groups' tends to suggest that the majority of the population do not have an ethnicity – or that one is shared by all those we are meaning to include in our designated group – and to carry overtones of inferiority, whereas 'Black' is a term that has been reclaimed by those struggling for the emancipation of oppressed people. Kum-Kum Bhavnani (1993), for example, has suggested that 'Black' is used in Britain as a political category encompassing all who experience the racism directed at non-white people – at racialised groups. She goes on to define racism as

> a system of domination and subordination based on spurious biological notions that human beings can be fitted into racially distinct groups. It is identified as a 'natural' process and is seen to be a logical consequence of

the differentiation of human beings into 'races'. Given that there is no sound evidence from the natural and biological sciences to justify the assumption that the human species can be divided up into separate 'races', both 'race' and racism come to be economic, political, ideological and social expressions. In other words, 'race' is not a social category which is empirically defined; rather, it is created, reproduced and challenged through economic, political and ideological institutions.

(p. 27)

Bhavnani goes on to suggest that four processes that feminists have revealed as resulting in the marginalisation of issues relating to women also apply to racialised groups:

1   *Erasure* is the process by which experiences are removed or 'hidden' from history.
2   *Denial* is the process by which differences between men and women, white and black, heterosexual and homosexual, young and old, working-class and middle-class are not acknowledged.
3   *Invisibility* is the outcome when differences are not considered as something worthy of research, for example, respondents in a survey are not analysed separately by racialised groups, or gender, or sexual orientation, or age – they are not considered important or relevant variables, and thus differences are rendered invisible.
4   *Tokenism* is when racial groups – or gender, or class – are analysed separately, but the need to modify or reformulate the analysis to take full account of difference is not recognised.

It would be problematic if feminists, while criticising the marginalisation of women, did not acknowledge that the same processes have marginalised racialised groups.

In the period after the Second World War, Britain encouraged New Commonwealth citizens to immigrate to fill the job vacancies in the growing economy. The initial immigration in the 1950s was mainly from the West Indies, and Asian immigrants (from India and Pakistan) came in the late 1950s and the 1960s. Immigrants were expected to come and fill the growing number of job vacancies and to take on the low-paid, low-skilled jobs that the native population were reluctant to fill. These immigrants were often met with hostility by the native white population, who regarded them as inferior and a threat to the British way of life. They were often seen as in competition for the scarce housing, educational and health services and blamed for the deteriorating state of the inner cities. While many, especially West Indians, had thought that coming to Britain would be like coming home, returning to the mother country, they have experienced hostility from the native population, a low standard of living, poor educational facilities for their children and unemployment. The daughters of immigrants have experienced even greater problems. Some are critical of the low-status, poorly paid jobs, the treatment from white society that their parents experience and the poor education that they frequently receive. Problems of finding employment often mean that their hopes and aspirations have been shattered.

Black women experience subordination and exploitation as women, as members of the working class and on the basis of their colour. Sociologists have been concerned to reject biological and psychological explanations for the subordinate and inferior position of Black women in Britain. Instead they have explored the social and structural aspects of social inequalities and examined how Black women became socially constructed as subordinate. They have considered differences in power, both in social and in economic terms, and examined the ways in which ideologies have come to construct Black women as inferior and to justify their inferior status. Women immigrants have not come to Britain just as the dependants of men. They make up about a quarter of the foreign labour force in Britain and over 40 per cent of all migrants (Phizacklea, 1983b). As Sheila Allen and Carole Walkowitz (1987) have argued, racialised and ethnic minority women tend to be concentrated in arduous and poorly paid work and experience high rates of unemployment as well as being engaged in unregistered home work (see Chapter 8).

The status of racialised groups has been explained by reference to biological factors – for example, that people in them are inherently less intelligent than white people, a proposition to which the work of psychologists such as Eysenck (1971) and Jensen (1973) has given some scientific credibility. An alternative explanation is one in terms of norms and values – that they do not share the values of white society and that this explains why they do not 'get on'. Similarly, racial prejudice has been explained in terms of the blind and irrational prejudice against 'outsiders' of bigoted individuals or the inability of groups to cope with the 'unusual' cultural character of a different racial group – that is, the group's way of life, including language, religion, family customs, clothes and so on. All these explanations tend to present non-white people as 'deviant' or as 'strangers' and seek to explain reactions to this status. This leads to a tendency to study the characteristics of ethnic groups themselves and to make a problem out of these very characteristics. Hence Asians are seen as too tied to tradition, hampered by 'arranged marriages', or too passive; West Indians are seen as disruptive or criminal, too active or militant. More recent work by Black writers has attempted an alternative approach: to analyse the institutional structures within *white* society – and this includes white sociology – which serve to oppress non-white people and to present 'the problem' in terms of them rather than in terms of white racist society (e.g. Centre for Contemporary Cultural Studies, 1982; Anthias and Yuval Davis, 1993).

Two major theories of ethnicity and race have emerged in sociology. Marxists argue that racial disadvantage can be explained by reference to the class structure under capitalism. Racialised groups are an integral part of the proletariat, the working class who are exploited by capitalists. Racial prejudice can be explained by reference to Britain's colonial past and the development of ideologies during the nineteenth century that justified Britain's exploitation of the Black inhabitants of the colonies by suggesting that they were inferior, less than fully human. The waves of immigration in the 1950s and 1960s must be seen in the context of the needs of international capitalism. The immigrants came to a country where ideologies of racial inferiority/superiority already existed. As the economic situation has changed and a shortage of jobs has arisen, prejudice has increased to some extent. Furthermore, marxists argue that the ruling class is able to exploit the ideologies of racial prejudice to maintain its position of dominance. Thus conflict between Black and white working-class people is based on the whites blaming the Blacks for their bad housing, lack of hospital resources, etc., while the Black population blame their plight on the prejudice of the whites with whom they come into contact. This, it is argued, deflects attention away from the 'real' causes of the problems, the lack of adequate provision for the working class as a whole.

Weberian sociologists reject the marxist theory of racial divisions. They argue that racial disadvantage arises out of competition between groups for scarce resources – such as housing, employment and education. A group seizes on identifiable social and/or physical characteristics of potential or actual competitors and use them to exclude them from the competition. (We have already seen in this chapter how men use social characteristics to exclude women from higher-class occupations.) In modern Britain the white native population has used social closure against racialised groups, especially those from the New Commonwealth and their descendants.

Weberian sociology better explains the diversity of ethnic divisions, but without adequately explaining why those particular characteristics rather than others should have been chosen. Marxists have provided a better historical framework, but they have to discard most of what is distinctive about the problem of race in order to explain it.

Black feminists have criticised both theories for taking no adequate account of gender differences and for not realising that the experiences of racialised women and the ways in which they are exploited are different from the case of racialised men. As Bryan *et al.* (1985, p. 1) say of their own experiences, 'we have seen the women's movement . . . documenting "herstory" from every angle except our own'. This criticism is now widely accepted by white feminists and one with which we agree. As two white women, we cannot write fully about the experiences of racialised women, and studies of ethnicity have ignored the specific position of racialised *women*. This limits the analysis we are able to provide.

Black girls and young women are disadvantaged in the schooling system, in housing, in employment and in the health service (see Chapters 4 and 8 below, and Bryan *et al.*, 1985). Black families are more likely to be seen as inadequate or incapable of caring for their children, and Black women are over-represented in the prison population, where they make up 40 per cent of female inmates (Bryan *et al.*, 1985). In employment, Black women may be in the same broad occupational category as white women, but this may conceal the fact that they are more likely to be in lower-status and lower-paid work *within* the category (Bruegel, 1979). It is important to recognise that the experiences of ethnic minorities are not all the same – they do not constitute a single economic labour market category (see Chapter 8).

Sociologists have argued that this situation is not just a result of individual prejudices, but of institutionalised racism being

> [t]he policies of institutions that work to perpetuate racial inequality without acknowledging that fact . . . Camouflaged racism . . . [is] concealed in the routine practices and procedures of organisations such as industries, political parties and schools.
>
> (Cashmore and Troyna, 1983, p. 60)

Examples of this would be the ways in which West Indian English becomes seen as 'broken' English, and the ways in which Immigration Acts have operated to exclude Black immigrants while still permitting white immigration. (Although Britain now restricts immigration of white non-EC nationals, for a considerable period of time it did not do so.)

Black feminists have argued that white feminist models of oppression are inadequate for accounting for the experiences of Black women. By setting up theories of women's oppression as applying to all women they have contributed to institutionalised racism. Black feminists have pointed out how women from Commonwealth countries, and particularly southern Asian ones, are perceived as dominated and oppressed by their traditional cultures. Assimilation into Western mores is therefore portrayed as a form of liberation, allowing them to rebel against their families, wear Western clothes, cut their hair and so on. This exaggerates the stereotype of 'traditional' society just as it exaggerates the 'liberation' of Western society. For white women, the nuclear family is the central site of oppression because of the way in which it defines women's sexuality in terms of monogamy and 'respectable' femininity and situates women in the privatised domain. Some Black women, on the other hand, have argued that the family – threatened by slavery, indentured labour and migration for work – was often something to be defended, a source of support and resistance in a racist society (Brah, 1986). Rather than the family being a marginalised and privatised domestic prison, in many ethnic communities it remains the central area of subsistence and is less likely to consist of an isolated couple and more likely to consist of a supportive network of kin.

Access to paid employment was seen as the way forward for many years in the women's movement, reflecting the aims of white middle-class feminists. Black women, by contrast, are more likely to have to go out to work and to define this as part of their role. The kind of work they are likely to do exploits them both as women and as workers, since they make up the lower-paid workers who also do the longest hours. The sexist assumption that employment cannot be combined with good mothering has not applied to Black women, who are often expected to work full-time for most of their lives. Indeed, 31 per cent of British West Indian households are single-parent units (Anthias and Yuval Davis, 1993, p. 117).

Black women are often perceived as sexually exotic by white men. Wealthy Western visitors are sold packaged holidays in Asia on this basis, and this imagery is hinted at in the advertising of airlines (Tyler and Abbott, 1994). Third World women are seen as more submissive, obedient and feminine than Western women, and *in extremis* this takes the form of white Western men applying for Third World women as wives by post – from the Philippines, for example. Thus for Third World women, their sexuality is often shaped by racist assumptions. Carby (1982) has questioned whether the whole notion of 'patriarchy' is really appropriate to the experiences of Black women. Black West Indian men never possessed 'patriarchal power' over their women in the way that white men did. However, many other Black feminists have argued not for the rejection of the concept of patriarchy but for an analysis that recognises the specific situation of racialised women. For example, Floya Anthias and Nira Yuval Davis (1993) point out how women are exploited as unpaid workers in family businesses in some ethnic minority groups and as low-paid workers in ethnic businesses. Often ethnic entrepreneurs have set up business as a way of avoiding exclusion and disadvantage, but they then exploit the unpaid labour of their own family members or the lowly paid labour of other women from ethnic groups.

What is evident is that it is very difficult to generalise about all racialised groups, which have very different histories and traditions. While Black West Indian women came to Britain explicitly as workers, some Asian women came to join families but later became workers as part of the economic strategy of survival.

SUMMARY

1 Studies of racialised groups have ignored the very different experiences of different women.

2 White feminist accounts of women's oppression have ignored the distinctive experiences of Black women. The sources of oppression of white women – for example, the nuclear family – are not necessarily the same for Black women.

3 Black women are oppressed not only by their gender but by the intersection of class, race and gender. On the whole, they suffer the worst of all groups in terms of disadvantage.

Women in 'The Rest'

'The Rest' refers to countries outside of the 'core' of Western industrialised nations; they are also referred to as 'the developing nations', or 'under-developed', or 'less developed', or 'non-industrial nations', or 'the Third World'. They include areas such as Latin America, much of Asia and much of Africa. We have chosen the term 'The Rest' because although it lumps together a large variety of cultures and countries it can be used as convenient shorthand for countries existing in a state of economic dependence upon the West – a state of dependence that has been created by imperialistic economic policies of capitalist countries and multi-national firms.

In 'The Rest' there is a large pool of cheap labour available and prepared to work for very little money – far less than workers in Britain. This potential labour pool has been exploited by Western capitalism in two ways: first, Western firms have moved factories to Third World countries, and second, Western countries have encouraged immigration from Third World countries to remedy labour shortages in their own economies. In the Third World taxation is very low as there is no welfare state, no pension and no social security system for the majority of the people. Employers can get away with production processes which are much more dangerous to people and the environment than would be allowed in the West – and therefore cheaper – since the industrial safety and environmental protection legislation is less stringently enforced than in Western nations. It is important to recognise that not only are Third World women exploited and racialised by capitalism, but that women in the West benefit from the exploitation of women in 'The Rest'.

While the situation of 'The Rest' generally receives little attention in the West, the position of women within it receives even less. However, gender serves to structure social relationships in all societies, and just as Western economic and cultural relations have penetrated Third World countries, destroying traditional ways of life and creating dependent economies, so Western notions of femininity and the family have likewise been imposed upon other models of gender and rendered them 'peculiar', 'heathen', 'un-liberated' or sexually exotic. On the other hand, the adoption of Western lifestyles and gender roles is often seen as evidence of 'progress'.

Sociology has concentrated on explaining why the poor countries of the world have not industrialised in the same way as the richer nations. Theories have tended to stress the lack of motivation or the inappropriate attitudes of 'The Rest', or suggested that they lack the economic foundation on which to build, or that they have been systematically exploited and under-developed by Western countries. Less attention has been paid to the role of women in 'The Rest' and what happens to them as countries attempt to industrialise and develop. In this section we shall attempt to look briefly at women in 'The Rest', illustrating our arguments with a few examples. It is not possible to make generalisations, because women's experiences in 'The Rest' differ according to their role prior to the beginnings of change. Many women working in agriculture or industrial production in their own countries are exploited both by the men of their own country and by Western capitalists, as women are seen as a source of cheap and docile labour, to be used to provide goods for Western markets.

Seager and Olsen (1986) suggest that we need to understand the ordinary lives of women and to recognise their common everyday experiences.

> They are the providers of food, fuel, water and often the whole family income – the sustainers and developers of their families, communities and countries . . . the fate of women is a critical determinant of the fate of whole societies.
> (Margaret Snyder, UN Voluntary Fund for Women, quoted in Seager and Olsen, 1986, p. 7)

Third World women are everywhere worse off than their men, have less power, less authority, do more work for less money and have more responsibility than men. In all societies women shoulder the primary responsibility for housework, nursing children and meeting the needs of their families, and in many countries women are also responsible for farming. According to the United Nations (see Brown, 1985) women constitute half the world's population but do nearly two-thirds of the world's work, receive 10 per cent of the world's income and own less than 1 per cent of the property. It has been estimated that women's unpaid labour adds a third to the world's economic product (Seager and Olsen, 1986).

Development is usually assumed to be 'a good thing' despite the enormous human costs. One area of interest to feminists has been the effects of socio-economic development on women. Susan Tiano (1987) has suggested that there are three competing perspectives on the impact that economic development has had on women:

1   the *Integration Thesis*, which argues that development results in female liberation and sexual equality as women become more centrally involved in economic and public life;
2   the *Marginalisation Thesis*, which holds that with capitalist development women become increasingly excluded from production roles and confined to the private sphere of the home – losing in the process their control over resources and becoming economically dependent on men;
3   the *Exploitation Thesis*, which argues that modernisation results in the creation of a low-paid female labour force – women become more central to industrial production but are exploited because they are seen as a secondary labour force.

In order to understand the impact of economic change on women it is necessary to have some understanding of women's lives in pre-/non-industrial societies. However, there is considerable controversy over the position of women in such societies. There is some agreement among anthropologists that gender inequalities were less prominent in hunting and gathering societies and in simple horticultural societies than in peasant-based agrarian ones. However, cultural factors, especially religion, are also important. Furthermore, the effects that economic change has on women also depend on class, as well as ethnic status. As a society undergoes economic change, so does the nature of work and so does the distinction between men and women. There is an increase in the sexual division of labour, and this occurs in a way which perpetuates female subordination. In areas where men and women work for wages, employment is segregated into industrial sectors and women are typically in lower-paid work than men and in work that is defined as less skilled than the work men do. In unwaged work women are increasingly seen as the domestic workers, and in many areas they lose the land they farmed to produce food for the family, to men who produce crops for cash. Thus women's economic dependency is increased. Often these changes are actively encouraged by aid agencies and Western employers, who work with Western ideologies of the family, the division of labour between men and women and the appropriate role for each gender (see Chapter 5). Thus in parts of Africa where women generally farmed to produce food for their families, aid agencies have trained men in farming and encouraged them to produce cash crops. In the process women have often lost control of their land or been edged out into more marginal land, which they till with no access to modern farming technology (Obbso, 1980). The very low pay of women employed in manufacturing industry can similarly be said to be based on the assumption that women either have only themselves to support or are partly supported by some man. Rae Lesser Blumberg (1981) suggests three reasons why economic development results in the marginalisation of women:

1   there is an increase in women's real workload;
2   there is a decrease in women's resource base;
3   there is a decrease in women's well-being and their opportunities as people.

As men are drawn into the cities to participate in the cash economy, women often have less control over resources. Men are less likely to help out as they are freed, by the demands of regular paid work, from traditional male domestic responsibilities. However, women are often expected to continue to grow crops to feed the family and carry out all the domestic work.

The impact of economic change on agriculture varies between regions. In Africa south of the Sahara and some of South-East Asia and Central America the 'slash and burn' technique has traditionally been used. Men cleared the land while women did most of the cultivation. Women had a central role in food production and therefore some influence in decision-making (Blumberg, 1981). European settlers, however, brought in the idea that farming is man's work and that crops should be produced for the market. Men took over control of the land from women and began to produce cash crops. Women continued to be expected to produce crops for home consumption, often on smaller plots of more marginal land. Women were also excluded from agricultural education; in Africa less than 5 per cent of trained agricultural personnel are women.

In India the 'Green Revolution' – the introduction of modern farming methods – began in 1964 (Beyres *et al.*, 1983), the goal being for India to become self-sufficient in the production of food grains. The changes this brought about had a considerable impact on women's roles. In India prior to the Green Revolution women were economically dependent on men in all classes, although the dependency varied in form and intensity between classes. In land owning and peasant households it was always men who owned the land and the means of production. In the dominant classes the dependency of women was further intensified by purdah (the concealment of women), which made it difficult for them to move outside their own homes, preventing their participation in the public sphere. Peasant women did work the land owned by their husbands, but only the wives of poor peasants and landless labourers worked for wages. In all households women would have been responsible for all domestic duties, including the processing of grain and looking after the poultry, cows, buffaloes and sheep.

The introduction of new technology has not affected all parts of India alike, but where it has been introduced it has resulted in a decline in employment for women. In rich peasant households women have been withdrawn from direct participation in farm work – labour has been hired to do the work previously done by women. This has reinforced women's economic dependence on men. In poor peasant and landless labourer households women have not voluntarily withdrawn from labour – their wages are essential for survival – but in many cases they have been squeezed out of employment by the new technology. Male labour is employed to use the new machinery.

Only a very small proportion of women in less developed countries are employed in factory work, but when they are they are employed in 'female' jobs. Most production in Third World countries is mass production for developed countries who have located some manufacturing in the Third World but control it from the West. The work exported is generally standardised, repetitive, calling for little technical knowledge, labour-intensive, and often using assembly-line operations which would be difficult and/or costly to mechanise still further. The aim is to exploit a suitable labour force – that is, one that is lower in costs of employment and/or higher in productivity. The wages in Third World factories are often as little as a tenth of those in the developed countries, and working hours up to 50 per cent higher, while productivity is as high as that of the First World or higher.

Female labour is cheaper than male labour, female productivity is higher than that of men, and women are thought to be naturally better at some tasks than men. Western owners do not have to bear the cost of training the female work force. The work is seen as unskilled, not because it does not require skill, but because the girls have already learned these skills in the home. Much of the relocated work is women's work or becomes seen as such because of the perceived advantages of female labour.

Conclusions

We recognise that women's experiences are structured by class and race – that racialised women in Britain suffer discrimination, exploitation and subordination because they are Black as well as because they are women. While middle-class women are more advantaged than their working-class sisters, this does not prevent them becoming poor if they become a head of a lone-parent family or from suffering relative poverty in old age. Third World women's subordination and exploitation are based not only on ideologies of women's role but also on ideologies of racial inferiority developed to justify the West's use of Black slaves and exploitation of 'The Rest'. Nevertheless all women's lives are structured by expectations of role-appropriate behaviour, the idea that women are – and should be – dependent on men, and the notion that women's fulfilment comes from marriage and caring for a husband and children. These assumptions are a key to women's subordination and exploitation – why women lack control over resources. This is equally as true in the West as in 'The Rest'.

SUMMARY

1   Women are generally worse paid and suffer worse conditions of employment compared with men, the world over.

2   'Development' has often worsened the situation of women because
    (a)   Western ideas of gender are imposed through the introduction of new forms of industry and through aid programmes.
    (b)   Women are primarily responsible for subsistence and household needs – maintaining the family economy and bearing and raising children – whereas men working as migrant labour may have to leave home altogether.
    (c)   Where women are engaged in production their wages are generally lower.

3   We have found little evidence to support the integration thesis; women do not seem to be liberated and to achieve equality with men as societies develop. There is some evidence for the marginalisation thesis – that is, that women are excluded from production roles and confined to the private sphere of the home, and this seems to be especially true in some rural areas. However, it seems that in urban areas and some rural ones modernisation results in the exploitation of women in new ways as they come to be seen as a cheap, expendable labour force, whether in the factory or on the land.

FURTHER READING

Anthias, F. and Yuval Davis, N. (1993) *Racialised Boundaries*, London: Routledge.

Payne, G. and Abbott, P. A. (eds) (1990) *The Social Mobility of Women: beyond male mobility models*, Basingstoke: Falmer.

Seager, J. and Olsen, A. (1986) *Women in the World: an international atlas*, London: Pluto Press.

Chapter four

Education

The sociology of education has been concerned primarily with examining class inequalities in educational achievement, and especially the relative failure of working-class children in obtaining educational qualifications. Until recently, sociologists have overlooked other important dimensions of educational differentiation – for example, gender and racial differences in achievement. Feminists have argued that girls are not only disadvantaged in the educational system, but that it is there that they learn to be subordinate and to accept dominant ideologies of femininity and masculinity. Girls, for example, come to see themselves as less important than boys and specifically as 'no good' at mathematics and sciences. Girls are apparently channelled into particular subjects that are seen as suitable for them and thus have their opportunities in the labour market severely reduced as a consequence. What needs to be explained is how girls come to accept this.

Feminist studies in the 1970s and 1980s concentrated on how girls came to be channelled into certain subject areas in spite of the equal opportunities legislation (the Equal Opportunities Act 1975). With the introduction of the National Curriculum following the 1988 Educational Reform Act, boys and girls now have to follow the same curriculum. Nevertheless the most recent research indicates that subtle processes are still at work that result in girls making choices that propel them into 'female' jobs and prepare them for subordinate roles in a patriarchal society, both at work and in the domestic sphere. Furthermore, the most recent research indicates that, despite anti-sexist work in schools and initiatives to encourage girls into science and engineering, the situation has changed only marginally and patchily. These processes are mediated by class and race, and girls do resist them. However, the majority of girls end up in 'female' jobs, whether these be the 'female' semi-professions, routine non-manual work or 'female' service work, and they come to see themselves as having chosen these jobs. Many girls continue to see their destiny as marriage and motherhood, and while some envisage this as being combined with a career or paid employment, others do not. It is not just what happens in school that prepares girls for their (subordinate) adult roles, but their experiences at home and with their peer group and the opportunities that are available to them in the labour market (see Lees, 1993; Bates, 1993).

Sue Lees (1993) has suggested four strategies that girls adopt in secondary school – strategies that indicate the complex ways in which class, race and gender articulate in structuring girls' schooling. She suggests that these are:

1   Girls who are pro-school and academically or work oriented. These are typically white girls from middle-class homes with strong parental support. They are oriented to academic success and occupational careers.

2   Girls who are anti-school but pro-work. These girls reject or feel rejected by the school but nevertheless are academically and/or career oriented. This is a typical response of able Afro-Caribbean girls, who reject the racist attitudes of school and teachers but have a strong commitment to academic success and an occupational career.

3   Girls who are pro-school but anti-work. These girls value school life as a place to have contact with friends and resist the attempt of teachers to harass them into working. Resistance was expressed, in Lees' research, both by disruptive classroom behaviour and by flouting the school regulations concerning dress, make-up and jewellery. Girls in this group often argued that academic work was not worth worrying about because they would only have part-time work, to fit in with family responsibilities, while others indicated that appearance was more important for girls in obtaining employment than academic qualifications. Some girls in this group also indicated that the behaviour of boys had prevented them from learning and that girls who resisted the boys were denigrated by other girls as well as by boys.

4   Girls who are anti-school and anti-work – who do not see school as a focus for their social life and reject education and any orientation to an

employment career. The majority of these are anxious to leave school and get a job and are already looking forward to marriage, motherhood and domestic labour. These girls regard low-paid routine work as preferable to school and are deterred from an employment career by their expectation that their major role will be raising children. In Lees' research these girls indicated that girls who did not accept the inevitability of a future as mothers and domestic labourers were deluding themselves.

Feminist research has demonstrated that schooling is centrally important in the processes by which girls come to take on a complex identity that is feminised, racialised and located within a class system. Schooling is an integral part of the patriarchal system within which women take on subordinate positions – a system that structurally disadvantages women. This happens irrespective of the attitudes and values of individual teachers or the policies of individual schools or local educational authorities (see Jordan, 1995). Although anti-sexist policies can mitigate the impact, they cannot eliminate it. Indeed, the within-school processes interact in complex ways with the influences of the home, the peer group, the labour market and wider social and cultural forces. These combine to 'produce' girls who are prepared to positively choose and take on women's jobs in a segregated labour market. While middle-class and Afro-Caribbean girls see their future in terms of an employed career and marriage, working-class girls see it in terms of child care and domestic labour, possibly combined with part-time paid work. The evidence from labour market participation would suggest that Chinese and non-Muslim Asian girls, similarly, anticipate combining a career with marriage, while Muslim Asian women tend to withdraw from the labour market permanently on marriage.

Girls' educational achievements

Girls now generally do better than boys in school, as measured by passes in school examinations – GCSE and GCE A levels; as girls and women have been granted more equal access to education so they have caught up with boys and men at each level, and at some levels they are now overtaking them. Young women obtain better results in 16+ examinations than boys, and they are overtaking them at A level GCE as well (Table 4.1). In 1991/2 31.4 per cent of females obtained one or more A levels as against 27.8 per cent of males. In Table 4.1 we have left in the figures from the 1990 edition of the book for comparison so that readers can see how the figures have

TABLE 4.1 Highest qualification of school leavers by sex

| | Boys | | Girls | |
	1985/6	1991/2	1985/6	1991/2
1 or more A levels or SCE Highers	18.5	27.8	18.5	31.4
GCSEs or SCE	68.4	65.2	71.5	62.6
Ungraded	13.2	7.1	10.0	6.0

Source: LSO, 1995.

changed in a very short time. Female enrolments are fast catching up with male enrolments in higher education too. Although the numbers in higher education in general have grown during the 1980s and 1990s, the biggest growth has been amongst women; there are now two-and-a-half times more women in the system than in 1970/1 (see Table 4.2). Indeed, in terms of applications to university in 1994/5, there were more female applicants than male ones. Even in post-graduate education, numbers of women going on to further degrees have increased dramatically since 1980. In 1970/1 there were twice as many male post-graduate students as female, but by 1992/3 there were only 11 per cent more (CSO, 1995). Estimates for 1994/5 (Department for Education, May 1995) indicate that for the first time there are more full-time female students actually on first degrees than male ones – 324.1 thousands compared with 320.6 thousands. (Men still outnumber women as full-time post-graduate students – 43.1 thousands compared to 35.8 thousands – and on non-degree full-time programmes – 58.6 thousands compared with 56.3 thousands.)

More girls stay in full-time education after the age of 16 than boys, although boys are more likely to have day release from an employer – reflecting the small number of girls who are taken on as apprentices. Women are more likely than men to take evening classes. Why do women do so well within the education system? One answer is that achievement and conformity at school contradict certain codes of masculinity, especially working-class

TABLE 4.2 Full- and part-time enrolments in higher education by sex 1970/1–1992/3 (thousands)

	Males	Females	% Females
1970/1	416	205	33
1980/1	524	303	37
1985/6	563	386	41
1992/3	759	685	47

Source: CSO, 1995.

masculinity (Willis, 1977). Additionally, the greater surveillance of girls and young women by parents also pushes them into doing homework. Girls are denied the freedom to 'go out' in the evenings that is extended to their brothers, and they tend to spend at least some of the time doing their homework. This differential policing of boys and girls and the ways in which it encourages girls to do homework is particularly evident in the fact that girls meet the deadlines for GCSE coursework which boys often miss (Gwen Wallace, 1996). This is a key finding from the recently completed *Making Your Way Through Secondary School* research project. However, some girls are disadvantaged and have difficulty in producing coursework or indeed in doing homework because of the large amount of domestic labour and child care that they are expected to perform at home (Lees, 1993; Bates, 1993; Wallace, 1996). Boys are generally not expected to contribute to the same extent – and indeed, girls may be expected to perform domestic labour for their brothers (Bates, 1993; Lees, 1993), although some of the boys Sue Lees interviewed in London did help with housework and thought that it was right that they should be asked to do so. Some research has suggested that Asian girls may be particularly disadvantaged by the amount of domestic labour they are required to perform (Wallace, 1996), and other research (Bates, 1993) has indicated that girls may be expected to take time off school for housework and child care.

Women tend to become qualified in different subjects from men. For example, women outnumber men at A level in domestic subjects, languages, English, art/craft/design and history. Men outnumber women in technical drawing, natural sciences, computer studies, geography and maths. This same pattern emerges in higher education. Table 4.3 shows the distribution of males and females in different subject areas in higher education. It can be seen that there are twice as many women as men in the arts and twice as many men as women in the sciences. In social sciences the numbers are evenly spread, but this again changes when we look more precisely at which subjects are being pursued – men are strongly represented in law and economics, women in sociology and psychology.

TABLE 4.3 Full-time first degrees by subject and sex 1992/3 (thousands)

	Males	Females	%Females
Arts	55	112	58
Science	158	85	35
Social Studies	70	72	50
Other	46	58	54

Source: CSO, 1995.

Therefore, the expansion of higher education has particularly benefited women, but women tend to be found in very particular sectors of education. It would seem that removing the barriers from female participation in education means that women start to do better at all levels of the education system. It has taken some years for women to catch up at the higher levels, however. They are now doing so, but studies have tended to show that they do not necessarily end up in the most prestigious academic positions in higher education (these are still heavily dominated by men, as we can see in Table 4.4). Therefore the academy is still very much a male-dominated domain with women holding fewer chairs or senior positions. Nor does a higher proportion of women obtaining degree level qualifications mean that there has been a significant increase in the proportion of women in the high-status jobs traditionally dominated by men. Women's jobs in the white-collar and service sector are the ones most likely to need qualifications, highly qualified women tend to end up in the female semi-professions.

A study by Kim Thomas (1990) looked at how different subjects in higher education are gendered. She compared undergraduates in physics and English/communications studies and looked at the different experiences of men and women in each subject area. She found that sciences were seen as embodying hard, incontrovertible and necessary knowledge leading to more serious, well rewarded and prestigious careers. Scientists saw themselves in a 'subject hierarchy' above 'vague and wishy-washy' subjects such as humanities. The minority of women who studied such 'hard' sciences were very determined to succeed but nevertheless felt marginalised in the male-dominated and competitive world of sciences. They were likely to see their career goals as conflicting with family goals if they were to marry. They were never seen as totally successful within physics and were often nonconformist in their behaviour within the science establishment. By comparison, only a small number of students of English were men but although this was seen as

TABLE 4.4 Percentage distribution of academic staff across ranks by sex in Great Britain 1991/2

| | Traditional academics | | Research only | |
	Men	Women	Men	Women
Professor	17.4	4.4	0.9	0.3
Reader/senior Lecturer	31.0	17.1	3.4	1.9
Lecturer	51.0	73.9	69.1	59.6
Other	0.6	4.6	26.6	38.2
Total number	25,579	5,234	12,385	5,923

Source: Universities Funding Council 1993, cited in Acker, 1994, p. 135.

a more vague, indeterminate and 'feminine' subject in the hierarchy of university values, men who behaved in an assertive, individualistic way with strong opinions were able to do very well. Here it was the men who tended to be more nonconformist. Thomas concludes that subjects were gendered in very particular ways and that masculinity and femininity took different forms within them.

It is interesting to note that women graduates are more likely to be in paid employment than women who completed only compulsory education – and this is true across the European Union. In Britain in 1991, for example, 90 per cent of women aged 20–39 without children younger than 15 were in paid employment, but 94 per cent of those with degrees. The difference for those with children is more startling – 56 per cent compared with 74 per cent. Graduate mothers are also more likely to be employed full time than non-graduate mothers (CEC, 1993).

It is also necessary to look at what happens to non-academic girls. Here it is evident that their main education is preparation for 'women's jobs'. Their aspirations are 'cooled out' not just by educational failure but also by the expectations of their future roles in the family. Many parents, teachers and employers ask: 'What is the point of girls striving for success at school when they will only get married and become dependants of men?' as do some girls themselves (Lees, 1993). Such expectations filter through to the girls, and domestic roles are seen as the alternative to academic success for them. In reality they are likely to spend much of their lives in paid employment (see Chapter 8), so this experience in the education system leaves them ready to accept lower-paid, lower-status jobs without promotion prospects. However, there has been something of a shift in attitudes. Research by Sue Sharpe (1995) suggests that while in the past young women saw marriage and motherhood as an inevitability and the latter as necessitating a break in their working life, they now expect to have jobs, babies *and* husband. Rather than marriage and motherhood being seen as an alternative career, it is seen as a parallel career. However, Sue Lees (1993) argues that while academic girls expect careers, non-academic girls anticipate part-time employment taken to 'fit in' with child care and domestic responsibilities. Mirza (1992) found that the Black girls she interviewed anticipated a career, but this was in marked contrast to the Irish girls in the study, who saw their futures as home-makers, child-carers and part-time workers. For these girls domestic fulfilment and commitment to the full-time labour market were seen to be incompatible.

In order to understand women's situation in the education system it is necessary to understand how gender interacts with ethnicity. What is evident is that Asian and West Indian women tend to have fewer academic qualifications than white women. However, West Indian women are more likely than West Indian men to have obtained GCSE grades A–C, to have vocational qualifications (a large percentage in nursing) (Mirza, 1992), and their performance is improving relative to their white peers. Furthermore, Afro-American women are also likely to be the higher achievers in continuing education in the USA (Mickelson, 1992). But in Britain, Asian women in the 16–24 age-group are much more likely than Asian men to have no academic qualifications (Brown, 1985). Therefore the way in which women perform relative to men in the educational system varies according to ethnicity (as does the value of having or not having educational qualifications).

The history of education for girls

Middle-class Victorian girls were inculcated from an early age with ideas of self-sacrifice and service while boys were encouraged to be independent. Middle-class Victorian boys and girls were separated at puberty, and girls were forced to cease any vigorous exercise, to dress in a more feminine way and to cease educational activity. This was because it was assumed that women were inherently weak and needed to reserve all their energies for their natural function of bearing children (see Chapters 5 and 7). At this time boys entered the all-male world of work or the public school, they were encouraged to increase their physical and intellectual activities and to become more active and independent. Thus middle-class young people had a prolonged period of education, but while boys went to boarding school or into employment young women were kept at home and prepared for domesticity.

Schooling for working-class children, by contrast, was not made compulsory till 1880, although the state permitted local school boards to build schools for them, by an Act of Parliament passed in 1870, and had required that factory children be educated for two hours per day by an Act of 1834. The main aim of education for working-class children was seen as teaching them to be obedient, punctual, clean and deferential to authority – to compensate for what were seen as the deficiencies of the working-class family. Literacy skills were taught, but there was more concern with moral education and discipline. While boys were taught gardening and carpentry, girls were instructed in needlework, cooking and other domestic skills. The aim was to produce a skilled and docile male work force and more domesticated wives, mothers and domestic servants. However, education was regarded as less necessary for girls than for boys by parents and employers. Truancy was treated with greater leniency when committed by girls since it was felt that if they were at home helping mother this was probably a useful education for them (Dyhouse, 1981).

Generally it has been argued that schooling was made compulsory for economic and political reasons, but Anna Davin (1979) has argued that in fact since women were not able to vote it is difficult to see why they were included in mass education at all. The explanation, she argues, is that this was a way of furthering the ideology of domesticity, since education was the way in which the middle-class model of the family could be imposed upon the working class. Education was designed, then, to prepare girls for mothering, so that they would bring up a healthy, properly socialised future generation. During the slow process of introducing education for girls in the nineteenth century, two alternative models of female education emerged. In the first model, based on the traditional view and embodied in the work of Miss Beale at Cheltenham Ladies' College, girls were equipped for their role in life as wives, mothers and companions to middle-class men. An education was supposed to make them more attractive to a potential partner by training them in domesticity and the feminine arts. This helped to foster the nineteenth-century ideology of middle-class domesticity. The second model was developed by Frances Buss at the North London Collegiate School. Miss Buss argued that girls often had to earn a living if they did not get married, and the usual career for a middle-class spinster was as a governess. The girls of Miss Buss received the same academic education as boys. However, girls were barred from higher education; Oxford did not allow them to become full members of the University until 1920 and Cambridge not until 1947. After feminist campaigns in the nineteenth century they were finally admitted to special women's colleges – such as Girton at Cambridge. Some colleges gave them the equivalent education to what was available at the men's colleges, but in others they received a different, less academically demanding intellectual diet.

The emphasis on differentiated curricula for boys and girls continued into the twentieth century. In the debates over education in the 1920s and 1930s, arguments concerning biological differences between boys and girls were used to strengthen the view that their curricula should be different. The 1927 Haddow Report accepted the evidence from teachers that girls were more passive, emotional, intuitive, lethargic and preferred arts subjects, despite alternative evidence from academic experts that natural differences in mental/physical capacity and educability were small and not relevant to the design of the curriculum. The 1943 Norwood Report accepted the view that while a boy's destiny was to have a job and be academically successful, a girl's was marriage and motherhood, and for this she did not need academic success.

The 1944 Education Act was the first formal recognition of the concept of equality of educational opportunity – that ability should determine the type of education that a child received. However, boys were (and are) admitted to the selective grammar schools on the basis of a poorer academic performance in the 11+ examination than was required of girls. If selection were accurately tied to ability at that age, then 30 per cent more girls than boys would have gone to grammar schools (Weiner, 1986). As far as less academic girls were concerned, official reports continued to emphasise the importance of education for motherhood. The 1959 Crowther Report argued that the curriculum for 'less able' girls should take account of their 'natural' domestic specialisation, and the influential Newsom Report, *Half our Future* (1963), argued that:

> we are trying to educate girls into becoming imitation men and as a result we are wasting and frustrating their qualities of womanhood at great expense to the community ... In addition to their needs as an individual, girls should be educated in terms of their main function – which is to make for themselves, their children and their husbands a secure and suitable home and to be mothers.

Two models of girls' education continued to exist in the early post-war period. A small minority of middle-class girls received a grammar school education, while for the majority of so-called 'non-academic' girls the emphasis was still on education for domesticity.

In the 1960s and 1970s there was a general move to comprehensive, co-educational schools, and this is the way in which most children are now educated. The comprehensive schools were introduced as a response to research that had demonstrated that the school system advantaged children who had fathers in non-manual occupations. However, subsequent research, both immediately following the reforms and more recently, indicated that comprehensive schools did not necessarily overcome class inequalities (Ford, 1969; Abrahams, 1995; Hargreaves, 1996), and feminists questioned whether the strategy benefited girls.

> for sociologists [the comprehensive system] has failed because it has not broken the cycle of social and economic reproduction, for feminists it has failed because it contributes to the continuing oppression of women, and for members of ethnic minorities it has failed because it does little more than perpetuate the institutional racism they confront elsewhere.
>
> (Ball, 1988, p. 24)

In secondary co-educational schools the choices made by boys and girls become even more sex-stereotyped – girls were even less likely to take science subjects than in the single-sex girls' schools. Furthermore, it has been reported that girls are academically less successful in co-educational schools (NUT, 1980; Harding, 1980; Kelly, 1981). It seems that in mixed classes girls were less able to develop an 'ethic of success', were less likely to have female teachers and heads as role models, and were more likely to come under the influence of stereotyped images of femininity which are antithetical to academic attainment (Shaw, 1976). Consequently, some feminists have argued for a return to single-sex schooling. Indeed some recent studies have indicated that women-only education may be in the best interests of women at all levels (Coats, 1994). Other research has questioned the extent to which anti-sexist strategies have had any impact and challenged the view that a compulsory National Curriculum will reduce subject stereotyping (Arnot, 1989).

Once educational equality was codified in the Sex Discrimination Act 1975 and the Race Relations Act 1976, the concept of equality of educational opportunity had been broadened to include race and gender as well as class. More recently there have been debates about the situation of lesbian, gay, bi- and trans-sexual people in education as well (Garber, 1994).

However, feminists have argued that processes within the school, the gendered labour market and the pressures on women to take up domestic roles mean that ensuring that boys and girls have the same curricular choice, or even an identical curriculum, will make little difference to patterns of inequality and that this is because of factors quite apart from whether boys and girls, working-class and middle-class, are educated together in the same classroom. Miles and Middleton (1990) point out that equal access to a common curriculum does not guarantee equal treatment in the classroom and wider society. Hilary Burgess (1990) concludes that co-educational schools are really boys schools and that girls have to 'fit in'.

Explaining girls' continued disadvantage

Christine Skelton (1993) has pointed out that girls' educational experience is different from and unequal to that of boys:

> Whether the focus of research has been on female pupils, teachers/ lecturers or students in further and higher education, the findings have all illustrated how females *receive* and *perceive* different messages about their aptitudes and abilities from those of males, which has implications for their place in the family and the labour market.
>
> (Skelton, 1993, p. 324)

Sandra Acker (1994) has indicated that feminists are not solely or mainly concerned with issues of achievement. She suggests that it is now indisputable that girls perform as well as, if not better than, boys in formal schooling. The debate is more complex however, it is about differential curricula: the avoidance by girls of science and technology; sexual harassment; the career prospects of women teachers and lecturers; the unequal treatment by teachers of boys and girls; and the weaving of gender differentials into the very fabric of school life (Acker, 1994). She suggests that there is a 'hidden curriculum' of gender differentiation that continues to operate and influence school processes despite the apparent gender neutrality of the official curriculum.

First, the academic hierarchy remains very firmly masculine. As illustrated in Table 4.5, the higher up the academic ladder we go, the more dominated it becomes by men. Primary and infant schools are more likely to have women teachers and women heads. At the other end of the spectrum, there are far fewer women professors than male ones and hardly any female vice-chancellors or college principals. Women are concentrated at the bottom rungs of the professional ladder within colleges, and this applies equally to any level of the educational system at which we choose to look. In primary schools where women predominate they are less likely to be in positions of authority than men. In 1990, 80.6 per cent of nursery and primary teachers were women, but only 48.6 per cent of nursery and primary heads (Acker, 1994). A third of male primary school teachers can expect to be promoted to head teacher, but only 7 per cent of females (Table 4.5). The proportion of female primary head teachers has actually declined since the 1960s, while the proportion has remained constant for men (Evetts, 1990). In 1990, 47.8 per cent of secondary school teachers were female but only 19.7 per cent of secondary school heads (Acker, 1994). Nearly 4 per cent of male teachers can expect to be promoted to head teacher, compared with 1 per cent of female secondary school teachers (Table 4.5). Furthermore, female teachers in secondary schools are less likely to teach science and technology – shortage subjects, the teachers of which are often given allowances to encourage them not to move (Acker, 1994). Female teachers are therefore concentrated in posts as classroom teachers and less frequently found in promoted posts. Teaching provides a job for female teachers but the potential of a career for men. The situation is even more stark in higher education, where during 1991–2 women comprised roughly one fifth of full-time academic staff but only about 5 per cent of professors (Acker, 1994). This means that the role models which boys and girls have available are ones suggesting that positions of high prestige are taken by men, reinforcing roles elsewhere in society.

TABLE 4.5 Percentage distribution of each sex across grades in England and Wales 1990

	Nursery and Primary		Secondary	
	Men	Women	Men	Women
Heads	32.4	7.4	3.8	1.0
Deputy heads	19.0	8.5	6.4	3.6

Source: Department of Education and Science, cited in Acker, 1994, p. 109.

Second, feminists have demonstrated that teachers have stereotyped attitudes to boys and girls and that the school reinforces rather than challenges gender divisions in the wider world. Ann-Marie Wolpe (1977) has argued that girls are encouraged to behave in a feminine way, and teachers see it as part of their duty to inculcate properly feminine standards of behaviour; more recently (1989) she has argued that in order to bring about change in girls' education it will be necessary to review and restructure the whole educational system systematically. Michelle Stanworth (1983) found, in her study of a humanities department in a further education college, that in an 'A' level class there was a tendency for both boys and girls to underestimate girls' academic performance and to regard the boys as more capable and more intelligent. Male teachers, when asked what they thought their pupils would be doing in future, tended to see even the most able female pupils' futures in terms of marriage, children and domesticity. When careers for girls were mentioned they tended to be sex-stereotypical – personal assistants and secretaries – even when these were not what the girls themselves wanted. However, the male pupils were seen as having careers ahead of them, with marriage hardly mentioned. This expectation of the teachers was in turn reflected in the expectations of pupils. Stanworth found that teachers seemed to be heavily influenced by the verbal contributions that pupils made in the class when making judgements about their academic ability, as were the pupils when making judgements about each other. The teachers agreed with the opinion of boys that they were more able than the girls and based this judgement on verbal contributions in the class, as the boys rarely had access to the girls' marks. This was despite the fact that some of the girls consistently got better marks for the written work than did the boys.

Sue Lees (1993) argues that there is an increasing body of evidence that mixed comprehensive education has increased sexism in schools. She indicates that teachers do little to challenge the sexual harassment that girls experience from boys, while Sandra Acker (1994) argues that many teachers do not challenge the view that boys and girls are naturally different and that girls' destiny is domesticity and motherhood. Margaret Goddard-Spear (1989) suggests that teachers think boys are more intelligent that girls. Her research demonstrated that teachers grade boys' science work more highly than girls. She asked a group of secondary school science teachers to grade a sample of written science work. The sex of the pupil was altered, and half the work was presented as boys' work and half as girls'. The most generous marking was by female teachers of work presented as being by boys, and the most severe by male teachers of work presented as being by girls. Valerie Walkerdine (1990) suggests that teachers know that girls are more able academically than boys, but they continue to undermine girls' achievements.

Third, textbooks embody various assumptions about gender identities.

Children's reading schemes have been shown to present boys and girls, men and women in gender-stereotyped roles. They also present far more male than female characters (Lobban, 1975). Science textbooks are also more likely to portray men than women, and where women are portrayed it is again likely to be in a stereotyped way (Kelly, 1985). Research in the late 1980s and 1990s suggests that, despite some attempts to produce reading schemes that are gender and race 'fair', racist and sexist schemes continue to be used (Skelton, 1993). Reading material and texts across the curriculum tend to portray boys and girls, men and women in stereotypical ways or, in some subjects, to ignore the contribution of women (Skelton, 1993; Abrahams, 1995). Michelle Commeyras and Donna Alvermann (1996) have demonstrated the ways in which 'textual inscriptions can define or relegate women and men to particular gendered positions and how the positioning serves to perpetuate imbalances in classroom talk about texts' (p. 31). They go on to point out that, despite thirty years of feminist historical writing, this has had little impact on secondary school textbooks. School textbooks and history curricula, with their emphasis on factual knowledge of key people and political development in Britain, perpetuate bias and influence students' interpretation of and attitude towards women in general by marginalising and ignoring their role. Indeed, they point out that the inclusion of one unit of non-European history in the primary National Curriculum and one at secondary level led critics to claim that too much attention was being paid to gender and race issues. Peterson and Lach (1990) have indicated that, despite thirty years of concern about gender stereotypes in children's literature, little has changed. However, Jackie Bradshaw and her colleagues (1995) argue that educational software manufacturers have made considerable efforts to exclude obvious gender bias from their products for primary schools. They point out, however, that there is a problem when packages are being used to deliver a content which is already gender-biased, and they found that gender-neutral characters were seen as male:

> The evidence for gender assignment is overwhelming, with 'male as norm' as the dominant strategy. Simply stripping images of obviously sex-stereotypical features does not rob them of their ability to carry gendered meaning . . . Our findings have potentially serious implications for girls, since the overwhelmingly male identification at the initial stage may make it more difficult for girls to identify directly with the images on the screen. The schema they bring with them already worked against seeing 'neutral' characters and gave rise to a tendency to translate sexual ambiguity into maleness. These readings may be one factor in the complex process whereby from an early age girls learn that computers are associated with maleness.
>
> (Bradshaw, Clegg and Trayhorn, 1995)

Fourth, although most schools are now co-educational, gender differentiation is nevertheless reflected in the organisation of the school – gender differentiation is a fact of life in schools. The outcome of gender differentiation is that, while girls, especially in primary school, are the 'model' pupils, both they and boys come to see boys as more important and to accept that it is boys/men who must be prioritised and who ultimately have authority.

Gender is routinely used in schools to divide children into groups for activities – for example, boys do football and girls do netball. Although in some schools girls may do football, boys rarely opt for netball, and mixed team games are uncommon after primary school. Segregation by sex is an administrative device that continues to be used in the majority of schools and by teachers in the classroom. Registers, record cards and cloakrooms are often divided on the basis of sex, and in primary schools children are frequently 'lined up' as girls and boys and given separate activities. Teachers consider separating children by sex as a routine and efficient means of organisation.

However, organisation by gender is only one of the features of school life that differentiates between boys and girls and reproduces ideas of 'femaleness' and 'maleness'. The very organisation of the school continues to reinforce gender. Staffing structures provide a model of male 'superiority', with the majority of authority positions occupied by men. Head teachers, heads of department, science teachers and the school caretaker are normally men, while classroom teachers (especially in primary school), auxiliaries, dinner attendants and school secretaries are women – 'women teach and men manage'. Hilary Burgess (1989) has argued that the organisation of the primary school mirrors paternal and maternal roles and reinforces the model of women as maternal and natural carers controlled by the paternal male authority figure. Primary classroom teachers are overwhelmingly female, while school management (head teachers) are frequently male. Child-centred primary education increases the identification of a class of children with a teacher as 'my children'.

However, despite the child-centredness of primary schooling, feminists have argued that boys are advantaged – it is not so much child-centred as boy centred (Skelton, 1993). Katherine Clarricoates (1980) has demonstrated, from her observation study of a primary classroom, that the key to understanding the way in which teachers organise and structure classroom life is to recognise that their central concern is to maintain control. Discipline is an important factor for teachers – both because it is necessary for them to carry out their teaching role and because of the expectations of their colleagues. The outcome is that boys receive more contact with teachers than girls because boys need more controlling. Teachers actually select material in lessons that will gain the attention of boys; this is both to help in the control of boys and to encourage them to work because girls score higher on tests. Not only the teachers but also the girls and boys recognise that certain subjects are 'boys' things' and others 'girls' things'. All of these are based on masculinist assumptions, which results in boys identifying with science and girls seeing it as a 'boys' subject'.

Maarit Lindroos (1995), in a study in Finland, has argued that the ways in which primary teachers interact with pupils produces different discursive spaces for boys and girls. She suggests that girls are interrupted more often than boys by teachers, as well as the teacher offering more space for the rest of the class to interrupt girls. The ways in which teachers enable girls to make contributions in class also serves to marginalise them, with teachers frequently interrupting them to make their points for them. She points out that:

> The boys did almost the same amount of talking as the teacher and used the longest terms . . . The teacher talked with the boys instead of the girls, who were just an 'addition' or something timid and in need of assistance.
>
> (Lindroos, 1995, p. 155)

She suggests that the outcome is that the boys are accorded authority while the girls are encouraged to be co-operative.

Research in secondary schools has also demonstrated boys' domination of the classroom and teacher time (Lees, 1993). At secondary school it is also argued that girls and boys develop subject preferences that prepare them for their future roles. Until the introduction of the National Curriculum the choices that girls made in the secondary school, as well as parental and teacher expectations (Kelly *et al.*, 1982) and the ways in which the timetable and subject choices were organised (Pratt *et al.*, 1984), prepared girls for 'female' jobs and domesticity. Traditional careers advice and teachers' attitudes tended to mean that girls did not choose science subjects; it is often suggested that girls are uneasy in handling science equipment and that they lack the familiarity with it that boys often have. The introduction of the National Curriculum has meant that boys and girls have to follow broadly the same curriculum until they are 16, science and technology being compulsory in the primary as well as the secondary school. However, this may have unintended consequences if the intent was to encourage girls to develop more positive attitudes towards science and technology. To the extent that science and technology are seen as masculine subjects, and teachers are likely to reinforce the view that they are so (Skelton, 1993), their explicit introduction into the primary curriculum may well ensure that these perceptions are developed at a younger age. The Association for Science Education found that there was little difference in the background knowledge that girls and boys brought to secondary schools but a significant difference in attitudes and interest, with boys already focused on physical sciences and girls on biological sciences. The report concludes:

> Teachers' own attitudes to science will be transmitted to their pupils in day-to-day classroom interactions. If women and men primary teachers display differing levels of confidence and enthusiasm in teaching biological and physical sciences/technology themes, then the early introduction of these subjects may reinforce rather than challenge the traditional gender bias.
>
> (ASE Educational Research Committee 1990 p. 4)

It is also likely, given the curriculum choices that are available and that the majority of schools no longer offer the three single science subjects at GCSE, that girls will opt for single rather than double science, thereby limiting the potential for them to take science 'A' levels. Indeed, Seers (1992) concluded that there were no changes between 1987 and 1992 in the proportion of girls taking science 'A' levels despite the changes in secondary education, including the introduction of GCSE balanced science courses and the implementation of the National Curriculum.

The statistical evidence on girls taking science subjects at school and in higher education indicates that, despite a number of initiatives designed to encourage girls into science and engineering, there was little change between the early 1980s and the 1990s. While the proportion of girls taking chemistry and physics 'A' levels increased marginally, it actually declined in biology – the only science 'A' level taken by more girls than boys (Shelley and Whaley, 1994). In higher education in 1993 young men outnumbered young women by 6 to 1 in engineering and technology, 3 to 1 in mathematical sciences, architecture and related skills and 2 to 1 in the physical sciences (Acker, 1994).

Judy Wajcman (1994) has indicated that the proportion of women taking computer courses in higher education has declined in the last twenty years, while at the same time information technology has become widely used in schools. She argues that access to computing at home and in schools is dominated by boys, that computing has become sex-stereotyped. She concludes that 'the absence of technical confidence or competence does indeed become part of the female gender identity as well as being a sexual stereotype'. The evaluation of projects such as *Girls in Science and Technology* (Kelly, 1987; Skelton, 1993), *Women in Science and Engineering* and the *Technical and Vocational Education Initiative* (Skelton, 1993) indicate that encouragement is insufficient to attract girls to science and technology. Jackson (1990) concludes:

> When we started there was a feeling that these poor unfortunate girls did not know the delights of a scientific (or engineering) career, and if only

we gave them the information they would all be converted. What we increasingly discovered is all the obstacles: peer pressures in schools, parental attitudes in some cases, inability to get to the apparatus because the boys grabbed it. Now I think we need to look at the training of teachers and the education of boys and men.

(Jackson, in Gold, 1990, p. 42)

Other researchers have suggested that science and technology teachers see girls as deficient, as lacking the necessary aptitude to do science and technology (Versey, 1990). However, the accumulating evidence is that the 'ability' to do science and technology has more to do with the differential opportunities that girls and boys have to tinker and play with construction toys (Riggs, 1994) and the gender stereotyping of subjects as 'boys' and 'girls' areas (Harte, 1992). Volman and Van Ecke (1995) suggest that the problem needs to be reconceptualised – away from seeing girls as the problem and towards seeing science and technology as the problem. The attitudes of girls to science and technology do not reflect misunderstanding or prejudice, but social realities. They conclude:

By starting from the assumption that girls are the problem researchers have been led into looking at them as an object. They have concentrated on explaining the 'behaviour' of girls. We think that approaching girls as agents, who can be asked what they think and feel, makes more sense if we want to understand how they experience mathematics, science and technology, different ways of teaching them and how and why they are compatible or not with being a girl. We think that this can help to avoid falling into the trap of concluding that education does not really make a difference and that it is only misunderstanding of girls themselves that they do not like mathematics, science and technology.

(Volman and Van Ecke, 1995, p. 292)

Fifth, there are different kinds of classroom interaction associated with the different genders. Detailed analysis of the moment-to-moment interaction in the classroom indicates that boys talk more and are allowed to dominate the classroom interaction, and this continues even when teachers are consciously trying to overcome it (Spender, 1982). Skelton (1989) has suggested that teachers typically work to interest boys for the sake of maintaining order. Goddard-Spear (1990) argues that boys are perceived as more active learners than girls, dominate teachers' time and are regarded more highly by teachers. Feminist researchers have pointed to the importance of language in the classroom. They have drawn attention to the tendency of girls to take a back seat in the classroom and to be more hesitant in making contributions than boys. Girls are often reluctant to speak in class, and diminished in the discussion which takes place. The classroom becomes seen as a man's world and girls are marginalised. Furthermore, teachers often use sexist remarks and sexist language in controlling girls. Katherine Clarricoates (1980) noted that:

> If boys get out of hand they are regarded as 'boisterous', 'rough', 'aggressive', 'assertive', 'rowdy', 'adventurous', etc. For girls the adjectives used were 'funny', 'bitchy', 'giggly', 'catty', 'silly'. It is obvious that the terms applied to boys imply positive masculine behaviour, whereas the categories applied to girls are more derogatory.
>
> (p. 161)

Sue Lees' 1993 research indicates that the situation has changed little and, despite the fact that they object to boys' domination of the classroom and their disruptive and sexist behaviour, in the end the girls have to put up with it. Indeed, Jackson and Salisbury (1996) suggest that teachers do little to challenge the disruptive, dominating behaviour of boys in the classroom – although they point out that it is not *all* boys who behave in this way.

Taken together, these indirect forms of socialisation are sometimes called 'the hidden curriculum'. While the overt message may be that the expectation of girls and boys is the same, this is subverted by a different message underlying the curriculum.

SUMMARY

1 Until recently girls were disadvantaged in the educational system because they were not provided with an education equivalent to that of boys.

2 Although there now appears to be more equality in terms of co-education and equal access, in practice girls are still disadvantaged in that they are channelled into particular subject areas and their participation is not taken seriously. They are 'cooled out'. This is on account of the 'hidden curriculum' which in the case of girls includes such factors as the organisation of the school, the expectations of teachers, the content of textbooks, the gender balance in the academic hierarchy and the way in which classroom interaction takes place. For both academic and non-academic girls the consequence is that their career and job opportunities are limited.

3   Several competing models exist as to how girls should be educated. The first model argues that they should be equipped for their lives as wives and mothers. The second argues that they should compete on equal terms with men by receiving the same education as boys. The third model argues that girls should be educated separately as a way of better enhancing their academic performance.

Feminist perspectives on education

Liberal feminists

Liberal feminist perspectives have been very influential in education, and indeed it was campaigns by liberal feminists that created opportunities for girls within the educational system. They argue that girls should have an equal chance to be educated in the same way as boys and that this will lead to equal opportunities elsewhere. They measure their 'success' in terms of the higher achievements of girls: better examination results and a higher proportion of girls entering higher education. However, these are only successes when seen from a middle-class perspective, and although more girls may be in the educational system this does not mean that they enter jobs as 'good' as those of boys (see Chapter 8). They simply enter feminine jobs at a higher level. Moreover, dominant expectations of femininity also follow them through the educational system. Hence, radical and marxist feminists argue that equality of opportunity is not enough and more fundamental changes need to be sought.

Radical feminist analyses of schooling

Dale Spender (1982) has argued that knowledge taught within the educational system is not neutral but rather that it reflects masculine assumptions about the world – for example, about the role of 'objective' interpretations rather than subjective, intuitive ideas, and about controlling nature through science rather than trying to live with it, and about the importance of political leaders as opposed to ordinary people. The school system, likewise, sets up teachers as 'experts' who pass on knowledge to others and who have authority over others, who determine what is a 'right' answer and what is a 'wrong' one. This also reflects a masculine view of the world – boys and girls learn that the 'great' artists, scientists, writers and sociologists were men. Men are portrayed as superior to women in all areas of knowledge, and women rarely find their experiences reflected in this knowledge. Knowledge, in this model, is packaged into discrete 'subjects' which become either masculine or feminine, and students are not encouraged to see the connections between them or to question these classifications. The importance of competitive striving for success in an individualistic way, which is embodied in the educational system, is for radical feminists an example of a male approach to the world. Other ways in which patriarchy is reproduced in schools include the ways in which boys come to dominate the classroom and teachers' time and the ways in which girls are sexually harassed in schools (Lees, 1993). The outcome of these processes is not so much that boys have the chance to reduce girls' possibilities for success, but rather that girls come to accept male power as inevitable. Teachers do not challenge the domination of boys in the classroom or their sexual harassment of girls. Girls withdraw and police themselves (Measor and Sikes, 1992) and develop strategies for coping.

Radical feminists have tended to focus on within-school processes and ignore the wider structural factors. By focusing on girls' experience they have ignored the experience of many boys who do not dominate or sexually abuse (Wolpe, 1989), and they probably underestimate the extent of girls' resistance (Measor and Sikes, 1992). However, Sue Lees (1993) does quote in her research examples of boys who objected to the sexual harassment of girls by boys and to the disruptive behaviour of (some) boys in the classroom.

Marxist and socialist feminist perspectives

Marxist and socialist ('dual-systems') feminists would both argue that this ideology of gender has to be seen in the wider context of a capitalist society. The school in capitalist society is the major ideological state apparatus that ensures that the relations of production are reproduced – that is, that the next generation of workers graduate not only with skills appropriate to the position they will take in the labour market but also with appropriate attitudes. Thus it is necessary to understand how schools provide different experiences for girls and boys so that gender as well as class relations are reproduced. This takes place through cultural reproduction – including the way in which those who develop anti-school attitudes and values and overtly resist the authority of the school nevertheless end up accepting low-paid 'women's' jobs.

Michelle Barrett (1980) has suggested that in relation to education three key questions need to be answered:

1   How is education related to the reproduction of the gender divisions of labour in capitalist societies?

2   What is the relationship between class and gender in schooling?
3   What role does education play in preparing men and women for a particular social order – one structured by class and gender?

In answering these questions marxist/socialist feminists have adapted the marxist theory of social class to analyse the question of gender relationships by examining patriarchal and class relationships within capitalist society. The aim is to provide an analysis of the role of education in creating a sharply sex-segregated, racialized labour force and to explain the processes involved in this. To do so they have adapted theories of social reproduction such as those developed by Bowles and Gintis (1976) and of cultural reproduction such as that developed by Willis (1977). In the process they have challenged the political neutrality of education, arguing that its structures and ideologies are already linked to the needs of the capitalist labour market and dominant class interests.

Bowles and Gintis have analysed the way in which the school acts as a selection and allocation device for the social reproduction of the class structure. The major function of the education system, they suggest, is to produce a stratified and conforming work force. Experiences at school prepare pupils for the labour market; for example, pupil/teacher relationships and the hierarchy of authority in the school prepare pupils for supervisor/manager/worker relationships. Different forms of education provided by different streams in the school system prepare children for different levels of occupation. Middle-class pupils are encouraged to develop the autonomy necessary for middle-class jobs, and working-class children are prepared for their subordinate position in the division of labour. Thus for Bowles and Gintis the school reproduces the relations of production.

In England, Paul Willis examined the way in which divisions are culturally reproduced. He asked not just why working-class boys finish up in working-class jobs, but why they see them as desirable jobs to take on. In other words, he argued that working-class boys were not forced into unskilled manual work but positively opted for it – seeing it a 'real men's work'. The study focused mainly on a group of twelve 'lads' in a school in Birmingham who constituted a small 'subculture'. It was evident that the lads experienced school not as a process of enlightenment but as a source of oppression. They reacted against teachers' authority by escaping from supervision and doing the things they valued most: smoking, drinking, swearing and wearing their own variation on the school uniform. While the teachers saw these lads as trouble-makers, the lads themselves were effectively driven by their experiences in the school to embrace male working-class culture. The lads were proud of their actions and saw those who conformed to school as passive and absurd 'ear 'oles'. The lads looked forward to starting work, their subcultural values and expectations reflecting those of the factory subculture.

Feminists have argued, in the same way, that school reproduces gender divisions; it prepares girls not only for their place in the work force but also for the sexual division of labour. Ann-Marie Wolpe (1977) argues that the family and the school prepare women for low-paid work in the secondary labour market and for domesticity. Michelle Barrett (1980) has pointed out that women have a dual relationship to the class structure. The education and training women receive by virtue of their class background prepares them for the places they will occupy in the labour market, but this is moderated by the expectation that all women will take on domestic labour and childcare and become economically dependent on a man. Thus working-class girls are prepared for low-paid secondary sector jobs, while middle-class girls are prepared for semi-professional 'female' jobs (see Chapter 8). More recent research by Bates (1993) indicates that despite Equal Opportunities legislation and educational reforms the situation remains largely unchanged.

Marxist feminists have criticised marxist models of work-role reproduction for not including any account of the reproduction of gender roles. They have examined the experiences of female working-class pupils in order to understand the ways in which they interpret and mediate the structures and ideologies transmitted by the school. The aim has been to understand how working-class girls come to have a particular definition of femininity which is constructed and negotiated in a competitive education system in which they 'lose out'. It is argued that the particular version of schooling that working-class girls get puts them in a position where they freely choose their own subordination – that is, they choose marriage and domesticity. The form of resistance that working-class girls develop is different from that of working-class boys. They form a subcultural ideology of love and romance – an exaggeration of the feminine stereotype. Most girls experience school as dull and boring, and their hopes for the future focus on romance, marriage and motherhood. Their ambitions are not focused on achievement and qualifications but on leaving school, 'getting a man' and setting up a home of their own. Girls also signify in other ways their opposition to a school system which aims to control expression of femininity in the interests of discipline and management. Girls use their sexuality to control the classroom; flirting with male teachers, for example, can be used to undermine the teachers' authority and control. Refusal to wear school uniform, or adapting it to the current fashion, wearing costume jewellery or certain kinds of shoes, are all forms of the same strategy.

However, some feminists have questioned the socialist feminist emphasis on class-based resistance. They have argued, for example, that all girls resent wearing school uniform and flout the rules on jewellery, and therefore the division between 'conformist' and 'resister' on the basis of academic performance found in the research on boys is not useful for describing the differences in girls' responses to schooling. Lyn Davies (1984) found that girls' responses to schooling in a mixed comprehensive school were similar to those of boys in the same stream in terms of attitudes to teachers, anxieties over achievement, the tedium of school assemblies, homework and so on. However, she found that girls had common attitudes to school uniforms regardless of ability group, and that irrespective of ability girls were pushed towards the same school subjects.

Black feminist perspectives on education

Black feminists have been critical of the way in which educational theories are assumed to apply to Black as well as white women (see, e.g., Carby, 1982; Bryan *et al.*, 1985; Amos and Parmar, 1981; Mirza, 1992). They argue that racism is as much if not a more central aspect of their experience than sexism. The differences between Black women, especially between Afro-Caribbean and Asian girls, who have very different cultural backgrounds, complicates this argument. Indeed, the cultures of Asian girls also vary considerably depending on the country from which their parents came and the religion of their family. However, Valerie Amos and Pratkha Parmar (1980) argue that all Black women share a history of subordination and of being treated in Britain as second-class citizens. They suggest that Black culture is blamed for the problems of Black people – that is, the educational failure of Black children is said to be because of their religion, their language, their communities, rather than being seen as a result of a racist society. In particular, Afro-Caribbean pupils are blamed for their supposedly uncontrollable behaviour. Gillborn (1995) argues that teachers have a general view that Black pupils are a disciplinary problem and that this takes on a reality for Black children, who are disciplined more frequently and more severely than white children – not always with justification. He quotes one teacher pointing out how an individual girl's behaviour becomes a generalised view. Following on from talking about one girl, the teacher suggested 'I think there is a problem with Afro-Caribbean girls in this school . . . I am not sure how to handle them, how to cope. You try hard not to sound racist but some of them are very lively' (p. 183). In Britain, to understand the experience of Black girls in school it is necessary to understand the racist, class and sex/gender system of which school is a part. Black girls experience racism in school not only from white pupils and some white teachers, but also from a racist and Eurocentric curriculum.

Thus Bryan *et al.* (1985) quote the experiences of a number of Black girls:

> School became a nightmare for me. They poked and pulled at me. 'Is your hair knitted, then?' 'Do you live in trees?'
>
> (p. 62)

> I remember my early school days as being a very unhappy time . . . There was a time when this teacher pulled me up in front of the class and said I was dirty and that she was going to make sure that my neck was cleaned – and she proceeded to do, with Vim.
>
> (p. 63)

> My memories of school are of being laughed at and everyone calling me golliwog.
>
> (p. 63)

They point out that the curriculum is racist and Eurocentric and Gillborn (1995) suggests that the National Curriculum has exacerbated this. Not only do reading books present women in sex-stereotyped roles; the majority of children and adults in reading schemes are white. History is taught from the perspective of white Britain. English books are selected on 'literary merit', which is judged from a white perspective. Black people are often portrayed as inferior:

> You will be getting deep into a story and suddenly it will bite you – a reference to black people as savages or something. It was so offensive . . . Sometimes you would sit in class and wait, all tensed up, for the next derogatory remark to come tripping off the teacher's tongue: Oh yes it was a 'black' day today, or some kid had 'blackened' the school's reputation.
>
> (Bryan et al., 1985, p. 65)

While few educationalists overtly accept the view that Black children are genetically less intelligent than white children, nevertheless teachers often expect less of them and Black children consistently underachieve at school. On the other hand, Afro-Caribbeans are expected to do well at games and are encouraged in this area of the curriculum. The result is that a substantial proportion of Black women underachieve at school and a relatively high proportion leave with few qualifications and are propelled into the very same jobs that their mothers were encouraged to come to Britain to take up in the 1950s and 1960s – dirty, low-paid jobs in the secondary labour market (Gillborn, 1995).

However, as with white working-class girls, some Black girls do resist the white culture. Mary Fuller (1980) has argued that some Afro-Caribbean schoolgirls' anger and frustration at the way they are treated at school leads them to a positive self-image – a positive embracing of being Black and female. They aim to achieve good educational qualifications, get decent jobs and move out of the subordinate position that their parents are in. Gaining educational qualifications gives them a sense of their own worth. However, this does not necessarily result in conformity to the norms of the school. They conformed to the ideal of the 'good pupil' only in so far as they did their school work. Apart from this their behaviour was designed to exasperate the teachers. In the class-room they gave the appearance of inattention, boredom and indifference; they expressed opposition to what they regarded as boring and trivial features of school by, for example, reading magazines or doing homework in class. They accepted the relevance of the school only in terms of academic benefit; they were able to exploit the school system without becoming subordinate to it.

Mirza (1992) has suggested that Black girls' academic achievement is due to their ambitions for themselves and their willingness to work hard despite a lack of encouragement from teachers. She points out that the ambitions of Black girls are not reflected in the jobs in which they end up. This is due to the location of the schools they attend, the racialised and sexualised labour market and the careers advice rather than to Black girls' expectations of marriage and motherhood. The Black girls she interviewed were committed to paid employment but made choices on the basis of realistic assessments of their abilities and the opportunities available to them.

Masculinity

A recent set of studies has considered how masculinity is constructed through schooling. Taking their lead from feminist studies of schools which have explored how femininity is constructed and perpetuated through education, these studies have considered masculinity as problematical. Beverley Skeggs (1995), for example, argues that masculinity is part of a set of codes and expectations found within the school system. Mairtin Mac an Ghaill (1994), in an empirical study of how masculinity is created within a school setting, found that the male peer group (with which the male teachers colluded) encouraged an atmosphere of hostility, homophobia and misogyny – in other words, male peer groups were created out of a resentment of gay men and hostility towards women. He suggests that rather than such peer groups being supportive, they tended to ridicule and intimidate boys who did not conform. In this way masculine culture and peer groups within the school served to create and police the boundaries of masculinity and ensure a heterosexual dominance. The 'normal' form of sex was intercourse with women, although women were discussed in an extremely insensitive way and the young men did not actually want to spend any time with women.

Ashwin: You have to prove yourself all the time. And it's different things to different groups. Like, everyone can look at a street gang and say, oh yeah, all their behaviour is about being hard. But in the top sets it's the same way, getting the best marks and all that. That would be seen as 'poofter' stuff to the gang but it is acceptable to the top set lot. But it's still about beating other people, doing better than them, and you're shamed if the girls get better marks. That would be real slack. You have to prove to them that you're better than them and the other boys.

(Mac an Ghaill, 1994, p. 93)

Other studies have suggested that harassment of women pupils and women teachers is a routine part of school life so that confrontational heterosexual norms were once again established – by the informal culture as well as the formal one. Mac an Ghaill indicates that there were indeed a number of codes of masculinity and that the middle-class and white boys subscribed to different ones than the Black boys and working-class boys. He explains this phenomenon by arguing that masculinity is in fact a *fragile* construct. Hence it has to be vigorously reinforced in these various brutalising ways which tend to perpetuate a certain kind of domineering manhood. Feminist studies in the classroom have shown, similarly, how formal and informal cultures, including the culture of masculinity, work together to produce and manage 'girls'. Ellen Jordan (1995), for example, has explored the ways in which boys in primary schools operate with a definition of masculinity that has feminity as the subordinate term. Boys therefore 'need' to dominate girls in order to demonstrate that they are masculine.

SUMMARY

1   Liberal feminists argue for equality of educational opportunity, and it is increasingly evident that more girls are found at all levels of the educational system than was the case in the past. The fact that girls are actually out-performing boys at some levels would be taken as a sign of the success of the type of reforms advocated by liberal feminists.

2   Radical feminists argue that in a patriarchal society the forms of knowledge processed at school reflect patriarchal assumptions. The educational system is set up in a masculine form and merely serves to reproduce gender differences. There can be no equality within the present educational system and women need to seek out their own forms of knowledge and styles of learning.

3   Marxist and socialist feminists have argued that schooling is essential to the maintenance of a capitalist society. They show that gender is part of the process of the reproduction of the work force, serving to create a docile, low-paid labour-force of women and preparing them for the private sphere for which women are responsible.

4   Black feminists have argued that white feminists have ignored the experience of racism suffered by Black girls as a distinctive form of subordination. They have shown that education is not just androcentric but also Eurocentric, denying Black women's experiences.

5   New approaches to gender in the sociology of education tend to emphasise the ways in which masculinity and femininity are produced as part of the education system, both through the formal organisation of schooling and through informal culture. The creation and policing of the boundaries of masculinity and femininity is one of the most important messages young people carry away with them from school and this also reinforces a dominant heterosexual ideology.

Young women entering work

Thus far we have indicated ways in which the organisation and culture of schools produce certain masculine and feminine outcomes. However, the relationship of education to the labour market is also important, with the latter, in articulation with parental and peer group pressure, setting up expectations which disadvantage young women from the very start. It is to these that we now turn.

The early literature about the transition from school to work was concerned mainly with 'occupational choice' (see Williams, 1974). This was later replaced by a model which emphasised class socialisation and considered the role of parental background and school career in determining the destination of school leavers (Ashton and Field, 1976; Willis, 1977). What all these studies have in common is a focus upon waged employment – and most of them focus explicitly or implicitly on young men. Feminists, by contrast, have tended to emphasise the role of the family in feminine socialisation. Young women, for example, may have to do housework or care for dependent relatives in a way seldom required of young men (Griffin, 1985; Bates, 1993). Once out of school, young women's occupational roles are circumscribed by the structure of opportunities for them in the labour market and by their anticipatory socialisation which leads them to think in terms of a very narrow range of careers. More recent research suggests that training schemes can also play an important role in this process (Bates, 1993). Their future roles in the home serve to limit both their own perceptions of the situation and the ways in which they are viewed by employers.

Young women are more likely than young men to continue in education and less likely to go into youth training schemes. Young women who do not go into higher education tend to enter different sectors of the labour market from young men. Those with educational qualifications are likely to take up clerical work. Shop and distributive work also absorbs a large proportion of young women, and the remainder enter unskilled assembly work, mostly in the engineering and textile industries. Those who do pursue some sort of extended education are likely to enter the 'semi-professions' of nursing, teaching and social work. There is a number of possible reasons for this pattern. First, there is discrimination by recruiting managers, who consider young women and young men appropriate for different jobs (Ashton and Maguire, 1980; Kiel and Newton, 1980). Second, there is the belief that young women are more nimble-fingered and patient than male workers (Pollert, 1981; Ashton and Maguire, 1980). Third, those entering traditional male jobs have had to contend with pressure and ribald commentary from male peers (McRobbie and McCabe, 1981; Cockburn, 1987). Fourth, informal and familial recruiting networks tend to have a conservative influence in that boys are recruited for boys' jobs and girls for girls' jobs (Kiel and Newton, 1980). As Roberts (1993) concludes, those young women who did attempt to break out of gender-stereotyped jobs or training soon discovered how bounded their options were and the extent to which they were destined to take up available gendered career opportunities.

However, differences between young men's and young women's experience in the labour market are not limited just to their initial point of entry. As they grow older these differences are likely to widen, for young women are less likely to receive any training, and such training as they do receive is of the 'sitting next to Nellie' sort (Pollert, 1981; Keil and Newton, 1980). In addition, young women are less likely to be promoted once in a job (Abbott and Sapsford, 1987a). The labour market destinations of young women are also structured by their own preferences, formed well before they enter the labour market. In the literature about young women's decision-making two bodies of opinion have emerged. One argues that young women simply enter the jobs available in the local labour market and adjust their expectations accordingly (Youthaid, 1981). The other argues that young women's preferences are unrealistic, reflecting ideas of glamour rather than labour market realities. Clerical and office work is seen as very desirable and 'feminine' by many young women, because it is clean, respectable and allows young women to 'dress up' (Griffin, 1985; Sharpe, 1976). Parents, too, feel that office work would be a 'nice' job for their daughters, and it sometimes gives the appearance of upward mobility. Other glamorous jobs mentioned by Sharpe's sample included air hostessing and modelling – all extensions of feminine roles. More recent research indicates that girls differ in the extent to which their career/job aspirations are realistic; the majority aspire to female jobs (Lees, 1993).

Marriage and motherhood cast a long shadow over their lives at this stage. Young women tend to regard marriage as a main concern and to find their expectations shaped entirely by marriage, which for them is a career (Sharpe, 1976). In the context of the 1980s and 1990s the fact that young women expect to get married need not necessarily mean that they also expect to give up work, nor that they structure their ambitions entirely around men. In Sharpe's sample of Ealing young women, the majority expected to stop work for only a few years when their children were small. Sue Lees' schoolgirls differed according to social class. Working-class girls expected to have part-time jobs to 'fit in' with domestic responsibilities; academic girls expected to have a career combined with marriage and children. Fuller's West Indian young women, by contrast, were very determined to continue working whatever their domestic responsibilities and exhibited high aspirations in career terms. These sentiments were reinforced by the belief that it was not good for a young woman to be too dependent on a man. In the words of one of her respondents:

> I want a proper job first and some kind of skill so that if I do get married and have children I can go back to it; don't want just relying on him for money, 'cause I've got to look after myself.
>
> (Fuller, 1980, p. 57)

The calls of the public and the private sphere may nevertheless remain in conflict for women. Anna Pollert (1981) found that working in a factory was not a 'nice' job for young women, as they were at the bottom of both the sexual and the occupational hierarchy. Romance offered an ideology of escape, but at the same time there was acceptance of the reality of manual labour as an inevitable part of their lives.

In the 1960s and early 1970s young women leaving school could look forward to employment – though this would in many cases have been an interval between dependence on parents and dependence on husbands. However, by the middle and late 1970s there was rising unemployment which hit young people particularly hard. The Government response to rising youth unemployment was to introduce training schemes to prepare young people for work and equip them with skills or to encourage them to remain in full-time education. Initially the Youth Opportunity Programme was instituted, then replaced by the Youth Training Scheme and later Youth Training. From 1988 changes in the state benefits system meant that all young people under the age of 18 were forced into YT unless they found employment or went into full-time education and continued to be supported by their parents (the alternative being no economic support whatsoever from the state). Trainees on YT are paid a training allowance, which increases in the second year. While the Government argues that the scheme provides training, preparing young people for the world of work, it has been argued by many young people and by trade unions and others that its main effect is to provide a source of cheap labour and keep the unemployment figures artificially low. However, even critics recognise that the places offered to young people are variable in the training they provide and that some do lead to 'real' jobs. In many areas the YT has become the main route by which people enter particular kinds of work – for example, the construction industry. In other parts of Europe, training was also introduced in response to the recession of the 1970s and 1980s. In countries where youth training had already existed, such as Germany, it was expanded (Bynner and Roberts, 1991).

During the 1980s the norm changed, from the majority of young people seeking paid employment at 16 to virtually all either remaining in education or moving on to a training scheme. Given that YT is presented as a period of training it might be thought possible for the sex-typing of jobs to be broken down and young women trained for employment in non-traditional occupations – that is, that it would provide opportunities for young women to train for jobs that are traditionally seen as male. However, despite YT having been set up with a commitment to equal opportunities, Cockburn (1987), in her research in London, found that this was not happening. Trainees were segregated by gender, young women taking up traditional female jobs and young men male ones. She suggests a number of reasons for this. The main one is what she calls the 'reality principle' in occupational choice – that is, that young people know how jobs are gendered. Other factors are the role models of parents, parental expectations, education and the demands of employers. Furthermore, her research into workshop YT schemes suggests that even when young women choose to train in non-traditional areas the attitudes of the other trainees and specifically the way they are treated by the young men and male instructors mean that it is difficult for young women actually to pursue their chosen area. In the words of one young woman:

> When I was at school this youth opportunities thing came up, I thought 'Great! Great! I can do my mechanics job', you know, but girls don't do that sort of thing. I thought 'Right, if anyone can do it, equal rights and all that' I thought 'I can get in there'. 'Cause, a garage wouldn't take me

113

on. But I got talked out of that. After that I went mainly for shop work, but really, you know, I would have been much happier working in a garage.

(Wallace, 1987, p. 193)

Cockburn (1987) also found that young women on YT were much less likely to be offered places in the higher-status employer-based schemes and more likely to end up in workshop schemes that were less likely to lead to a job or to be seen as providing a 'proper' training. West Indian young women found more problems than white ones because their colour was used as a screening device by employers, while Bryan *et al.*, (1985) argue that West Indian young women are likely to end up on training schemes that do not adequately prepare them for the jobs they want. Others have shown the young women's disillusionment and their attempts to confront sexist hierarchies which ultimately failed and have described how different YT schemes perpetuate different styles of femininity. Young women on 'care' schemes, for example, are tough, used to death and the harder sides of caring, including the dirty work, and they spurn the idea of complaint. On the other hand young women on, say, fashion courses are much more motivated by the ideology of the scheme and put all their effort into training, even though few ever become 'fashion designers' as such.

Thus young, non-academic women are trained for women's jobs – low-paid work that is seen as suitable for women. While the specific experiences of young women may have changed, nevertheless they have always been and continue to be conditioned by the assumption that a woman's major role in life is to be a wife and mother – their experiences at school, at home and in the peer group combine to prepare them to perceive themselves as willingly taking on low-paid women's work (Bates, 1993).

Conclusions

This chapter has tried to show the persistent inequalities existing in education and provide some explanations for it. Although women's performance in education is very high and they are already outperforming men in many fields and levels of education, women nevertheless do *not* get better jobs and careers afterwards. The relationship between education and the labour market means that a set of assumptions and constructions of masculinity and femininity tend to affect both, and that there is a continuity between sexism and disadvantage in education and sexism and disadvantage in the labour market. Future domestic roles play a part in depressing young women's expectations and career or education prospects, even though, for contemporary young women, child care responsibilities necessitate only a short break – if any – in an employment career, and marriage is no longer seen as a reason for giving up paid employment.

SUMMARY

1   Although young women are more likely to be qualified than young men, they find themselves in parts of the labour market – notably the service sector – where wages are lower and prospects bleaker.

2   Youth Training, introduced from the 1970s as a response to unemployment, tends to reinforces gender inequalities by emphasizing particular kinds of masculinity or femininity, in spite of a formal commitment to equal opportunities.

3   Women's careers are conditioned by the expectation of marriage and motherhood, even though in contemporary Britain, childcare is less likely to lead to a significant career break than in the past. Contemporary young women expect to have everything – an interesting job, children and marriage – rather than choosing between a career and motherhood as in the past.

FURTHER READING

Acker, S. (1994) *Gendered Education*, Buckingham: Open University Press.

Bates, I. and Riseborough, G. (eds) (1993) *Youth and Inequality*, Buckingham: Open University Press.

Measor, L. and Sikes, P. (1992) *Gender and Schools*, London: Cassell.

Weiner, G. (1994) *Feminisms in Education*, Buckingham: Open University Press.

Chapter five

Women and the
life course

Age is usually seen as a natural or biological status, yet historical and cross-cultural research has shown that the way in which different societies divide up the life course is highly variable, as is the behaviour associated with different age groups. Age status is of particular importance to women, who are more often defined in terms of ascribed biological characteristics than of social achievements. For example, a sexually attractive woman is usually assumed to be a young woman, whereas an attractive man can be of any age. Thus age–status transitions serve to define different kinds of femininity and what it means to be a woman. In this chapter we look at the life course: childhood, youth, marriage and motherhood, middle age and old age.

Childhood

Children are perceived to be less than full social beings – for example, they are seldom questioned in sociological surveys, presumably on the assumption that they are incapable of making rational responses in the same way as adults. But children also have a privileged status as representing the future hopes and aspirations of a society or social group and as such are accorded particular help and protection. This has not always

been the case. For Rousseau, the eighteenth-century French philosopher, children were primitive savages waiting to be civilised through education.

It is generally argued that before the age of modernity there were no distinctive phases of childhood and adolescence; rather, from the age of about 7 children became part of adult society, expected to undertake work roles and contribute to the maintenance of the family (Aries, 1962). Children were punished for crimes in the same way as adults, being deemed morally responsible for their actions. By the nineteenth century they had come to have a special status as the idea of 'childhood' spread from the middle classes to the lower classes. Nevertheless, children of this age were still usually prosecuted in the same way as adults.

> On one day alone in February 1814 at the Old Bailey sessions, five children were condemned to death: Fowler aged 12 and Wolfe aged 12 for burglary in a dwelling; Morris aged eight, Solomons aged nine and Burrell aged 11 for burglary and stealing a pair of shoes.
>
> (Pinchbeck and Hewitt, 1973, quoted in Muncie, 1984, p. 33)

Children in pre-industrial Britain, whether they remained at home or went into service, had little freedom. At the age of 6 or 7 years they were sent away to work in other households as servants or apprentices and this continued until they were able to marry, usually in their late twenties. The rising middle class frequently sent their sons to be apprenticed, and from the sixteenth century increasingly to boarding school, although the main growth of these came in the nineteenth century. Middle-class girls were mainly kept at home, while the small number of girls' boarding schools trained girls for domesticity. Girls were controlled either by their fathers or by their masters. Wages were nominal, and many girls would have been expected to send things home to their parents.

In the early nineteenth century working-class children provided cheap labour in the factories. However, from the 1830s, Factory Acts limited the age from which children could be employed (to 10 years) and the hours that young people could work, making children under the age of 10 economically dependent on their parents. However, young people continued to work in paid employment well into the century; young girls were frequently sold into prostitution, and the use of children as chimney sweeps was not outlawed until late in the nineteenth century. Families were often dependent on the wages of their young, and this situation continued up to World War One and beyond (Humphries, 1977). Girls would also have been expected to help their mothers with domestic tasks and to help in the care of younger siblings.

Welfare reformers were instrumental in creating an idea of childhood through their campaigns to save children from hard labour, from prostitution and vice, from exploitation by adults. In so doing an idea of an ideal sheltered and innocent childhood was constructed with children, and later adolescents, being segregated into schools and penal institutions separate from adults where they could be reformed and saved. Campaigns to help young people were also based upon the idea that their leisure time could be used productively in clubs and organisations and that this along with special institutions for the young could prevent them from developing bad working habits and falling into crime and sinful activities. The child-savers and youth-savers, whose activities were later institutionalised in social policy, therefore helped to impose the middle-class notion of a sheltered and innocent youth onto other sections of the population.

By the twentieth century childhood had become identified by psychologists and the medical profession as a crucial period of language and identity formation. As the welfare state developed, children were singled out as particular objects of welfare intervention needing special diet, dental and medical assistance. The expanding social services were concerned with the moral and social welfare of children, and the education system began to concern itself not only with their erudition but increasingly with their well-being more generally. Associated with this was the development of various experts and professions who specialised in the care, treatment and nurturance of children and later of adolescence.

Other trends served to change the status of childhood. The decline in infant mortality and the decline in the birth-rate more generally after the Second World War meant that families were able to invest more in their children in the reasonable certainty that they would survive (Gittens, 1985). Under these circumstances, children became objects of fun and pleasure for adults, a sort of household luxury, an object of conspicuous consumption. Children became the main purpose and focus of family life, so that rather than supporting families through their work, they became the dependants of families for whom other consumption priorities should be sacrificed.

The separation of home from the workplace resulted in the segregation of women and children. The home in middle-class households was supposed to represent a haven from the fierce competition of the market place and public world which men were able to visit but in which women and children were cloistered and sheltered. This middle-class, cloistered and sheltered view of home and childhood later spread to the working class.

Also from the late nineteenth century children began to be recognised as having rights of their own. Various legislative measures were designed to protect the child from his or her own family and from exploitation or neglect by other adults. However, the welfare of children was also linked to their social control, and the 1908 Children's Act was intended both to protect children from becoming criminal adults and to separate them in 'reformatories'.

'Problem' children were to be both protected and reformed. The young offender was handled differently from adult offenders, tried in 'juvenile courts', and schools were supposed to monitor the progress of children in order to identify 'problem' cases. This was partly because it began to be argued that disturbed children would become delinquent adolescents. Hence, childhood came to be associated with developmental and psychological stages which had to be correctly negotiated, if necessary with professional help (Rose, 1986; Sapsford, 1993).

In the late twentieth century we have a view of childhood as something cloistered and innocent. Hockey and James (1993) indicate that it is associated with a subordinate and dependent status in a age-structured society. Children are themselves subject to a process of infantilisation whereby authority remains in the hands of adults. In addition this sheltering is associated with innocence so that childhood is supposed to represent a happy part of a person's life. Finally the globalisation of childhood through media communications means that children in other parts of the world – often Black or differently coloured – are presented as victims of war, famine or other hazards in contrast to the safe and happy world of Western childhood. The Western model of childhood is taken to be the ideal and the norm.

Female and male children are marked as different with different clothes and toys, subject to different kinds of socialisation. Until the last couple of decades young boys and girls led institutionally segregated lives, having different schools, different curricula, different youth clubs, and so on. Many of these institutional differences have been eroded along with a move towards co-education in schools, but in other respects girls are more specially treated and subject to control and surveillance than are boys of the same age. This is on account of increasing anxieties about sexual threat in contemporary society resulting from moral panics following the disclosure of cases of child physical and sexual abuse, which take up much news time. Girls are sheltered more than boys from the real or imaginary dangers of the outside world or from sexual threats. This sexualisation of adult contact with children means that children are segregated more strongly from the adult world than previously, as a result of recent public anxiety about their protection. Girls are seldom allowed to walk alone or spend much time on their own, autonomously, outside of adult surveillance.

However, this vigilance and anxiety on the part of adult protectors distracts attention from the fact that children are most likely to be physically or sexually attacked by the adults who are supposed to be protecting them. The tremendous psychological anxiety roused by sexual abuse means that gullible social workers or Satanic rituals are more easily blamed than loving parents. Physical abuse cases have also received a great deal of publicity, especially following the widely publicised cases of the deaths of Maria Colwell in January 1983 at the hands of her stepfather (Parton, 1985), and Jasmine Beckford in 1985 from neglect and injury by her parents; the setting up of telephone 'childlines' for the victims of sexual abuse has resulted in intervention once more to protect children from adults and a renewed debate about the status of childhod.

Anxiety about the innocence of children can be exemplified in the recent and much discussed case of James Bulger, the Merseyside toddler who in 1993 was abducted from a shopping centre, tortured and killed by two boys, aged 11 and 9 years. In addition, reports of quite vicious bullying of children by other children in school has also helped to raise the question of what childhood is. This has raised public anxiety and renewed debate about the age at which children could be said to be responsible for their actions as well as denting their image as 'innocent'.

This illustrates the profound ambiguities in relation to childhood in our culture. Children have more cultural autonomy but less financial independence. They are supposed to have sheltered, innocent lives but are victims of their own violent impulses and the sexually predatory actions of those who are supposed to protect them. They have more autonomy and wealth inside the home and yet less autonomous freedom of movement outside the home. With the fall in birth-rates and the increasing costs of raising children in a consumer oriented, competitive society, children become the sole object of family life.

SUMMARY

1   Childhood is not simply a biological category but was constructed as a social category, one of particular concern, from the sixteenth century onwards. This process continued in the late nineteenth century and later with the growth of the welfare state and education.

2   Childhood gradually became identified with a special psychological process of development and particular professionals such as psychologists and social workers became 'experts' on assisting with children.

3   Children then started to become objects of special attention within families, the focus and purpose of family life rather than an economic resource.

4   Childhood is now a period of segregation, dependence and subordination.

Adolescence

Just as childhood is a socially and historically specific phenomenon, so too is adolescence, although it too is usually assumed to be biologically defined. 'Adolescence' is sometimes portrayed as a phase in which people have to make difficult psychological adjustments to the physical changes in their bodies. For girls and young women it is associated with the development of secondary sexual characteristics – breasts, body hair – which are also thought to cause particular problems.

In legal terms the status of adolescence is ambiguous. Young people are seen as responsible for their criminal activities from the age of 10. However, a young woman cannot give consent to sexual intercourse with a man until she is 16, although a doctor may give her advice on contraception and provide contraceptives before she reaches that age (but see Hawkes (1985), for example, for an account of the covert regulatory practices adopted by 'family planning' professionals towards those whose lifestyle they deem 'irresponsible'). Young men and women may marry at the age of 16 but need their parents' consent. A young man used to be liable to conscription into the armed forces at the age of 16, but the age of voting for members of Parliament is 18, and this is also the minimum age for standing for election. The legal point of transition from childhood to adulthood is 18 years – reduced from 21 in 1970. However, homosexual relationships between men are not legal unless both parties are 18 (lowered from 21 only in 1994), but not illegal at any age if both parties are women. It is already evident from this that young men and young women have a different status in law reflecting different assumptions about masculinity and femininity.

Youth is getting longer and longer. The protracted period of growing up which follows childhood is extending. As the years in full-time education increase (often through statutory changes but also as a result of more young people choosing to stay on at school), as the number and range of vocational and technical education courses increases, as the number and range of training schemes increase, so young people spend longer and longer charting a course through the complex maze of opportunities and possibilities. The numbers going into higher education have increased too (see Chapter 4). However, with changes in the labour market discussed in Chapter 8, the chances of finding full-time work are increasingly remote, especially in the case of young people, who are the most affected by unemployment. Hence they spend longer and longer being trained and educated for more and more uncertain futures. This is particularly the case for young women who are continuing in education and training in increasing numbers.

The fact that young people are increasingly found in education and training, or unemployed, rather than at work changes our view of youth. To put it starkly, in 1945 80 per cent of 14-year-olds were at work in Europe. Now 80 per cent of 14–18-year-olds are in full-time study. We would now think that people of this age are 'too young' to work!

The general tendency in state and welfare legislation is to recognise young people as independent actors – to give them more autonomy and decision-making power. However, this is also a contradictory process since efforts to cut welfare expenditure have meant that benefits have also been taken away from young people on the assumption that they should be more dependent upon their families. This process of increasing autonomy is reflected in the cultural and social experiences of young people as part of a process of individualisation. This means that although young people may be dependent upon their parents for longer and longer periods of time, they have more autonomy and space within the home for longer periods of time. Thus it is not uncommon for adolescents, especially in middle-class families, to have their own rooms, their own videos, their own CD players and so on through which they can lead lives increasingly independent of the rest of the family without ever leaving home. It becomes increasingly difficult for parents to control their activities.

Adolescent rebels?

The idea of adolescence as a period of storm and stress is part of common-sense ideology. However, the anthropologist Margaret Mead challenged this view. In her study of adolescent young women in Eastern Samoa (1943) she found no evidence of role confusion, conflict or rebellion. On the basis of this study she suggested that adolescence was not universal and biologically determined but culturally variable, and that the stresses of adolescence are socially determined and relate to the ambiguous status to which young people find themselves consigned by particular societal forms. Whether adolescence is a period of strain, stress and conflict even in the Western world is questionable. Coleman (1980), in a review of a number of studies, suggested that difficulties between young people and their parents have generally been over-stated by academics and the media because of almost exclusive concentration on 'bizarre' behaviours and spectacular youth cultures. Young people tended to be conformist rather than deviant or radical. The majority disagreed with taking drugs, did not drink much alcohol, believed themselves to behave responsibly and mainly turned to 'Mum' when in trouble (cited by Springhall, 1983, p. 34).

Young women in teenage culture

In the period after the Second World War, with increased affluence in the 1950s and 1960s, considerable attention was paid to youth. They were portrayed as the 'affluent consumers' who were able to stimulate the pop music, magazine and fashion industries with their new-found spending power (Wallace, 1989). Media, political and sociological attention has always focused on specific 'problem' groups such as muggers, football hooligans and drug-takers. These groups of young people are seen as deviant, as holding anti-social values and as challenging adult society. In the 1950s it was the 'Teds', in the 1960s the 'Mods' and 'Rockers', followed by the 'punks' in the 1970s. During the 1960s the 'hippies' – a more middle-class subculture – and the student movement rejected middle-class ideas of the protestant work ethic and 'respectability' in a consumer society. The problems with these groups were portrayed as problems of 'the youth of today' in general. In this way the idea of adolescence as a universal phenomenon was reinforced. However, marxist sociologists at the Centre for Contemporary Cultural Studies (e.g. Hall and Jefferson, 1976), analysing these subcultures, argued that they were not examples of 'universal' problems of youth but rather of particular class fractions. Thus the Teds and Skinheads were examples of working-class youth subcultures and the hippies of a middle-class one, rather than a reflection of the behaviour, attitudes and values of all young people.

The 'subculture' literature does not take young women into account; it focuses entirely on male subcultural activity. McRobbie and Garber (1977) wondered whether this was because young women are really not active in sub-cultures, or because they are rendered 'invisible' by male researchers? They answer their own question by arguing that young women are not present in male subcultures, except as girlfriends and hangers-on, because they have their own cultural forms of expression based upon the retreat from male-defined situations into an alternative culture of 'femininity' based around the young women's bedrooms and being a 'fan' of popular cult heroes or music groups. This subculture is therefore negatively defined in the literature:

> They are marginal to work because they are central to the subordinate and complementary sphere of femininity. Similarly, marginality of girls in the active, male-focused leisure subcultures of working-class youth may tell us less about the strongly present position of girls in the 'complementary' but more passive subcultures of the fan-club.
>
> (McRobbie and Garber, 1977, p. 211)

The behaviour of teenage women is at least in part an outcome of the ways in which they are treated differently from boys. Because young women are seen as more in need of care and protection, parents 'police' their daughters' leisure more strictly than that of their sons. This is linked to the dominant ideological definition of 'appropriate behaviour for women'. Sue Lees (1986) has also shown how boys control young women in the public sphere through the threat of labelling them as sexually promiscuous. It is expected that boys will 'sow wild oats', but similar behaviour attracts censure in young women and is likely to lead to derogatory labels such as 'slag', 'slut', 'scrubber', 'easy lay'. Indeed, this sexual labelling has less to do with the actual sexual practices than with the extent to which young women's behaviour deviates from the popular ideas of femininity – for instance by the use of swear-words or loud behaviour for which they could be labelled as 'sluts' or 'slags'. To remain desirable – a 'nice' girl – young women must suppress any real sexual desire and conform to expectations of romantic love and monogamy. This double standard serves to constrain the private and the public lives of young women to ensure conformity based on a model of sexuality which ultimately takes its form from the ideology of the nuclear family.

Criticisms of the sociology of youth by feminists have raised issues of gender in a new way. Feminist sociologists' arguments showed that ideas of 'masculinity' and 'femininity' which had been taken for granted as natural were in fact social in origin: these roles had to be learned by young people. Feminist critics such as McRobbie and Garber argued that young women did not 'rebel' in the way that young men did, but rather used romantic fantasy as a source of escapism. Other studies such as those of Sue Lees (1986), Christine Griffin (1985) and Claire Wallace (1987), by contrast, have argued that the ideology of romantic love plays a more complex role in the lives of young women. In many respects young women are not deceived by the images of life portrayed in women's literature but have very realistic ideas of what married life might hold in store for them. Second, they argue that young women do have a number of strategies of resistance, such as becoming tomboys or even getting pregnant, both of which flout the 'nice girl' stereotype. Third, these studies have emphasised the importance which jobs hold for young women, as a source of status and independence both outside and within the family. Marriage and motherhood are not their only goal in life. For example a re-study of the original 1980s sample in the 1990s by Sue Sharpe (1995) carried out in London found that in contrast to the earlier study, young women she interviewed no longer saw marriage and motherhood as their only goal in life. More recent studies of young women have tended to emphasise the variety of feminine identities available to them and the way in which they can switch between these, manipulate them or change them as it suits them. These studies, in line with more recent social theory, have therefore tended to emphasise the way in which feminine identities are chosen rather than pre-determined.

Young women, consumption and the media

Young women are important consumers of media materials. They are targets for a range of magazines such as *Jackie* or *Seventeen* which single them out in terms of age groups. Teenage girls are the main consumers of a variety of romantic magazines which give instruction on hygiene and behaviour and provide romance cartoons and stories as well as information about favourite pop-stars and actors. Main features in such magazines are articles about fashion and appearance. Through these strictly age-graded magazines, it is argued, young women learn their roles in life, and this encourages them to see romance as normal and desirable and to see the ultimate goal of romance – to get married or have a steady relationship with a male companion – as their hearts' desire. For these young women the main interest of their teenage years is in getting a man, and to this purpose they become absorbed into the ideology of romance – 'falling in love with love'. This preoccupation with appearance and boyfriends appears to be more important for working-class young women than middle-class ones (Sarsby, 1983; Sharpe, 1976; McRobbie and Garber, 1977).

However, more recent studies have tended to emphasise the fact that young women are not the victims of media manipulation. McRobbie has revised her earlier study of *Jackie* readers as passively manipulated, seeing them instead as active and critical consumers of such magazines. They pick out what they want and leave the rest. Nor are they very convinced by the slushy romance of some of the stories. Rather, this is harmless escapism. McRobbie also argues that the magazines themselves have changed with more space given to real problems, often using real photograph stories rather than idealised romances. Recent studies have tended to emphasise the pleasures of consumer culture and romance for young women instead of portraying these as a source of oppression.

SUMMARY

1   Adolescence and youth are socially constructed age-status transitions. The period of adolescence and youth has been extended through increasing educational and training opportunities linked with the disappearance of a youth labour market.

2   Adolescence and youth are associated with distinctive subcultural activities in which young women play particular roles.

3   Young women are the main consumers of magazines and particular
     parts of media culture but they also actively use these artifacts to shape
     their own lives and identities.

Adulthood

Adulthood is associated with taking up full status in society – with having
sexual relationships, getting married, having children, holding a full-time job
and living in an independent household. It is also associated with citizenship
status – the right to vote, to take out loans or to enter a legal contract. Such
life transitions are not marked by 'rites de passages' as in traditional, non-
Western societies, but there are ritual markers associated with them. These
can take three forms: private markers such as first menstruation, first sex,
first cigarette; public markers such as marriage or graduation; official markers
such as the right to vote, or, in some countries, military service for men.

These transitions take place in different ways and have a different
meaning for women than for men. Entering adult society usually takes place
a few years earlier for young women than for young men since they generally
marry earlier, have sex earlier, enter youth cultures earlier and so on. For
young women such life transitions are accelerated and this is particularly the
case for working-class young women, while for middle-class young women
life transitions are more protracted. This also varies across cultures – for
example, in Germany or Denmark young people get married and start households later than is the case in Britain.

These life-status transitions also have different meanings for different
sexes. While the beginning of sexual activity can be a source of great pleasure
and pride for young men, something to be publicly trumpeted, for young
women it is a very difficult territory to negotiate – a complex series of bargains
and transactions and sometimes physical violence which involve not being
seen as a frigid 'drag' on the one side but also not a promiscuous 'slag' on the
other (Cowie and Lees, 1985; Halson, 1991). It is entirely oriented around
heterosexual sex, with penetration being the final and ultimate goal. This too
has a different meaning for men than for women; it has little to do with female
pleasure (Ussher, 1989). Marriage too has different meanings for men and
for women, as do childbirth and parenthood, since women have the main
responsibility for these and often have to interrupt their careers to care for
children. Increasing numbers of women are raising children without a male
partner for at least some period of time – the majority (90 per cent) of lone-
parent families are headed by women.

Although the bodies of both men and women change as they progress through the life course, women's careers are perceived as more intimately tied to their biology and reproductive cycles than are men's. Men being perceived as the universal rational beings who are defined in relation to their performance and action in the labour market and public life, their reproductive functions and bodies are seldom referred to and are seen as unproblematic. Women's bodies and reproductive functions, on the other hand, are constantly discussed and seen as in some ways determining their lives (Ussher, 1989).

Ussher argues that in the nineteenth century women were seen as prey to their wombs through hysteria, an illness caused directly by emanations from the womb, and to their peculiar disposition to illnesses such as neurasthenia which required them to take constant rest and special diets. However, in the 1980s and 1990s they are still seen as victims of various biological processes. If we begin with menstruation, women are frequently seen as victims of 'raging hormones' either because 'periods' are just beginning, because they are causing 'pre-menstrual tension' or because they are declining as in the case of menopause. In each condition women are said to suffer from temporary indisposition which can sometimes become insanity. Thus pre-menstrual tension is given as the reason for road accidents or murder and for moodiness or inconsistency at work.

On account of these biological 'problems', women's life course is more likely to be subject to medical intervention or to be seen as a kind of disease. Women are recommended hormone replacement therapy or hysterectomies as a solution to menopausal problems. Women are given hormone treatment or special diets for pre-menstrual tension or irregular menstruation. The fact that many problems associated with such life-changes can also be traced to social and psychological issues is overlooked in the enthusiasm to find medical explanations and 'cures'. For example, Ussher (1989) found that pre-menstrual symptoms were very varied and there was no one pattern or experience of them for women. For some women it was a pleasurable and for some women a miserable experience. Some women did not even notice it. Experience of menstrual tension depended to a great extent on what other things were taking place in a woman's life. Nevertheless this 'problem' is subject to medical diagnosis and help.

Nelly Oudshoorn (1994) points to the ways in which science has constructed the hormonally controlled female body and the ways in which medical science has come to manufacture and mass-produce drugs (especially the contraceptive pill) in order to control sex and the female body. The introduction of the hormonally controlled body concept, the idea that hormonal treatment can cure many of the problems from which women suffer – 'female problems' – has resulted in the notion that control can be exercised from menstruation to menopause. 'Women's problems' – pre-menstrual tension, unwanted pregnancy, hot flushes and so on – can be controlled by medication. The natural female body can be controlled by male scientific knowledge, and in the process women's lives come even more closely under the scrutiny of (patriarchal) medical science. This, of course, reinforces the notion that women are different from and inferior to men.

> Imagine what might have happened in a world with different cultural and moral attitudes towards gender and responsibilities for family planning and children. It is not beyond imagination that we would have ended up with a male contraceptive pill, a medical treatment for male menopause and a classification system of multiple sexes.
>
> (Oudshoorn, 1994, p. 151)

Aging itself is a problematic process for women in a society which values physical attractiveness as the defining feature of women. Losing this attractiveness is a major source of anxiety, and women are constantly exhorted through advertising to control their bodies with the help of creams or potions, dieting, exercise or even plastic surgery. Although men are also increasingly purchasing such cosmetics, it is to women's anxieties that most of the advertising is directed (Arber and Ginn, 1991).

Women who have passed the menopause are seen as having no use anymore for their reproductive functions and therefore as uninterested in sex. Doctors are more likely to recommend hysterectomies for them, and sex is seen as of no more importance to them. In medical textbooks their ovaries and reproductive organs are seen as 'shrivelled' or 'senile', metaphors which imply that they are used up and useless. Men's organs, on the contrary, are never described like this, although they too undergo physiological changes with age. The removal of sexual organs is never recommended for older men in the same way that hysterectomy is for older women, as though they had no use for such organs (Martin, 1987).

Women are classified as 'pre-menstrual' in their youth, as 'pre-menopausal' in their thirties, 'menopausal' in their forties and 'post-menopausal' in their fifties, as though the experiences of their reproductive organs define their lives and can be used as a classificatory system for women generally. The menopause is seen as a loss of function, a decline of some kind. However, women have more recently tried to redefine this life phase and to see it instead as a new beginning, a new period of growth in their lives. Far from it being associated with a loss of sexual activity, some women report that sexual desire becomes stronger and more interesting, but this depends crucially upon the presence of an interested and available sexual partner (Ussher, 1989).

Women who have children find themselves defined in terms of their roles as mothers and carers. Once pregnant, their bodies are the subject of continuous examination and supervision by medical experts, and the experience of birth itself is increasingly one controlled by technology and remote expertise rather than by the woman herself. The time and location of the birth is chosen frequently by doctors rather than by the woman herself.

On the other hand, childless women are seen as frustrated mothers, as somehow incomplete, condemned to a marginal life. Having children is seen as women's ultimate goal, irrespective of whatever else they may have achieved in life, so that the lack of children often has to be explained by some problem – the woman's psychological inadequacies or her lack of feminine qualities. Now that women are able more easily to have careers, they are often described as selfish for committing themselves to a career instead of having children. Men are not seen as suffering from such problems, whether or not they father children.

These biological theories of femininity can be seen as ideologies and discourses which construct women's lives in particular ways – ways which are derogatory and which see them as biologically controlled. This also helps to provide legitimation for medical control and intervention in women's lives – their problems (which can have many sources) are explained and treated in terms of their biology. Biology is not seen to affect men's lives in the same way, although they too undergo physiological changes in the process of aging. This reinforces the idea raised in Chapter 1 that men do the analysing and it is women as the 'Other' who need explaining. What needs explaining is why their bodies are different from men's, which are seen as the normal ones. These biological discourses surrounding women's bodies help to prevent women's sexuality or reproductive cycles from being seen in any other way. Although they are presented as 'scientific', they in fact reflect a male view of the world (Sayers, 1986).

SUMMARY

1   Women's lives are seen as shaped by their biological bodies and the changes these bodies undergo. Men's lives by contrast are seen as shaped by their achievements.

2   Women's life course is seen as related to their reproductive cycles through menstruation, fertility, menopause. These processes are seen as inherently problematical. These are seen as ways of defining and classifying different groups of women and explaining their social behaviour.

3   The fact that women are seen as being at the mercy of their bodies justifies medical intervention and control of their lives to a much greater extent than men's.

Women and later life

An increasing proportion of the Western world consists of elderly people. People live longer and longer. This is an issue for older women because the majority of elderly people are women. The proportion of people aged over 65 has grown both in absolute terms and as a proportion of the UK population. In 1988 the UK population was estimated to stand at 57.1 million, of whom 18 per cent were aged 65 years and over (Arber and Ginn, 1991), compared with 5 per cent of the population in 1901. As part of this trend there is an increase in the numbers of those aged 85 and older, most of whom are women. Two per cent of women and 0.5 per cent of men are of this age group and the proportion of people in it is expected to rise by 62 per cent in the next twenty years. About half of these need assistance with their daily living.

A high percentage of elderly people live alone – especially older women. Fifty per cent of older women (aged 65+) are widowed and 37 per cent are married, and the same proportion live alone. While 66 per cent of severely disabled older men receive personal care from a spouse and 65 per cent domestic care, only 28 per cent of older women receive personal care and 20 per cent domestic care from a spouse (Arber and Ginn, 1991, p. 148).

Just as the earlier stages of the life course are socially constructed, so are the later stages. This can be illustrated by looking at how older people are differently treated at different points in history and in different cultures. Among the Venda-speaking people in Africa, elderly people have a particular authority within the society because of their proximity to the spirit world: grey hair is seen as a positive sign of status rather than a negative one and is a source of pleasure (Hockey and James, 1993). However, in most societies older men have more status and power than do older women. In our own society, the treatment of later life can be shown to have varied considerably too over time. Giarchi (forthcoming), for example, identifies three main historical periods – pre-modern, high modern (or Fordist) and postmodern or post-Fordist periods.

In the pre-modern era aging was seen as negative, but it was not seen as being attached to any particular chronological age – rather, it was seen as a general deterioration, but also a sign of wisdom and authority. Although the old body occasioned disgust, the old woman's body excited particular disgust because beauty and love were associated with younger bodies. Erasmus (1466–1536), for example, wrote of older women:

> . . . these broken-down women, these walking corpses, stinking bodies. They display their flaccid, disgusting breasts and sometimes they try to stimulate their lovers' vigour with quavering yelps.
>
> (cited in Giarchi, forthcoming)

In the modern period, associated with industrial capitalism, a number of transformations took place.

- First, old age was medicalised – it came to be seen as a medical condition requiring medical intervention and control, despite the fact that most elderly people are healthy.
- Second, the body was seen as a machine, one where the parts were wearing out or breaking down. The broken down, unproductive body was one to be discarded or no longer used in the industrial process – it was relegated to a different area of life. (Women, of course, are seen to have unproductive bodies when they have been through the menopause; at a younger age than men they are seen as past being productive workers.)
- Third, there was the development of the welfare state, which sections off old age according to legal norms of retirement (between 60 and 67 in most European countries) and entitlements to pensions and other benefits. In most countries women are compelled to retire earlier, despite the fact that they are most likely to live longer and therefore for women the period of retirement can be very long indeed. The vast array of care systems associated with the development of the welfare state serves further to relegate older people to being burdens, in need of assistance and a drain on the productive population. However, many of the carers are themselves older women over the age of retirement, as are those employed in the care system. Both the carers and the cared-for are women in later life.
- Other cultural changes included the change in the nature of family life, with elderly people increasingly disengaged from the family – hence 50 per cent of women over the age of 60 live alone. The shift towards youthful fashions and the pre-eminence of the ability to participate in consumer culture tends to marginalise older people who have lower incomes (Giarchi, forthcoming).

The result has been a tendency to 'infantilise' the elderly – to treat them in the same way as children: as having less authority, less status, as being unable to make decisions for themselves and even as being people who are not suited for sexual activity (even though the majority lead active sex lives if they have a partner). Thus, according to a New International Report in 1982 'at least 47 per cent of couples in their sixties and 15 per cent of couples in their eighties still enjoy regular and frequent sex' (cited in Giarchi, forthcoming). This is particularly problematical for older women, who are seen as no longer sexual beings; men in their seventies are seen as justified in their sexual libido as long as it is with younger women.

Giarchi (forthcoming) goes on to identify a third phase of postmodern-isation in which the life course is deconstructed and rigid demarcations of age disappear as life gets longer and early as well as later retirement becomes more common. During this phase, alternative, pluralistic significations of age emerge with older people associated with a range of activities including continuing education. However, the continuity of ideas associated with modernity and Fordism tends to slow down the liberating potentialities of this postmodern age.

The increasing numbers of elderly people and their changing position has lead to increasing questioning of the position of the elderly and the formation of pressure groups such as the 'Grey Panthers' to defend their interests. In the words of Grey Panthers leader Margaret Kuhn:

> Our oppressive, paternalistic society wants to keep the elderly out of the way, playing bingo and shuffleboard ... We are not mellowed, sweet people. We're outraged.
>
> (quoted in Giarchi, forthcoming)

Consequently, older people are challenging the notion that they are dependent and lonely, that they are in ill-health or that they are mentally confused or demented. Arber and Ginn (1991) argue that an increased political conscious-ness may be developing amongst older people around such issues. Many of the diseases of old age can be traced to environmental problems such as pollution rather than old age *per se* and affect only some old people just as they affect some younger people.

Poverty and later life

Old age is traditionally associated with poverty, with lowered incomes and inability to earn money. While many older people do suffer poverty, in fact many do not. Just as the older person freezing to death through lack of heating is a popular image in our society, so is the affluent elderly person who has retired on a generous occupational pension and now travels the world or spends the winter in Portugal and Spain to avoid the cold. Consumer culture has spread to incorporate these older consumers. There is great variation, with 47 per cent of retired households having half the income of the other retired households (Victor 1991). The situation of women in later life in fact magnifies their inequalities at earlier stages of the life course. This is linked to factors such as gender, class, race and how old they are (see Black Report, 1978; Whitehead, 1987).

Poverty is particularly a problem for older women. First, they are likely to live longer than older men and to find themselves in the category of the very old elderly, who are generally poorer. Second, due to their interrupted careers in the labour market and their positions, which are generally in lower-paid, lower-status jobs, they are less likely to benefit from occupational pension schemes, which are the ones which bring affluence in old age and are earnings-related (Groves, 1991, 1992; Walker, 1992). However, as Simone de Beauvoir (1977) has pointed out, old age has been regarded as 'a moral problem'. Women have been ignored in studies of the transition from employment to retirement, even though the numbers of women in paid employment and therefore undergoing the transition to retirement have been growing steadily. Furthermore, the ways in which male transitions to retirement impact on women in the domestic sphere have also been ignored.

Older people are more likely to be living in poverty than other age groups, and older women are especially vulnerable to poverty and necessity in all societies (Storey-Gibson, 1985). In Britain in 1987, for example, more than one older woman in three (35 per cent) was living on an income at or below supplementary benefit level, compared with a quarter of men (Johnson and Webb, 1990). Older women living alone are even more likely to be living in poverty – just under 50 per cent, compared with 40 per cent of single older men. In 1988 three times as many older women as men were living in households with below average incomes (House of Commons Social Security Committee, 1991, p. xxxix).

> In addition to sex-based inequalities in income and household resources, older women in general are more disadvantaged than men . . . They are three times more likely than older men to be living alone, and only half as likely to have a spouse. Older women report more illness and long-standing health problems and consult their GPs more frequently than men . . . Older women are also more likely than older men to suffer from psychological problems such as loneliness and anxiety and to have lower levels of morale or life satisfaction.
>
> (Walker, 1992, p. 181)

Conclusions

This chapter has demonstrated that women's lives are heavily structured by age stages which are seen as 'natural'. Women are seen in relationship to the age stage and 'the natural' – girls are pre-pubescent, young women are pubescent, adult women are maternal/pre-menopausal, middle-aged women are menopausal, and older women are post-menopausal. Physical/sexual attractiveness is related to age – only young women are conceived as sexually attractive. At each stage of the life course women are said to be controlled by their hormones – to be determined by biology. Feminists have challenged this and argued that life stages for women are *socially* constructed, as they are for men. Malestream theories have either not challenged biological explanations for women or have constructed the 'scientific' knowledge which sustains the view that women are controlled by their biology. Knowledge about women constructed by men has been used to control and subordinate them.

SUMMARY

1   Women in later life are classified as less productive citizens, more in need of medical help, as burdens on the community and as sexually undesirable. These classifications apply more to elderly women than to men because women are more often defined by their bodies and their physical attributes.

2   Old age is particularly a problem for women because the majority of the elderly are women and the majority of the poor elderly are women since they lack the pension benefits that men enjoy.

3   The numbers of elderly, especially elderly women, are increasing.

4   On the one hand the crisis of the welfare systems in Europe means that there may be less scope for caring for the elderly in future and concerns about how to pay their pensions; however, there are also 'postmodernising' tendencies which could lead to the liberation of elderly people.

FURTHER READING

Arber, S. and Ginn, J. (1991) *Gender and Later Life: a sociological analysis of resources and constraints*, London: Sage.

Hockey, J. and James, A. (1993) *Growing Up and Growing Old: aging and dependency in the life course*, London: Sage.

Wallace, C. (1987) *For Richer for Poorer: growing up in and out of work*, London: Tavistock.

Chapter six

The family
and the household

The family is a concept that is familiar to all of us – at least, in industrialised countries. Most people regard themselves as members of one or more families. We are constantly bombarded with images of a particular type of family – what the anthropologist Edmund Leach (1967) has called 'the cereal-packet norm family' – consisting of husband as head of household and children being cared for by a smiling wife. We come to think of this as the normal, natural and inevitable family form. In fact only one in twenty households in Britain at any one time consists of a father in paid employment, a dependent wife and two children. Consequently we need to distinguish 'the family' – a group of relatives – from 'the household' – a technical term used to describe all the people living in one home, who may or may not be related. The nuclear family (the cereal-packet family) is often the unit which is assumed in advertising, housing and social policy when we talk about 'the family', and it is to this that we shall mainly be referring here. However, this is an ideal – an ideal of a happy family which does not often fit the reality and one which is not descriptively neutral but value-laden. Dianne Gittens, in challenging the view that the family is a universal institution which performs essential functions for individuals and societies, has pointed out that:

Social recognition of mating and of parenthood is obviously intimately bound up with social definitions and customs of marriage. It is often assumed that, in spite of a variety of marriage customs and laws, marriage as a binding relationship between a man and a woman is universal. Yet it is estimated that only ten per cent of all marriages in the world are actually monogamous; polygyny and polyandry are common in many societies, just as serial monogamy is becoming increasingly common in our own. Marriage is not always a heterosexual relationship. The Nuer ... practise a custom known as 'ghost marriages' whereby when an unmarried or childless man dies, a relation of his then marries a woman 'to his name' and the resulting children of this union are regarded as the dead man's children and bear his name.

(Gittens, 1992, p. 69)

Sociologists have tended to assume that the modern Western middle-class idea of the family and family life is what is, if not the norm, then what *should* be the norm, elsewhere as here. Thus they do not take account of the diversity of the ways in which co-residence, economic relations, sexuality and reproduction can be organised. Gittens goes on to suggest, referring to modern Britain, that:

Ideals of family relationships have become enshrined in our legal, social, religious and economic systems which, in turn, reinforce the ideology and penalise or ostracise those who transgress it.

(Gittens, 1992, p. 74)

Politicians in many countries, following the Judaeo-Christian or many other religious traditions, see the family as extremely important. Both the major political parties in Britain have expressed their support for the family and argued that state policies must strengthen it. The British Conservative Party, since its election in 1979, has stressed that it is 'the party of the family' and argued that people must be discouraged from choosing alternative lifestyles such as cohabitation or homosexuality. They argue for the traditional patriarchal nuclear family – that is, one in which the father sets and enforces standards of behaviour. In this type of family there is assumed to be a gendered division of labour such that the man takes on the major responsibility for earning a wage and the woman for caring for the 'breadwinner' and the children. This view of the family is one that is widely shared as an ideal. Hence, although other family forms such as single-parent families, extended families or re-formed families are increasingly common, they are not seen as normal or desirable. Indeed, these and other families in which no father exercises control are often seen in Western Europe as the cause of many social problems

– especially crime, juvenile delinquency and people's inability to take on responsibility for their own economic and social support (Abbott and Wallace, 1989, 1992).

Sociological perspectives on the family

Sociologists in Western Europe studying the family have claimed that it is a central and necessary institution in society. However, they have tended to take the domestic division of labour for granted. Feminist sociologists, by contrast, have highlighted the position of women in families and argued that the family is the main way in which women are oppressed – although some Black feminists (e.g. Carby, 1982) have argued that the family provides a source of support against racism. Sociological theories of the family have been dominated by the structural-functionalist school of sociology and in particular the work of Talcott Parsons. In this perspective the co-resident nuclear family with a gendered division of labour is seen as the one most suited to the needs of industrial society. Marxists challenged this picture to the extent that they suggested the family met the needs of capitalist society – that is, that it served the interests of the ruling class by helping in the maintenance of the capitalist system. These traditional sociological theories of the family have tended to look at the relationships between family and society and have not examined relationships within the family, nor how these relationships both structure and are structured by external social, economic and power relationships. The domestic sphere has tended to be regarded as a private area – not only outside public concern, but also outside the concerns of sociologists.

The symmetrical family

One of the most influential studies in the sociology of the family in Britain was undertaken by Willmott and Young in the 1960s (Young and Willmott, 1973), building on previous studies they had carried out in London into families in the 1950s (Willmott and Young, 1957). This study was carried out in a period when re-housing policies and increased affluence meant that most young people, when they married, could set up home independently, and more geographical mobility meant they often did so at a distance from kin. It was argued, partly as a consequence of this and partly because more married women (including those with children) were taking paid employment, that the division of labour between men and women in the domestic sphere was changing: men would take on more domestic work and women would be more likely to work outside the home. Willmott and Young argued that the family would become more democratic, with both partners sharing decision-making and financial resources. It was suggested that rather than having segregated conjugal roles, where husband and wives did different jobs within the house and had separate activities and friends, husbands and wives were increasingly spending their spare time together and had friends in common. The main conclusion of the Willmott and Young study was that the British family was becoming increasingly symmetrical – that is, that the roles of husbands and wives were becoming more alike and would eventually become identical. Willmott and Young were careful to argue that this was the *coming* family form – the way that the family was developing, not the way that it was already – but argued that in Britain there was a definite progression in this direction.

Feminist approaches to the family

Feminists have challenged the view that the family is becoming more egalitarian and symmetrical. Feminists argue, by contrast, that the family is a site of inequality where women are subordinated and women's roles perpetuated and also that it institutionalises heterosexuality – the idea that heterosexuality is both the norm and normal. It is suggested that there are two interlocking structures of subordination of women in the family:

1   women's position as wives and mothers;
2   socialisation processes in the family during which children internalise male and female attitudes and transmit them to their own children, thus perpetuating male domination and female subordination.

While marxist feminists stress that women's exploitation in the family serves the interest of capitalism, radical feminists stress that it serves the interests of men, who benefit from the unpaid labour of women in a system of patriarchy. They are agreed, however, that the family oppresses women and that women are exploited and subordinated within it. Feminists argue that women's position in the family as wife/mother results in a position of subordination to men/fathers, at least in part because of economic dependency, but also because of widely shared ideologies of the family. Thus feminists have questioned not only sociological assumptions concerning the family, but common-sense ones as well.

Barrie Thorne (1982) has argued that four themes are central to the feminist challenge to the conventional sociology of the family:

1   The assumptions concerning the structure and functioning of the family. Feminists challenge an ideology that sees the co-resident nuclear family

with a gendered division of labour as the only natural and legitimate form of the family. Feminists argue against the view that any specific family form is natural – that is, based on biological imperatives. Rather, they would claim that forms of family organisation and ideology are based on social organisations and assumptions about people's roles held by the people of a given society. For example, there is no inherent (biological) reason why men cannot do housework; it is just that people in our society believe that it is not the right thing for them to do and hence that they are incapable of it.

2   Feminists have sought to claim the family as an area for analysis; this challenges the gender-based categories of analysis in malestream sociology.

3   Feminists argue that different members of families experience family life in different ways. They argue that women's experiences of mother-hood and family life have demonstrated that families embody power relationships that can and do result in conflict, violence and the inequitable distribution of work and resources.

4   Feminists question the assumption that the family should be a private sphere. While women and children are often cut off from outside con-tact in the modern nuclear family, this is partly an illusion at the level of public policy. The form that the family takes is heavily influenced by economic and social policies and the family is permeable to outside intervention.

It is argued that common-sense beliefs about the nature of the family deny women the opportunity to participate in the wider society and gain equality with men. It is in this way, also, that we can explain women's exclusion from the labour market, youth cultures, political life and other areas of social life discussed elsewhere in this book.

Industrialisation, the family and the origins of the family wage

Feminists have examined the history of family life and changes in the organisation of families, from the perspective of women. There is some dis-agreement as to whether or not women have always been subordinated and exploited in the family, or whether their subordination is a result of the growth and development of capitalism. Radical feminists argue that patriarchy (the domination of women by men) in the patriarchal mode of production (the family) existed long before the development of capitalism. Marxist feminists argue that the economic dependency of women on men which enables them to be dominated and exploited in the family is a result of the growth of industrial capitalism. Dual-systems feminists suggest that the ideology of patriarchy predates capitalism but that the way in which women are exploited and subordinated in industrialised societies is the result of the interaction of this ideology with the material relations of production (the way in which goods and services are produced and the relationship between the workers and the owners of the means of production in capitalist society).

For feminists the great change that has occurred in the family since the seventeenth century has been the institutionalisation of the 'housewife and mother' role. Before industrialisation the product of labour was regarded as the joint property of the family and not seen as the property of individuals to be divided up. Every member of the family worked to produce what the family needed – there was no distinction between production and consumption. With industrialisation the home became separated from the place of work – consumption from production. Gradually women became associated with the domestic sphere, the care of the home and children, and men with the public sphere, earning a wage and participating in politics. These changes were gradual and affected different classes at different times. The change that occurred was summed up in a satirical gibe by John Roby (quoted in Pinchbeck, 1977, p. 37):

1743	1843
Man, to the plough	Man, Tally Ho
Wife, to the cow	Miss, piano
Girl, to the yarn	Wife, silk and satin
Boy, to the barn	Boy, Greek and Latin
And your rest will be netted	And you'll be gazetted.

Most middle-class women in Britain accepted the housewife role by the beginning of the nineteenth century, and the number of working-class women in officially recognised paid employment (as recorded by the Census) declined rapidly after 1850. Roberts' 1982 research demonstrates that by 1900 the majority of working-class women thought that ideally a wife should stay at home to care for her husband and children, although there were regional variations.

The changes brought about by the industrial revolution altered not so much the type of work that women did as the context in which that work was carried out. Women became economically dependent on the wages of their husbands and no longer had direct control over economic resources. The legal subordination of women to men continued; women had limited rights in property, and the ability of women to participate in public life was very restricted. Until 1884 a married woman had no right to her own property in

Britain – this passed from her father to her husband – nor did she have any right to custody of or access to her children. It was not until the passage of the Marital Causes Act 1928 that women could divorce their husbands on the same grounds as their husbands could divorce them, and not until 1882 that an Act was passed instituting maintenance for women from the husband in case of legal separation, and even then only on the grounds that he had committed aggravated assault on her.

The industrial revolution resulted in the growth of towns and cities, in a vast increase in population, in the development of new and better methods of transport (roads, canals and railways), and in new class relationships – the emergence of a working class (factory workers), a middle class (clerks, administrators and professionals) and an upper class (the owners of factories and productive land). Changes in the relationships between men and women, husbands and wives, parents and children happened in the context of these changes as well as the new economic and political structure that developed.

In the pre-industrial period middle-class women helped their men in productive roles. An example is the Cadbury family. Before the nineteenth century they all lived above the chocolate shop and the wives and daughters were actually involved in the running of the business. However, when with the growth of the town the Cadburies moved to the suburb, the men went to work at the shop and the women stayed at home. Mrs Cadbury and her daughters undertook domestic tasks and the supervision of domestic servants, and the daughters were instructed in feminine graces. The women became involved in religious and philanthropic activities. The Cadburies wanted to have a different kind of home life. With increased affluence they no longer needed the labour of the female members of the family and could afford to bring in labour. They also valued the domestic ideal – the home as a retreat from work and a view of women as delicate and needing protection from the world as a place of danger and sin. The Cadburies did not *have* to move from the shop, but for other middle-class families new methods of production meant that the factory was separated from the home, and the home, the domestic sphere, became seen as the place for women.

For the working class the changes were very different. In pre-industrial Britain the family had been a unit of production. There had been a division of labour by gender, and men were generally seen as having a dominant role, but women were not regarded as the economic dependents of men. In the early stages of industrialisation, men, women and children all worked together in the factories. Men generally managed to secure for themselves the jobs that were seen as the most skilled. Gradually during the course of the nineteenth century women and children were excluded from factory jobs and became increasingly dependent economically. The working class came to share the domestic ideals of the middle class and to see a non-working wife as the ideal – a wife who could care properly for her husband and children and provide a home for them. The reasons why this happened are complex, and feminists do not agree on them precisely, but two factors do emerge as very important:

1 Middle-class philanthropists attempted to shape working-class life to fit their ideas of what family life was like, and put pressure on government to implement reforms that reinforced these conceptions. The 1834 Poor Law assumed that a woman was dependent on a man, for instance. Factory legislation restricted the hours women and children could work, lessening their worth as employees. Women were assumed to be responsible for caring for their husbands and children, and middle-class women set out to teach working-class women how to do this. Towards the end of the nineteenth century and into the early twentieth the poor health of the working class was blamed on negligent mothers, especially those who worked.

2 From the mid-nineteenth century sections of the male working class began to argue that a man should be paid sufficient to support a wife and children, so excluding the necessity of his wife or children taking paid employment. Most feminists argue that the 'family wage' principle resulted in the exclusion of women from paid employment and their economic dependence on men, thus giving men power over their wives. Women perform domestic and other duties in exchange for being maintained by their husbands (see Chapters 6 and 8).

Barrett and McIntosh (1980b) argue that women were disadvantaged by the growing idea that a man should earn a family wage, and that the capitalists and the organised male working class benefited. Capitalists benefited because women at home caring for their husbands and children helped to maintain a fit and active workforce, and working-class men because they gained the unpaid services of their wives. It also enabled men to have economic and social power in the home. They argue that this ideology of the family wage is still powerful and is a major aspect of inequality for women – not only because married men are supposed to support wives and children, but because men are thought to be entitled to earn a 'family wage' while women are not. This justifies the low pay that attaches to 'women's jobs' (see Chapter 8) and restricts women's choices and reduces their economic power within marriage.

In the former Communist societies industrialisation also resulted in the exclusion of women from paid employment (Voronina, 1994). However, Communist governments introduced equal rights legislation, and the majority of women came to have full-time employment. Being engaged in full-time employment, however, did not liberate women from domestic work (Khotkina, 1994), and indeed the hours of domestic labour put in by women in Eastern Europe probably exceeded those of their sisters in Western Europe (Einhorn, 1993). Zoya Khotkina (1994) has suggested that while there was equality according to the constitution, there was patriarchy in real life. Women were (and are) not only expected to carry out all the domestic labour but were also restricted in their work opportunities (Voronina, 1994).

Women's experience of family life

To understand the feminist criticisms of the family it is necessary to examine the disjuncture between ideologies of domesticity and women's personal experiences as wives and mothers. Betty Friedan (1963) referred to the distress suffered by middle-class American mothers in the 1960s as 'the problem that has no name', while Liz Stanley and Sue Wise (1983) have argued that many women distinguish between the family as an institution and their own family. The former is seen as desirable, while the latter is often experienced as not meeting their expectations of family life.

Girls grow up expecting and wanting to get married, seeing the wedding day as the supreme moment of their lives. Married life rarely turns out to be what they had expected, however – the reality is very different from the dream. Jessie Bernard (1973) has suggested that there is 'her' marriage and 'his' marriage, two different things, and that men benefit more from marriage than women do. Married women are more likely than single women or than single men to suffer from mental illness, while married men are the least likely to do so. Women often get married from economic necessity, because they cannot earn sufficient to live on and therefore it is only through marriage that they have potential access to a decent living wage. Single women are thought to be in need of the protection of a man, and this is an additional pressure towards marriage. Men, on the other hand, gain both economic and social advantages from marriage – they are cared for, they enjoy the 'unpaid' domestic labour of their wives, and often 'unpaid' help with their employed role as well. Women 'help' their husbands by entertaining colleagues and clients, by doing unpaid clerical work, by acting as a telephone answering service, and in some cases a wife is seen as essential or nearly essential for a man to be able to carry out his work role (Finch, 1983a). Most wives are expected to organise their lives around the demands of their husbands' jobs – preparing meals and other activities to fit in with their partners' working hours – and to tailor what they do to his 'needs'.

Housework, the 'unpaid' labour of a wife, is worth quite a lot if it had to be paid for at market rates. In 1987 the Legal and General Life Assurance

Company estimated that a 'dependent' wife was worth £19,253 a year in earnings (quoted in *Sunday Times*, 29 March 1987). The Company located on a computer the 'average' wife, a 37-year-old mother of two named Rosalind Harris. Her work was found to start at 7 a.m. on Monday when she began to prepare the breakfast and to end at 9 p.m. that day (a 14-hour working day). During the week she worked as a shopper, a window-cleaner, a nurse, a driver, a cleaner, a cook and a child-minder. Her total working week was of 92 hours' duration. (This excludes periods 'on call', with the children in bed.)

Feminists have suggested a number of reasons why married life does not turn out to be the ideal that is portrayed for women. Ann Oakley (1982) has suggested that women experience four areas of conflict in family life:

1   The sexual division of labour means that women are expected to be responsible for domestic work and childcare. This means that women become economically dependent on men and have no access to money that they see as their own.
2   Conflict arises over the different emotional needs of men and women. Women are expected to deal with the frustrations and anger of husbands and children but have no one to whom they can turn themselves.
3   Economic and physical differences in power between husbands and wives mean that women can experience lack of control over financial resources, an inability to engage in social activities and even physical violence from their husbands.
4   Male control of sexuality and fertility means that men's needs are assumed to be the more important. Women are expected to 'please' their husbands, to give in to their sexual demands, and to have and to care for their children.

Indeed, it could be argued that married women do not have a separate identity either in their own eyes or the eyes of others. Married women generally put the needs of their families before their own needs and desires and they are identified by others with their families. In Britain married women generally take their husbands' name and often become seen as an appendage of their husbands and children, being 'John Smith's wife' and 'Jean and Billy Smith's mother' – having no separate social identity of their own. This identification with the family often carries over into paid employment (see Chapter 8). Men, on the other hand, tend to take their main identity from their employment. Wives are frequently asked what their husband does for living, as if that were a major source of their identity, and seldom what they do themselves.

Familial ideology

Ideas about women's role are reinforced by the mass-media presentation of women in a narrow range of roles, with an emphasis on the wife/mother role. This is especially noticeable in television commercials and popular soap operas. What is equally important is the range of roles that women are *not* portrayed as playing, or seen as exceptional if they are so portrayed. Even in programmes such as 'The Gentle Touch' and 'Cagney and Lacey' the 'tough' women not only have male bosses but are portrayed in domestic roles as well. Similarly, children's reading schemes have often been shown to portray men and women, boys and girls in typically segregated masculine and feminine roles (see Chapter 5).

Veronica Beechey (1986) has suggested that two assumptions underlie familial ideology:

> 1 [that] the co-resident nuclear family . . . is universal and normatively desirable,
> 2 [and that] . . . the form of sexual division of labour in which the woman is the housewife and mother and primarily located within the private world of the family, and the man is wage-earner and bread-winner and primarily located in the 'public' world of paid work, is universal and normatively desirable.
>
> (p. 99)

She suggests that the assumption is that the family is biologically determined and argues that this view of the family is part of our taken-for-granted common-sense assumptions. This patriarchal family form is reproduced by social and legal institutions in Western society because it is assumed that this is both how people *do* live their lives and how they *should* live their lives. For example, these assumptions about families underlie patterns of schooling, labour markets and ways in which the social security system is organised, as well as the type of housing that is provided in both the private and the public sector. Their force is three-fold: to set up the role of housewife and mother as an available lifestyle for women, to declare it a lifestyle which is inherently satisfying for women and one with which they ought to be satisfied, and to place on women as individuals any blame for the lifestyle's failure to satisfy them. In other words, like any ideology the familial ideology has the effect of converting the interests of a dominant group into the self-perceived interests of a subordinated one and making the dominated group responsible for any consequent failures – in this case by individualising a set of discontents which might otherwise be thought to have their base in collectively experienced structural pressures rather than in individual failures.

Boys and girls, men and women take it for granted that men are strong and tough and should be 'breadwinners' and that women are submissive and gentle and should care for men and children. Even when people's own experiences do not live up to this ideal they still see it as how things ought to be. It is also assumed that this type of family best serves the interest of its individual members and of society generally. Feminists question the assumption that a particular set of living arrangements is natural and universal and that this form of living arrangement necessarily best serves the interests of women.

The diversity of family forms

Feminists have argued that while the nuclear family may be the moral norm in Britain, anthropological research has demonstrated that there is a wide variety of living arrangements throughout the world, as well as kinship systems. Ann Oakley (1972) concludes from a review of the anthropological evidence that while in all societies there are rules about what is suitable for men and women to do, there is also a wide variation between societies as to what is considered suitable for each gender.

Even within contemporary Britain there is a diversity of family forms and ways of organising roles within the family. Nevertheless, families that do not conform to the nuclear family norm are seen as deviant, strange and a less desirable form of living arrangement. This applies not only to those who choose not to get married, but to families of Asian origin who choose to live in extended family form or to retain close family connection, to West Indian families which are often assumed to be matrifocal (mother-headed), and in which the mother chooses to work full time, especially when the children are young. It extends also to families where the father takes a considerable responsibility for domestic work and child-care, or where the mother is 'the breadwinner' and the father the homemaker. Explanations for 'deviant' family forms tend to focus on deviant cultures – working-class, Afro-Caribbean, or Asian. However, culture becomes the explanation only when 'deviant' behaviour is being explained – white, middle-class behaviour is seen as natural (see, e.g., Phoenix, 1992).

More and more households do not conform to conventional norms. More people are cohabiting (living together without formal marriage); the proportion rose from 2.7 per cent of couples aged 18–49 in 1979 to 5 per cent in 1985. Claire Wallace (1987) found it a normal prelude to marriage for almost all young couples. In 1991, 7 per cent of non-married women aged 16–59 were cohabiting, while 30 per cent of single women aged 25–34 were doing so (CSO, 1995, Table 2.20). More people are having children without being married. Whereas only 6 per cent of all live births in 1961 were outside marriage, by 1991 32 per cent of live births were outside marriage (CSO, 1995, Table 2.27). Britain had the third highest proportion of live births outside marriage in the European Community in 1992; Denmark had the highest, at just over 45 per cent, France marginally more than Britain, and Greece the lowest at less than 4 per cent – the EC average was 20 per cent (CSO, 1995, Table 2.27). However, the fact that these births are also increasingly registered in the father's as well as the mother's name implies that they are taking place within stable relationships, perhaps to couples who are cohabiting. Many of the respondents in Wallace's study reported that they might have children and then see how well they got on with their partners, rather than getting married:

> What's the point of getting married to someone if you haven't lived with them? You don't know what they're like, do you?
>
> (Wallace, 1987, p. 161)

However, these *de facto* relationships are of a form which mirrors the conventional nuclear family, including its sexual fidelity. Children may now be born outside marriage, but traditional roles of motherhood are usually the same, and indeed children are now more likely to be brought up by their biological mothers than to be sent away for adoption as in the past. The result of increasing divorce and increasing birth outside marriage, however, is that more children grow up for at least part of their childhood in lone-parent families, and these are almost invariably headed by women. They have risen from 8 per cent of all families with dependent children in 1972 to 21 per cent in 1992 (CSO, 1995, Table 2.11). Many people have argued that the trends cited here are evidence of the breakdown of the family.

Despite all the arguments about the decline of marriage, the increase in illegitimacy and so on, it continues to be the case that most people in Britain grow up, get married and form a nuclear family for part of their adult life. Nine out of ten people get married at some time in their lives; 90 per cent of women are married by the age of 30 and over 90 per cent of men before the age of 40. Most couples who get married (or have stable cohabitation relationships) have children. Thus nine out of ten married women have children, and four out of five children live with their two natural parents. Seventy-nine per cent of families with children are headed by a married couple and 21 per cent a lone parent. The majority of lone-parent families (90 per cent) are headed by a woman, and the major reason is separation or divorce from the male partner, although some female family heads are single or widowed (Family Policy Studies Centre, 1988). In 1991 three-quarters of children lived in a married-couple family with both their natural parents,

3 per cent lived with both their natural, non-married parents, and 6 per cent were step-children in a couple family. The remaining 17 per cent of children lived in a lone-parent family (CSO, 1995, Table 2.10).

In some respects marriage is more popular than ever. The age at which people marry had fallen during this century, so that in the 1960s one bride in three was a teenager, although it is now rising again – in 1992 the median age at first marriage was 26 years for women and 28 years for men (CSO, 1995, Table 2.16). There are both gender and class differences in age of marriage, with working-class couples marrying on average at a younger age than middle-class ones. People are also marrying more than once, and the percentage of remarriage has risen from 14 per cent in 1961 to 38 per cent in 1992 as the divorce rate has increased. The number of divorces nearly trebled between 1961 and 1971, doubled between 1971 and 1981 but increased by only 11 per cent between 1981 and 1991. The rise in the divorce rate correlates with legal changes that have extended the grounds for divorce and made it easier to obtain one. A majority of divorced people either remarry or cohabit.

However, it is important to examine household structures as well as familial relationships, given the continuing emphasis on the moral superiority of the nuclear family. It is also important to note that there is a variety of family forms in modern Britain: single-parent families, extended families, role-swap families, dual career families and re-formed families as well as conventional nuclear ones. Furthermore, while the ideal may be that (married) women with young children should not be in paid employment, an increasing number are. Indeed, it is the norm for mothers of school-age children to have paid employment, and most non-employed women with young children expect to work when the children grow older (Abbott and Ackers, forthcoming).

Power and the division of labour in families

The choices about who works in the family and who stays at home to care for the household and children are based on an ideology of appropriate gender roles. However, this is reinforced by labour market factors; men can generally earn more than women, so that it is generally the case that men have the paid employment and women care for the children. This traps women in a situation of financial dependency. Employment, taken to fit in with domestic responsibilities, rarely pays sufficient to give a woman financial independence, and most women do not feel they are entitled to control the spending of the 'family wage'. Even where it is the norm for married women to have full-time paid employment the horizontal and vertical segregation of the labour market means that wives generally earn considerably less than their husbands (see, e.g., Abbott and Ackers, forthcoming; Khotkina, 1994). The family wage is supposed to be large enough to support a man, his wife and his children. The man's need to earn a family wage is used in wage bargaining by trade unions, and a wife's earnings are seen as supplementary – money with which to buy luxuries. Hunt (1980) found that the husband's money was spent on the essentials and the wife's on extras, so it was the man's employment that was seen as essential and the wife's as something that could be given up if necessary. However, not all married men with a family earn a 'family wage', and many men and some women without familial responsibilities do earn one. In 1977 the Equal Opportunities Commission estimated that the number of families living in poverty (i.e. below the supplementary benefit level) would have been three times greater if it had not been for married women's earnings (see Land, 1978). Women without a male head of household are more likely to be living in poverty than those with one.

The 'family wage' is not paid to the family, but to the (male) wage earner. How this money is distributed within the family depends on power relationships between husband and wife and who is seen as having the right to decide how and where the money is to be spent. Jan Pahl (1980) has described the different ways in which husbands and wives manage their income. In some cases the husband hands over the wage packet and the wife gives him back his 'pocket-money'; in others the husband gives the wife housekeeping money; in a third type of case resources are pooled and spending decisions made jointly. Pahl has pointed out that in some cases the husband does not maintain his wife. Graham (1984) and Pahl (1983) have also found that women with children whose marriages have broken down have sometimes found that they are better off on supplementary benefit than they were when they lived with their husbands.

Furthermore, research shows that resources are not shared equally within families. Women tend to put their husbands and children first and their own needs last. When money is tight, women go without food, clothes and other necessities. Women rarely have personal spending money in the way that men do, and they feel that if they spend housekeeping money on themselves they are depriving their children (Brannen and Wilson, 1987). Men and children have pocket money, women have housekeeping money. More recent research has confirmed that women's wages are often seen as covering the extras, however essential they are (e.g. Brannen and Moss, 1991; Pahl, 1989). Even where, in theory, women have control over resources, or joint control, men expect to be consulted and have the final say over the purchase of large household items such as washing machines, refrigerators or cars (Hunt, 1980; Edgell, 1980). When the household has a car, it is generally the husband who has the use of it, even if the wife can drive. In many cases the car is a 'perk' of the job, and the wife has no claim over it in any case (Graham, 1984).

Within the home, men tend to have more space that they regard as their own – a den, a study or even a garden shed.

Women accept the lack of control because they are not the breadwinners. However husbands and wives handle their money, it is unusual for a married woman to have money for her own personal use. As Lee Comer has said:

> If any sociologist . . . had inquired into the financial arrangements in my marriage I would have lain my hand on my heart and sworn that we shared money equally. And in theory I would have been telling the truth. In fact, it would no more have occurred to me to spend money on anything but housekeeping as it would for him . . . not to . . . a reality in which a husband can spend money however he wishes but a reality . . . in which she makes do because to do otherwise is to encroach too far into the man's rights. The only money she spends guiltlessly is on food for the family and clothes for the children.
>
> (1974, p. 124)

Obviously women's lack of power over financial resources relates not just to ideologies concerning the appropriate roles of men and women but also to the realities of who is seen as earning the money and who is seen to be 'not working'. Women's domestic labour is not seen as 'real' work because it does not bring in money, and women are not paid for it. They are maintained by their husbands in exchange for the labour. However, it is men's control over financial resources that gives them such power in marriage and makes it difficult for a wife to leave her husband even if he is mentally or physically violent to her or she is just unhappy in her marriage. Again this is compounded by the kind of job that she would be able to get if she left, and if she had children.

The division of labour in the home

To understand the division of labour within the family we need to examine not just who does what job, but who is seen as responsible for ensuring that a particular job is carried out, and to challenge the view that there is an equitable division of labour between 'man the breadwinner' and 'woman the carer'. The imbalance comes about partly because women in Western Europe increasingly have paid employment as well as doing housework, cooking and childcare, and partly because women's domestic labour requires far more hours of work than men's paid labour (see Chapter 8). Feminists often point out that it is women who are generally responsible for the necessary, repetitive jobs that have to be done on a regular basis, while men do those that are creative and can be done when convenient. Often this division is based on what men and women are thought to be naturally good at. Women are said to be naturally good at cleaning, sewing, washing up, shopping, washing, caring for children, cooking and so on.

Ann Oakley (1974a,b) was the first feminist sociologist to examine the division of labour in the household seriously and to look at domestic labour as work (see Chapter 8). She has also challenged the view that women have a private domain of their own – a domain which they rule and where they make the decisions. In fact, she suggests that as men spend more time in the home, take more interest in their children and have more joint activities with their wives, so women's power is diminished.

David Young and Peter Willmott (1973) have suggested that men and women in Britain now share childcare, domestic tasks, and the 'breadwinner' role and make decisions jointly, but Ann Oakley (1982) has argued that even when conjugal roles are shared, men are generally said to be 'helping' their wives. Women are held responsible if essential tasks are not carried out, and men will frequently 'make do' for meals if their wives are absent. Stephen Edgell (1980) has argued that wives are left to make the more minor decisions, about meals or purchasing children's clothes, while the major decisions such as moving house are made by the husband. However, even in the more minor areas of decision-making a husband's wishes may be paramount. Pauline Hunt (1980) has suggested that women prepare meals that are the ones their husbands like and discount their own preferences. Research in a number of other countries suggests a very similar picture (see, e.g., Einhorn, 1993; Voronina, 1994; Khotkina, 1994).

Even when they have paid employment women continue to do most of the domestic work – to take on the dual role. Martin and Roberts (1984) asked the husbands and wives in their sample if they shared housework equally. Twenty-six per cent of wives and 27 per cent of husbands considered that they shared equally, but 73 per cent of wives and 72 per cent of husbands said that the wife did all or most of the housework. The reported division of labour did change when the wife was in paid employment; 43 per cent of wives in paid employment and 44 per cent of husbands whose wives were in paid employment said they shared domestic tasks. However, this still left a majority saying that wives did the majority of the domestic work. (When the wife was in part-time employment only 23 per cent of wives and 24 per cent of husbands reported an equal sharing of household duties.)

Similarly, Audrey Hunt (1975), in a study of female managers, found that they did not get much help at home. Anna Pollert (1981) found that even married women working full time in a factory regarded themselves primarily as housewives and their husbands as workers. Even if they said their husbands 'did a lot', they still seemed to do most of the domestic labour:

A closer look showed that Sheila still did most of the daily drudgery of cooking and housework and with most of the women it became apparent that 'sharing' meant a limited delegation of specific tasks to their husbands, while they bore the responsibility for the endless, undefined, niggling work.

(Pollert, 1981, p. 198)

On a larger scale, the British Social Attitudes Survey (Jowell *et al.*, 1991) found that the majority of married people thought that women had more responsibility for household tasks than men, though only for ironing did a majority of respondents (58 per cent) think the task should be allocated mainly to women. The only task that a majority of respondents thought should *not* be allocated mainly to women was washing up, where 12 per cent thought it should be allocated mainly to men and 76 per cent that it should be shared equally. The reality was rather different, however – the only tasks not actually *done* mainly by women were shopping and washing the evening dishes, but only 8 per cent of households indicated that shopping was done mainly by the men (compared with 45 per cent where it was done mainly by the women) and 28 per cent of households indicated that the evening dishes were done mainly by the men (compared with 33 per cent where they were done mainly by the women – see Table 6.1).

While it is evident that men are not sharing domestic work with their wives, even if their wives are in full-time employment, it is even more clear that they are not taking on responsibility for tasks. Men seem to be able to choose what domestic tasks they undertake and often take on those that women find more enjoyable, such as bathing children, rather than tidying up

TABLE 6.1 Division of household tasks, 1991 – actual and ideal

	Actual allocation %			Ideal allocation %		
	Mainly men	Mainly women	Shared	Mainly men	Mainly women	Shared
Household shopping	8	45	47	1	22	76
Makes evening meal	9	70	20	1	39	58
Does evening dishes	28	33	37	12	11	76
Does household cleaning	4	68	27	1	36	62
Does washing and ironing	3	84	12	–	58	40
Organises household money, bills	3	40	28	17	14	66
Looks after sick children	1	60	39	–	37	60

Source: Jowell *et al.*, 1991

the toys or cooking the meal. The jobs men do in the home – 'do-it-yourself', for example – are those that have a lasting output, while women are responsible for the day-to-day repetitive, never-ending ones. This division of labour is considered 'natural' by both men and women.

Motherhood and mothering

For many feminists, women's subordination and exploitation arise because women have children. It is this biological fact which enabled men to subordinate women, with women placed thereby under the protection of men. Firestone (1974), for example, has argued that women will be able to free themselves from men's control only when they are freed from reproduction (see Chapter 2). Not all feminists accept this biological argument as an adequate explanation for the subordination and exploitation of women. Nevertheless, the assumed centrality to women's lives of having and rearing children is an important aspect of women's lives. It is generally assumed that women will get married and have children. Women who choose not to do so are seen as strange, as unnatural.

Feminists have pointed out that there is a need to distinguish between the biological capacity to have children and the social role of motherhood. It is assumed that because women have children they will look after them. But, as Miriam David (1985) has pointed out: 'Motherhood is a social concept, fatherhood barely recognised. To father a child refers only to the act of procreation' (p. 32). Not only is motherhood a social construction, it is also a historically specific concept, in terms of being seen as a woman's chief vocation and primary identity. It developed among the middle classes during the industrial revolution as part of the new ideology of domesticity and womanhood. By the end of the nineteenth century a woman's primary duty was seen as having and caring for her children.

Mothering is seen as a *vocation* for women in Western Europe and North America. Indeed, in the former Communist states it is increasingly argued that women ought to remain at home and care for their children. It is regarded as something that women are naturally good at and derive great emotional satisfaction from. Women are seen as responsible for the care and control of their children. When something goes wrong, the mother is blamed; she is seen as inadequate or negligent. In the early part of the twentieth century in Britain women were blamed for the high infant mortality rates and the poor health of their children. While there was considerable evidence that the real underlying causes were poor housing, poverty and appalling environmental conditions, women were blamed for not being hygienic in the home and for not providing adequate nutrition (see Chapters 6 and 7). In the period after the

Second World War the popular interpretation of psychoanalysts such as Winnicott and Bowlby led to an emphasis on the need for mothers to care for their pre-school children full-time. Mothers who did not do so were in danger of raising delinquents and badly adjusted children. These ideas continue to have widespread popular appeal despite considerable evidence that it is the quality of care and not the quantity nor the biological identity of the person giving it that is important, and indeed that young children need to form attachments to a variety of adults and children. Interestingly, upper-class parents who employ nannies and send their children away to boarding schools at a young age are rarely accused of neglecting them.

The ideal of motherhood as a full-time vocation has shaped our thinking about women and mothering. Women's primary identity is as a wife and mother – a vocation that 'enables them to fulfil their emotional needs'. However, feminists have pointed out that there is a wide gap between the ideal and the reality. Mothering is hard work – children require constant care and attention – and is generally carried out in isolation. Ann Oakley has suggested that, given the disjuncture between the ideal and the reality of mothering, we should not be surprised at how many women suffer from post-natal depression, but at how few do so. A response in Boulton's 1983 interview study expresses the immediacy of the mothering role:

> There are times when I feel like saying, 'I will feed you twice as much today so tomorrow I can just have a break'. Before, I could say 'The fridge badly needs to be cleaned but I can leave it'. With children they need feeding when they need feeding. Their nappies have to be washed every day. It's as simple as that. When they cry, you can't say 'Well, I'll see you in an hour'. That is when it hits you. The fact that it's seven days a week, twenty four hours a day, and they make the rules.
>
> (p. 69)

Research by Brown and Harris (1978) found that women at home with pre-school children stood a high risks of suffering from clinical depression. A report to the government by the Women's National Commission suggested that women were twice as likely as men to suffer from stress, because 'they are the buffer and absorber of stresses of the other members of the family'. They suggested that women often coped by turning the stress in on themselves, and this could result in alcohol or cigarette addiction. Hilary Graham (1984) has argued that working-class mothers with young children smoke cigarettes as a way of coping – sitting down with a cigarette is the one peaceful time they have. Despite all this evidence the myth persists that motherhood is a satisfying and fulfilling role for women. Helen Roberts (1985) found that general practitioners could not understand why the married women who came to them were dissatisfied and that a married woman with a good husband, lovely children and a nice home was not necessarily happy.

It is important, however, to separate out mothering from the conditions of isolation under which it is practised, and indeed from the associated drudgery of housework that accompanies it. Ann Oakley, in her study, found that the housewives enjoyed childcare more than the other work. Nevertheless, many of them felt isolated and missed the company of other adults during the day. Feminists have suggested, given the amount of time women spend with children and the ideologies of mothering, that it is hardly surprising that some women do physical harm to their children. It is a result of frustration and desperation, not of individual pathology. Ann Oakley (1982) quotes a letter from a mother, in the *Sunday Times*:

> When I read a study of baby battering I can't help thinking, 'There but for the grace of God go I' . . . If all mothers who have ever shaken a screaming baby, or slapped it, or thrown it roughly into its cot, stood up to be counted, we would make a startling total.

Because motherhood is presented as a natural and desirable role for women, abortion of unwanted pregnancy is often seen as unnatural and even horrific (although in many Central and Eastern European countries lack of contraception has meant that women have had to use abortion as a way of controlling their fertility, as indeed they did in Western European countries before contraception became widely available during the course of the twentieth century). Feminists have campaigned for many years in Britain and the United States, for example, to defend the right to abortion, but it is still difficult for married women to get abortions, since it is thought that they should want children (MacInytre, 1977). The assumptions about women's natural roles structure women's lives, not only in families, but in education and the world of work. Women are seen as 'natural' carers because of their maternal role. Employment opportunities are limited because employers assume that motherhood is more central to women's lives than a career. This affects all women, and indeed the limited job opportunities and the low pay that women receive may actually push women into marriage and motherhood (Walby, 1986, 1990). Ann Oakley (1974a) found that many of the housewives she interviewed reported that when they got married they wanted to have children in order to escape from boring jobs. (Interestingly, many of them found being a housewife even more boring and could not wait to get back to work!) It could also be argued that because most women have to get married, to have access to a living wage, having children is the price they have to pay. Other women may, on the other hand, regard marriage as the price they have to pay to have children.

Femininities

The idea of the family as the natural and normal place where sexual relations take place has tended to privilege heterosexual relations and to render deviant any sexual relations which take place outside this context. Although more people now accept pre-marital sexual relations as normal, this also means that courting has become sexualised and the 'norm' of sex between a man and a woman, sanctified by romantic love, has been reinforced. In Victorian England women were not supposed to enjoy sex at all and it was only men who were thought to have an uncontrollable sex drive which impelled them to the many prostitutes who patrolled the streets. From the 1920s the 'sexologists' such as Havelock Ellis started to argue that sexual satisfaction was important for both partners, and this became incorporated into ideas of what an ideal marriage should be – a satisfying sexual partnership. However, this companionate sexuality was defined according to masculine norms: women should enjoy penetrative sex with men; if they did not then they were 'frigid'. Frigidity is assumed usually to be the woman's problem rather than her partner's. Furthermore, this whole discourse reinforced the idea that heterosexuality was the natural, biologically determined human relationship.

Sexuality more generally, however, continues to be defined in male terms. Women's bodies, conveying sexual promise, are presented as desirable and are used to sell anything from cigarettes to spare parts for cars. We are constantly presented with the idea of woman as sexually passive but attracting the man and thus needing to beautify herself by, for example, purchasing exotic underwear. Men are presented as sexually active and predatory, at the mercy of their 'uncontrollable lust' which can be satisfied only by penetrating women, whether the women are willing or not. Radical feminists have argued that unwanted sexual advances by men could be construed as a form of rape and that our society condones and indeed institutionalises rape (see Chapter 9). The sexual abuse of women and girls in the home is likewise a product of the presentation of men as having uncontrollable sexual appetites and women as victims of this, since most of the abusers are men and most of the victims are female. Many feminists have thus argued that constructions of sexuality serve to define women's identities and that this derives from the ideology of the family and experiences of family life.

Conclusions

Feminists have argued that family ideology has constructed the bourgeois nuclear family as natural and inevitable. While some feminists have located the cause of women's subordination in the family, others have argued that wider social and economic processes and structures influence women's decisions to get married and have children. Women's experience of family life is mediated by their differing locations within patriarchal, racist and capitalist society. Despite social and economic changes that make it easier for some women to live independently of men, and changes in social attitudes and law that make divorce socially more acceptable and easier to obtain, many women choose to marry or at least cohabit, seeing it as an attractive option. In spite of social and economic changes in the last thirty or so years, gender divisions remain pervasive features of families – women continue to be responsible for the greater part of domestic labour and in the main are at least partially economically dependent on their male partners.

SUMMARY

1   Feminist sociologists have explored women's role in the family critically, seeing the family as the central area of oppression for women, whether it is capitalism, men as a class or both that benefit from this.

2   They have looked at various factors associated with women's position within the family: mothering, the domestic division of labour, economic dependency.

3   These things which characterise women's position within the family also characterise their position outside in the labour market, the education system and political and public life.

4   In reality there is a wide variety of household arrangements and feminists have been concerned to endorse these. However, there is also a strong familial ideology which is reinforced through state legislation, advertising and institutional structures. This ideology represents the patriarchal nuclear family as the natural and normal way to live.

FURTHER READING

Barrett, M. and McIntosh, M. (1980) *The Antisocial Family*, London: Verso.

Coron, C. (1992) *Super Woman and the Double Burden*, London: Souvenir Press.

Gittens, D. (1985) *The Family in Question: changing households and familial ideologies*, London: Macmillan.

Chapter seven

Women, health and caring

Health is an issue of central concern to women. Women form the majority of health care workers, are responsible, in the family, for the health of others and are the major consumers of formal health care (Foster, 1995). However, until the development of feminist sociology little attention was paid to gender as a key variable. Feminists have reopened the history of women healers, explored the roles that women play in the health care system, analysed the ways in which health inequalities affect women, pointed to the ways in which medical power is used to control women and the ways in which doctors have taken away control over pregnancy and childbirth from women and medicalised what women have perceived as a natural process. More recently, feminists have focused on the informal health care work done by women, pointing out that much of the caring work women do in the domestic sphere is concerned with promoting the health of household members. Women also play a key role in the lay referral system – the system in which decisions are made about whether to visit the doctor or not, or what other action should be taken. In the process of highlighting the key role that women play as unpaid health care workers, feminists have also highlighted ways in which conflicts develop between informal and paid providers, and the extent to which paid providers are unaware of the needs of the unpaid carer. The unpaid carer is often invisible, the focus of attention

being the patient, so that the needs of a woman caring, for example, for 24 hours a day, seven days a week for a disabled relative are completely ignored. A key point here is that the paid providers are themselves often women, yet because they work within the dominant medical paradigm they fail to identify with the unpaid carers and assume that women are ready, willing and able to provide the constant care demanded of them. The implementation of the National Health Service and Community Care Act 1990 has reinforced this view of women as carers, with its emphasis on the role of informal care. Furthermore the increased emphasis on care in the community means that resources are being concentrated on those who would otherwise have to be taken into residential care. The rhetoric may emphasise supporting informal carers, the reality is that often the resources are not available (Ackers and Abbott, 1996).

The multiple roles that women play affect their physical and mental well-being. However, most research into work and ill-health has focused on male-dominated occupations. Little attention has been paid to the health hazards of work roles where women predominate, and even less to those of the housewife (see Doyal, 1995). Similarly, research into health inequalities has focused on differences between social classes or between deprived and non-deprived households; little attention has been paid to differences in the health experiences of women and men, nor has account been taken of the ways in which resources are distributed within households, often meaning that some members are deprived while others are not. Indeed, poor women with young children bear a particularly heavy burden (Blackburn, 1991; Graham, 1993; Payne, 1991) and this has adverse consequences for their health. Jennie Popay and Jill Jones (1990) have reported on the poor health of mothers bringing up children alone, compared with those in two-parent families. There is evidence to suggest that when resources are limited women do without in order to ensure that their husbands and children are adequately provided for (see Chapter 6), while Brown and Harris (1978) suggest that women at home with young children are more likely than others to suffer from clinical depression (see also Bernard, 1973; Nairne and Smith, 1984).

The discourse of health assumes that women will care for the members of their family when they are unwell and takes for granted, as natural, the health care work that women do in the domestic sphere. It also assumes that mothers will prioritise the needs of their children, putting their needs and care above their own needs – that women will, if necessary, sacrifice themselves for their children. It also, paradoxically, defines as health care the formal health care provision supplied by the state and private paid medicine. Health care is seen as provided by doctors, nurses, health visitors and so on; the health care provided by women in the home is not defined as such but seen as an integral aspect of their caring role in the family (see, e.g., Graham, 1984).

Women and medicine

During the course of the nineteenth and twentieth centuries, scientific medicine has come to dominate health care in the Western world and doctors have achieved a high social status and considerable power. In Britain the National Health Service provides health care free at point of delivery to all citizens, and we generally regard this as 'a good thing'. We regard medicine as something good that has improved the health of the nation and alleviates pain and suffering. We tend to argue that what we want is more: more hospitals, more doctors, more nurses, more research and so on; then there would be improvement in health. Historically, however, improvement in health has often come from raised living standards, changes in behaviour and general public health reforms rather than from specific advances in medical knowledge. Jane Lewis (1980), for example, suggests that the decline in the maternal mortality rate in Britain in the 1930s and 1940s was as much due to improvement in the diet of pregnant women as to medical advances. Today, a decline in female deaths from lung cancer, for example, is much more likely to come from women stopping smoking, and indeed from the elimination of pressures in women's lives that led them to smoke, than from advances in treatment. This is not to deny that medical advances improve health in some instances and reduce mortality (death) and morbidity (illness), but to point out that preventive measures are often more effective than curative ones and indeed less costly in the long run.

Western scientific medicine is said to be objective and value-free, and doctors are seen as medical scientists who are objective about their patients in much the same way as any other scientists are about their subject matter. Medical science progresses via the scientific method (the experiment), resulting in the acquisition of certain, objective and unchallengeable facts and an autonomous and value-free body of knowledge. However, there are problems with this view of science, which sociologists have challenged in general and specifically with respect to medicine. Sociologists argue that all scientific activity is inevitably influenced by the society in which it is carried out and that the scientist often plays a major role in explaining and ultimately justifying various aspects of the way in which a society is organised.

Furthermore, feminists regard medical knowledge as part of the means by which gender divisions in society are maintained – modern medicine acts as a form of patriarchal control over women. Medicine not only reflects discriminatory views of women but serves to reproduce these views by actively stereotyping and controlling women who deviate from them. The way in which women were seen as weak and in need of constant rest by the medical profession in the nineteenth century, thus justifying, for instance, their exclusion from higher education, is one example. More recently the US radical feminist Mary

Daly has argued that modern medicine has actually exercised control over women as a response to the rise of feminism. She argues that there is:

> every reason to see the mutilation and destruction of women by doctors specialising in unnecessary radical mastectomies and hysterectomies, carcinogenic hormone therapy, psychosurgery, spirit-killing psychiatry and other forms of psychotherapy as directly related to the rise of radical feminism in the twentieth century.
>
> (Daly, 1978, p. 228)

Women experience the health care system as paternalistic, and their own experiences and knowledge are ignored or downgraded. This has been especially highlighted in the area of pregnancy and childbirth and it is also true with respect to contraception. In terms of women's informal caring roles their own knowledge and understanding of the patient is dismissed as irrelevant. Often, feminists argue, medical intervention does more harm than good, and in other cases it offers palliation rather than a cure. In childbirth, for example, it has been suggested that many procedures that have become routinised, such as routine episiotomy, are of dubious benefit to mother or child. More recently there has been considerable debate about the prescribing of hormone replacement therapy (HRT) for menopausal women, which has recently become seen as a panacea for menopausal problems. In medical literature the menopause has been transformed from a natural, non-problematic event to a deficiency disease – curable by HRT (Foster, 1995). While there is considerable clinical and patient evidence that HRT alleviates physical menopausal symptoms, there is less evidence that it assists with psychological problems (Ussher, 1989). Claims have also been made that HRT reduces the possibility of older women having heart disease, strokes and osteoporosis, but less emphasis has been placed on the possible long-term and horrific side-effects – increased risk of both endometrial and breast cancer and even less on the immediate ones – fluid retention, weight gain, breast tenderness, abdominal cramps, irritability, nausea and vomiting (Kahn and Holt, 1989, p. 98). Peggy Foster (1995) concludes that:

> it is perfectly logical to support the prescribing of HRT as a treatment for the more severe physical symptoms of the menopause while opposing its growing use as a panacea for all the problems women associate with aging, including losing their looks.
>
> (p. 82)

Similarly, the giving of tranquillisers to housewives with depression only renders the intolerable more tolerable; it does nothing to alleviate the underlying causes of depression.

Women and health inequalities

Gender inequalities in health care provision and the ways in which the specific health care needs of women are ignored have been highlighted by feminists. So also have the ways in which medical intervention is used as much to increase the power and prestige of medical men as to improve the health of women, and the questionable benefits of much medical intervention to its receivers. Marxist feminists have highlighted inequalities in health care and the ways in which the health care system serves the needs of a capitalist society. A 'cultural critique' has questioned the view that medicine, as a science, is value-free and objective, that doctors as professionals are knowledgeable and concerned with meeting the health care needs of clients, that medical intervention is always of benefit to clients and that the dramatic reductions in ill-health and general improvements in health achieved in industrial countries in the last hundred years are due to advances in medical knowledge. The concern that feminists have expressed, then, is not just that women's health needs are ignored, nor that medicine is sexist, but that modern medicine itself may be less valuable than is claimed. The actual technical competence of doctors and of modern medicine needs to be scrutinised. It is argued that doctors exhibit massive ignorance on such subjects as birth control, menstruation, breast feeding, the management of childbirth, the menopause, vaginal infections, which are the dangers that women face across the life course. (See, e.g., Foster, 1995; Doyal, 1995.)

The publication of the Black Report (1978) on health inequalities in Britain stimulated investigations into the existence, extent and causes of health inequalities in Britain and Western Europe more generally (see, e.g., Abbott and Giarchi, forthcoming). The main focus of attention has been on social class differences, and sociologists have developed materialist and structuralist accounts to explain these. They have argued that the major causes of health inequalities are material inequalities – that the reason why the working class have higher mortality (death) rates and higher levels of morbidity (illness) is material deprivation. Research by Peter Townsend and his colleagues (1987), Pamela Abbott and her colleagues, and others has found that there is a high correlation between local government wards that have high levels of material deprivation and wards that have poor health experience relative to the rest of the wards in a defined area.

However, the priority in such research has been on investigating men's health, and specific studies of work hazards have concentrated on male-dominated occupations. Little attention has been paid to the health hazards of women's paid and unpaid work. Furthermore, women are expected to look after the health of men and children. While it is recognised that men and women do have different health experiences, little account has been taken of the sex/gender system in examining the pattern of health and illness. Thus the research has failed to explain why it is that although men die on average at a younger age than women, women appear to suffer more ill-health than men. In 1989 the life expectancy of a British man was 73.7 years, and the life expectancy of a woman was 78.1 years. However, there are social class differences between women in this respect. Women married to men employed in semi- or unskilled jobs are 70 per cent more likely to die prematurely than those whose husbands are in a professional or managerial occupation (OPCS, 1986). Furthermore, women in social classes IV and V have higher mortality rates than men in social classes I and II, despite the overall tendency for women to live longer than men. This pattern is found in other European countries – women on average live longer than men and there are social class differences between women (Abbott and Giarchi, forthcoming). However, studies in Britain and elsewhere have indicated that women rate their own health as worse than men rate theirs (Blaxter, 1990; Whitehead, 1987). Thus despite their longer life expectancy, women report more illness and disease than men.

Women of all social classes consult their general practitioners more often than do men (Table 7.1), consume more drugs and medicines than men, occupy acute hospital beds slightly more often and are admitted to psychiatric units more often than men (Kane, 1991). Female consultation rates with GPs for depression are three times those of men (Royal College of General Practitioners, 1990). One in twenty women aged between 25 and 74 seeks help from her GP for emotional problems, compared with one in fifty men in Britain. Across a number of developed countries women are twice as likely as men to be prescribed tranquillisers (Ashton, 1991). Again there are social class differences. Women married to men in the lowest social classes suffer three times more longstanding illness than do those in the highest social classes. However, it is not the case that we can determine the relative health experience of different groups from the amount that they consult doctors or make use of the health services. Women of the lowest social classes, for example, make more use of the health services than the more affluent, but not to the extent that their much greater health problems would suggest that they should (LeGrand, 1982). The preventive services are used least by the women who suffer most from the problems that these services are intended to forestall (Doyal, 1987). A good example here is screening for cervical cancer. Although women married to men in social class V are four times more likely to die of cancer of the cervix than women married to men in social class I, they make much less use of the screening facilities than middle-class women; the difference in death rate between working-class and middle-class women is not fully explained by differential use of the preventive services. There is also a marked social class gradient in the use of services connected with

TABLE 7.1 Social class, gender and GP (NHS) consultations in Great Britain, 1980

Socio-economic group	Average consultations per person	
	Males	Females
Professional	2.9	4.1
Employers/managers	3.5	4.4
Intermediate/junior non-manual	3.7	4.6
Skilled manual	3.7	4.9
Semi-skilled manual/personal service	4.0	5.4
Unskilled manual	4.3	5.5

Source: adapted from Hilary Graham, 1984.

fertility control. Women married to men in middle-class occupations are much more likely than women married to manual workers to attend family planning clinics or discuss fertility control with general practitioners. Inequalities are also evident with regard to abortion. While working-class and Black women argue that they are pressured into having abortion, other women point out how difficult it is to get one – especially on the NHS. Fifty per cent of abortions are in fact performed outside the NHS (Doyal, 1987).

It is necessary to consider, if women's greater use of health services suggests that women are sicker than men, why working-class women make less use of preventive services than middle-class ones, and why working-class women make less use of the health services than their health problems would suggest they need. Some feminists have suggested that women's life experiences mean that they suffer more ill-health than men. Others have argued that this is an artefact – that women's greater use of health services is due to factors other than that they are suffering more ill-health than men. Explanations that stress the different life experiences of women are:

1   the biological – that women suffer more problems with the reproductive tract than do men (Kane, 1991); and
2   that the isolation of women in unpaid domestic labour seems to be linked with a higher incidence of depression among women (Brown and Harris, 1978; Ussher, 1989).

Peggy Foster (1995) has pointed out that the biological and feminist models of women's need for health care both assume that it is women who rely on health care providers. She argues that:

> any dependency relationship between women and health care providers is at least partly the other way round . . . all those employed in the

manufacturing and delivery of health care need women to consume their works as much as, if not more than, women need the type of products and services provided.

(p. 3)

Those that stress the artefactual nature of the difference suggest:

1   that women often visit the doctor on behalf of others, especially children (Graham, 1984);
2   that female socialisation in Western cultures makes it more acceptable for women to adopt the 'sick role';
3   that women are subject to the 'medicalisation' of normal childbirth (Leeson and Gray, 1978; Oakley, 1980);
4   that women live longer than men (the ratio of women to men aged 75+ is 2:1), and older people tend to have more health problems than younger ones (Leeson and Gray, 1978).

Indeed, Leeson and Gray (1978) report that the hospitalisation rate is higher for men than for women, if maternity and disorders of the breast and reproductive tract are excluded. For example, in Britain in 1972, 816 per 100,000 men were hospitalised compared with 710 per 100,000 women, counted on this basis.

Other research suggests that consultation rates are a poor guide to the amount of illness suffered in the community, and that women are more likely than men to 'suffer in silence'. Scambler and Scambler (1984) found that women do not necessarily visit the doctor when they are unwell (see Table 7.2). Helen Roberts (1985) found that women differed in the extent to which they visited the doctor and divided them into the frequent attenders and the infrequent attenders. She did not find that the latter group suffered less ill-health than the former, but rather that they differed in their views as to when the doctor should be consulted. The infrequent attenders argued that the doctor should only be visited when this was essential, the frequent attenders that the doctor should be visited when one was unwell, before things became too bad. Both groups were concerned with not wasting the doctor's time, but while the former group argued that this meant only going when it was essential, the latter argued that the doctor should be visited at the first signs of illness to prevent a lot of time having to be spent treating a serious illness.

Scambler and Scambler found that women differentiated between illness that required a visit to the doctor and illness where alternative methods were indicated. Thus women often experience suffering but do not regard themselves as ill. A similar situation was noted some sixty years ago in the Workers' Health Enquiry into the lives of working-class women (Spring-Rice, 1939):

TABLE 7.2 Ratio of symptoms noted to consultations with medical practitioners (based on health diaries kept by 79 women aged 16–44)

Symptom	Ratio of consultations to occurrences
Tiredness, lack of energy	No consultations
Nerves, depression or irritability	1:74
Headache	1:60
Backache	1:38
Sleeplessness	1:31
Aches or pains in muscles or joints	1:18
Cold or influenza	1:12
Stomach pains	1:11
Women's complaints (e.g. period pains)	1:10
Sore throat	1:9

Source: adapted from Scambler and Scambler 1984.

many women replied 'yes' to the question, 'Do you usually feel fit and well?' In answer to the next question, 'What ailments do you suffer from?', the same women listed a whole series of problems including anaemia, headaches, constipation, rheumatism, prolapse of the womb, bad teeth and varicose veins.

(p. 69)

As is the case today, certain 'ailments' had to be suffered, but the women were 'well enough to carry on'. Women's domestic and caring roles mean that they cannot be ill because they have to care for their families. Williams (1987) found in Aberdeen that fatigue or weakness did not constitute 'illness', and 'fit' meant being able to work. Jocelyn Cornwell (1984), in her study in Bethnal Green, also found that women regarded themselves as 'not ill' if they could carry on. Pill and Stott (1986) suggest, from their study of 204 women in Cardiff, that working-class women have a low expectation of health and that the women were not accustomed to thinking particularly about their health. Women are also the ones who decide when their husbands and children are ill and may adopt the sick role (Locker, 1981).

It is also important to consider why working-class women are less likely to make use of the health services than middle-class women. There has been a tendency to blame the working-class woman, to suggest that she is less able to perceive the benefit of the services offered, especially preventive ones. However, feminists have suggested that it is necessary to turn the question around and ask what is wrong with the way the services are provided. They argue that often the provision does not meet the needs of the woman, that there are no arrangements to care for the young children they often have to bring with them, that working-class women find it difficult to communicate with middle-class professionals, and that the women are aware that the main causes of their ill-health (children, housing, lack of money and so on) lie outside the province of the medical profession and also outside their own control (Pill and Stott, 1986; Blaxter, 1985; Cornwell, 1984). While working-class and Black women experience the greatest control from health professionals – at the extreme, being pressured to have unwanted abortions or prescribed depo-provera (a long-term birth control measure with serious side effects, banned in the United States) without informed consent – feminists argue that all women are controlled by medical ideology. A key example here would be the way in which male doctors have come to control pregnancy and childbirth, reducing women to reproductive machines (see, e.g., Oakley, 1980, 1984a).

Radical feminists emphasise the ways in which male medical ideology is used to control women, and feminists in the United States in particular have strongly attacked the exploitative nature of the American health care system. Marxist feminists, meanwhile, have been concerned to point to health in-equalities between women from different social classes and ethnic groups and the ways in which the state controls the health care system to meet the needs of capitalist society. Lesley Doyal (1987) suggested that the NHS was a powerful mechanism of social control both because it appeared to be a major move to meet the needs of the working class and because it served the interests of the capitalist class by ensuring a healthy work force (although she was also critical of the male doctors' patriarchal, sexist attitudes towards their female patients). However, despite forty years of the NHS the inequalities in health between women from different social classes persist, and while the health of all women has improved, the relative inequalities have remained the same – or even increased to some extent (Whitehead, 1987). Indeed, it could be argued that the NHS has failed to meet the specific needs of women because the ways in which services are provided do not enable women to make full use of them. Lack of facilities for caring for young children, the timing of appointments, the centralisation of provision and the attitudes of the profession have all been cited as reasons why services have not been used (Graham, 1984).

Iatrogenic medicine

Some medical intervention, it is suggested, is *iatrogenic* – that is, it causes more harm than good; the treatment actually does more harm than the original illness. We have already mentioned the side-effects of hormone replacement therapy, prescribed for menopausal women. Another good example is the recent use of a particular drug to treat arthritis. Some patients prescribed the drug, which relieves the pain of arthritis, have ended up with poor health as a result of the so-called 'side effects' of the drug – such as an inability to tolerate daylight. However, with women's health there is greater concern because some drugs or treatments that are prescribed on a routine basis, not to treat illness but to prevent unwanted pregnancies, have been found to be iatrogenic. The 'coil', for example, has been found to cause extensive menstrual bleeding and low back pain in some women. However, the main cause for concern has been the contraceptive pill, the most reliable method of contraception available to most women. The pill was introduced into the USA in 1960 and has subsequently been used by millions of women throughout the world. It was seen as an effective, modern and scientifically respectable method for controlling fertility and was freely prescribed by doctors to women of child-bearing age. However, by the mid-1960s it began to be suspected that there was a link between the pill and cancer of the cervix and circulatory (heart) diseases. Attempts to assess the validity of this suspicion uncovered serious deficiencies in the testing of contraceptive drugs. It was found that they had not been tested on women for the whole period of the reproductive cycle, so that the possible effects of taking the pill for twenty or thirty years was unknown. A study by the Royal College of General Practitioners in 1974 found that the risk of dying from circulatory disease was five times greater for women taking the oral contraceptive pill than for others. Women who were over 35 years old who had been taking the pill for five or more years and who smoked were found to be at the greatest risk. The pill has also been found to have a number of side effects – depression, a loss of libido (sex drive), headaches, nausea and excessive weight gain – but there has been little research into these. Furthermore, the subjective experiences and feelings of women have often been dismissed as irrelevant or 'not real' by medical men. Indeed, research indicates that GPs strongly prefer the pill, especially for young women, and the medical profession seem to have few doubts about its safety (Reid, 1985) and feel that women are unnecessarily worried about it (Tindall, 1987). Similarly, there is medical confidence in depo-provera and the IUD (see Wilson, 1985; Guillebaud and Low, 1987; and an editorial in *The Lancet* for 28 March 1992). However, in the United States most drug companies are ceasing to research, develop and manufacture contraceptive drugs because of the escalating costs of testing the product and the high price of the insurance needed to protect them against lawsuits from those damaged by their products (Lincoln and Kaeser, 1988).

It has by now, and as a result of availability of such devices as the pill and the coil, become generally accepted that it should be women who take the responsibility for birth control precautions, and it is women who suffer the serious consequences if contraception fails. (This may be changing to some small extent, however, with the AIDS risk and the emphasis on using condoms and barrier cream.)

It seems unlikely that what are often referred to as the 'side effects' of female contraception would be so readily ignored if men were the users. It would be interesting to know how many men would be prepared to use the intrapenile device described by Dr Sophie Merkin:

The newest development in male contraception was unveiled recently at the American Women's Centre. Dr Sophie Merkin of the Merkin Clinic announced the preliminary findings of a study conducted on 763 unsuspecting male undergraduates at a large mid-Western university. In her report, Dr Merkin stated that the new contraceptive – the IPD – was a breakthrough in male contraception. It will be marketed under the trade name Umbrelly.

The IPD (intrapenile device) resembles a tightly rolled umbrella which is inserted through the head of the penis and pushed into the scrotum with a plunger-like device. Occasionally there is a perforation of the scrotum, but this is disregarded as the male has few nerve-endings in this area of his body. The underside of the umbrella contains a spermicidal jelly, hence the name Umbrelly.

Experiments on 1000 white whales from the continental shelf (whose sexual apparatus is said to be closest to man's) proved the IPD to be 100% effective in preventing the production of sperm and eminently satisfactory to the female whale since it does not interfere with her rutting pleasure.

Dr Merkin declared the Umbrelly to be statistically safe for the human male. She reported that of the 763 undergraduates tested with the device only two died of scrotal infection, only twenty developed swelling of the testicles and only thirteen were too depressed to have an erection. She stated that common complaints ranged from cramping and bleeding to acute abdominal pains. She emphasised that these symptoms were merely indications that the man's body had not yet adjusted to the device. Hopefully the symptoms would disappear within a year. One complication caused by the IPD and briefly mentioned by Dr Merkin was the incidence of massive scrotal infection necessitating the surgical removal of the testicles. 'But this is a rare case,' said Dr Merkin, 'too rare to be statistically important.' She and other distinguished members of the Women's College of Surgeons agreed that the benefits far outweighed the risk to any individual man.

(From *Outcome* magazine, the East Bay Men's Centre newsletter, and *The Periodical Lunch* published by Andrew Rock, Ann Arbor, Michigan, USA)

This is of course a spoof – no such device has actually been invented. The account was published to illustrate the fact that most men would not be expected to suffer what many women experience with an IUD, such as heavy bleeding, backache and vaginal infections. Indeed, any development at all in this direction is highly unlikely, given that little attempt has been made to develop and market new methods of contraception for men; less than five per cent of research budgets are devoted to this (Bruce, 1987).

While it may be true that women choose what method of contraception to use, their choice is limited by what is available. Modern methods do enable a woman to have control over her own fertility, rather than relying on her partner or risking having an abortion after conception, but her choice is limited by decisions that have already been made by drug company executives, doctors, researchers and others about which methods will be developed and made available. Further, given that most methods have their own problems, the choice is often a negative one. Women choose the method that affects them least – so one may choose the pill because the IUD caused excessive bleeding, while another may make the reverse decision because the pill resulted in excessive weight gain. Medical control of many of the newer methods of birth control means that women are dependent on their doctors for advice, and doctors are generally inadequately trained in this area. Most women will have to make a judgement based on what their doctors tell them, and doctors often become resentful if female patients question their advice or reveal that they are knowledgeable in the area. Doctors frequently expect patients to accept that they know best. Yet they rarely talk to their female patients about birth control in detail and are inclined to dismiss subjective experience and base their advice on what they regard as sound scientific judgement. (A further restriction of women's ability to choose which method of contraception to use is the preference of their partners. Pollack (1985), for example, found that many men preferred their partners to use the pill rather than spoil their fun and use a sheath.)

Nevertheless, doctors' non-medical values do influence the decisions they make about sterilisation and abortion, for example (and about the issue of less drastic means of contraception – see Hawkes, 1985). While white middle-class women have been demanding the right to choose to be sterilised or to have an abortion, working-class and Black women have pointed out that they have often been pressurised into having an abortion or being sterilised against their inclinations (Bryan *et al.*, 1985). On the other hand, Rose Shapiro (1987) has suggested that:

> The need of family planning organisations and doctors to prevent pregnancy is so powerful that it manifests itself almost as an irrational fear. The impression given is that accidental pregnancy is the worst thing that could ever happen to women and that abortion is an absolute disaster.
>
> (p. 41)

However, in other parts of the world abortion has been the main or only form of contraception available to women. Lesley Doyal (1995) indicates that, world-wide, abortion ranks fourth after female sterilisation, IUDs and contraceptive pills as a method of contraception. In Russia, abortion has been seen as the main form of contraception; it 1987 it is estimated that the number of abortions rose above eleven million.

While many women have undoubtedly benefited from the development of modern forms of contraception and these have enabled women to avoid unwanted pregnancies, they have nevertheless extended medical and social control over women. The world-wide market for contraceptive pills and devices is worth billions of dollars, and it is in the interests of multi-national companies to encourage the medical profession to prescribe and women to use high-tech contraception. Women's ability to control their own fertility has been restricted and heavily controlled by the medical profession and the multi-national pharmaceutical companies.

Gender, power and medicine

Medical images of women

The way in which medical men 'construct' women is a powerful element in their control of their female patients. While in the nineteenth century medical men argued that women were physically frail, in the twentieth century they have suggested that they are mentally weak and easily dissatisfied with their domestic roles. Medical images of women are of course reinforced by the ways in which medical education is carried out and the contents of what is taught. Female medical students (and feminist doctors – see Eisner, 1986) have argued that sexism is rampant in medical training and that women are often treated as sexual objects of ridicule by (male) lecturers. Men are seen as the norm against which women are seen as abnormal.

Analysis of medical textbooks shows that they include 'facts' about women that are little more than prejudices. They stress the superiority of doctors' objective knowledge and clinical experience over women's own subjective perceptions – even when women's own experience is under examination. Little attention is paid in the medical curriculum to problems specifically suffered by women except those relating to pregnancy and childbirth; thus common female problems such as cystitis (bladder infection) or vaginal infections are not taken seriously and there has been little basic research into incontinence and osteoporosis. Even the menstrual cycle has not been extensively researched (Koblinsky *et al.*, 1993). Gynaecologists and obstetricians are considered to be experts on women, yet it is a male specialism. They exercise great power *vis à vis* women and are in a position to define 'normal femininity' and 'normal sexuality'. Not only are they often given little training on female sexuality, but an analysis by Scully and Bart (1978) of the major gynaecology textbooks suggests that what they are taught is out of date. They found that myths about female sexuality continued to be stated as facts even after major surveys had revealed them as myths. Lesley Doyal (1995) points out, furthermore, that when health problems do affect both men and women, possible gender differences are never explored. For example, coronary heart disease, more common among women than men, has been researched in the main on male-only samples.

Doctors tend to see women's medical problems as emotional and mental rather than physical. Susan Penfold and Gillian Walker (1984) review a number of cases where women received a psychiatric diagnosis but were subsequently found to have a physiological problem. Furthermore, women's depression is assumed to arise because of their inherent weakness – because they cannot cope with the demands of a family, the isolation of domestic labour, and so on. However, the research of Brown and Harris has suggested that depression in women relates primarily to their life circumstances, while the American feminist Jessie Bernard (1973) has argued that being a housewife makes women sick because they become depressed and suggested that paid employment protects women from depression. (However, Arber *et al.* (1985) have suggested that married women under the age of 40 with children may suffer more physical illness if they have full-time paid employment.) Maggie Eisner (1986) has referred to the attitude of male general practitioners and suggested that it is because women have to cope with their families' problems that they turn to the GP for emotional support:

> A speaker said that women ask their GPs for more emotional support than men do, implying that women, being weaker than men, have greater need for such support. I pointed out that the women spend a lot of their time and energy giving emotional support to many people in their lives and often have no one but the GP to turn to for their own emotional support.
>
> (p. 121)

Scully and Bart (1978) suggest that doctors 'blame' women's emotional and hysterical behaviour on the female reproductive tract, and this was certainly the case in the nineteenth century. Nineteenth-century doctors argued that women were controlled by their biology – women, it was argued, were entirely under the control of their reproductive organs, and so doctors could provide a 'scientific' explanation of this truth. A malfunctioning uterus or ovary could result in the spread of disease throughout the body. Some

Victorian doctors thought that women did not have sexual feelings, while men had strong sexual urges. Instead of sexual urges, women were said to be endowed with a strong maternal instinct, and their most important duty in life was motherhood.

The upper-class woman in particular was portrayed as frail and sickly – her delicate nervous system was seen as needing protection as much as her sickly body. Middle-class women were encouraged to have long periods of rest – especially at times of menstruation. It was thought especially dangerous for women to engage in intellectual activity. Higher education was seen as a special danger, and women were excluded from the universities on the grounds that they were a risk both to their health and to their femininity. It was claimed that a woman who developed 'masculine' intellectual qualities would necessarily underdevelop her 'female' qualities, endangering both her fertility and her capacity for motherhood. While middle- and upper-class women were encouraged to be idle, working-class women were expected to work, but the work assigned to them was hard manual labour. Thus the inherent inferiority of women was used to justify the two very different lifestyles enjoyed by middle- and working-class women in Victorian England.

The cult of frailty among upper-class and upper-middle-class Victorian women was strengthened by the view that a man should be able to support a leisured life; to be able to afford domestic servants was a status symbol. Some Victorian wives rebelled, but the majority did not because they were totally dependent on their husbands/fathers. The boredom and confinement of upper-class women resulted in a cult of hypochondria, and especially hysteria. Doctors argued that it arose from a morbid condition of the uterus, which began at puberty and ended with the menopause. Medical intervention was said to be necessary to establish personal and social control. 'Cures' included hysterectomies, clitorectomies, ovarectomies and other forms of genital mutilation. While most women were not 'treated' surgically, they did consult medical men and came to define themselves as inherently sick – a view that was reinforced as hysteria was represented as a contagious disease and isolation from other women was considered essential to successful treatment.

The portrayal of women, and especially upper-class and middle-class ones, as inherently sick created more work for medical men, which enhanced the status and income of those who were doctors to wealthy women. It also underpinned doctors' campaigns against midwifery, as they claimed that all women's complaints, including pregnancy, were diseases and demanded the care of a doctor. It was thus in the financial interest of doctors, as well as sustaining their claim to exclusive right to treat the sick, to maintain the view that women were not only weaker than men but also inherently sick. It also justified the exclusion of women from the public spheres of education, business and the economy and reinforced the view that woman's role was in the domestic sphere and that women's fulfilment came from motherhood. This view is still evident in the ways in which women are treated during pregnancy and childbirth by the medical profession to this day.

Women, medicine and reproduction

As Lesley Doyal (1995) has pointed out,

> If women are to maximise their health and their autonomy they must be able to determine the nature of their reproductive lives . . . they must be able to control their own fertility without risking unpleasant or danger-ous side effects and they must be able to pass safely through pregnancy and childbirth.
>
> (p. 93)

Medicine is involved in three areas of reproduction:

1   contraception – the prevention of unwanted pregnancy;
2   pregnancy and childbirth;
3   reproductive technologies designed to enable women who could not otherwise do so to become pregnant.

While feminists have been critical of medical intervention in these areas, it is nevertheless important to recognise that there have been positive aspects to this intervention. In the nineteenth and early twentieth centuries women did face extreme hazard in childbirth, and many, including upper-class women, had severe complications and long-term ill-health as a result of pregnancy and childbirth, including prolapse of the uterus and irreparable pelvic tears. Medical advances have made pregnancy and childbirth a much less hazardous process for both the mother and the child (Himmelweit, 1988; Llewelyn Davies, 1915). Medicine cannot take all the credit – improved diet, hygienic conditions and a general rise in the standard of living have all played an important role in reducing maternal and infant mortality and morbidity. Nonetheless, credit is due.

However, medical dominance in these areas of women's lives means that women are controlled to a large extent by medical men, and they rely on doctors for advice and information. For example, pregnant women are treated 'as if' something is going to go wrong – women are required to make regular ante-natal visits and are virtually forced to have their babies in hospital, where doctors control the management of labour and childbirth. As Ann Oakley (1987) argues, motherhood has become a medicalised domain.

The key point is not that medical intervention has played no role in making pregnancy and childbirth safer, but that doctors have taken over total control of the management of pregnant women, so that women are unable to make informed decisions about their lives. This came out clearly in the case of Wendy Savage, the consultant obstetrician who was suspended on a charge of incompetence (of which she was eventually cleared) after a campaign by her male colleagues, who objected to the ways in which she practised (see Savage, 1986). During the campaign to clear her and the subsequent Inquiry it became evident that the key issues surrounded how pregnancy and child-birth were to be managed. Savage argued that women should be allowed to make informed choices during pregnancy and childbirth, that ante-natal care should be provided in clinics near women's homes and that they should be allowed to give birth at home if they wanted to do so. The role of the doctor was to assist women, not to control them and make decisions for them.

Feminists have argued not only that women do not feel in control during pregnancy and childbirth, but also that there is little evidence to support the view that technological intervention in childbirth is beneficial for mother and/or child. Ann Oakley (1982), reporting on research carried out in 1975, found that 69 per cent of first-time mothers did not feel in control of themselves and what was going on in labour. She also quotes research carried out in Wales, finding that the increased use of induction (artificial starting of labour) did not reduce perinatal mortality (death of the baby in the first two months of life), but did increase the number of low birth-weight babies. Induction carries risks to both maternal and foetal health – for example, the tearing of the perineum in the mother and an increased likelihood of a forceps-assisted birth with its associated risks. There has also been an increase in the use of caesarian section without clear evidence that this has improved the health of babies or mothers. Other routine procedures such as foetal heart monitoring and routine episiotomy (cutting the perineum to prevent tearing) are also of doubtful benefit.

Feminists have suggested that women and doctors have very different views about pregnancy and childbirth. During pregnancy, they suggest, the mother is seen by doctors as a life-support system for the foetus, and the emphasis is on the needs and health of the baby rather than those of the mother. Doctors regard themselves as the experts on childbirth and preg-nancy. Medical practice is based on the assumption that doctors have access to a scientific body of knowledge about childbirth, but doctors deal mainly with illness and they tend to treat pregnancy as if it were a sickness. This means that they are more interested in the pathological than the normal, in using technology, and in women taking medical advice.

Graham and Oakley (1981) argue that while doctors see pregnancy as a medical problem, women see it as a natural phenomenon. While for the doctor pregnancy and childbirth are medical events starting with diagnosis and ending with discharge from medical supervision, for women they are parts of a process which has to be integrated with other social roles. They are accompanied by a change in status, to mother, with the obligations that this imposes permanently and comprehensively on a woman's life. While for medical men the success of pregnancy and childbirth is measured by low perinatal and maternal mortality rates and low incidence of certain kinds of morbidity, and a 'successful' outcome is a healthy mother and baby in the immediate post-birth period, for the mother success is measured by a healthy baby, a satisfactory personal experience of labour and delivery, the establishment of a satisfactory relationship with the baby and integrating the demands of motherhood into her lifestyle. While the doctor sees himself as the expert, possessing superior knowledge and therefore in control, the mother sees herself as knowledgeable about pregnancy, as perceptive about the sensations of her body and its needs. However, mothers felt they were not in control. Pregnant women spoke of problems in communicating with their doctors, of not being able to ask questions, and of being treated as ignorant. They also disliked being seen by different doctors at each visit and complained that they felt like battery hens – as just one unimportant item in a factory production system.

While feminists have argued that doctors have medicalised childbirth and in the process taken away control from women, they have also pointed to medical control in other areas of reproduction. Doctors control the most effective means of birth control – the pill, the coil, the cap, and sterilisation. Women have to seek medical advice to be able to use these methods of controlling their fertility. The 1968 Abortion Reform law made abortion on medical grounds legal and more freely available, but the decision as to whether a woman can have an abortion is made by doctors. Doctors also control the new reproductive technologies concerned with helping women to conceive and have children. Doctors often refuse sterilisation or abortion to young married women while single women and women from ethnic minority groups are positively encouraged to have abortions. Doctors also decide which women should have access to reproductive technology, and the decision is often based on moral rather than medical judgement. Also, access to reproductive technology and abortion is mediated by ability to pay; NHS provision is greatly outstripped by demand, so many women are forced to turn to private practitioners. This option, however, is available only to those with money. Scientific and medical advances in the area of reproduction have on the one hand given women the possibility of deciding if, when and under what conditions they will have children. On the other hand, however, the dominance of so much of reproductive technology by the medical profession and the state has permitted doctors to have even greater control over women's lives.

The development of *in vitro* fertilisation in the late 1970s, which was seen as a 'miracle cure', has led feminists more recently to turn their attention to what are commonly described as the 'new' reproductive technologies. These include not only technologies that make it possible to extend parenthood to people who have been unable to realise their wish to have a child, but also techniques that can be used to diagnose genetic or chromosomal abnormalities *in utero* and which at the same time enable the sex of the child to be determined.

While some feminists have been concerned about the availablity of the services on the NHS and the ways in which access to them is controlled by the medical profession, others have raised questions about the impact that they will have on women's lives. Access to infertility treatment is restricted and a majority of infertile women who undergo techniques such as IVF and GIFT still do not have a child – 90 per cent of treated women do not have a baby (Page, 1989). Furthermore, women having IVF in the 1980s were 27 times more likely to have a multiple birth than other pregnant women (Oakley, 1993). Some have suggested that the new technologies will be used by men to control and exploit women even further. Amniocentesis, it is argued, will be and has been used to determine the sex of the unborn foetus and force women to have an abortion if the foetus is not of the desired sex – generally male – while it is virtually impossible for a single woman to get IVF treatment, reinforcing the patriarchal ideology of the heterosexual nuclear family (Leila and Elliott, 1987).

Other feminists (e.g. Michele Stanworth, 1987a) have suggested a more cautious approach. While recognising the strong desire of some women to have children and the ways in which they will be assisted by the new technologies, Stanworth suggests that insufficient attention has been paid to questions of safety, women's health and their ability to make informed decisions. Also, it is necessary to recognise that there is a range of reproductive technologies – not just the various 'new' techniques that have been the focus of public attention. While many of these techniques are flawed and their safety questionable, nevertheless they provide an indisputable resource on which women draw according to their priorities. What is necessary is for women to be better informed about these technologies so that they can make better informed decisions. While science may be seen as helping women, the control over it is not in their hands, but those of doctors. These issues can be illustrated by reference to ultra-sound – a method of enabling doctors and patients to see an image of the foetus on the screen. Doctors use it to detect abnormalities and to date conception exactly (women's knowledge of when they became pregnant is regarded as unreliable, and some women cannot give an exact date for the first day of their last period, which is used to date conception). Women gain great benefit from seeing their own baby in this way (Petchesky, 1987), but, as Ann Oakley (1987) has pointed out, it is not entirely certain that the procedure is completely safe – it may cause some risk to the health of the mother and/or the foetus.

Women, health and domestic violence

The ambivalent attitude that feminists adopt to the medical profession and medical interventions has been highlighted in the recent attention given to domestic violence (assault on a wife by her male partner) as a health problem. Feminist research on domestic violence has highlighted it as a serious problem and indicated that it is probably the single most common cause of injury to women (Stark and Flitcraft, 1988), although health professionals, at least in Britain, appear not to recognise it as such (Borkowski *et al.*, 1983). Doctors tend to treat the physical injuries and not their cause – the abusive relationship (*Gender and Society*, 1989; Pahl, 1995). Doctors do not see domestic violence as an area for medical intervention, as Mildred Dealey Payclaw has suggested:

> Physicians will often say, 'I'm not a law enforcement officer, and I'm not a social worker. I'm here to treat the body, and she needs to see a psychiatrist.' (quoted in *Journal of the American Medical Association*, 1990)

The issue, as Jan Pahl indicates, is 'What can health service professionals do to help women?' (1995, p. 127). She suggests that health professionals must respect women's accounts, know the relevant information to enable them to help women, keep careful records of injuries and give the time to help women (Pahl, 1995). In North America, Needs Assessment Profiles have been developed for use with women whom doctors or other health care workers suspect of having been abused (Jezierski, 1992; Lazzaro and McFarlane, 1991; Flitcraft *et al.*, 1992).

> If abuse is to be prevented, the cycle of violence interrupted and the health and well being of women provided, nurses in all settings must take the initiative in assessing all women for abuse during each visit [for ante-natal care] and offering education, counselling and referral.
> (Lazzaro and McFarlane, 1991, p. 28)

However, while health professionals may be able to provide immediate treatment, the long-term help they can provide is limited, given that the long-term solution to wife abuse is giving more power to women, individually and collectively:

Violence against women is the product of the subordination of women. Short-term measures may have short-term effects . . . but it is certain that no long-term measures will be successful unless there is a fundamental change in the social and economic structures that maintain the subordination of women within marriage and in wider societies.

(United Nations, 1989, p. 108)

The danger is that health professionals will medicalise domestic violence, lay the blame for the violence on the woman victim and ignore the perpetrator of violence and the context in which the violence took place. Thus on the one hand feminists recognise that health professionals are in a powerful position to provide help and support for women who are abused by their partners, while on the other hand they are wary of the extent to which professionals will be able to move outside patriarchal assumptions about the family and the causes of domestic violence.

Women as providers of health care

Women form the majority of health care workers, both formal and informal. Over 75 per cent of all employed health care workers in the UK are women (Orr, 1992). Women are concentrated in the lower-paid, lower-status jobs. While 90 per cent of nurses are female, only 25 per cent of doctors are. Also, the majority of cleaners and kitchen hands are women. Black women tend to be in the lowest-paid, lowest-status jobs (Doyal *et al.*, 1981). Thus there is horizontal and vertical occupational segregation in the health service (see Chapter 8). Within particular types of work there is further vertical segregation; while women constitute 25 per cent of doctors, they form only 9 per cent of consultants and 15 per cent of gynaecologists.

Women are also the major providers of unpaid health care in the home (Graham, 1984). Even excluding those caring for dependent children, about 75 per cent of adults caring for an elderly or disabled relative in the home are women (Arber and Ginn, 1991). Much health education is directed at women, who are assumed to care for other relatives in the household. Health visiting was developed in the early part of this century specifically as a way of educating mothers in how to look after their babies and young children. Girls' education at school has been seen as part of the process of training them for motherhood. Mothers have been blamed for the poor health of their husbands and children, and maternal education has been seen as a way of improving the nation's health. Often the poor material and economic circumstances under which women are caring for their families have been ignored and the blame for the poor health of children has been placed on the ignorance of mothers rather than on poverty.

Women as healers, men as professionals

Feminists have rediscovered the historical role of women as healers, showing that until the eighteenth century healing was mainly women's work, but that since then men have come to play a dominant role in medicine. However, long before this men had tried to prevent women practising medicine, and from the eighteenth century they challenged their right to practise midwifery autonomously.

While there is evidence that women practised medicine in medieval Europe (Verslusyen, 1980), a law was passed in England in 1421 preventing this practice. Pressure for this law to be passed came from male doctors (Verslusyen, 1980), and in this they were supported by the Christian belief that women were inferior and had an evil nature (Daly, 1978). However, health care given by women, as today, extended far beyond professional work. Women cared for the sick members of their families and community and played a central role in childbirth, which until the seventeenth century was seen as the exclusive concern of women. Women learned about helping the sick and assisting women in childbirth from other women in the community who had acquired the necessary skills and expertise. Thus while women were barred from formal institutions of learning, they learned from each other (Ehrenreich and English, 1979). Indeed, the poor had little access to formal medical care until the nineteenth century, with the growth of the voluntary hospitals, and the available evidence suggests that women continued to rely on informal knowledge in areas such as birth control and abortion until well into the twentieth century.

A key question that has concerned feminists is how men came to usurp women's traditional role as healers. It seems unlikely that this happened because men's skills and knowledge were superior, as there is little evidence that qualified doctors had effective treatments to apply before this century, although the claims made by male medical men that they had superior skills may have been believed by some patients. Also, the ability to afford the high fees charged by physicians may have been a way of achieving and maintaining a high status in middle-class society.

Ehrenreich and English (1979) have suggested a link between the campaigns against witches that occurred in Europe between the fourteenth and seventeenth centuries and the suppression of female healing. They argue that women healers were singled out to be executed as witches and that thousands of women peasant healers were seen as part of a subversive social movement threatening the (male) authority of Church, Crown, the aristocracy and the few university-trained physicians. However, there is no clear evidence that all or even most women healers were regarded as witches during this period, and indeed there is considerable evidence that unqualified women healers continued to practice in England after the witch-hunts had ceased.

Other feminists have argued that the changes that accompanied the Industrial Revolution were a major factor in men achieving control and dominance in medical practice. Alice Clark (1919) argued that the displacement of women healers by qualified medical guilds (the precursors of the Royal Colleges) was part of the process whereby skilled workers in general moved out of the family into the market-place and excluded the unskilled and unqualified from practice. Margaret Verslusyen (1981) also points to the development of hospitals. Before the eighteenth century medical men treated only the wealthy, in their own homes. By the end of the eighteenth century hospitals had begun to be built in the growing towns. These hospitals were built with charitable money donated by the wealthy for the exclusive use of working-class patients. In them, medical men began to treat 'charity' patients who were their 'inferiors'. Doctors were therefore able to develop and test new ideas on these patients. At the same time the growth of the middle class meant that there was an increase in the number of fee-paying patients for doctors to treat at home. The growth in clientele and the claims to new scientific knowledge provided a base from which qualified doctors pressed for the banning of their unqualified female rivals.

Anne Witz (1985) has argued that the ways in which medical men struggled to establish and sustain a sexually segregated division of labour provides an example of social closure and demarcation (and that they were aided in applying this closure by the state) – closure in that women were excluded from practising medicine, and demarcation in that doctors defined what was medical work and therefore the preserve of medical men and what was ancillary and could be carried out by female nurses and midwives. In 1858 the Medical Act established the exclusive male prerogative. The Act defined a person who could practise medicine as one who was a qualified medical practitioner by virtue of possessing a British university degree or a licentiate membership or fellowship of one of the medical corporations. The Act did not exclude women in itself, but women were not allowed in practice to go to universities or become members of medical corporations.

The exclusion of women from medical practice was challenged by women who conducted a protracted struggle to gain admittance to the medical profession. The first qualified female medical practitioner to practise in Britain was Elizabeth Blackwell, who qualified at a US medical school in 1849. Elizabeth Garrett (Anderson) qualified in 1865 with the Society of Apothecaries, the only medical corporation not explicitly excluding women.

However, the Society immediately changed its rules so that the same could not happen again.

Women campaigned to be allowed to qualify as doctors on the basis of equal rights claims – a common demand of feminists in the nineteenth century and based on the dominant liberal political philosophy (see Chapter 10). Women also argued that women and children should have the right to be treated by a woman doctor. They had to gain the support of male members of Parliament to introduce legislation. In 1875 an 'Enabling Bill' was passed, permitting universities and medical corporations to admit women, but this did not force them to do so. (In 1899 an Act of Parliament removed all the remaining legal barriers to women training as doctors, so that they had in theory to be admitted to training, but the *de facto* barriers remained.) In the late 1870s Sophia Jex-Blake and other women established the London School of Medicine for Women. However, even when women were admitted to medical training and became qualified medical practitioners, they tended to confine their practice almost exclusively to women and children, working in hospitals or in dispensaries they themselves established, or as medical missionaries.

While women won the right to train as doctors and practise medicine, it continued to be a male-dominated profession. There has been a steady increase in the number of women training as doctors and in the proportion of female to male medical students; nevertheless the high-status jobs continue to go to men. Female general practitioners argue that they are frequently expected to look after women and children, yet they want to deal with the full range of patients and medical complaints dealt with by general practitioners (see also Chapter 6).

Nurses, midwives and medical men

A key feature of health care is the dominance and control that doctors exercise over paramedical workers, including midwives and nurses, a position that is sustained through state support (Johnson, 1972; Larkin, 1983). Nursing was established as a profession supplementary to medicine (Gamarnikow, 1978), and the Midwifery Act of 1903, which required that only registered midwives be permitted to practise, placed them finally under medical control. Jeff Hearn (1982) has argued that the process of professionalisation is a process of male assumption of control over female tasks. Thus as male doctors acquire the status of a profession they not only exclude female healers from practising but gain control over other female workers, who take on a subordinate role in the medical division of labour.

Women healers retained control over childbirth for a much longer period than they did over healing generally, but even in midwifery they began from the 1660s to have their dominant role challenged by male midwives (obstetricians). It is possible that the origins of male midwifery relate to the invention of the obstetric forceps, or more simply that it was just another example of males attempting to take over a field previously dominated by females. However, there was opposition to male midwifery (1) from the general public, who thought it indecent, (2) from female midwives because of the threat to their livelihood, and (3) from established medical men who saw it as degrading women's work and not part of medicine at all.

The invention of the obstetric forceps was certainly an important 'break-through'; prior to their invention, an obstetric delay (slow birth) resulted in the death of the mother and/or the child. The use of them was restricted to barber-surgeons and therefore to men, and the number of cases helped was small and the risk of infection and death as a result of their use was enormous. The growth of the lying-in hospitals where male midwives delivered women also played a role in raising the status of male midwifery, especially as women were excluded from the scientific knowledge they claimed to have. Probably more important was the fact that from the seventeenth century a fashion gradually developed for the wealthy to use male midwives, giving support to the male midwives' claim that their knowledge was superior to that of female midwives. This was supported by the argument that only the male midwives could do surgery if complications should arise.

It was in the late nineteenth century that medical doctors accepted that midwifery should be undertaken and controlled by men. During the nineteenth century the Colleges of Physicians and Surgeons both argued against doctors' involvement in midwifery, but by 1850 lectures in midwifery were being given in British medical schools and by 1866 proficiency in it was necessary for qualification as a medical practitioner. The claim by doctors to control childbirth was made on the basis that medical men had superior knowledge. By 1880:

> a great advance had been made in the science and art of midwifery. This was due chiefly to the introduction of male practitioners, many of whom were men of learning and devoted to anatomy, the groundwork of obstetrics.
>
> (Spencer, 1927, p. 175, quoted in Oakley, 1980, p. 11)

This claim was not justified on medical grounds. In the nineteenth century a quarter of women giving birth in hospital died of puerperal fever, and those delivered at home were more likely to be infected if they were attended by a male doctor rather than a female midwife. (Puerperal fever is an infection transmitted by doctors from other areas, and especially from dead bodies, to women in childbirth.) Nevertheless medical men were determined to gain control of midwifery and to determine the role of female midwives – to establish the division of labour between themselves and the female midwives. Thus they set out to demarcate what areas were rightfully theirs at the same time as defending the medical prerogative. The struggle between medical men and female midwives since the seventeenth century had begun to establish a distinction between *assistance* at childbirth and *intervention* in childbirth – one between normal and abnormal childbirth. Only male doctors (qualified medical practitioners) were allowed to use forceps and to intervene surgically.

The Midwifery Registration Act of 1902 resulted in the registration and education of midwives coming under the control of medical men, and a doctor had to be called in if anything went wrong with a delivery. A major reason why doctors did not usurp the role of midwives was that they realised that there was no way in which they could meet the demand – in the late nineteenth century seven out of every nine births were attended by female midwives. Also, many doctors did not want to attend poor women. Doctors thus deskilled midwives, and while female midwives continued to attend poor women in childbirth, doctors attended the wealthy. Medical domination of childbirth continues in the late twentieth century, and indeed it could be argued that it has increased, because the majority of births are in hospital under the (official) control of a consultant, and because of the increased use of medical technology. While most women are actually delivered by a (female) midwife, the ultimate control remains in the hands of the (generally male) obstetrician.

Nurses, too, play a subordinate role in the medical division of labour. Nursing has always been and continues to be a predominantly female province. Most nursing is of course done by women, as unpaid carers in the domestic sphere. However, nursing in the public sphere is also predominantly a female occupation. While caring for the sick was undertaken in a variety of institutions in the past, it was not until the middle of the nineteenth century that nursing emerged as a separate occupation. Prior to that, nursing in hospitals was seen as a form of domestic work that required little specific training and was usually undertaken by married women, doing little different for their patients than they did for their families at home. The demarcation between nurses and patients was blurred – able-bodied convalescent patients were expected to help the nurses with the domestic work on the wards. Florence Nightingale suggested that in the mid-nineteenth century nursing was mainly done by those 'who were too old, too weak, too drunken, too dirty, too sordid or too bad to do anything else' (quoted in Abel-Smith, 1960, p. 53). The argument that nurses needed training and the recognition by doctors that bedside medicine meant that patients needed monitoring developed before Florence Nightingale's reforms. However, she did attempt to develop nursing as a profession and to recruit middle-class women, who received a training. These reforms took place in the voluntary hospitals, and it was not until late in the nineteenth century that nurses in workhouse hospitals were trained.

While Florence Nightingale recognised the need for trained nurses, she trained them in obedience, so that in the division of labour between nurses and doctors, nurses were seen and saw themselves as the subordinates of doctors and as under medical control. Nor did Nightingale challenge the link between womanhood and nursing. Eve Gamarnikow (1978) has pointed out that in the Nightingale model nurses were still responsible for the cleaning of the wards as well as the care of the patients. She suggests that the relationship between doctor and nurse parallelled the relationship between the Victorian husband and wife in the family. The nurse looked after the physical and emotional environment, while he, the doctor, decided what the really important work was and how it should be done. Thus the good nurse was the good mother, concerned with caring for her patients (family).

In the twentieth century, while nurses no longer see themselves as handmaidens of doctors, they have remained trapped in their status as subordinate to doctors. In 1918 the Nursing Register was introduced, and the Nurses Act 1943 established state enrolled nurses as well as state registered ones, but neither kind is recognised as independent practitioners. Anne Williams (1987) has argued that the subordinate role of nurses is exemplified in the ways drugs are administered in hospitals:

> doctors prescribe drugs and nurses administer drugs. Here is an example of nurses as 'handmaidens' to doctors. They have no say in prescribing drugs. They are not authorised to prescribe what they give. Yet they are accountable for what they give, how much, etc., etc.
>
> (Williams, 1987, p. 107)

Ann Oakley (1984b) confessed:

> In a fifteen-year career as a sociologist studying medical services, I confess that I have been particularly blind to the contribution made by nurses to health care. Indeed, over a period of some months spent observing in a large London hospital I hardly noticed nurses at all. I took their presence for granted (much as, I imagine, the doctors and patients did).
>
> (p. 24)

Nursing in the late twentieth century is seen predominantly as a lowly paid female occupation, but there are clear ethnic and class divisions in nursing. The greater emphasis on community care for frail elderly people has also resulted in home helps taking on personal care work, creating even greater divisions between women who perform paid caring work and those who supervise it (Abbott, 1995). Working-class women and women from ethnic minorities are concentrated in the assistant grades and white middle-class women in the registered grade in the prestigious teaching hospitals. Furthermore, more men are entering nursing, and the new managerial structures introduced in the 1970s have resulted in a disproportionately large number of men appointed to management posts. Although men have been able to become general nurses only since 1943, they have increasingly moved into senior posts in what was once, as far as the nursing of physical illness was concerned, an all-woman and woman-managed occupation (see Chapter 8).

Women, motherhood and 'informal' care

Women are seen as primarily responsible for maintaining the health of their families, and as informal, unpaid carers they play a major role in caring for the sick, the disabled, the elderly and other dependent groups. Hilary Graham (1987a) argues that women are providers of informal health care in the domestic economy and that this role is shaped by the sexual division of labour, such that men are seen as providers and women as carers, and by the spatial division of labour, where the local community is seen as the setting for routine medical care and centrally located institutions of medicine for the application of specialist medical skills. Graham suggests that there are three aspects to women's health work: providing for health; teaching for health; and mediating professional help in times of crisis. Thus she argues that much routine domestic labour and caring is about health maintenance, while women are seen as responsible for the health education of their children and are generally the ones who decide whether it is necessary to consult a doctor and indeed take the children to the consultation.

The welfare state was built on the assumption that the traditional nuclear family was the norm and that women would care and provide for the members of this family. As is pointed out in Chapter 8, more recent policies of community care are built on the assumption that women are prepared to care for dependent members of their families (including the wider, extended family). The Health Education Council's 'Look after Yourself' campaign in the early 1980s was also directed at women, assuming that they wanted to care for and look after the health of their men and children.

Women are also blamed when their families are seen as unhealthy. They are seen as responsible for bringing up healthy children and maintaining the health of their men for the nation. Health visitors, social workers and other professional state employees 'police' the family to ensure that women are carrying out their task adequately. Since the early twentieth century motherhood has been a medical domain not just in terms of ante-natal care and delivery, but in terms of bringing up healthy children. When in the early twentieth century considerable concern was expressed about the poor health of the working class, made visible in public by the poor state of men volunteering to enlist in the army at the time of the Boer War, the blame was placed on negligent mothers. It was argued that women should put caring for their families first, should give up paid employment and be trained in domestic skills and childcare. The government advocated the employment by local authorities of trained health visitors under the control of the district medical officers, building on the voluntary movement that had developed in the nineteenth century which visited the houses of working-class families with young children. Scant attention was paid to the poverty and appalling conditions in which working-class women were struggling to bring up their children and the poor health experienced by most of these women. The available evidence suggests that, then as now, women put the needs and demands of their families first and gave little consideration to their own needs.

While it is rarely given official recognition, and the tendency is to see paid health workers as the primary providers of health care, women provide most health care, within the confines of the family. The unpaid, rarely recognised health care work of women in the domestic sphere is extensive. The welfare state is built on the assumption that women will perform this work and that women naturally want to care for their partners and their children.

While feminists are correct in arguing that male medical men have usurped women's role as healers in the public sphere, women continue to have the major role in the private sphere. However, women are under medical dominance and control in the medical division of labour, whether they are paid workers in the public sphere or unpaid workers in the domestic one.

Conclusions

Women play a dominant role in health care systems, both as providers of care and as patients. Women have the major responsibility, in the domestic sphere, for providing informal health care for husbands, children and other dependents. Within the formal health care system women predominate, but they are concentrated in the least prestigious and powerful jobs – as nurses, junior doctors, care assistants and domestics. Black women are found disproportionately in the least prestigious jobs – that is, those that are poorly paid, often part time, and insecure. Medical knowledge has played a powerful role in constructing popular images of women as 'inferior' to men and as controlled by their bodies.

SUMMARY

1   Women are some of the main workers in the health services. The medical services are highly segregated by gender, with employment such as nursing associated with feminine roles – caring, nurturing, domestic work and so on – being associated with female workers while high-status posts associated with specific expertise such as consultancies are associated with male professionals.

2   Women are the main consumers of health services because:
    (a)   they are responsible for the health of the family and are likely to see the doctor on the family's behalf;
    (b)   women are themselves more likely to suffer from a variety of ailments;
    (c)   women live longer than men.

3   Western medicine is defined according to masculine models of health and illness. It is not concerned with the well-being of the individual but rather with curing disease.

4   Women are more likely to be the informal carers and the ones responsible for health outside of the formal services – for example, treating the illnesses of family members.

FURTHER READING

Doyal, L. (1995) *What Makes Women Sick*, London: Macmillan.
Foster, P. (1995) *Women and the Health Care Industry*, Buckingham: Open University Press.
Graham, H. (1993) *Hardship and Health in Women's Lives*, Hemel Hempstead: Harvester/Wheatsheaf.

Chapter eight

Women's work

Sociologists divide people's lives into 'work' (paid employment), 'leisure' (the time when people choose what they want to do) and 'obligation time' (the periods of sleep, eating meals and other necessary activities). Feminists have pointed out that this model reflects a male view of the world and does not fit the experiences of the majority of women. This is partly because unremunerated domestic labour is not recognised as work – it is 'hidden' labour – and partly because married women participate in few leisure activities outside the home (see, e.g., Deem, 1987). Most of the classical sociological studies of paid employment have been of men – coal-miners, affluent assembly-line workers, male clerks – and the findings from these studies have formed the 'hard data' on which general theories about all workers' attitudes and behaviours have been based. Even when women were included in samples, it was (and still often is) assumed that their attitudes and behaviours differed little from men's, or married women were seen as working for 'pin money', paid employment being seen as relatively unimportant in their lives as they are assumed to identify primarily with their domestic roles as wives.

A growing body of feminist research challenged and continues to challenge these assumptions and provides more detailed information on women as workers. Feminists have argued that domestic labour is work and should be regarded

193

as such. They have also maintained that the majority of women do not take on paid employment 'for pin money' but from necessity, and that paid work is seen as meeting important emotional and identity needs by many women. This does not mean that women's experiences of paid employment are the same as men's, however, nor that their attitudes and values are identical.

The sexual division of labour

All societies have a division of labour based on sex – work that is seen as women's work and work that is seen as men's work; labour is gendered. However, the nature of the work that is done by men or women varies from society to society and has changed historically. In almost all societies the care of babies and young children is seen as women's work, but in many societies men take on the task of caring for young boys, in others older children generally look after younger ones, and in others again the older women care for the children. Cooking is mainly seen as women's work, except the preparation of feasts and ceremonial meals which is frequently seen as men's work. In many but not all societies hunting and fishing are regarded as men's work, but planting and harvesting are frequently undertaken by women either alone or alongside men. Women, in many societies, are responsible for the care of livestock. On the basis of this evidence Ann Oakley (1982) has suggested that the sexual division of labour is socially constructed and not based on natural biological differences. Jobs become identified as men's jobs or as women's jobs; *then* it is argued that men and women do these jobs because of natural biological differences.

In Western societies, with industrialisation, work became separated from the home, and work done in the public sphere – paid work – became more highly valued than unpaid work done in the domestic sphere. Women became seen as those who were 'naturally good' at domestic work and caring, and men as the providers – those in paid employment in the public sphere. Male trade unionists, employers and the state were able to restrict women's paid employment and exclude them from certain occupations. Consequently, men were able to define the conditions and rules of the game, so that for women to succeed in the male world of paid work it is necessary for them to play the same game. In order to have a career, to be seen as promotable, women have to be prepared to work full-time and to have no 'career breaks'. Even then, women face problems because they are likely to be excluded from the informal world – drinking in bars, pubs and clubs – and not to have a 'wife' to entertain for them and look after the home. It is not just the problem of getting promoted, however, that women face. Women are often refused training, and recruited on the assumption or given work experience on the basis that they do not want a career because they will have career breaks – because their main role is as wives and mothers. In manual work, 'skill' is socially constructed, so that jobs that involve tasks associated with masculine expertise – such as driving – are seen as more skilled than jobs that involve feminine dexterity – such as sewing.

In Western societies both men and women believe that work is less important for women than for men and that men should have higher wages and more secure employment because of their role of supporting the family. Men are seen as 'breadwinners' whereas women are seen as domestic carers. There is no necessary reason why this should be the case. It would be quite possible for men and women to be seen as equally responsible for the economic support of the household and for the necessary domestic labour and childcare. Indeed, there is a gap between the ideology that a woman's place is in the home and the reality for many women who have paid employment. However, the ideology still has real consequences for married women; most assume, as do their husbands, employers and the state, that even if they have paid employment they are still solely or primarily responsible for childcare and domestic labour. This ideology is so pervasive, so much a part of taken-for-granted common sense, that it is rarely questioned or challenged. It has important consequences for the type of paid employment that most married women seek and are offered. It influences the type of occupations that young women enter on leaving school, not only because of their own aspirations but also what career officers, their parents, school and employers see as suitable for them (see Chapter 4). While it is the case in many of the former Communist societies that married women had full-time employment, they were nevertheless still expected to do the bulk of unpaid domestic labour and were generally in jobs paid at a lower rate than men's (see Einhorn, 1993; Khotkina, 1994; Voronina, 1994; Abbott and Ackers, forthcoming).

Employers clearly have views of what is appropriate work for women, and women generally share these views (Chaney, 1981; Yeandle, 1984; Massey, 1983; Beechey and Perkins, 1982). Many 'female' occupations are clearly regarded as using the 'natural' abilities women require in the domestic sphere – caring for young children, nursing, preparing and serving food, and so on. Much of the growth of part-time work in the recent restructuring of the labour market is dependent on the needs of women with domestic responsibilities to take on paid employment even if the pay is low and the conditions of employment poor (Land, 1987; Beechey and Perkins, 1986). Obviously these assumptions are not only sexist but also frequently untrue. Not all women marry. Many (including some who do marry) have a life-long commitment to the labour market (Dex, 1987; Martin and Roberts, 1984). Many women work out of economic necessity; their families would be in poverty without their additional income (Land, 1980).

A history of women and employment

An analysis of the history of women's work reveals a complex relationship between work in the home and in the labour market. In pre-industrial Britain there was no clear separation between work and the home; economic production was not concentrated in factories, offices and other places of employment. Most people worked in or near the home. Nor was there a gendered separation between productive work and unproductive work. All work was seen as contributing to the maintenance of the household, although some tasks were seen as men's and some as women's. However, with the Industrial Revolution in the nineteenth century, paid employment became separated from the home – in factories, offices and so on. Men, women and children (at least in the working class) went out to work. Production and consumption, productive and unproductive (domestic) work became separated, and gradually men became associated with the former and women with the latter. Women were excluded from paid employment, and it became seen as 'natural' that women, or at least married women, should stay at home and care for their children. (Most nineteenth-century and early twentieth-century feminists accepted this and argued for women having a choice – the choice between paid employment and marriage.) What aroused concern in the nineteenth century was not whether or not women should work – women's work in the domestic sphere and the home caused no concern. It was the public appearance of wage-earning working women that produced hostile comments. Working wives and mothers in particular were regarded as unnatural, immoral and negligent home-makers and parents. They were also accused of taking work from men.

This concern was underpinned by a developing domestic ideology which was formed among the middle class between 1780 and 1830 and gradually spread to all classes and to both sexes. The ideology maintained that the world was divided into two separate spheres, the public and the domestic. Men should be involved in the public sphere of work and politics, making money and supporting their families (Davidoff *et al.*, 1976). Women should stay at home in the domestic sphere, caring for their children and husbands and dependent on their husbands for financial support.

Although many single and even married working-class women had to work, by the end of the nineteenth century they would not have expected to be life-long workers and generally shared the domestic ideal. Married women believed that their primary commitment was to their families and worked only when this was essential for the maintenance of the family; while 25 per cent of married women worked according to the Census of 1851, this had fallen to 10 per cent by 1901. However, poverty did drive many married women to work, and it is estimated that in the period 1890 to 1940, when the Census recorded 10 per cent of married women as working, 40 per cent worked at some time during their married lives. It is also probable that the Census underestimated women's employment, partly because of the nature of it – e.g. domestic service, taking in washing – and partly because of the increased status of a man who earned enough to support his wife and children, so that men might have been reluctant to record their wives as working on the Census forms. However, female participation in the labour market was quite high because the majority of single women worked and they comprised as many as one in four women at some points in the nineteenth century. In 1871, 31 per cent of women aged over 10 years were in employment, and in 1931, 34 per cent of women over 14 were in employment. (The school leaving age was 10 in 1871 and 14 by 1931.)

By the end of the nineteenth century women had become segregated into a small range of lowly paid, low-status occupations. The low pay of women is partly explained by the comparative youth of female workers, as most women gave up employment on marriage. The male trade unions kept women out of higher-paid jobs and fought for a family wage for men – that is, one sufficient for the support of a non-working wife and children. Even when women did the same work as men they did not receive the same pay. Equal pay for male and female teachers, for example, was not fully implemented until 1962. The state also played a role in 'creating' occupational segregation and making men more desirable as employees. Restrictive legislation, supposedly introduced to protect women, also excluded them from certain occupations, restricted the hours they could work and set the hours between which they could work. The Mines Act 1884 forbade women to work underground, but women were still able to work above ground as pit-brow girls. The protection afforded by legislation did not extend to housework, or to domestic servants, or to preventing women doing dirty and dangerous work (in agriculture, for example).

Most men saw working women and especially married working women as a threat to their own paid employment and status as breadwinners. They argued that there was only a limited amount of paid employment, and if women were allowed to work then some families would be left without an income. Women were also thought to lower the level of wages in general because they could work for less than men. Consequently, it was argued that women should be excluded from paid employment or confined to low-status, lowly paid jobs – women's jobs. The trade unions were dominated by men and were concerned to protect men's conditions and wages. Women were prevented or discouraged from joining trade unions, and in any case trade unions were seen as not concerned with representing women's interests. Thus the protective legislation could be said to be designed as much to protect male workers from female competition as to protect women.

Not all women were passive. Women at all levels fought for the right to participate equally with men in paid employment. Women, for example, fought for the right to go to university and qualify as medical doctors. Women formed their own trade unions and fought against the conditions of their employment. A notable example of this is the Match Girl Strike. However, on the whole men, the trade unions and the state succeeded in creating a segregated labour market, and the domestic ideology was generally accepted by the end of the nineteenth century by men and women in all social classes. Although women worked in large numbers during World War One, they accepted that after the war men should have priority in the labour market. Many employers, including banks and the government, operated a marriage bar, so that women had to give up employment on marriage; the marriage bar on female teachers was not removed until the 1944 Education Act. Since the Second World War increasing numbers of women have taken on paid employment, especially married women. However, despite the Equal Pay and Equal Opportunities legislation, a segregated labour market persists and domestic ideology is pervasive. Furthermore, there is little evidence that men are taking on more responsibility in the private sphere; women are still expected to take on the double burden (Martin and Roberts, 1984; Arber, 1990; Benigni, 1989). To the extent that men do undertake a greater share of the work in the private sphere, they tend to take on those aspects of child care that women find most rewarding and enjoyable, not the routine drudgery of domestic cleaning (Edgell, 1980; Langberg, 1994; Abbott and Ackers, forthcoming).

Domestic labour

Understanding women's role as unpaid domestic workers is crucial to understanding their position in Western societies and their role in the labour market. However, it is only recently that housework has become a topic of serious academic concern. Functionalist sociologists argued that it was necessary for women to undertake the physical and mental servicing of men in complex industrial societies. Marxists argued similarly that this was necessary in capitalist societies; women were responsible for the reproduction of labour power – both for the bearing and rearing of children and the mental and physical refreshing of employees. While both marxists and functionalists argued that domestic labour was a private 'labour of love', the marxists pointed out the ways in which it related to the economic system of employees – ensuring that there was a continuing supply of well serviced workers to meet the demands of capitalism.

The view that domestic labour is the responsibility of women is also widely held by the British people – although this may be changing slowly.

A comparative study of attitudes in Europe (Deshormes LaValle, 1987) found that 41 per cent of those interviewed said that men and women should have equal roles in the home and in paid employment, and 47 per cent of married men said they would prefer a wife in paid employment; half of the married men inteviewed in the UK said they would prefer a working wife. Of course, wanting a wife in paid employment does not necessarily indicate a willingness to share in domestic labour. Despite an increased participation of men in domestic work, women retain the responsibility for most work in the home (see Chapter 6).

Feminists have examined empirically what housewives actually do and developed theories that explain the relationship of housework to the social structure and the economy in general. All feminists have argued that housework is hard, physically demanding work and that the notion of the weak housewife has developed because housework is hidden from public view and done out of affection and duty rather than for payment. Crucially, feminists examined the relations and sexual division of labour between men and women in the domestic sphere and defined women's unpaid activity within the home as work. Research by Gavron (1966), Oakley (1974a,b), Pahl (1980) and others rigorously analysed what work was done in the domestic sphere, for whom, to whose benefit and at whose cost.

The vast majority of 'housewives' are women. Housework is seen as women's work and it is assumed that women will do it if they live in the household. The general assumption is that women can do domestic tasks naturally and men cannot. Furthermore, Oakley (1974a) argued that the refusal to acknowledge that housework is work is both a reflection and a cause of women's generally low status in society. She points out that housework is largely under-rated, unrecognised, unpaid work that is not regarded as 'real' work. However, domestic labour involves long hours of work: in 1971, in Oakley's sample, women did 77 hours a week on average. The lowest was 48 hours, done by a woman who also had a full-time job, and the highest was 105 hours (Oakley, 1974a).

Ann Oakley (1974a,b) studied housework within the framework of the sociology of work. She spoke in depth to forty mothers in London aged between 20 and 30. The majority of them were full-time housewives, and half had husbands in working-class occupations and half in middle-class ones. The women described housework in terms similar to the way in which male assembly-line workers have described their work, reporting even more monotony, fragmentation of tasks and excessive speed of work than the assembly-line workers in Luton (Goldthorpe *et al.*, 1969). However, unlike male manual work, domestic labour is not closely supervised and is performed largely on the basis of personal rather than contractual relationships. It is unpaid, with no fixed remuneration linked to the hours put in or the quantity or quality of the goods or services produced. Women got little pleasure from housework as work, although working-class women invested more in the role and searched for satisfaction in it. Overall the nature of the tasks included in domestic labour were rated negatively even amongst women who claimed to be satisfied as housewives. Seventy per cent were dissatisfied with the role, the commonest complaint being loneliness. Autonomy was the most valued aspect – the control over one's own pace of work – and the women set themselves routines and standards of work to which they forced themselves to adhere. Oakley suggests three explanations for this task-setting strategy:

1   it was one way of gaining a reward from housework tasks – a woman gained satisfaction if she reached her own 'high' standards;
2   self-imposed standards were a way of emphasising the housewife's autonomy; and
3   it was a method of overcoming the fragmentary nature of housework and imposing a unity on it.

However, Oakley argues that these self-imposed rules come to take on an objectivity, become seen as external and actually diminish the autonomy and control that women have, by enslaving them to what were originally their own standards.

Domestic labour, then, is seen by feminists as real work. They also argue that the demands of housework and the economic and personal conditions under which it is performed mitigate against the formation of a sense of solidarity among women. Domestic labour is a solitary activity, and women are bound to housework by ties of love and identification. Women like to feel reasonably good about their domestic work; in the absence of clear standards or the praise of employers, women tend to use other women as the standard against which to measure their own performance in a competitive way. Housework consequently tends to divide women rather than to unite them.

Explaining the division of labour in the domestic sphere

Feminists argue that all men derive benefit from the expectation that women will perform domestic labour. Men work to earn a living and expect not only an income from their employment but personal service from a wife at a cost to themselves of less than the market value of the goods and services provided. Christine Delphy (1977) argues that gender inequalities derive from the ways in which husbands appropriate their wives' labour. The wife does not receive an equitable return for the domestic labour and childcare she does for her husband. Delphy argues not only that domestic labour is work just as much as factory labour is work, but also that it is provided in a distinct 'mode of production' – the domestic mode. In the domestic mode of production the husband appropriates the labour power of his wife; in return for the economic support provided by husbands, women are expected to provide domestic services. The marriage contract is a labour contract the terms of which only become fully apparent when it is alleged that the wife has failed to fulfil her side of the bargain. According to the radical feminists men benefit from the unpaid labour of women in the domestic sphere, and therefore they have a vital interest in maintaining the sexual division of labour. Consequently men resist equal opportunities legislation, support policies that protect men's privileged position in the labour market and 'allow' their wives to work – but still expect them to do the housework (see Chapter 10).

Marxist feminists argue that it is the capitalist system that benefits from the unpaid domestic labour of women. Not only does women's domestic labour reproduce the relations of production, but it also contributes to the maintenance of tolerable living standards for men and may reduce political pressure for radical change. Women expend considerable effort and energy stretching the household income and maintaining the household's standard of living.

There are a number of problems with this perspective, since domestic work is not fully equivalent to work outside the home in that it is not subject to measurement, control or rates of payment in the same way. Rather, it is done out of a sense of love, obligation and duty, so the relationships are different. The major problem with marxist theories is that they fail to take account of men's interest in perpetuating women's role as domestic labourer. Also, they tend to derive women's oppression from capitalism, when women's oppression predates capitalism. The radical feminists, on the other hand, tend to ignore the benefits that capitalists derive from women's domestic labour and their accounts tend to be descriptive rather than explanatory. Also, they assume that it is men who benefit from the unpaid labour of women, but employers also benefit, as well as other dependent groups.

Women's unpaid 'caring' work

Women are expected to care not only for their husbands and children but also for other dependants, and in a voluntary capacity for people generally in the community. Women are also frequently seen as necessary to their husbands' work role. As Janet Finch (1983a) has demonstrated, this extends beyond the wives of managers and businessmen who are expected to entertain for their husbands. Men in many occupations 'need' a wife, and the employer benefits from this labour. Finch refers to the village policeman's wife who not only manages a police home but substitutes for him, to the doctor's wife, the clergyman's wife, and so on. Goffee and Scase (1985) have suggested that wives play a vital role in helping self-employed husbands, who are often heavily dependent on the (unpaid) clerical and administrative duties undertaken by their wives. Wives are often forced to abandon their own careers to underwrite the efforts of the 'self-made' man. Furthermore, given the long hours self-employed men work, wives are left to cope single-handed with the children and the domestic chores. Sallie Westwood and Parminder Bhachu (1988) have pointed to the importance of the labour (unpaid) of female relations in the ethnic business community – although they also point out that setting up a business may be a joint strategy of husband and wife.

Women are also expected to care for relations who cannot look after themselves. Policies of community care that have been advocated by successive governments since the 1950s have a hidden agenda for women. Such policies, which involve closing down or not providing large-scale residential care for the mentally handicapped, the mentally ill, physically handicapped people and the elderly have frequently assumed that women are prepared to take on the care of dependent relatives. While it is generally suggested that 'the family' should care where possible, in practice it is women who perform the care. It is generally assumed that it is part of a woman's role and that women are natural carers; that carers should be women is an unquestioned assumption.

While it is probably true that many women take on the caring role relatively willingly, it nonetheless radically alters their lives. Michael Bayley (1973), in a study of the family care of mentally handicapped children in Sheffield, argued that community care means in reality care by mothers. Nissel and Bonnerjea (1982), in a study of 44 married couples caring for an elderly dependent relative, found that wives spent on average 2–3 hours a day doing essential care for the relative, whether or not they were in employment. (Husbands spent on average eight minutes a day.) Abbott and Sapsford (1987b) found that in families with a child with learning difficulties the mother took on most of the responsibility for the child, with if anything less help from the community than received by mothers of other children. Abbott (1982) suggested that 'normalising' life for people with learning difficulties denormalises it for 'Mum'. Married women who have to care for a relative can no longer look forward to the time when the children are older, when they can have more freedom to develop their own lives, return to paid employment and enjoy a measure of economic freedom. The physical and mental demands of the caring role combine with the expectation that, where necessary, the carer will cover 24 hours per day, seven days a week. Even when day-care or schooling is provided the carer is not freed; she has to be there to see the child/elderly person on the transport and be at home when the dependant is returned.

What is at stake is not just the loss of potential earnings or the amount of labour involved, but the fact that women are trapped in the domestic sphere. Janet Finch and Dulcie Groves (1980) have argued that in the context of public expenditure cuts, policies of community care are incompatible with equal opportunities for women, because community care means care by the family, which in practice means care by women. Processes of labour market segmentation mean that most women cannot earn as much as their husbands, making it economically non-viable for the men to give up their jobs even if they were prepared to take on the caring role. Nor would the provision of additional services radically alter the situation; more provision of day-care, respite care, home nursing and the like would ease the immense burden on a woman caring for a dependent relative, but it would not liberate her from the domestic sphere nor from her responsibilities for taking on the main burden of caring.

Sally Baldwin and Julie Twigg (1991) summarise the key findings of feminist research on community care and indicate that the work on 'informal' care demonstrates:

> that the care of non-spousal dependent people falls primarily to women; that it is unshared to a significant extent by relatives, statutory or voluntary agencies;
> that it creates burdens and material costs which are a source of significant inequalities between men and women;
> that many women nevertheless accept the role of informal carer and indeed derive satisfaction from doing so;
> that the reasons for this state of affairs are deeply bound up with the construction of female and male identity, and possibly also with culturally defined rules about gender-appropriate behaviours.

(p. 124)

Janet Finch (1984) and Gillian Dalley (1983, 1988) argue that community care inevitably exploits women and therefore that institutional care should replace it. Dalley argues not only that familial lifestyles and responsibilities inevitably exploit women but that the collective way of living has a value in its own right, suggesting an alternative both to 'families' and to 'institutional' care. Susie Croft (1986), however, has raised the issue of the rights of people for whom care is provided and of their needs. Sally Baldwin and Julia Twigg have pointed to the range of support services available for people living in the community and their carers. However, the extent to which these services are provided for informal carers may be very limited, and many of the providers of the services are lowly paid female workers (see, e.g., Abbott, 1995).

SUMMARY _____

1   Women do substantial amounts of unpaid work in the home, and this is concealed by the fact that it is assumed to be part of their 'natural' function.

2   The work women do in the home as housewives – partly in maintaining the domestic dwelling and partly in caring for the other family members (husbands, children, other dependants) – is different from that done in the paid economy. Although all the same services could be bought outside the home, within the home they are provided out of 'love' and 'duty' rather than for a wage.

3   There is some debate as to who benefits from this unpaid and hidden work. Marxist feminists argue that capitalism benefits economically from housework in terms of improved profits. Radical feminists argue that men are the main beneficiaries.

Women and paid employment

There has been a steady increase in women's rate of participation in the labour market in Britain during the twentieth century, especially in their part-time employment. The most dramatic rise has occurred in the participation rates of married women, since the Second World War. Familial ideology may see a woman's primary role as that of wife and mother, but the majority of women (including married women) have paid employment for the majority of the years during which they are employable. According to the 1991 Census women formed 47 per cent of the labour force, though with substantial age, regional and ethnic variations (Stone, 1983; Massey, 1983; Abbott and Tyler, 1995).

In 1991 in Great Britain, 73 per cent of eligible women aged over 16 (i.e. excluding those who were inactive students, the permanently sick or disabled, and retired women not economically active) were in employment or registered as unemployed (OPCS, 1993a, Table 10). Fifty-two per cent of *all* women over the age of 16 were economically active. However, there were marked variations in economic activity rate by age, with about 60 per cent of women aged 16–24 economically active, 74 per cent of those aged 25–49, but only 49 per cent of those aged 56–65 and 7 per cent of those older than 65 (see Table 8.1 for the estimated figures for 1993 – the most recently available at the time of writing). These figures may be an underestimate, because women who have casual employment or are home workers may not be recorded, and women who are unemployed and seeking work may not be registered as unemployed. Compared with other European Union countries a high proportion of women in Britain are economically active. Greece has the lowest proportion of economically active women, at 32.6 per cent, and Denmark the highest at 61 per cent. However, nearly half of the employed women in Britain are in part-time work, compared with only 7 per cent of men (Table 8.2). Most women in part-time jobs had taken them because they did not want full-time ones.

Married women are less likely to be in employment than those who are not married. In Britain in 1991 57 per cent of married women were economically active (Abbott and Ackers, forthcoming, Table 4). The only country in Europe with a higher proportion of married women in employment is Denmark, where 69 per cent are in paid employment.

There are also variations between women from different ethnic backgrounds, both in participation in the labour market and in whether they engage in full- or part-time work. Afro-Caribbean and British Indian women are more likely to be in the labour market than white women. Muslim women are less likely to work, but the figures do not take account of the home working in which they may engage. Also, Afro-Caribbean and Asian women are more likely to work full-time than white women if they do work. (See Tables 8.3 and 8.4.) Of white women in employment, 40 per cent are in part-time work, 21 per cent of West Indian women and between 20 and 25 per cent of British southern Asian women (OPCS, 1993a, Table 10). Women of West Indian origin are more likely to work while they have young children than are other women. (The figures from the 1991 Census suggest a smaller proportion of women working part-time in 1991 than the OPCS figures for 1994. This may be a real change, but it is more likely to be a result of using different definitions of what counts as full- and part-time work.)

Women are more likely than men to be in non-manual occupations. Seventy-five per cent of women are in non-manual jobs, compared with 46 per cent of men. However, men are more likely than women to be in professional or managerial occupations; 27 per cent of men are in such occupations, compared with 12 per cent of women. Women are more likely to be in routine non-manual (clerical and related) occupations – 63 per cent of employed women are in this type of job, but only 20 per cent of employed men. Within the manual category, men are much more likely than women to be categorised as 'skilled' (craft and similar) workers, 23 per cent of employed men compared with 3 per cent of employed women. West Indian and Asian women are more likely than white women to be in unskilled manual work, and West Indian women are less likely than white or Asian women to be in the highest social class (see OPCS, 1993, Table 16; Abbott and Taylor, 1995, Table 8.9).

TABLE 8.1 Civilian labour force economic activity rates by gender and age – estimates for 1993

Age	16–19	20–24	25–34	35–44	45–49	50–59	60–65	Total 16+
Men	63.9	83.8	92.5	93.6	90.3	75.4	52.2	71.9
Women	63.8	70.7	70.7	77.0	74.8	54.6	24.8	52.6

Source: OPCS, 1995, Table 4.4.

TABLE 8.2 Percentages of full- and part-time employment by gender in 1994

	Full-time	Part-time
Males	92.8	7.2
Females	53.8	46.2

Source: OPCS, 1995, Table 4.12.

TABLE 8.3 Economic activity as a percentage of the total population of women aged 16+, by ethnic group

Ethnic group	Percentage of total female pop. who are economically active	Percentage of eligible[a] female pop. who are economically active	Amount worked (percentage)	
			Full	Part
All	50	73	61	31
White	50	69	60	40
Black (Caribbean)	67	82	79	21
Black (African)	60	74	78	22
Black (Other)	63	76	78	22
Indian	55	82	76	24
Pakistani	27	32	73	27
Bangladeshi	22	28	73	27
Chinese	53	68	66	34
Other Asian	54	64	75	25
Other	50	68	73	27

Source: derived from OPCS, 1993b, Table 10.
Note: [a] i.e. excluding inactive students, the permanently sick or disabled and retired women.

TABLE 8.4 Economic activity rates in the female population of working age, 1994, by ethnic group and age

	16–24	25–44	45–59
All	65	74	70
White	67	75	70
Black[a]	51	71	72
Indian	51	69	53
Pakistani/Bangladeshi	35	24	–
Other[b]	34	57	54

Source: OPCS, 1995, Table 4.3.
Notes:
[a] African, Caribbean and other Black people of non-mixed origin
[b] Includes Chinese and other ethnic minority groups of non-mixed origin, plus people of mixed origin.

Women's labour-market participation is clearly affected by their domestic responsibilities. It is not so much marriage as having dependent children that conditions participation – see Table 8.5. Women with young children tend to withdraw from the labour market, returning to part-time work when the children reach school age and to full-time work when the children are older. Not only do a high proportion of women return to paid employment after having children, but many return between births, and the time that women are taking out of the labour market for childbirth and child-rearing is decreasing. Women are spending an increasing proportion of their lives in employment, though very few have continuous full-time careers because of their domestic responsibilities (Martin and Roberts, 1984).

The pattern of women's paid employment across the life course is changing in all Western European countries, but there are clear differences between countries. Denmark and Portugal are the two countries where female participation most nearly matches the Inverted U curve – that is, the majority of women do not take 'career breaks' – although participation rates are higher in Denmark. In France, the United Kingdom, Germany and the Netherlands the activity pattern of women most clearly resembles the M-shaped curve, with a high proportion of women having a career break, although the Netherlands has a higher rate of participation among women aged 40–50 than the other three countries. In the remaining countries – Italy, Spain, Greece, Ireland, Luxembourg and Belgium – despite the increase in female economic activity rates, there continues to be a peak in female employment at about age 25 and a decline thereafter.

Married women are less likely than single women or men to be in paid employment, in all EU countries. Having children also affects women's

TABLE 8.5 Economic activity status of women aged 16–59 by age of youngest child, 1994

		Working full-time	*Working part-time*	*Temporarily unemployed*	*Economically inactive*
All women	%	36	29	5	30
Child aged					
0–4	%	16	30	6	48
5–10	%	20	45	6	29
11–15	%	34	40	4	22
No dependent children	%	46	23	5	25

Source: OPCS, 1995, Table 4.5.

economic activity (European Commission, 1993). Forty-four per cent of mothers with children aged 0–9 are in employment, compared with 92 per cent of fathers (Table 8.6). In the United Kingdom activity rates increase significantly with the age of the youngest child: while less than a third of mothers work whose youngest child is less than 3 are in paid employment, 70 per cent of those whose youngest child is 7 or older are (Joshi and Davies, 1994). The highest level of mothers' employment is in Denmark, where 75 per cent are in paid employment, while Ireland (30%) has the lowest employment of mothers.

Two-thirds of employed mothers have part-time jobs. Over 50 per cent do so in the UK, Germany and the Netherlands, and a significant minority in Denmark; however, less than 15 per cent of employed mothers do so in Italy, Greece, Portugal and Spain. Over 50 per cent of mothers who work part-time work twenty hours or more a week – 14 per cent working more than thirty hours. Only 14 per cent work less than ten hours a week. Mothers working part-time in the Netherlands and the UK tend to work short hours – over 20 per cent less than ten hours and the majority less than twenty. In contrast, over 25 per cent of part-time working mothers in France, Italy, Denmark and Greece work longer than thirty hours a week (European Commission, 1990).

In explaining the patterns of women's labour-market participation, supply factors are obviously important. Women's participation is obviously affected by family responsibilities and especially the existence of dependent children. Studies such as those carried out by Susan Yeandle (1984), Judith Chaney (1981) and Veronica Beechey and Teresa Perkins (1982) show that women in Britain have a clear view of what kinds of job are appropriate and available and that they search for work accordingly. These studies also show that demand-side factors are also important. Employers also have a clear view about what is appropriate work for women, and they work to 'activate' a supply of female labour. Many jobs, especially part-time, lowly paid ones,

TABLE 8.6 Percentages in employment of mothers and fathers with children aged less than 10, 1988

	Men with children aged <10	Women with children aged <10
Belgium	94 (1)	60 (22)
Denmark	92 (2)	85 (28)
France	92 (1)	59 (16)
Germany	94 (1)	55 (24)
Greece	96 (1)	41 (3)
Ireland	81 (2)	30 (9)
Italy	95 (2)	42 (5)
Luxembourg	97 (-)	40 (13)
Netherlands	92 (8)	40 (35)
Portugal	96 (1)	69 (6)
Spain	91 (7)	33 (4)
United Kingdom	88 (1)	51 (35)

Source: derived from Roll, 1992.

Note: Figures in brackets are those in part-time work.

are created as women's jobs, often with hours to suit women with domestic commitments.

Children have a very large effect on women's ability to participate in the labour market – although child-care is clearly not the only factor and clearly interacts with cultural attitudes to married women's having paid employment. Maternity leave is a universal right for all employed women in the European Union, although the length of time and degree of income entitlement vary significantly from country to country. All the EU countries with the exception of the UK and Portugal provide publicly funded child-care for over 50 per cent of children aged from 3 to the compulsory age of school entry. Only Denmark provides a significant amount of publicly funded child-care for children under the age of 3 or out-of-school care for those of primary-school age. Although the availability of child-care is clearly a factor in explaining women's varied participation in paid employment, it is not by itself a sufficient explanation. Ireland and the Netherlands, for example, have significantly more places for pre-school children in publicly funded care than the UK, but much lower employment rates for women aged 25–49 – 45 and 58 per cent respectively, compared with 73 per cent (Maruani, 1992).

However, it is clear that the availability of child-care is a significant factor in enabling women to participate in the labour market. In France, for example, the almost universal availability of pre-school publicly funded child-care, combined with long school hours, has enabled French mothers to work full-time. By contrast, in Britain the low level of pre-school provision and a relatively short school day accounts both for the continuing M-shaped pattern of the female activity-rate curve and for the high level of part-time employment of women with children. It is also likely that the provision or not of child-care by the state interacts with cultural attitudes to whether married women or women with children should participate in paid employment. The low employment rate of married women in Ireland would seem to be heavily influenced by cultural factors.

Women's experience of work

The increased labour market participation of women does not mean that women's experience of work is the same as men's. Employed mothers are concentrated in an even narrower range of occupations than women in general in all European Union countries (Abbott and Ackers, forthcoming). They are to be found in large numbers in three main types of economic activity: 45 per cent in 'other services', 20 per cent in 'distributive trades', and 11 per cent in 'other manufacturing'. The type of work, the hours that women work and the return that they receive for their labour all differ from men's. Even where women are employed in the same occupation as men and have equal pay, their experiences may differ greatly from men's. Crompton and Sanderson (1986) argue that many married women have semi-professional jobs while their husbands have careers. In many occupations women are found predominantly on the lower rungs while men hold a disproportionate percentage of senior posts – this is most notably the case in teaching, nursing and social work. However, women and men are frequently concentrated in different jobs, often with men supervising or controlling women. Women often work part-time, while the vast majority of men work full-time. Women, as a result, often do not enjoy the same conditions of employment as men, or even (if they work less than 16 hours per week) the protection of employment legislation. The most exploited of women are not only without fringe benefits; they also lack seniority and are unlikely to be promoted, and this is the case for part-time professional and managerial employees as well as those further down the occupational scale (Martin and Roberts, 1984). In addition women are more likely than men to be doing homework – producing industrial goods at home – on piece-rates that may work out at as little as 40p per hour (Allen and Walkowitz, 1987). It is estimated that there are anything up to half a milion home workers in Britain, though it is impossible to estimate the exact numbers because much of this work is subcontracted or concealed.

Women's orientation to work

Martin and Roberts (1984) provide some information on women's attitudes to work. They found that social and domestic circumstances had a considerable influence on the way women thought about it. Some, for example, find it difficult to cope with paid work and domestic responsibilities. However, type of job and the employment situation also affected women's orientation to work. Contrary to popular opinion, they found that the majority of women, including married women, were highly dependent financially on their wages from work, and that the majority of women were fully committed to work, but this varied over the life-cycle, the most highly committed being childless women older than thirty.

Irrespective of whether they worked full- or part-time, women thought that the most important aspect of employment was doing 'work you like'. Part-time employees thought 'convenient hours' was equally important but were less likely than full-timers to see pay and job security as important. Part-time employees also stressed having friendly people to work with as important. Both full- and part-time employees gave low priority to the career aspects of the job or the opportunity to use one's abilities, although these were seen as important by younger women and women in full-time work. Women who were forced to work out of economic necessity, who tended to be in low-status, lowly paid jobs, reported a general sense of dissatisfaction with their jobs. Women who worked because they enjoyed working, and were often in more highly paid jobs, reported a higher level of satisfaction.

Feminist studies of women factory workers (e.g. Anna Pollert, 1981; Sallie Westwood, 1984; Ruth Cavendish, 1982) suggest that women's orientation to work is primarily as housewife. Women on the shop floor have a shared culture of romance, marriage and family. However, studies such as the one by Jean Martin and Ceridwyn Roberts, and Ann Oakley's study (1974a,b), demonstrate that paid employment is central to the lives of women employees. Women are expected, however, to cope with the double shift, and this influences their ability to demonstrate total loyalty to the job in the way in which many men can. They have to juggle their responsibilities to their families and to their employers in ways that men rarely have to do.

Women in employment

As with malestream studies of male workers, feminist sociologists have tended to study female factory workers, and there is a growing number of ethnographic studies of women in factories. There has also been some attention paid to female office workers and women in the professions. However, there are large gaps and much research still needs to be carried out to fill in our knowledge about women in paid employment.

Women factory workers

A number of studies of factory workers (e.g. Cavendish, 1982; Pollert, 1981; Coyle, 1984; Westwood, 1984) show a similar pattern: women and men working in separate occupations, with men working in jobs classified as skilled and women doing work classified as semi- or unskilled and earning substantially less than men. They all agree that 'skill' is constructed in such a way that it is seen as a characteristic of men's work and not of women's work. Ruth Cavendish (1982), describing a London factory, notes that the complex skills expected of women on the assembly line actually took longer to acquire than those of the male skilled workers. She provides a graphic account of what it is like to do unskilled factory work. The factory in which she worked employed about 1,800 people, of whom 800 worked on the factory floor. Virtually all the women were immigrants – 70 per cent Irish, 20 per cent West Indian and 10 per cent Asian, mostly from Gujarat in India. She notes that the men enjoyed significantly better working conditions than the women – their jobs enabled them to stop for an occasional cigarette, to move around and to slow down without financial penalty, while the women were tied to the line. Male-dominated trade unions and management worked together to protect the interests of male workers. Women were also frequently supervised by men, so that the women were controlled by men at the workplace.

All the women were semi-skilled assemblers with very few exceptions. Men, on the other hand, were spread throughout the grades and were divided from each other by differences of skill and pay. Even in the machine shop where men and women worked together on the same job the men were paid at a higher rate than the women on the grounds that they could and the women could not lift the heavy coils of metal. While young men were trained as charge hands, the young women were not; the latter lacked the possibilities for promotion that were open to the former.

The women were controlled by the assembly line and the bonus system. The views of the women workers were not sought when new designs and new machinery were introduced. The women had no chance to move or think while they were working and no time for a quick break, and if they could not keep up with the line then they were dismissed. At work the women were controlled and patronised by the men, but other women were generally supportive and friendly. The most important things in the women's lives appeared to be their family and home; the single women looked forward to marriage and domesticity. All the women shared a general interest in a cult of domesticity.

Anna Pollert, in her study of a tobacco factory in Bristol, found, similarly, that the women worked for money, but the men thought that they worked for 'pin money' and that women's work in the factory was routine, repetitive, fiddly, low-grade work that would not be done by men. They thought that women should be paid less than men because they had babies, were inferior and did not have to support a family. If women were paid the same as men they would price themselves out of paid work, they argued.

The women accepted the low pay, because they compared it with the wages of other female jobs. While they rejected the idea that their place was in the home, they thought of themselves as dependent on men and conceived of their pay as marginal to a man's – even though two-thirds of the workforce were young, single women. They saw marriage and a family as their 'career' and conceived of themselves as at the bottom of the labour market in class and gender terms. The unmarried girls looked to marriage as an escape from low-status, monotonous work (even though they worked alongside married women for whom this had proved not to be the case). Val, one of Anna Pollert's informants, expressed this well:

> Get married [laugh]. Anything's better than working here. Well, most women get married, don't they? Not all of them works all their lives like a man. Put it this way, I don't want to work when I'm married. I don't really believe in married women working. Well. 'Cos there's not much work anyway, and they ought to make room for people what have got to lead their own lives.
>
> (p. 101)

Romance permeated the talk of the women on the shop floor. Appearance, courting and marriage dominate the conversation and work was seen as temporary. Among the married women, who all did the double shift (as both housewives and paid workers), their main identity was as housewives.

Women and personal care work

Personal care work such as that of care assistants and home helps is predominantly performed by women; indeed, the jobs have generally been created as women's jobs and are assumed to require the 'natural' abilities of women. Women working as home helps, nursing auxiliaries, care assistants and the like are employed in the female peripheral labour market – low-status jobs with poor and insecure conditions of employment. They are often supervised and controlled by other female workers who have more secure employment in the core labour market (Abbott, 1995).

The client group is mainly elderly; care workers are working with elderly, degenerating bodies and polluting substances. The work is often repetitive and involves dirty tasks. While many of the women undertaking this kind of work are positive about it (Abbott *et al.*, 1992), feminists have tended to see it as exploitive and therefore to see the women who do it as powerless victims of patriarchal social structures. Hilary Graham (1991) has pointed out that feminists have tended, unintentionally, to take on policy-makers' definitions of care and to equate it with work carried out in the domestic home, for relatives and family, involving normative obligations of kinship. This, as she points out, has meant that they have ignored the class and racial factors that impact on care and care work and the ways in which paid domestic labour in the private home results in a blurring of the boundaries between the domestic and the public spheres. Feminists have also tended to ignore paid care work in residential settings and the ways in which the structuring of work in these settings and the meaning given to it blurs the public/ private distinction.

Care work in both the domestic and the public sphere is principally women's work. It is not just that it is mainly women who undertake it, but that it is seen as naturally women's work. In both spheres care work involves both physical and emotional labour and is pre-eminently concerned with hygiene and health promotion. Caring involves physical and emotional support of others – caring for the whole person. The skills of caring are not seen to be derived from the qualities of being a care assistant, a nursing auxiliary or a cook, but from the qualities of being a woman. Women judge themselves and are judged by others in terms of their ability to care.

Paid care work is, however, different from unpaid care work in that it is (of course) remunerated, it takes place in given localities, with given hours of employment and is supervised and regulated. However, it is about more than the performance of tasks: it is about creating order, routine and discipline. The smooth working of care relationships is based on individual clients allowing the carers to control them and their movements – to order their lives. Clients have to accept care, and the acceptance and being (usually) grateful for the care provided appears to be part of the reciprocal relationship expected by paid carers (Lee-Treweek, 1994). However, the skills that women deploy in carrying out paid care work are not recognised – they are categorised as unskilled workers. This ignores the process by which women have learned the required skills – as part of the socialisation process in the home and experientially in caring for their own families (Abbott, 1995).

Women and clerical work

In clerical work, one of the major types of work done by women, women are found in lowly paid dead-end jobs, seen as 'female jobs'. Women are often recruited on the basis that they will not be promoted, while men are recruited on the assumption that they will. Once in employment, women are less likely than men to be offered structured work experiences and the opportunity to study that would enable them to seek promotion and to be seen as promotable. As clerical work has declined in status and the tasks it involves become standardised, fragmented and rationalised, so increasingly women have been recruited to office work. The de-skilling of office work is mediated for men by the possibility of promotion. While women are recruited to the lowest grades, paid at lower rates and replaced by other young women when they leave to have children, men, it is assumed, will be mobile out of clerical work.

One of the major debates in malestream sociology since the Second World War had been whether or not clerical workers have been proletarianised – that is, whether the pay, conditions of employment and nature of work of clerical workers are comparable to those of manual workers. British sociologists, following a weberian analysis, have looked at the market situation, work situation and status situation of male clerical workers and argued that they are middle-class because they enjoy superior conditions of work, are accepted as middle-class and do not identify themselves as working-class (see Lockwood, 1958; Goldthorpe et al., 1969). Braverman (1974) argues that clerical workers have been proletarianised and that the feminisation of clerical work is part of this process. Reviving the debate, Crompton and Jones (1984) argue that while female clerical work is proletarian, men's is not – primarily, they suggest, because male clerical workers have the possibility of upward mobility out of clerical work. They suggest that this situation may change as more women seek and are seen as potential candidates for promotion. However, the view that female clerical workers are proletarian holds only if they are compared with male manual workers. Martin and Roberts (1984) and Heath and Britten (1984) argue that female clerical workers enjoy pay and conditions of work more comparable to women in professional and managerial work than to women employed in manual work, where few are in work defined as skilled.

Women in the professions and as managers

Women tend to be concentrated in the 'female' semi-professional occupations rather than in the male-dominated professions. Semi-professional occupations have less autonomy than professional ones, lower status and less pay.

Women are often seen as 'naturally' suited to the 'caring' work involved, for example, in nursing, primary school teaching and social work. However, even in these occupations the women tend to be concentrated in lower grades and to be controlled by men.

In the established professions there has been an increase in recent years in the number of women. Medicine is the profession that has the largest proportion of women. In 1976, 23 per cent of all doctors on the General Medical Council Register were women, and the proportion of women entering medical school has increased from between 22 and 25 per cent in the years from the Second World War to 1968 to 37.8 per cent in 1978 (Elston, 1980) to 46 per cent in 1985 (Allen, 1988) and 50 per cent by 1990 (Hockey, 1993). However, despite being 25 per cent of medical graduates in the 1960s, women were still under-represented in top posts in the 1980s; only 15 per cent of hospital consultants, 3 per cent of consultant surgeons and less than 1 per cent of general surgeons were women (Hockey, 1993). Women are also unevenly distributed across the medical specialities, and this is not solely the outcome of chance and personal preference. Women are heavily represented in community medicine and the school health service, in general practice and in certain hospital specialisms such as anaesthesia, radiology, mental illness and children's mental illness (Mackie and Pattullo, 1977; Evetts, 1994). These tend to be the specialisms where women's real or potential conflict between home and work can be reduced, and the areas that are less 'popular' with men – women tend to be concentrated in the same specialisms as immigrant doctors. It is also sometimes argued that women have the 'innate characteristics' necessary for such specialisms, but women's assumed 'married' destiny and assumed specialist knowledge do not lead to many women specialising in plastic or neurosurgery, nor in obstetrics, gynaecology or paediatrics (Young, 1981). Indeed the small percentage of obstetricians and gynaecologists who are women (12 per cent) has remained stable throughout the 1970s and 1980s (Montague, 1992).

It is often argued that the reason for women's lack of career prospects is their domestic commitments, because they take time out to have children, seek part-time work and are not 'really' committed to their work. It could, however, be argued that women are disadvantaged because the training and promotion are based on assumptions about continuous, full-time work, that part-time training is not provided in many medical specialisms and that candidates for promotion are expected to have had certain experiences by a certain age – difficult for a woman who has had a career-break or worked part-time for a period.

Isobel Allen (1988) found that from the point of entry to medical school through to hospital consultant posts, women doctors face sexist attitudes, have to compete within an 'old boy network' of patronage, are asked discriminating questions at interviews – for example, questions about childcare arrangements were asked of women some of whom did not even have children – and that they were frequently treated in less favourable ways just because they were women. Barbara Lawrence (1987), in a study of single-handed female general practitioners, found that they had decided to set up on their own to avoid being dominated by male partners. They had found that in mixed group practices they were paid less than their male colleagues and were expected to see the women and children. Young (1981) has suggested that sexism is built into the medical curriculum and that women are portrayed as inferior.

In contrast to the male-dominated professions, women form the majority in the 'female' semi-professions. Jobs such as nursing and teaching are seen as 'good jobs for women' because of the hours worked, the demands on interpersonal skills and the relatively steady employment prospects. However, these occupations lack the autonomy enjoyed by professionals and women in them are often dominated by men – nurses by (male) doctors and teachers by (male) headmasters. While the pay is relatively high in these occupations, compared with the pay of women in general, it is poor in comparison with the salaries enjoyed by those employed in the 'male' professions. In both nursing and teaching women are under-represented in the top grades when account is taken of the ratio of men to women in the occupation as a whole. In 1990 women made up 81 per cent of the primary and nursery teaching force, but only 48 per cent of teachers in secondary schools. In secondary schools women held just over 30 per cent of senior posts, but only 20 per cent of headships. Thirty-four per cent of deputy headships and 65 per cent of senior mistress/master posts were held by women; however, these posts often involve pastoral responsibilities which are assumed to be a 'feminine' skill (DES, 1990). In 1976 only 10 per cent of nurses were men, but men held 29 per cent of regional and district managerial posts. In hospital nursing, 10.7 per cent of the nursing force were men, but 25 per cent of nurses above the professional grade (staff nurse), and 72 per cent of male registered general nurses were in grades above staff nurse, compared with 47 per cent of female registered nurses. Men are promoted to the position of nursing officer more quickly than women; men on average take 8.4 years to reach this grade, and women 17.9 years (Hockey, 1995). Community nurses, who appear to enjoy more autonomy and are predominantly female, are likely, however, to be under the control of the general practitioner to whom they are attached (Maguire, 1980). (See Chapter 7 for further discussion of doctor/nurse relationships.)

Women are marginalised, then, in professional and managerial work as well as in skilled manual work. They occupy the lower-status, less well remunerated levels within all sectors of the labour market.

Women and unemployment

Traditionally, in sociology, unemployment has not been thought to pose a problem for women, or at least for the majority of married women. This is because it is argued that women's wages are marginal, not essential to the family, that women's main identity and status is derived from their role as wives and mothers, and that women can 'return' to their primary domestic role. Women's unemployment is also hidden – a high proportion of women seeking employment are not registered as unemployed – in the Martin and Roberts survey (1984), 50 per cent.

However, feminist research has challenged this view and has argued that work and work identities are central to many women's lives and that the money women earn is essential. Angela Coyle (1984), in a study of 76 redundant women, found that only three, two of whom were pregnant and one near retirement age, took the opportunity to stop work. All the others sought alternative employment – and found work that was less skilled, had poor working conditions and was less well paid than their previous posts. The women said that they worked because a male wage was inadequate for the needs of the household and because they valued the independence they gained from paid employment and having their own income. She concludes that paid work was seen as central to the lives of these women and that redundancy was viewed as an unwelcome interruption to their working lives.

Women and labour market segmentation

Feminists have pointed out that the labour market is segmented horizontally and vertically (see, e.g., Hakim, 1979; Abbott and Tyler, 1995). Women tend to be concentrated in lowly paid, low-status occupations and into work done only by women. Within each occupational stratum women also tend to be concentrated at the lower levels (Martin and Roberts 1984; Payne and Abbott 1990a; Siim 1987). Furthermore, the work that women do is less likely to be classified as skilled than the work men do (Phillips and Taylor 1980). The gender pay gap has not narrowed significantly in the last ten years; while some women have secured employment in the higher-paid professional employment categories, women are still over-represented in lowly paid jobs (see Table 8.7). The pay gap varies from country to country and from manual to non-manual work. It is on the whole wider for non-manual than manual work – probably reflecting women's concentration in routine non-manual (clerical and secretarial) work. In the UK and Italy, for example, female non-manual workers earn less than 60 per cent of the earnings of male ones,

TABLE 8.7 Female earnings as a percentage of male earnings across Europe, 1980/91

| | Manual workers | | Non-manual workers | |
	1980	1991	1980	1991
Belgium	70.2	75.6	61.9	65.2
Denmark	86.0	84.5	n/a	n/a
Germany	72.1	73.1	66.0	67.1
France	78.3	80.2	61.1	67.2
Greece	67.5	79.2	n/a	68.5
Ireland	68.7	69.5	n/a	n/a
Italy	83.2	79.3	n/a	n/a
Luxembourg	64.7	68.0	49.7	55.2
Netherlands	73.0	76.2	59.1	64.8
Spain	n/a	72.2	n/a	60.9
Portugal	n/a	70.8	n/a	70.7
UK	69.8	67.2	54.5	58.3

Source: derived from European Commission, 1994, p. 8.
Note: The '1991' figure is in fact from 1990 for Netherlands and Luxembourg, and 1989 from Italy; n/a indicates data not available.

whereas in Portugal they earn over 70 per cent of male non-manual earnings. In manual work, women in all EU countries earn over two-thirds of male earnings, the widest gap being in the UK, where women manual workers earn about 67 per cent of male earnings – compared with Denmark, where they earn 84.5 per cent.

In all community countries, irrespective of women's participation rate in paid employment, most women are concentrated in a narrow range of occupational sectors and in a small number of jobs. They have also made few inroads into the higher-level jobs; the possibilities for women of gaining access to top jobs remain very few. The growth in part-time employment reinforces job segregation; where part-time employment develops, women become confined to an even more limited range of jobs, especially in part-time service work, where jobs have often been created as 'women's work'.

In Britain in 1991 women made up 75.8 of all junior non-manual workers and 82 per cent of all personal service workers, whereas men constituted over 80 per cent of professional workers, foremen and supervisors, skilled manual workers, 'own account' manual workers, farmers and members of the armed forces. Only in routine non-manual and unskilled manual work did the proportion of women in the category exceed their proportion overall in the work force (44 per cent). Furthermore, 62.7 per cent of employed women are in routine non-manual work – see Table 8.8. (This pattern of labour market

TABLE 8.8 Labour market distribution by gender in the UK, 1991

Socio-economic Group	Men %	Women %	Percentages of total group	
Employers and managers				
Large establishments	6.1	3.1	71.4	28.6
Small establishments	12.7	7.4	68.7	31.3
Professional workers				
Self-employed	1.5	0.3	86.6	13.4
Employees	5.6	1.6	81.7	18.3
Other non-manual				
Intermediate	9.8	18.4	41.4	58.9
Junior	9.0	36.0	24.2	75.8
Personal services	1.4	8.3	18.0	82.0
Manual workers				
Foremen and supervisors	3.0	0.8	83.8	16.2
Skilled	20.0	2.6	90.9	9.1
Semi-skilled	11.3	9.2	61.1	38.9
Unskilled	3.9	7.1	41.1	58.9
Own account	9.1	2.8	80.5	19.5
Farming				
Employers and managers	0.6	0.1	85.8	14.2
Own account	0.7	0.2	86.4	13.6
Labourers	0.9	0.5	70.1	29.9
Armed forces	1.4	0.5	92.5	7.5

Source: derived from OPCS, 1993b, Table 92.

Note: Of those classified as 'in employment' in the original table, 1.0% of men and 0.8% of women were 'unclassifiable', and 1.6% of men and 1.2% of women were on government schemes. These are not shown in the table above but have been included in the total on which the percentages are based.

segmentation is similar across the European Union – see Abbott and Ackers, forthcoming.)

Patterns of labour market segmentation in Britain do vary for women by ethnic group, but within the overall pattern of the gendered and segmented labour market (see Abbott and Tyler, 1995). For example, 62.7 per cent of all employed women are in routine non-manual work, compared with 20.2 per cent of employed men (Table 8.8). When this is disaggregated by ethnic group (Table 8.9), it is evident that this concentration of women in routine non-manual work is common across ethnic groups. There is, however, some variation: for example, only 48.4 per cent of women of Indian origin are in routine non-manual work, compared with 67.4 per cent of Black Caribbean women.

TABLE 8.9 Women in routine non-manual work, by ethnic group

Ethnic group	% in routine non-manual work
White	63.6
Black (Caribbean)	67.4
Black (African)	63.1
Black (Other)	66.9
Indian	48.4
Pakistani	50.5
Bangladeshi	61.4
Chinese	57.2
Other Asian	65.6
Other	66.6

Source: OPCS, 1993a

Segmented labour markets mean, then, that women are concentrated in certain occupations (horizontal segmentation) and at a lower level within occupational strata (vertical segmentation). Despite the increasing population of women in the work force and of women with a life-long commitment to and expectation of an occupational career, women are much less likely to be upwardly mobile during their working lives than men (Abbott and Sapsford, 1987a; Payne and Abbott, 1990a; MacEwan Scott, 1994) – to be promoted, in other words. While there has been and continues to be an increase in the number of managerial and professional jobs available, and women have increased their proportion of the jobs in these categories, the numbers remain small. Crompton and Sanderson (1990) suggest that women are more likely to remain at their 'entry level', while men have linear careers. Furthermore, the Hansard Society Commission of Women at the Top (1990) documents how women were found in declining numbers at the top of the hierarchy in all the professions studied. This appears to be the case even in those professions where women predominate, and in some cases the proportion of women gaining promoted posts in these professions has even declined.

Overall, the evidence with respect to the opportunities for promotion for women is that women are less likely to be promoted than men and indeed are concentrated in jobs that are less likely to lead to high remuneration and promotion (Crompton and Sanderson; 1990; Evetts, 1994). Women, then, experience labour market segmentation and marginalisation even in professional and managerial jobs. Furthermore, when a professional occupation becomes seen as 'a female one', it declines in status – although men continue to dominate the senior posts.

Routine non-manual, service and manual occupations are more clearly and explicitly gendered than professional and managerial ones. Employers clearly have a view of what is appropriate work for women, and women generally share this view (Chaney, 1981; Yeandle, 1984; Beechey and Perkins, 1982). Many 'female' occupations are clearly regarded as using the 'natural' abilities women are seen as requiring in the private sphere: caring for young children, nursing, preparing and serving food, and in general securing the needs of others – 'emotional labour'. As with professional and managerial occupations, the movement of women into an area of employment tends to result in a decline in its status and relative remuneration. This process is clearly evident in the history of clerical work. It is not self-evident, however, that any less skill is involved now than was the case in the past, though the skills required may indeed be different ones. (This contrasts with the ways in which male printers have retained their high status and remuneration with the move from typesetting to computers – see Cockburn, 1983.)

Sexuality and women's employment

Small-scale studies of the everyday relations of work have given us a greater understanding of the relations of occupational segregation by sex. Male power and sexuality are evident in the workplace – sexual harassment, for example, is one way in which men subordinate and control women at work (Mackinnon, 1987; Stanko, 1988; Ramazanoglu, 1987). Indeed, men actively employ a number of tactics, including sexual harassment, to offer active resistance against moves towards sexual equality in organisations (Ramazanoglu, 1987; Cockburn, 1990).

Sexuality affects a woman's position in the labour market in a number of ways, from being judged by her looks when she applies for a job to experiencing sexual harassment when she is in it. Women are recruited, and have to dress and behave, in different ways from men in the same occupations (Tyler and Abbott, 1994). Examples of sexualised labour include the jobs of airline hostesses, restaurant and bar staff, and secretaries (Adkins, 1995). However, women are employed more generally as sexualised actors. Clara Greed (1994) points to a comment frequently made by the male surveyors she interviewed: 'attractive women make unattractive property more attractive'.

Studies of women and employment have identified three broad ways in which sexuality and gender can be theorised as impacting upon 'women's work': essentialisation, feminisation and sexualisation (Tyler and Abbott, 1994).

Essentialisation refers to the way in which female jobs are or come to be defined as requiring skills and abilities which women are deemed to possess by virtue of their biology. Occupations such as nursing, social work and primary-level (especially infant) teaching are perceived as requiring essential female qualities. Similarly, 'unskilled' work such as is delivered by care assistants, home helps, ward orderlies and waitresses is essentialised – seen as 'naturally' women's work.

Feminisation is the process by which jobs previously performed by men or by both men and women have come to be seen as essentially women's jobs (Adkins and Lury, 1992). This process of feminisation can be related to the redefinition of whole sectors of work as 'women's work'. Davies (1979), exploring how and why clerical work became feminised, argues that it has come to be perceived in terms of gendered attributes which are learned and shared by women, such as the ability to 'organise', for example.

The third process, *sexualisation*, may be perceived as the outcome of the cumulative impact of essentialisation and feminisation, so that what constitutes 'women's work' has come in some cases to be defined both in terms of biological sex and of gendered social identity. Indeed, what is purchased by employers from female workers and sold to male customers is sexuality (Tyler and Abbott, 1994). Furthermore, emotional labour – managing one's own and others' emotional needs – becomes sexual labour when it is commodified and sold within a gendered, commercial labour market – when women provide services for male customers (Hochschild, 1983) and have to work 'sexually' (Adkins, 1992).

Feminist workplace studies have enabled us to understand the gendered experiences of women and the ways in which women at work are subordinated. Studies undertaken in the 1970s, mainly influenced by socialist feminist perspectives, examined gender divisions within the capitalist workplace and class relationships in capitalist society (e.g. Pollert, 1981; Cavendish, 1982). Subsequently, studies within the same theoretical perspective were concerned to understand the ways in which women's experiences within the workplace were structured by class, gender and race (e.g. Westwood, 1984). More recently, feminist studies of the workplace have been undertaken from a radical feminist perspective and have been concerned to examine sexuality and male power (e.g. Pringle, 1989; Adkins, 1992, 1995). These studies have been concerned to understand the ways in which the deployment of sexuality is used by men to control women in the office, in the community and on the factory floor (e.g. Ramazanoglu, 1987; Hearn and Parkin, 1988) as well as the ways in which women's sexuality is commodified (Pringle, 1989; Adkins, 1992, 1995; Tyler and Abbott, 1994).

These more recent workplace studies have demonstrated the ways in which men use sexuality to control women in the workplace as well as in the domestic sphere. In the labour market women are judged by their looks, are employed to deploy their sexuality both in providing services and in selling goods, and are controlled by sexual harassment in the workplace. While socialist feminists have argued that sexual relations are determined by the unequal power relations between men and women, radical feminists argue that they do not just reflect but also determine the inequality of power relations. Boys are socialised to see heterosexuality as an integral aspect of being masculine, of being 'a real man' with all its associated privileges, status and rewards. They are socialised to believe that men have sexual access to women as of right and to see women's bodies as sexualised. Thus women's bodies are objectified (through pornography and advertising), defined as 'other' and as accessible for men. Conversely, girls are socialised to see women as providing service and pleasure for men in the private and public spheres; they are socialised into service roles and to service men.

However, female labour market participation and labour market segmentation, as well as women's experiences of paid employment, systematically correlate with both supply and demand factors as well as with family and sexual ideologies: with the search for profit in the capitalist mode of production and the power of men to exclude women and define 'skill' (see Beechey, 1987; Walby, 1986). In order to understand women's position in the labour market and their experiences of paid employment, we need to understand the ways in which patriarchy and capitalism articulate together to subordinate and exploit women. Put simply, patriarchy is concerned that women shall be subordinated to and serve the needs of men, including their sexual needs, and capitalism with securing a flexible, cheap labour force. It is in patriarchy's interests to keep women in the domestic sphere, and in capitalism's to employ them in the labour force. According to Walby (1990), there has been a move in Britain away from the 'private patriarchy' of the nineteenth century – the non-admission of women to the public sphere – to a public patriarchy in the twentieth where women are not excluded from the public sphere but disadvantaged in it. In terms of employment this has meant a move from strategies designed to exclude women from paid employment to segregationist and subordinating strategies. Women are exploited and dominated by men in both the private sphere (as wives, mothers, daughters) and in the public sphere, as well as meeting the needs of capitalism for a cheap, flexible labour force. The relationship between capitalism and patriarchy is dynamic and changing, and it impacts differentially on different groups. In the nineteenth century it was mainly middle-class women who were excluded from paid employment, while in the late twentieth century British Afro-Caribbean women are most likely to experience public patriarchy and Muslim British women private patriarchy. Patriarchy and capitalism have competing interests but reach accommodations; thus men (as husbands) clearly benefit from the additional income generated by their wives' paid employment – especially as research suggests that women retain the major responsibility for childcare and domestic labour. Conversely, employers have been able to 'create' jobs that use the assumed 'essential' skills of women, justifying low wages. Men benefit from the servicing and emotional labour women provide in the public sphere as well as enjoying and controlling women's sexuality. Employers are able to sell goods and services by exploiting women's sexuality, and potentially disruptive men are controlled by women's sexualised servicing.

Conclusions

Thus although Victorian feminists fought for the right for middle-class women to work, on the assumption that work would lead to liberation, and many latter-day marxists – including those in the Soviet Union – have done the same, we can see that work is not necessarily a source of liberation for women. The work that women do merely reinforces their traditional roles within the family. We can also see how important it is for sociology to be aware of women's work as well as men's; some of what has been described here is very much at variance with the traditional 'sociology of work'.

SUMMARY

1   When women are in paid work they do different jobs from men.

2   Jobs that women do receive less pay and are of lower status than men's jobs.

3   'Skill' is used as a way of justifying differences between men's and women's jobs. However, feminists argue that skill is an idea constructed by male workers.

4   Women experience work in different ways from men because of their different relationship to the labour market.

5   Feminists argue that malestream sociology has 'naturalised' the real work that women do in the domestic sphere – made it seem the exercise of a natural function rather than the performance of real work.

FURTHER READING

Dex, S. (1985) *The Sexual Division of Work*, Brighton: Wheatsheaf.

Walby, S. (1986) *Patriarchy at Work*, Cambridge: Polity.

Westwood, S. (1984) *All Day Every Day: factory and family in the making of women's lives*, London: Pluto Press.

Chapter nine

Women, crime and deviance

Explaining crime – women as criminals

We are all concerned to explain or make sense of criminal behaviour – to make sense of actions that appear to us as unnatural or strange. Of course, some behaviours may seem more problematic than others: for example, we may find it relatively easy to understand why a lone-parent mother on supplementary benefit stole food from the local supermarket, but much more difficult to understand why our next-door neighbour beat his wife. When we try to explain the criminal behaviour, we tend nonetheless to use a few single-factor motivational or trait categories – sickness, jealousy, hate, greed, over-permissiveness and lack of social (especially parental) control. We tend to assume that the behaviour can be explained by characteristics of the individual or her life experiences. Sociologists and other criminologists tend to argue that lay explanations or common-sense theories are simplistic and inadequate. Despite this, there are close parallels between common-sense and social science explanations.

Much crime seems to us inexplicable; we cannot understand how any human being could have committed it. We hear the details of the behaviour with incredulity and see the perpetrator as less than human, as an animal. Theories of crime that see criminal behaviour as innate (genetic/biological) were developed at the end of the nineteenth century by the Italian criminologist Lombroso and other degeneration theorists. Criminal conduct was seen as caused by biological or physiological characteristics of the individual. The biological factors were said to project the individual into a life of crime. Lombroso argued that criminals were atavistic – that is, genetic throwbacks to an earlier form of man (*sic*). While Lombrosian theories of crime are no longer given wide credence, biological theories continue to have some influence. The psychologist Hans Eysenck (1971), for example, argues that extraverts are more likely to commit crime than other types for ultimately biological reasons – differences in neural organisation with behavioural consequences – and Katarina Dalton (1961) has suggested that some female crime can be explained by hormonal changes during the menstrual cycle (pre-menstrual tension).

Another way in which we try to account for what appears to be totally incomprehensible behaviour is by seeing the perpetrator as mentally sick and suggesting that he or she is mad and therefore not responsible for his or her actions. Some criminological theories have suggested that criminal behaviour is caused by serious mental pathology or at least is the result of some emotional disturbance. These types of explanation have been especially prevalent in explaining female criminality, and we discuss them more fully below. Here we shall note only that while it must be acknowledged that some lawbreakers may suffer from mental disturbance, the same can be said of many non-offenders.

A further way in which criminal behaviour is explained is by suggesting that it is a result of the social conditions in which the offender lives or of life experiences of individuals. Two sets of explanations are frequently encountered: those that 'blame' the socialisation of the individual and the family, and those that see the immediate 'bad' social environment as the cause. Thus wife-beating is frequently explained by reference to the socialisation of the offender in a home in which he either saw his mother beaten or was beaten himself. Child abuse is sometimes similarly explained, or sometimes explained by reference to the current living conditions of the family – for example, living in poverty in one room.

In the 1960s some sociologists began to challenge the idea that it was possible to establish the causes of social behaviour in the same way that it was possible to establish causes in the natural sciences, as the theories described above have done. The positivistic mode of analysis had argued that it was possible to discover the causes of criminal behaviour in the same way that it is possible to establish laws in physics, and that it was possible to be value-free and objective about the social world (see Chapter 11). The new criminologists, as they became known, argued that in the guise of value-freedom sociologists had studied things from the perspective of those with power in society and had ignored the perspectives of the powerless. Furthermore they pointed out that by paying attention to violations of law criminology had ignored the legal system and devalued the place of human consciousness and the meaning that criminal activities had for those engaged in them.

The new criminologists were concerned to examine the relationship between law and crime, the purpose and function of the legal system and the relatively autonomous role of individual meaning, choice and volition. Labelling theorists suggested that if criminals do differ from non-criminals in social characteristics, this is not the cause of their law-breaking but because these very characteristics are used by society to label some people as criminal and ignore others. Maureen Cain (1973) and Steven Box (1971), for example, suggest that the police are more likely to suspect and arrest a working-class man than a middle-class one. Furthermore, it was suggested that the only way that criminals differed from non-criminals was that the former had been involved in the criminal justice system. Sociologists, then, became concerned to identify the key mechanisms by which crime is socially constructed through law creation, law enforcement and societal reaction.

More recently some sociologists, from what is called a left realist position (see, for example, Matthews and Young, 1986), have argued that the new criminology was idealistic and romanticised the criminal. They point out that the people who suffer most from criminal acts are working-class people. We can also add that the new criminology, like most of the old, neglected women and crime. Women are relatively powerless, yet these sociologists rarely considered them. Furthermore, women frequently are the victims of abuse from men, both in the domestic sphere and in public. While the new deviancy theorists were challenging the view that is is possible to establish the causes of men's lawbreaking, their failure to include women in their analysis meant that biological and pathological explanations continued to be accepted as explaining female lawbreaking.

Women and crime – the evidence

One of the reasons that 'women and crime' has been a neglected area in sociology is that women appear to be remarkably non-criminal. With the possible exceptions of shoplifters and prostitutes, women convicted of crime are seen as exceptions and extreme deviants both from the law and from femininity – that is, acceptable female behaviour. This is probably, at least in part, because so few women compared with men are convicted of crimes, but it also relates to what is seen as acceptable behaviour from women as compared with men. Much male deviance is associated with what it means to be 'a man' – theft using force, fighting in gangs, football violence, and so on.

The Home Office's annual statistics on crime provide information on convictions for criminal offences. These are broken down by age, sex and type of offence but not by social class or ethnicity. We can ask three questions of the statistics which will enable us to begin to determine whether women are less criminal than men and how female criminality differs from male:

1   are there differences in the amount of crime committed by men and women;
2   are there differences in the kinds of crime committed by men and women; and
3   are there any recent changes in the amount or kind of crime committed by men and women?

The crime statistics for England and Wales for 1993 (Home Office, 1994; CSO, 1995) suggest that women are considerably less criminal than men, and this appears to be as true for the more serious (indictable) offences as for the less serious (summary) ones – see CSO (1995), Figure 9.15. (Indictable offences are those for which an offender has the right to have, or must have, a trial before a jury in a Crown Court; summary offences are triable only in a Magistrate's Court.) Table 9.1 shows that in 1993 87.7 per cent of those convicted of indictable offences were men, and 12.3 per cent were women; the proportion of women would be a little higher if we included cautions as well as convictions, as women are more likely than men to be cautioned rather than prosecuted, but men would still form the vast majority. There are some age differences: boys and young men are even more likely to have been convicted of an indictable offence than girls and young women. Women and girls are more likely than boys and men to receive only a caution if apprehended by the police, but the difference is only slight in the youngest age group.

Women are convicted of all categories of crime, but men commit a far higher number of crimes in all categories (Table 9.2). There are only two categories of crime, 'Theft and handling stolen goods' and 'Fraud and forgery', where less than 90 per cent of those convicted were men. Theft and handling stolen goods is the offence for which both men and women had the highest conviction rates. However, the category accounted for 58 per cent of all females convicted and only 37 per cent of all men convicted; 82 per cent of the people convicted in this category were men and 18 per cent women. Furthermore, Table 9.3 shows that women are mainly convicted of shoplifting in this category – 64 per cent of all women convicted of theft or handling stolen goods were convicted of shoplifting, compared with 26 per cent of men. Even in this category far more men are convicted of shoplifting than women, however – 46,018 men compared with 29,189 women. (The figures are for 1986.)

TABLE 9.1 Persons sentenced or cautioned for indictable offences in 1993, by sex and age, in England and Wales

Age	Offences no. (000)			Percentage cautioned		Percentage sentenced	
	Male	Female	Total	Male	Female	Male	Female
10 and under 14	22.2	7.7	29.9	90	97	90.6	9.4
14 and under 17	78.0	21.6	99.6	62	84	89.6	10.4
17 and under 21	77.3	13.0	90.3	32	52	89.4	10.6
21+ years	243.7	51.3	295.0	25	46	86.9	13.2
Total	421.2	93.6	514.8			87.7	12.3

Source: Home Office, 1994, Table 7.4.

TABLE 9.2 Offenders found guilty of indictable offences at all courts in England and Wales in 1993, by type of offence – percentages by gender

Offence	Males		Females	
	No. (000)	%	No. (000)	%
Violence against the person	35.5	91.3	3.4	8.7
Sexual offences	4.3	97.7	0.1	2.3
Burglary	39.2	97.5	1.0	2.5
Robbery	4.8	94.1	0.3	5.9
Theft and handling stolen goods	99.5	81.8	22.1	18.2
Fraud and forgery	13.6	77.7	3.9	22.3
Criminal damage	8.6	91.5	0.8	8.5
Drug offences	19.9	90.9	2.0	9.1
Other (excluding motoring)	34.2	90.5	3.6	9.5
Motoring offences	10.3	95.4	0.5	4.6
Total	269.8	87.7	37.8	12.3

Source: Home Office, 1994, Table 5.9.

The statistics on sentencing also suggest that there are differences in the types of crime committed by men and women. Adult women (aged 21+) are more likely to be given a caution by the police than men – 46 per cent of all persons sentenced or cautioned in 1993, compared with 25 per cent – or if brought to court then given a conditional discharge – 18 per cent of women compared with 14 per cent of men – or a probation order – 9 per cent of women compared with 7 per cent of men. Men were more likely to be fined

TABLE 9.3 Offenders found guilty of theft offences in all courts in England and Wales in 1986, by sex and type of offence

Offence type	Males		Females	
	No. (000)	%	No. (000)	%
Theft from the person	1.9	1	0.4	1
Theft in a dwelling	2.5	1	0.7	2
Theft by an employee	5.8	3	1.5	3
Theft from mail	0.2	0.1	<0.1	0.1
Abstracting electricity	2.6	2	1.0	2
Theft of pedal cycle	3.3	2	0.1	0.2
Theft from vehicle	11.6	7	0.2	0.4
Theft from shops	46.0	26	29.2	64
Theft from meter, etc.	5.2	3	1.3	3
Theft of motor vehicle	28.8	16	0.7	2
Other theft	48.5	27	6.5	14
Handling stolen goods	22.9	13	3.9	9

Source: Home Office, 1987, Table 5.1.

than women – 28 per cent compared with 17 per cent – and more likely to receive a community service order – 8 per cent compared with 3 per cent – or a prison sentence, immediate or suspended – 13 per cent compared with 4 per cent (Home Office, 1994, Table 7.5). Men were also likely to receive longer prison sentences than women.

The official statistics on convictions suggest that women are far less criminal than men and that while women do commit all crimes, the majority of women convicted of a crime are found in the one category – theft and handling stolen goods. It also seems that women, on the whole, commit less serious crimes than men.

The final question concerns changes in women's behaviour – has the number of women convicted of criminal offences changed in recent years, and how does this compare with men? Numbers convicted fluctuate from year to year, and trends are therefore difficult to determine. However, between 1977 and 1986 the number of women found guilty of crime in England and Wales increased steadily from 207 thousands in 1977 to 277 thousands in 1986 but has since declined to about 251 thousands in 1993 (Home Office, 1994, Table 5.8). During the same period there has been a decline in the number of men convicted – from 1,744 thousands in 1977 to 1,617 thousands in 1986 (with a high point of 1,842 thousands in 1982) to 1,174 thousands in 1993. However, if we look just at indictable offences (a rough indication of the incidence of more serious offending) a different pattern emerges. Here the number of women convicted has declined from 68 thousands in 1977 to 50 thousands in

1986 and some 38 thousands in 1993; the major increases have been in summary offences. Conversely, for men we find that from 1977 to 1986 there was an increase in the number convicted of indictable offences from 358 thousands to 385 thousands in 1985 (but this has since declined to 270 thousands in 1993), while there was an overall decrease in the number of men convicted of summary offences (see Table 9.4). The official statistics on conviction rates do not suggest that there has been a large increase in female criminality in recent years. They do suggest that, to the extent that there has been an increase, it has been in the more trivial offences.

A major problem with the official statistics on convictions is that they tell us only the numbers arrested and convicted for crimes. There is a large amount of unsolved crime, and we know nothing about those who perpetrate it. In 1986, for example, 3,847 thousand crimes were recorded by the police, while there were only 1,895 thousand convictions. Much of the crime recorded by the police is never 'cleared up' – that is, no one is ever convicted of it. Furthermore, self-report and victim surveys suggest that there is a large amount of crime that is never reported to the police. The problem is that we do not know the size or distribution of this hidden crime. Known crime is like the top of an iceberg, that which is visible; research suggests that some crimes, visible ones, are more likely to be reported to and recorded by the police than hidden crimes, those that take place in private. A mugging is much more likely to be reported than an assault on a wife, for example. The police and public are more likely to suspect some people of crimes than others – working-class men and ethnic minority men are more likely to be suspected and arrested than middle-class white men (Box, 1971; Chapman, 1968). The crime statistics do not, then, represent the 'real' amount of crime, nor are those convicted of crime necessarily representative of all lawbreakers.

We can ask, then, if the differences between the conviction rates of men and women represent a 'real' difference in the lawbreaking of men and women, or just reflect the fact that women are better at hiding their crimes and less likely to be suspected of crimes – that is, that they do not fit the stereotype of the criminal. Pollack (1950) argued that women were not less criminal than men. He argued that women were naturally good at concealing their actions and naturally secretive because they had to hide the fact of menstruation. Women commit large amounts of crime that remain hidden, he argued, especially child abuse and murder of spouses. However, even if this were the case it seems unlikely that the amount would be sufficient to increase women's incidence of lawbreaking to that of men, especially as there is also hidden male crime, for example male middle-class crime, wife abuse and other domestic crimes. Self-report studies suggest that women are indeed less criminal than men. Mawby (1980), for instance, found that both young men and young women in Sheffield admitted to more crime than would seem to be

TABLE 9.4 Offenders found guilty at all courts in England and Wales, by sex and type of offence, 1977/93

	1977	1979	1981	1982	1983	1985	1986	1987	1989	1991	1993
MALES (Figures are numbers of offences, in **tens of thousands**)											
Violence	3.9	4.5	4.7	4.8	4.7	4.4	4.0	4.4	5.1	4.3	3.6
Sexual offences	0.7	0.7	0.7	0.7	0.6	0.6	0.5	0.6	0.7	0.6	0.4
Burglary	6.8	5.7	7.4	7.4	6.7	6.4	5.5	5.3	4.2	4.5	3.9
Robbery	0.3	0.3	0.4	0.4	0.4	0.4	0.4	0.4	0.4	0.5	0.5
Theft and handling	18.0	17.5	18.4	19.0	18.0	17.4	14.8	14.4	10.8	10.8	10.0
Fraud and forgery	1.6	1.6	2.0	2.0	2.0	2.0	1.8	1.8	1.8	1.7	1.4
Criminal damage	0.8	0.9	1.1	1.1	1.1	1.1	0.9	1.0	0.9	0.9	0.9
Drugs	*	*	1.3	1.5	1.6	1.7	1.5	1.5	2.0	2.2	2.0
Other (excl. motoring)	1.4	1.4	1.2	1.3	1.6	1.7	1.3	1.7	2.6	3.2	3.6
Motoring	2.3	2.0	2.7	2.9	2.9	2.8	2.7	2.8	1.1	1.1	1.0
Total indictable	35.8	35.1	39.9	40.9	39.8	38.5	33.4	33.9	30.0	29.6	27.0
Total summary	138.6	131.8	146.6	138.7	144.4	127.8	128.3	99.3	101.6	97.4	90.4
All offences	174.4	167.0	186.4	179.6	184.2	166.2	161.7	133.2	131.0	126.9	117.4
FEMALES (Figures are numbers of offences, in **thousands**)											
Violence	3.5	3.5	4.0	4.1	4.0	3.6	3.3	3.4	4.4	3.9	3.4
Sexual offences	<0.1	0.1	0.1	0.1	0.1	0.1	0.1	0.1	0.1	0.1	0.1
Burglary	2.4	2.6	2.6	2.6	2.4	2.2	1.7	1.6	1.3	1.4	1.0
Robbery	0.2	0.2	0.2	0.2	0.2	0.2	0.2	0.2	0.2	0.3	0.3
Theft and handling	54.0	51.7	48.2	49.0	45.3	42.2	34.9	32.1	26.6	25.5	22.1
Fraud and forgery	4.5	4.4	5.5	5.2	5.5	5.4	4.8	4.9	4.7	4.5	3.9
Criminal damage	0.6	0.7	0.8	0.8	0.8	0.8	0.7	0.7	0.7	0.9	0.8
Drugs	*	*	1.9	2.0	2.1	2.3	2.2	2.2	2.4	2.1	2.0
Other (excl. motoring)	1.7	1.7	1.3	1.2	1.3	1.1	1.2	1.3	2.1	2.8	3.6
Motoring	0.8	0.7	0.9	1.0	1.0	0.9	0.9	0.9	0.4	0.5	0.5
Total indictable	67.7	65.5	65.5	66.1	62.7	59.0	50.0	47.5	43.0	41.9	37.8
Total summary	139.7	144.0	175.6	169.4	190.4	189.3	227.4	175.2	179.2	194.1	213.3
All offences	207.4	209.5	241.0	235.5	248.4	248.4	277.4	222.7	222.2	236.0	251.1

Source: Home Office, 1987, 1994, Table 5.8.
Note: *: figures not available.

indicated by the official statistics, but that the ratio of male to female crime seemed about right. Feminists conclude that on balance the available evidence does indicate that women commit less, and less serious, crime than men. Also, while there was a period when it was true that more women became involved in crime, this seems to have been mainly petty crime, and male crime also increased during the same period (Box and Hale, 1983). Thus there is no evidence to support the claim that as women become more liberated they increasingly develop the same patterns of criminality as men.

The need for feminist theory

Feminists have suggested that to understand the issues surrounding women and crime two key questions need to be considered:

1   why do so few women commit crimes; and
2   why do those women who commit the crimes do so?

They suggest that malestream theories have either failed to tackle these questions or provided inadequate answers.

Thus psycho-positivistic (biological/psychological) theories of female criminality have stereotyped women and do not provide an adequate explanation. However, they continue to hold a dominant place in the explanation of female crime long after they have been seriously challenged as adequate explanations for male criminality. Thus Hilary Allen (1987) has argued that women accused of serious violent crimes are much more likely than men charged with comparable crimes to be portrayed in court reports as suffering from psychological problems that suggest they are not responsible for their actions. Furthermore, women are more likely to be found insane or of diminished responsibility and, if convicted, more likely to be given psychiatric treatment in place of a penal sentence than is a man. Another example is premenstrual tension (PMT): women have successfully defended themselves against criminal charges by pleading diminished responsibility on the grounds that they were suffering from PMT at the time they committed the crime. The success of these pleas, feminists argue, depends not only on the evidence of expert witnesses, but also on the courts' preparedness to believe this evidence because it fits their stereotype of female criminals. This stereotype has itself been informed, at least in part, by psycho-positivistic theories of crime, theories which argue that female lawbreakers are either biologically different from those who do not break the law or that they are out of their minds – mentally ill – and therefore not responsible for their actions.

Sociological theories, on the other hand, have with few exceptions ignored women. They have not seen gender as an important explanatory variable and have assumed that theories based on male samples and a male view of the world can be generalised to women. In some cases they have implicitly or explicitly accepted biological theories, as for example Durkheim (1897) did in his study of suicide, when he agreed that women were less likely to commit suicide than men because they were biologically at a lower stage of development than men and therefore less influenced by the social forces that resulted in people committing suicide. Even major critics of conventional criminology have failed to raise the issue of women and crime (e.g. Taylor, Walton and Young, 1975).

Feminist theories of crime

Feminists have argued that a paradigm shift is essential so that gender can be seen as an important explanatory variable in explaining why some women are lawbreakers; women have their experiences mediated by gender and class relationships. They are also agreed that patriarchal relationships, ideologies of femininity and women's assigned role in the family all play key roles (see Chapter 6). While the individual must be seen as free to shape her own actions, destiny and consciousness, this happens in an economic, ideological and political environment which she does not control (see Chapters 1 and 8). Furthermore, it is recognised that empirical studies of women who have engaged in lawbreaking are essential so that it is possible to determine under what circumstances women do break the law. An analysis which makes connections between women's lawbreaking and how women are handled in the criminal justice system is also essential. Finally, while the double control of women in the class and gender system may explain why most women do not break the law, theories need to be developed that explain why some women do break it.

The ideology of femininity constructs girls and women in a particular way. The natural role for women is seen as that of a wife and mother. Girls and women are seen as needing protection and care. Consequently, young girls tend to be controlled more than their brothers and given less freedom. Of especial concern is the protection of girls' virginity. While boys are expected to 'sow wild oats', girls are expected to remain virgin until they marry – or at least to have a 'steady' relationship. While young men who come before the courts and are handled in the juvenile justice system have generally committed criminal offences, girls are more likely to come before the courts for being in need of care and protection, including from their own promiscuity – what are referred to as 'status offences', coming within the ambit of the law only because of the age of the 'offender'. This seems to remain true even when the girls have in fact committed criminal offences (Shaklady Smith, 1978).

This alerts us to the important fact that the boundary between normality and abnormality is elastic – that is, what is seen as normal for men may be seen as abnormal for women, not to mention class and ethnic variations as well. Crime and deviance are not immutable but historically and culturally variable. Whether or not behaviour is seen as criminal/deviant depends both on the context and on the individual doing the behaviour. The stereotype of the criminal as male, and of female criminals as being psychologically inadequate, influences not only sociological theories, but also the people involved in the administration of the criminal justice system on the one hand and our common-sense view of the nature of women on the other.

However, studies of women who have been convicted of criminal offences and who have been imprisoned (e.g. Dobash *et al.*, 1986; Carlen, 1983; Carlen *et al.*, 1985, Mandaraka-Sheppard, 1986) have confirmed the main feminist criticisms of traditional criminology. Four major characteristics of female offenders have been highlighted:

1   that women who engage in property crime are motivated by economic factors – that is, they steal because they need or want the goods they steal;
2   that women commit all types of offences;
3   that women do fear and feel the impact of the stigma of the 'criminal' label; and
4   that women are seen as doubly deviant – deviant for breaking social rules, and also 'unfeminine' and 'unnatural' because they have offended against rules of feminine behaviour.

Feminists argue that what is necessary is eventually to develop theories that are adequate for explaining and understanding the lawbreaking of both men and women. This does not mean that feminists are looking for a universal theory that will explain all criminal behaviour in all circumstances. There is no reason to assume that all criminal behaviour can be explained in the same way. What is necessary is theories of crime that take account of gender, ethnic and class divisions and studies that are situated in the wider moral, political, economic and sexual spheres which influence women's and men's status and position in society. However, as Carol Smart (1976) argues, initially it will be necessary to carry out research on women, in order to make women visible and to find alternative ways of conceptualising the social world so that the interests and concerns of women are adduced and included rather than subsumed or ignored.

However, some feminists have argued that existing theories of crime can be developed to the point where they account adequately for women. There is no reason, they suggest, why explanations for female crime should be different from those for male crime. Morris (1987), for example, argues that Disorganisation Theory and Differential Association can both be extended to account for female crime. Leonard (1978) has suggested that a reformulated Labelling Theory with elements of critical theory can be developed, and Shaklady Smith (1978) has used labelling theory to explain female juvenile delinquency.

Disorganisation theory

Cloward and Ohlin (1961) argued that crime occurs because not everyone is able to achieve the accepted goal of society (economic success) by the legitimate means (hard work), especially via the gaining of educational qualifications. Cloward and Ohlin suggested that crime happens because, just when working-class adolescents have been encouraged to adopt a set of economic and material aspirations of which the larger society approves, the means of achieving these goals is locked off from them – that is, they do not gain the necessary qualifications to embark on a career that will enable them to achieve economic success by legitimate means. In reaction to this, adolescents most at risk of becoming criminals develop an alternative authority to that of the state – the delinquent gang.

Given that women experience unequal opportunities even more than men, then this would seem to be a possible explanation for female crime. Indeed, given that opportunities are more restricted for women than for men, we might expect women to exhibit a higher rate of crime than men. The fact that they do not can be explained, however, by their limited access to illegitimate opportunities.

There are major problems with this theory, however. It assumes that there is universal agreement on societal goals and accepted means of achieving them, and that crime is committed mainly by working-class men and women. While it is recognised that there may be differential access to the goals, based on gender as well as class, it fails to recognise differential access to the means. More important, however, it fails to take account of the key fact that social goals are different for men and women. Girls are socialised into a world that sees marriage, child care and domesticity as the main goal. Indeed, girls who reject the societal view of appropriate feminine behaviour and who consequently endanger their chances of achieving these goals are seen as deviant (Lees, 1986).

Differential association

Sutherland (see Sutherland and Cressey, 1966) developed Differential Association as a theory of crime as a result of his criticisms of sociological theories of crime which regarded crime as a male working-class phenomenon. He argued that the official statistics under-represented middle-class criminals because their crimes were often dealt with by the civil rather than the criminal courts – or out of court altogether, by the 'private justice' of employers, clubs and private institutions. Sutherland argued that criminal behaviour was a result not of poverty or inadequate socialisation, but of the people with whom one associates. Behaviours, values and justifications were picked up by association with others. Sutherland argued that people who committed crime have more contact with those who condoned criminal behaviour than with those who opposed it. He also suggested that this approach applied equally to women and men. However, his theory fails to explain why brothers and not sisters become criminals, why the wives of criminal men do not become criminals, and so on.

Critical (marxist) criminology

Critical criminology has sought to understand the basis of social inequality and power relationships within capitalist societies. It has explored the class dimension of crime and has illustrated the ways in which the criminal law is selectively enforced against the powerless. However, women are not easily accommodated within these accounts, as women are relatively powerless in capitalist societies and also rarely commit crime. Thus despite the relatively subordinate social and economic position of women and their exploitation and domination by men, women appear in the crime statistics much less frequently than men.

Leonard (1978) and Gregory (1986) have argued that marxist theory needs to be reformulated so that the considerable impact of gender as well as class position on crime is taken into account. What is needed, they suggest, is a 'dual-systems' theory (see Chapter 2) that can understand women and crime adequately. A theory is needed that enables us to understand why women are relatively uninvolved in crime and what structural factors influence the particular pattern of the crimes in which women do participate. It is necessary to understand the way that legitimate and illegitimate means to socially valued goals are different for women than for men and how women's associates affect them as compared with men's. It is necessary to take into account the ways in which the distribution of wealth and power affect women in capitalist societies and how this influences their criminality. It is necessary to consider why women who are relatively powerless are nonetheless infrequently labelled criminal. Finally, it is necessary to consider what role women play in a class society, the difference in the oppression of working-class women and working-class men, and the way in which women are controlled and handled in the legal system and in society generally.

Using a dual-systems perspective, Dee Cook (1987) has studied women who committed fraud against the supplementary benefit system. She argues that the majority of women claiming supplementary benefit are single-parent mothers. They are seen as deviant because they are not living in families that conform to ideas of a normal family in capitalist societies (see Chapter 6). The major reason for these women fiddling supplementary benefit, she argues, is economic necessity. When they are caught for fiddling they provoke a negative reaction because of their deviant personal status as well as because of their criminal acts. Social security fiddling for women is seen within a framework that takes into account their class situation and patriarchal ideology.

Labelling theory

Leonard (1978) has argued that labelling theory is potentially valuable for understanding female crime. Using labelling theory it is possible to look at the inherent bias in the law, its relativity, and the different ways in which it is enforced. Within such a framework it would also be possible to examine social reaction to female criminals and how this influenced their self definitions.

Labelling theory developed in the 1960s as one response to positivistic criminology. It was argued that crime was caused by a number of factors, that it was impossible to obtain a representative sample of people who commit crimes from which to generalise, and that deviancy theorists should concentrate on studying societal reaction to crimes and criminals and how labelling as an outsider resulted in changes in self identity. Labelling theorists also argued that crime and deviance were relative and not universal categories. Finally, they rejected the view that value-free research was possible in the social sciences and argued that it was important to look at things from the perspective of the underdog.

Labelling theorists have been criticised for ignoring female deviance and crime. Milkman (1976) has suggested that while labelling theorists presented sympathetic accounts of male deviants, they failed to do so for female ones. She points out that labelling theorists portrayed prostitutes, for example, in a stereotypical way and through the eyes of ponces and pimps rather than through their own self-perceptions.

However, labelling theory has been used by feminists carrying out research on young people. Sue Lees, in her study of teenage girls (1986), has argued that the ways in which young men and young women label young women act as a powerful mechanism of social control (see Chapter 4). Shaklady Smith (1978), in a small ethnographic study of teenage girls, argues that labelling theory can be used to understand the pattern of female delinquent activities. Using open-ended interviews she studied three groups of young women in the Bristol area in 1970 – thirty girls on probation orders, fifteen girl members of gangs and thirty girls who had never been referred to any agency dealing with juvenile delinquency, as similar as possible to the first group. She found that girls committed all the kinds of offences with which young men but not girls are usually associated; for example, 63 per cent of the probation group and 73 per cent of the gang sample had deliberately damaged property (see Table 9.5). An analysis of the responses of the gang and probation samples demonstrated that many of them had committed most of the offences for which male juveniles are usually taken to the courts. However, an analysis of court records suggests that girls are much more likely to be brought before the court as in need of care and protection than as charged with offences, but if charged more likely to be given a custodial sentence.

Her data also suggest that girls tend either to be conformist or very delinquent. Girl delinquents were labelled, she argues, by parents, teachers and non-delinquent girls alike as unfeminine and to be disapproved. However, the labelling of them by others as unfeminine did not result in further status loss, nor did they become promiscuous. Rather, they responded with aggressive behaviour and remained popular among their peers. Nonetheless

TABLE 9.5 Self-report of delinquent acts and offences committed by girls in research by Shaklady Smith

Type of offence	Control sample	Probation sample	Gang sample
Total numbers:	30	30	15
	%	%	%
Skipped school	63.3	90.0	93.3
Shoplifting	36.7	90.0	80.0
Breaking and entering	10.0	33.3	26.7
In car without owner's permission	16.7	60.0	60.0
Deliberate property damage	26.7	66.7	73.3
Running away from home	3.3	76.0	53.3
Sex under age of consent	13.3	70.0	73.3
Taken drugs	3.3	10.0	33.2
Taken part in a fight	23.3	63.3	73.3

Source: Shaklady Smith, 1978.

they did suffer a double rejection; they were rejected both on account of their violation of the law and because they rejected femininity. The girls saw themselves as tough, dominant and tomboyish.

Once labelled, these girls became isolated from their normal peers; parents of non-delinquent girl forbade their daughters to mix with the girl juvenile delinquents. The girls became more and more dependent on the delinquent group:

> social definitions of female delinquency lead not so much to a total rejection of femininity in that a male role is aspired to, as a rejection of certain elements of the culturally stereotyped female role which is perceived by the girls as too constraining.
>
> (p. 84)

Labelling propelled them into more extreme forms of delinquency. Shaklady Smith suggests that the protective attitudes of probation officers, social workers and other agencies paradoxically resulted in the same labelling of behaviour as 'common' or 'sluttish'. Long before they reached court girl juvenile delinquents had 'experienced a continued defining process which classified them as unfeminine'.

Carlen *et al.* (1985) have also shown the ways in which labelling influences the patterns of female crime and the ways in which female criminals are labelled unfeminine. However, labelling theory does not explain why people become criminal in the first place, nor does it take full account of power (class and patriarchal relations) in advanced capitalist societies.

Social control theory

Heidensohn (1986) has suggested that the question we should be asking is not why some women commit crime, but why women are so non-criminal. In other words, we should be explaining why women do not become criminal. She suggests that the reason is because of the ways in which women are controlled. She argues that women are controlled within the family and within society generally. She suggests that there are two types of theory of social control. Some theories emphasise the ways in which societies are cemented together by a shared value system. These values or ideologies are transmitted via the media, the educational system, the family, courts, police and so on. A second type of theory emphasises bonding in relationship to the family, the peer group and the school, whereby people are bound in to society's norms and values. Thus women are controlled by ideologies of appropriate behaviour for women and by their role in the family.

However, Pat Carlen (in Carlen and Worrall, 1987) has suggested that the problem with control theory is that it does not explain why some women *do* become criminal. She attempts to develop feminist control theory so that it can do this. She suggests that:

1   Women generally conform while they perceive it to be worth while to do so. Such calculation takes into account the costs and benefits of criminal behaviour.

2   Working-class women are controlled within two areas, the workplace and the family – that is, they are doubly controlled. They thus have to make a 'class deal' – to accept a wage for work – and a 'gender deal' – to take on feminine behaviour.

3   Most working-class women make the class deal and the gender deal because the exploitative nature of these two deals is obscured by the ideology of familialism and community working together in women to engender an attraction to the (imaginary) norm of respectable working-class womanhood.

4   A commitment to the norms of respectable working-class womanhood is most likely to happen where girls are brought up in families where there is a male breadwinner and a female carer – although girls can learn appropriate behaviour from the mass media, especially women's magazines and pop songs which report marriage coupled with wage-earning job as a deal to which young women should aspire. Thus the woman most likely to become criminal is one brought up in care or taken into care in adolescence.

5   The majority of women are not criminalised even when caught breaking the law. While they remain in the family as a daughter or wife they are seen as having made the gender deal. It is unassimilated women, women who have been in care or rejected 'normal' family life, who are likely to be seen as recidivist lawbreakers.

6   Women who see themselves as marginalised and consequently have nothing to lose may turn to lawbreaking and see it as preferable to poverty and social isolation.

Social control theory emphasises the ways in which girls and women are controlled within both the public and the private spheres and how they are therefore likely to be more conformist than men. The stereotype of women and a woman's role plays an important part in explaining the ways in which the control of women is achieved. These assumptions underlie the law governing sexual behaviour, the social benefit system, the interventions of health visitors and the ways in which the criminal justice system handles and disposes of female offenders. The normal woman is seen as a wife and mother who is in need of protection, while the deviant woman is seen as needing to be trained to perform domestic tasks and child-care. However, it is evident that more research needs to be carried out before we can answer the key questions that have been raised concerning women and crime: explanations for the patterning of crime; explanations for why women's crime differs so much from men's; and assessment of how far and in what ways gender differences in crime are linked to class, age and race.

However, it is clear that explanations which see female crime as a result of a failure of individual women to adapt themselves to their supposedly natural biological role are inadequate and misleading. Women's behaviour, criminal and non-criminal, needs to be explained by reference to a social formation which imposes restrictive and exploitative roles on women. Furthermore, it must be recognised that in certain economic and ideological circumstances crime may be a rational and coherent response to women's awareness of the social disabilities imposed on them by class and gender roles.

Radical feminists

Radical feminists have paid more attention to analysing crimes of which women are victims rather than looking at female criminality – that is, to manifestations of male power, and especially to domestic violence, rape and pornography. However, a radical feminist account would emphasise patriarchal power relationships and women's exploitation and subordinate position in examining female crime.

Sue Edwards (1987) has carried out research into women and prostitution. She argues that explanations for why women become prostitutes are an extension of explanations of the oppression and exploitation of women in patriarchal society: she suggests that because of women's low earning potential, a decline in job opportunities for women and the erosion of welfare benefits, more girls and young women drift into prostitution. Prostitutes, she argues, are harassed by the police if they walk the streets and controlled by pimps if they work off-street. While women prostitutes face high risks of prosecution or exploitation, the pimps and ponces and others benefiting from prostitution remain relatively free to exploit prostitute women, as they are placed in an increasingly valuable position in both the law and the economy.

SUMMARY

1   Most theories of deviance have been developed to account for male crime and deviance.

2   Women appear less often in official statistics of crime, and the evidence suggests that they do in fact commit fewer crimes. The pattern and nature of their crimes are likewise different from men's.

3   Feminists have tried to extend mainstream theories of deviance – such as the labelling perspective – to fit female crime. However, they have also highlighted the importance of taking other factors into account – such as the economic position of women, and their role in the family – in understanding women's crimes.

Crimes against women

Women are likely to be victims of all forms of crime, but they are especially vulnerable to violent attacks by men, both sexual and physical and by the men with whom they live as well as men not previously known to them. It is not just that women are the victims of violent men, but that fear of violent crime is a powerful control over women's lives.

Feminists have been interested not only in explaining why men are violent towards women, but in exposing the ways in which women who have been attacked by men are treated in the criminal justice system and by welfare agencies. Frequently, it is argued, women who have been assaulted, whether physically or sexually, end up feeling that they themselves are to blame. Indeed, attacks on women are frequently explained by saying that 'she deserved it' – for example, rape victims are blamed because they went out late at night alone, or wives who have been beaten by their husbands are blamed because they failed in their wifely duties, or daughters who are the victims of incest are said to have tempted their fathers with their flirtatious behaviour.

Sue Lees (1989) has analysed cases in which men have pleaded provocation as mitigating circumstance when they are being tried for killing a wife, lover or former lover. (A successful plea of provocation means that the jury returns a verdict of manslaughter rather than murder. The former carries a mandatory life sentence, but in the case of the latter a judge can give any sentence from a conditional – or even in theory an absolute – discharge to life imprisonment.) Lees quotes a number of cases in which male killers who have used the plea of provocation have been given relatively light prison sentences on being found guilty of manslaughter. She argues that the evidence for provocation is often based on the uncorroborated assertion of the accused and his friends, and that verdicts of manslaughter (unpremeditated killing) are often brought in even when there is evidence of premeditation. She points out that if a man kills his wife on finding her in bed with another man he can successfully plead provocation and be found guilty of manslaughter. She suggests that:

> The concept of provocation is based on three very questionable assumptions. Firstly, that a reasonable man can be provoked into murder by insubordinate behaviour – infidelity, bad housekeeping, withdrawal of sexual services and even nagging . . . The law provides for a legitimation for men to behave violently in the face of insubordination or marriage breakdown . . . If it can be successfully alleged that the victim was unrespectable, negligent in her wifely duties, then provocation is usually accepted. Secondly, the idea that women can be similarly provoked even when they have been beaten up or raped is seldom entertained. This would be a 'licence to kill' rapists or wife batterers. Thirdly, although the main distinction between murder and manslaughter revolves around whether the killing is premeditated or not ('malice aforethought', or intention to kill, is murder, but if someone kills by accident or through negligence, or is provoked, it is manslaughter) a defence of provocation on the basis of 'loss of self-control' in practice . . . often over-rides evidence of premeditation.
>
> (pp. 2–3)

Three major forms of explanation of violence towards women have been developed – the first two within malestream theory, and the third (by feminists) as a critique of the malestream theories and an alternative account:

1 *The traditionalist* In this perspective crimes such as rape and assault on wives are seen as infrequent. While not all women are seen as the cause of the violent behaviour, many are. Thus rape victims are said to have enticed the rapist and 'caused' him to have uncontrollable sexual urges. This can be either because of their behaviour in public places or by 'leading on' the man with whom they have been out, encouraging him to expect that he will be given sex. It is accepted that some victims are innocent, but they are expected to demonstrate this by resisting the attack and showing considerable evidence of physical injury.

Assaults on wives are also seen as being deserved by the wife for failing in her duties, and men are assumed to have responsibility for controlling their wives. Indeed, until the nineteenth century in England the debate concerned not *whether* a man could beat his wife but *how much* he could beat her. The saying 'a rule of thumb' comes from one legal judgement that a man could legally beat his wife with a stick provided it was no thicker than his thumb. It was not until the end of the nineteenth century that assaults on wives of this nature became illegal. In the traditionalist perspective, as with rape, it is accepted that some men beat their wives without just cause, but this is thought to be a relatively small proportion.

2 *Liberal/psychiatric* This perspective accepts that violence towards women is a social problem, but it sees it again as a relatively minor problem. In this view either the male perpetrator is seen as sick or disturbed or the female victim is seen as seeking out violence. Thus for rape the rapist is seen as mentally ill or socially inadequate, or female victims are said to be masochistic. Similarly, men who beat their wives are said either to have been brought up in a home where they were battered as children or to beat their wives as a result of being drunk, or the wives are said to want to be beaten.

In this perspective men who are violent to women are seen as sick and as needing treatment, or to be the 'victims' of women who invite violence.

3 *Feminist perspectives* There is no single feminist perspective, but all feminist approaches locate violence to women by men within the broader context of women's position as subordinate to men. In the 1970s feminists tended to try to explain rape and assaults on wives as serious indications of men's violence towards women. However, more recently feminists have broadened this view and suggest that anything that frightens or intimidates women must be seen in the context of men's control of women's behaviour. Thus women's fear of violence acts to control their behaviour, so that they restrict and limit their activities, and if they do go out at night they place themselves in the protection of a man. Furthermore, the advice to women is always not to go out when another woman has been raped in an area; it is never suggested that men should stay in so that it is safe for women to go out. Feminists have also become more concerned with doing research that explores how women experience male violence and power and how fear of rape and attacks from men restrict their behaviour, rather than in developing explanations for male violence. Feminist research has also demonstrated the limited value of legal reforms aimed at helping women who are the victims of male violence and the failure of the police and the courts to deal adequately with such men.

Until the 1970s the victimisation of women by men remained hidden. (See Chapter 10, however, for the nineteenth-century feminist campaigns around these issues.) With the rise of second wave feminism, the extent of assaults on wives, of rape and of child sexual abuse has become more evident.

Women have become more prepared to report men who commit violence against them and, more importantly, welfare agencies, the police and the courts have become more prepared to believe women and children. However, feminists argue that the extent of these crimes is still grossly underestimated and that the criminal justice system is still reluctant to accept how widespread violence against women and children is and to deal with the offenders. Feminists argue that rape and assaults on wives are serious crimes and should be treated as such. The perpetrators of these crimes should be charged and punished in the same way as they would be for any other serious violent crime.

Rape

Feminists argue that:

> the fear of rape affects all women. It inhibits their actions and limits their freedom, influencing the way they dress, the hours they keep, the routes they walk. The fear is well founded, because no woman is immune from rape.
>
> (Clarke and Lewis, 1977, p. 23)

In Britain rape is legally defined as unlawful sexual intercourse (which in turn means that the penis must penetrate the vagina). The Sexual Offences (Amendment) Act 1976 says that a man commits rape if:

1   he has sexual intercourse with a woman who at the time of intercourse does not consent to it; and
2   at the time knows that she does not consent to the intercourse or is reckless as to whether she consents to it.

In Britain until 1990 a man could not be charged with raping his wife, as the law assumed that the marriage contract gave him the right to have sexual intercourse with her. (Although the law has not been changed to make it a criminal offence, it has now become established in case law through convictions in the courts.) Feminists have been concerned to examine three issues: first, to ask why rape occurs and what attitudes and beliefs support it, second to examine the social and legal constraints which prevent women obtaining their legal rights, and third, to understand the experience of rape victims.

Rape is commonly viewed as the outcome of the male sex drive – that men have uncontrollable sexual urges. However, Barbara Toner (1977) suggests that anthropological evidence shows that the strength of the male sex drive depends on cultural attitudes and values. She points out that amongst the Arapesh of New Guinea rape is virtually unknown, while amongst the Gusii of Kenya it is a major form of social control.

Feminists argue that rape is an act of violence and domination which devalues and dehumanises the victim. Susan Brownmiller (1976), a radical feminist, argues that men are natural predators and women their natural prey. Men have the ability to rape women, but women cannot retaliate in kind. Rape, she argues, is used by men to generate fear in all women, and this is a conscious process of intimidation. Women, she argues, continue to be subordinated by men through the threat of rape. Women will be able to overcome their subordination only when they are fully integrated into the state apparatus for legislating against rape and for enforcing that legislation. The state will then be able to protect women from rape. In this view the cause of rape is male sexuality itself, and the solution sometimes advocated is political lesbianism.

Many feminists, however, reject biological explanations for rape and argue that rape is sustained and justified by patriarchal ideology and patriarchal relations. Lynne Segal (1987), for example, suggests that the problem is masculinity – that male sexual violence is about roles and gender, not essential biological characteristics such as innate violence and/or uncontrollable sexual urges. Feminists argue that patriarchal ideology defines women as either mothers who are respected or sexual objects for men's pleasure. Men want to gain sexual possession of women, and men control women's sexuality for their own purposes. They argue that while patriarchal ideology overtly condemns rape, it covertly legitimates it by viewing it as normal. In courts of law rapists often use the excuse, successfully, that the victim 'asked for it'. Furthermore, feminists argue that the rape law is concerned to protect the interests of men as much as the honour of women. Rape is viewed as a crime against property – daughters and wives; the father's/husband's property is damaged. Rape, they argue, is a political act that takes away a woman's autonomy to decide what to do with her own body. It is an act of aggression which carries with it the threat of death. Rape victims are chosen indiscriminately, in that no woman is immune from rape. Rape teaches all women that they are subordinate to men and it keeps women in a state of fear. It is thus an effective way of controlling women and restricting their freedom.

However, Joni Lovenduski and Vicky Randall (1993) point to the ways in which women in Leeds actually rejected the attempts by police and others to control their behaviour as a result of the 'Yorkshire Ripper' murders. They argue that while 'A lot of women were controlled by the "Ripper" murders: they gave up jobs and evening classes, women students left university and returned to homes in other parts of the country', other women acted differently and 'organised life for each other and lent each other their guard dogs. Instead of a siege mentality, there was the development of a sense of collective strength, a sense of shared experience' (pp. 331–2).

Feminists argue that the victims of rape are frequently 'put on trial' by the court procedures and blamed for the crime themselves. This is especially the case if the woman leads a sexually active life or her behaviour is seen as having 'caused' the rape by, for example, hitching a lift at night. Recent changes in the law so that a woman's sex life could not automatically be examined in court have not protected women from this, as most judges have in practice given permission for the woman to be questioned about her sexual history (Edwards, 1984). Helen Kennedy QC has pointed out that:

> In rape trials women are asked all sorts of irrelevant and inappropriate questions which have nothing to do with the crime – and which are never put to men. Barristers home in on their lifestyle to show that they encourage rape.
>
> (quoted in Bouquet, 1995, p. 46)

Sue Lees, indeed, has argued that:

> Women who are brave enough to take their cases to court go through a form of judicial rape. They are subjected to ruthless character assassination and humiliation.
>
> (quoted in Bouquet, 1995, p. 46)

Carol Smart (1995) has argued that actors in rape trials share a view of sexuality which emphasises the pleasure of penetration and intercourse. The assumption, then, is that rape must be pleasurable for women because it involves penetration. The core of the trial the centres around pleasure and the meaning of a woman's 'no'. The Court, Smart argues, shares an understanding that women are capricious about sex and may say 'no' when they mean 'yes'. The key issue becomes whether a woman's 'no' meant 'no'. Clearly this issue is central to what has become known as 'date' as opposed to 'stranger' rape. In the former case it is frequently argued that the woman 'really' wanted sex, that she has clearly indicated this despite the fact that she said 'no'.

Also, in rape trials the rules of corroboration play a key role. Until the Criminal Justice Act 1994 juries were warned by the judge that it was dangerous to convict on the uncorroborated evidence of the complainant, but that they might do so if they were satisfied that it was true. The dangers of convicting on the basis of uncorroborated evidence are present in all trials, but the law required the jury to be warned of this only in rape trials, treason trials and when the evidence has been given by children or accomplices. In rape trials the implied insult, that rape victims were no more reliable as witnesses than children or accomplices, was compounded by the jury being told that the experience of the courts was that women accuse men of rape for totally malicious reasons and innocent men must be protected from such allegations. Given that there are rarely witnesses to rape, and often the victim's and accused's accounts differ only as to whether she consented to sexual intercourse, rape convictions are difficult to obtain unless there is corroborative evidence – for example, if the victim received injuries. Indeed, Home Office research has indicated that rapists are rarely convicted and imprisoned unless the victim is sexually inexperienced, was raped by a stranger and sustained injuries (Bouquet, 1995).

Indeed, long before the crime comes to trial women are degraded and disbelieved. Women are reluctant to report rape in the first place because of the ways in which rape victims are questioned by the police and the ways in which medical examinations are carried out. The police are less likely to believe the rape allegation of some women than others. For example, Ann Burgess and Linda Holmstrom (1979) studied the cases of 146 women and girls who reported to a hospital emergency room (casualty reception) in the United States as having been raped. They suggest that the responses of the police and the decision as to whether to prosecute or not were based on stereotypes of rape. The woman was believed and the police carried out an investigation if the woman was previously a virgin, if she was judged emotionally stable, if the rapist was a stranger and if the rapist used or threatened to use a weapon. The case was dropped if the victim had gone willingly, if she was unmarried and sexually experienced, if she had emotional problems, if she was calm when she was making the report and if the rapist was known to her. Barbara Toner (1977) found that the police in Britain held similar stereotypes of rape. Women reporting rape are more likely to be taken seriously if they report the offence immediately, are upset, did not know the rapist and show signs of having put up a struggle. (However, feminists have suggested that women do not want to be beaten, and victims of rape have often said that they were too frightened to resist and that they were afraid they would be killed if they did.) Toner found that women who reported rape often felt they were treated unsympathetically by the police and found the medical inspection conducted in an insultingly matter-of-fact way. Research carried out for Thames Valley Police by Oxford Brookes University in 1994 found that only a fifth of rape victims reported the crime to the police. Over half of the victims thought they were unlikely to be treated fairly by the courts (Bouquet, 1995). Catherine Mackinnon (1987) has suggested that women do not report rape or at least do not proceed with allegations because of the type of evidence that they will be required to give in court.

Feminists have challenged a number of myths about rape:

1   Rape is widely believed to be impossible. It is argued that women can always avoid being raped by running away or resisting and fighting back. This ignores the aspect of fear, that women are too frightened to run away and are scared of the consequences if they resist.

2   It is believed that women enjoy rape. However, studies of women who have been raped suggest that they felt humiliated and frightened. Also, men benefit from the belief that women want intercourse.

3   It is believed that rape is a rare act. However, victim studies and the experience of rape crisis centres suggests that only a small number of rapes are reported to the police. Ruth Hall (1985), in the only published UK incidence report, found prevalence figures of 17 per cent for rape and 20 per cent for attempted rape.

4   It is believed that rape is committed by strangers. Statistics show that the rapist is as likely to be known to the victim as to be a stranger. Also, rapes are as likely to happen indoors as in the open. For example, Amir (1971) found that 57 per cent of rapists were known to their victims.

5   It is believed that rape is committed only by psychopaths. However, studies suggest that few convicted rapists are mentally abnormal. Carol and Barry Smart (1978) point out that rapists are not treated differently from other offenders by the legal system and generally receive short sentences, and that few are dealt with under the mental health legislation. Furthermore, the criminal records of convicted rapists often include non-sexual as well as sexual crimes.

6   It is believed that rape is an impulsive act, the result of uncontrollable sexual urges, and to be unplanned. Women are said to 'cause' the urges which men cannot control. However, research has demonstrated that most rapes are planned. For example, Amir (1971) found that 70 per cent were planned, 11 per cent partially planned and only 16 per cent what he called 'explosive'.

7   It is believed that rape is a problem of the lower classes. However, men of all ages and all social classes attack women.

Assaults on wives

The extent to which wives are violently assaulted became evident in the early 1970s when women's liberation groups began to respond to the obvious need for refuges for women who wanted to leave violent men. As Dobash and Dobash (1980) observe:

In 1971 almost no one had heard of battered women, except of course the legions of women who were being battered and the relatives, friends, ministers, social workers, doctors and lawyers in whom some of them confided. Many people did not believe that such behaviour actually existed, and even most of those who were aware of it did not think that it affected sufficient numbers of women or was of sufficient severity to warrant wide-scale concern.

(p. 2)

The women who come to refuges – about 12,000 in any one year (Lovenduski and Randall, 1993, p. 309) – have often been living with men who have beaten them violently for years. Many have tried unsuccessfully to leave their husbands or partners on a number of occasions, but the problem of finding accommodation and supporting themselves and their children has frequently driven them back to the violent home. Welfare agencies, the police and the courts were seen as at best unhelpful and at worst likely to advise them to 'make the best of it'.

This comes about at least in part because violence in the family is seen as a private affair, something to be sorted out by the husband and wife themselves, rather than something needing intervention by welfare agencies, the police and the courts. The police frequently refer to such incidents as 'domestic' rather than regarding them as serious cases of assault. Furthermore, calling them domestic shifts the blame for the violence from the husband to the husband-and-wife and normalises it as part of family life. Police reluctance to take assaults on wives seriously is also evidenced by their reluctance to charge husbands with assault and take them to court. They argue that this is because wives usually refuse to testify and forgive their husbands. However, evidence from states in the USA where police are required to charge husbands who assault wives does not support this contention, and nor does research in Britain that has examined this 'attrition rate'. In Britain the practice of 'no criming' 'domestic' disputes is gradually being abandoned (Edwards, 1989; Bourlet, 1990). A series of Home Office memos to police forces between 1983 and 1990 instructed them to take domestic violence more seriously, and in 1991 the Home Office instructed police forces to set up data-banks of women at risk. However, the response of police forces, organised regionally, has been mixed, with a few forces having very good practices and others having made no changes. In some forces there are *no* Police Domestic Violence Units, while in others not only are there such Units, but domestic assault on women is treated as seriously as assaults on strangers (Lovenduski and Randall, 1993, p. 314).

In the United States it is estimated that between two and four million and possibly as many as eight million women are battered every year by the men with whom they live (Sassetti, 1993). It is likely that it is the single greatest cause of serious injury to women, accounting for more injuries that car accidents, muggings and rape combined. Domestic violence also accounts for between 30 and 40 per cent of female murder victims in the United States every year. Twenty-five per cent of all violent assaults in Britain are domestic assaults on women, over a *thousand* women a week in London alone telephone the police with a domestic violence complaint (Lovenduski and Randall, 1993, p. 317), and one in five murder victims is a woman killed by her partner or ex-partner (Smith, 1989). Strauss and Gelles (1986 – see also Strauss *et al.*, 1980; Strauss, 1980) have indicated that while wives and husbands are almost equal in their violence, wives' violence is generally in response to a physical attack – that is, defensive – while husbands' violence is generally offensive. Also, women are much more likely to experience severe attacks from their partners than are men. Similarly, in Britain research into domestic violence indicates that in the overwhelming majority of cases men are the perpetrators and women the victims (Smith, 1989), and this holds true for different ethnic and cultural groups. Mama (1989) has indicated that:

> the prevalence of violence against women in black communities illustrates the full meaning of triple oppression along the dimensions of race, class and gender.
>
> (p. vii)

Mama, like the Southall Black Sisters (Sahgal, 1989), has been critical of pressures put on Black women to keep quiet about their experiences of male violence. Indeed, she argues that because of the focus on fighting against *police* violence against Black community activity, it took:

> a long time to address a reality in which black women are more likely to be assaulted by their male partners than to be attacked by racists.
>
> (p. 16)

Most research into assaults on wives has been carried out by interviewing women in refuges. In the main the research has been carried out by academics. Indeed, the Department of Health and Social Security has been criticised for commissioning research on wife-assault from academics rather than involving the women in the refuge movement, it being suggested that the DHSS spent large sums of money on research that could better have been spent helping the victims of abuse (Hanmer and Leonard, 1984). The findings of research, they suggest, have added little that the women in the refuges did not know already.

Feminist researchers have rejected individualistic explanations for domestic violence. The largest single feminist study of wife-beating was carried out by Rebecca and Russell Dobash (1980) in Scotland. They argue that the problem of violence against women is a deep-rooted societal one arising out of the patriarchal family system, a system in which the husband's authority over the wife creates a particular marriage power relationship and a subordinate position for wives and mothers. They argue that men are more powerful than women and exploit the labour of women in marriage – that is, women are expected to service their husbands by providing domestic services for them. They argue that one of the major factors precipitating male violence to their wives is husbands' perceptions that a wife is not performing her wifely duties satisfactorily – for example, a house seen as not cleaned properly, a meal not prepared promptly or a wife suspected of not being sexually faithful. Jan Pahl (1985), in her research, also found that men who beat their wives had frequently tried to control their behaviour and expected them to stay at home and not go out alone. Henrietta Moore (1995) has suggested that interpersonal violence can always be seen as evidence of the struggle for the maintenance of power – in this case, the power of men to control women.

Feminist researchers have also explored why women find it so difficult to leave violent men. They argue that there are economic, social, ideological and legal factors which all interact to make it difficult for women to leave violent men. In economic terms it is difficult for a woman to support herself and her children, but more urgent is the problem of finding housing. Indeed, Jan Pahl found that the women she interviewed were frequently surprised to discover that they were financially better off on supplementary benefit than they had been when living with their husbands (Pahl, 1985). Housing was a major problem; in the past the women had left home but had been forced back because of their inability to find suitable accommodation. The refuge provided a warm and friendly environment that battered wives could turn to, but it was not suitable for the long term.

In social terms wives who have been assaulted often feel that they cannot admit that their marriage has failed. They blame themselves and see it as an individual problem. Also, a woman's relatives and friends may well tell her that she has herself to blame for being in the situation and that she must put up with it (Homer et al., 1984).

Mama (1989) and Maguire (1988) have pointed to the additional problems of Black women leaving violent partners. Mama, for example, documents incidents where the collective pressures of the extended family make it difficult to leave, and Maguire points to the problems that women who have come to Britain to marry confront – of deportation, of stigma and of their family's response if they have to return to their own countries.

Patriarchal and familial ideology also influence the response of welfare agencies to wives who have been assaulted. Johnson (1985) argues that social workers have not been trained to deal with assaults on wives, that they lack the resources to help women victims and at best they can refer the women to a hostel. A large proportion of assaulted women seek medical help – for example, 80 per cent of the Dobash and Dobash (1980) sample had been to the doctor, and 64 per cent of the women Jan Pahl (1985) interviewed – although they rarely mentioned that they were beaten by their husbands. Doctors do not see marital problems as part of their concern; this is not the kind of problem that 'real' medicine is concerned with. In a number of studies women have been critical of the response of doctors to their attempt to seek help, and especially of the medical practice of prescribing tranquillisers (Dobash and Dobash, 1980; Pahl, 1985). Non-medical advice, when it was offered, was generally to leave the man, but no account was taken of practical problems. The police were also frequently criticised in these studies and by the women who had been assaulted. Police, it is argued, are reluctant to intervene in what they regard as domestic disputes and will rarely take the men to court (Dobash and Dobash, 1980; Edwards, 1989; Bourlet, 1990). This is a problem because women frequently turn to the police for help, and while the police response is improving, this is probably happening only slowly and patchily in Britain (Johnson, 1995).

In the 1970s the one major response of the government to the problem of assaults on wives was a set of legal reforms designed to give women greater protection from violent men and to make it easier for women to leave them. An analysis of how the legal reforms have worked in practice demonstrates, feminists argue, both the limitations of reform and the ways in which patriarchal ideology influences judicial decisions.

Three Acts were passed in the late 1970s, all designed to assist women assaulted by their husbands: the Domestic Violence and Matrimonial Proceedings Act 1976, the Domestic Proceedings and Magistrates' Courts Act 1978 and the Housing (Homeless Persons) Act 1977. The 1977 Housing Act made it the responsibility of local authorities to rehouse certain categories of people – mainly families – providing they had not intentionally made themselves homeless. The Act explicitly stated that women who had left a violent man should not be seen as having intentionally made themselves homeless and should be rehoused if they had dependent children. However, many local authorities have not rehoused women and their children. Furthermore, even if they are prepared to accept the woman as homeless the problem is not solved. The woman and her children will have to live in accommodation designated for homeless persons for some time and then to accept the first offer of permanent accommodation, however unsatisfactory the woman may find it. Also, while she is in temporary accommodation the husband may be able to gain custody of the children; still living in the matrimonial home, he may be able to convince the court that he can better provide for his children than can his wife. If the wife no longer has custody of the children, she is no longer entitled to be rehoused by the local authority.

The Domestic Violence and Matrimonial Proceedings Act (DVMPA) and the Domestic Proceedings and Magistrates Act (DPMA) were both designed to give battered women greater protection. The DVMPA applied in the County Courts and permitted courts to issue non-molestation and exclusion injunctions independently of any other proceedings before the court. Injunctions were to be available in an emergency, could have powers of arrest attached, and men could be sent to prison for breach of an injunction. Relief was available to married and cohabiting women equally. The DPMA extends similar powers to Magistrates' Courts. This meant that women had a local, inexpensive, simple and quick access to relief if they were assaulted. However, the provisions applied only to married women, magistrates had no powers to exclude men from certain localities, and husbands could be arrested only if they inflicted actual physical injury on their wives.

In practice these Acts have not extended much greater protection to wives. Case law has established legal precedents which demonstrate judges' and magistrates' reluctance to prevent a man entering his property. It has been made evident that the courts see the protection of children as the most important factor. There has been a reluctance to use the emergency powers, and injunctions are frequently issued without powers of arrest attached, which means the police argue that they cannot enforce the injunction. Over and above this, the police have been reluctant to intervene even when powers of arrest have been attached.

Social policy changes introduced by the Thatcher Government in Britain have also impacted on the ability of women to live without men. These policies, aimed at reducing state spending and the role of the state, have included the sale of council houses, cuts in local authority spending resulting in them being able to provide less support for refuges, and legislation requiring divorced and separated women to claim maintenance for children from their former partners. The sale of council housing, with a prohibition on local authorities using receipts from the sales to build more housing, makes it more difficult for women leaving violent homes to be offered adequate accommodation by local authorities, despite their statutory obligation. Reductions in grants to refuges make it more difficult for the refuges to provide an adequate service for the women seeking their help, or for more refuges to be opened.

We can conclude, then, that the current state of English law on domestic violence is one of a legal system which provides all the necessary remedies, but which in its operation fails to protect women as fully as it should and leaves them vulnerable. What we must bear in mind is that abused women are not just victims but also survivors – Hoff (1990) describes them in her study as 'crisis managers rather than helpless victims' (p. 56), and Dobash and

Dobash (1992) reject the view that abused women become the victims of learned helplessness.

Women, violence and male power

Some feminists have argued that by concentrating on rape and assaults on wives the real extent of male violence against women is obscured. They argue that all women are affected by male violence and that the crime statistics and official victim and self-report studies seriously underestimate the extent of violence towards women by men. Violence is a powerful mechanism of social control; women's movements are severely restricted by the actual violence they experience and by fear of male violence. Violence, it is argued, encompasses more than actual physical assault and includes all behaviour designed to control and intimidate women carried out by men. The extent to which men control and intimidate women only becomes evident when we include sexual harassment, obscene telephone calls, flashing and other behaviour by men designed to control women. Liz Kelly (1988) has offered the following definition of sexual violence:

> [Sexual violence] includes any physical, visual, verbal or sexual act that is experienced by the woman or girl, at the time or later, as a threat, menace or assault, that has the effect of hurting her or degrading her and/or takes away her ability to control intimate contact.
>
> (p. 4)

Research by Jalna Hanmer and Susan Saunders (1984) and by Jill Radford (1987) has found that women's behaviour is very much restricted by their fear of men – both in the domestic sphere and in the public. Women do not go out at night, or to certain places, not only because they fear attack, but also because the men with whom they live try to prevent them going out alone. They also found that women experience considerable amounts of violent behaviour from men, but that much of this is hidden – it is not reported to the police, nor do women reveal their experience of violence in response to surveys such as the British Crime Survey. They suggest that this is because women are reluctant to reveal the extent to which men are violent and there is no reason to suppose that the women who have not reported the violence to the police are more likely to reveal it to a survey. In their research they acknowledged the reasons why they were doing the research in advance and left the women to define violence themselves. They argue, therefore, that their findings reflect more accurately the experiences of the women and their perceptions of violence.

Jacqui Halson (1989) argues that her research among 14-year-old girls in a co-educational school confirms that sexual harassment is a form of sexual violence commonly experienced by young women both in school and outside. The young women experienced sexual harassment from both male teachers and male pupils, and she argues that the school sanctioned it by not intervening and therefore reproduced the existing imbalances of power between women and men. The girls felt uncomfortable and threatened by the behaviour of one male teacher, who was referred to as 'a right Casanova'. The boys leered at the girls, verbally harassed them and physically assaulted them, although the behaviour usually stopped short of rape. Often one girl was sexually harassed by a gang of boys, and this increased a sense of powerlessness and meant that the girls policed their own behaviour so that they were not likely to meet a group of boys when on their own. The girls did not find the boys' behaviour flattering, but offensive and humiliating, and in no way could it be said to be experienced as 'friendly', 'inoffensive' or 'just teasing'. Nor was it mutual, and it could not be dismissed as banter or mutual flattery. The girls were not empowered to challenge the boys because the school's attitude was that such behaviour was harmless, not a serious problem, and there were no school rules forbidding it.

Halson suggests that one incident reveals the lack of understanding by the school authorities of how seriously the girls viewed sexual harassment. Some graffiti were put up in the school – 'Mary is a slag'. The young woman concerned was extremely upset, and her mother came to the school and threatened to take action. However, a senior member of the staff suggested that the mother was making a lot of fuss over nothing and that 'slag' was a common term of abuse used to refer to girls – precisely missing the key point, that terms like 'slag' are used to diminish women, to humiliate them and to enable men to control them.

Liz Stanley (1984) has argued that the type of research that seeks to reveal how women make sense of their experiences when confronted by violent behaviour is essential. In analysing her own experience of receiving obscene telephone calls she argues that the police response of advising women to hang up is inadequate, not only because the police fail to understand how women actually feel when they receive such calls, but also because it does nothing to deal with the problem. She found that it was frequently some time into the conversation before it became evident that the call was obscene, and that hanging up does not cut the line; consequently when the telephone was picked up some time later the caller was still there. Her strategy for dealing with such calls was to challenge male power by pretending that she could not hear the caller and asking him to speak up. The usual response of the caller was to hang up after a few minutes.

However, not all male violence is as easy to challenge as that of obscene telephone callers. Carol Ramazanoglu (1987) has pointed out how difficult it is for female academics to challenge sexual harassment from male colleagues, and in other situations women do not have the physical strength to fight men. Other researchers have argued that the response of women to other forms of violence is eminently rational when seen from their perspective. Women who are raped or flashed at say that they are scared of being killed and this conditions their response. Women do not report incidents of violence to the police because they are aware of the patriarchal response that they will elicit. Women who are the victims of male violence are likely to see themselves as blamed for it. Feminists are aware that neither changes in legislation nor asking men to change their behaviour are likely to make much difference, although both are important. They therefore argue that women should organise to help themselves, for more refuges run and controlled by women, for rape crisis centres, and for women to be taught self-defence techniques.

What is vital also is to challenge the view that assaults on wives and rape are in some sense different from other violent crimes. They are, of course, in that they are examples of the ways in which men use violence to maintain or reassert their power over women and control women, but they are not less serious. Indeed, it could be argued that they are more serious. What must be challenged is the common-sense view that crimes in the domestic sphere are a private matter and not the concern of the police and the criminal justice system, and that rape is a sexual crime, the result of men's innate sexual urges.

Feminists are challenged by those who argue that women can be violent to men and that this is also hidden. Rebecca and Russell Dobash (1980) say that they have frequently been asked about assaults on husbands when they give lectures on wife-battering. They argue that there is no evidence to suggest that this is a serious problem. Mildred Pagelow (1985) in her research in the United States found no evidence to suggest that assaults on husbands were common. Perhaps, however, the most telling thing is that there are no refuges for battered husbands and no apparent demand. It has been suggested that this is because men are unwilling to confess that they are beaten by their wives. However, a man can much more easily leave a violent home than can a woman. Men are not expected to care for the children and they have the economic means of supporting themselves that women lack.

Conclusions

In this chapter we have dealt with two aspects of feminist work on crime. In the first half we discussed feminist work on women and crime, and in the second half work on male violence towards women. The two halves reflect very different feminist approaches. The work on women and crime is heavily academic in orientation and concerned with either incorporating women into existing theories of crime or arguing the need to reformulate sociological approaches to crime in order that they can adequately explain both why women are so non-criminal and the behaviour of the women who do break the law. The work on women and violence has to a large extent been carried out by radical feminists (see Chapter 2 for more details) who are concerned not only with researching the problem of men's violence to women but also with developing strategies for dealing with it. They argue that male violence affects all women, irrespective of age or social class, and that it is one of the major ways in which men control women in patriarchal societies. We have included such material in this chapter on women and crime because we want to demonstrate not only the ways in which malestream sociology has ignored or marginalised the crimes that are committed by men against women; but also the ways in which the legal system marginalises, trivialises and belies women's victimisation, and how it blames it on the victim. Men who are attacked on the street are not told that they should not have been out there; women are. Men who are beaten up are not told it was because of the way they behaved; women are. Men are not advised not to go out at night alone or not to visit certain places; women are. Women's behaviour is controlled by men and this control is reinforced not only by the media, the police and the courts but by other women. Control of women is a key aspect of understanding women's behaviour – why women break the law and why they do not, and why they are attacked, beaten and abused by men.

SUMMARY

1   Feminists have highlighted aspects of crime hitherto ignored or considered 'normal' – for example, rape, assault on wives, and sexual harassment.

2   Feminists have argued that these need to be explained in the context of male power and the fact that sexual and physical violence is considered normal behaviour for men in our society, in some sense, but not for women.

FURTHER READING

Dobash, R. E. and Dobash, R. P. (1992) *Women, Violence and Social Change*, London: Routledge.

Heidensohn, F. (1986) *Women and Crime*, London: Macmillan.

Kelly, E. (1988) *Surviving Sexual Violence*, Cambridge: Polity.

Chapter ten

Women and politics

Women are notably absent from what is conventionally seen as 'politics' in Britain. Despite the fact that the former Conservative Party leader, Mrs Thatcher, was Prime Minister from 1979 to 1991, there are and have been few other women in key positions of political power in contemporary Britain, few women trade union leaders and few members of parliament (though the number of women local government councillors has increased). Women are assumed to be less able at carrying out political tasks than men and less interested in politics. Political sociology has tended in the past to accept this common-sense view of women's relationship to politics and to give it scientific authority.

Sylvia Walby (1988a) has argued that there have been four kinds of approach to gender issues in political sociology:

1   women have been seen as irrelevant to politics, or when mentioned seen as behaving in less authentically political ways than men;

2   criticisms have been raised of the ways in which women have been distorted in political sociology and especially in voting studies;

3   there have been feminist studies of women's political activity; and

4   analyses have been made of gendered politics, examining

not only women's political activity but also patriarchal resistance – that is, the power struggle between feminism and patriarchy.

To this we would add a fifth: an analysis of the role of the state in creating and maintaining the nuclear family and the role of women as wives and mothers.

In this chapter we shall examine the feminist criticisms of malestream political sociology and feminist research on women's politics.

Women and voting studies

Siltanen and Stanworth (1984) have suggested that women's political capacity has been underrated in the malestream literature. Malestream research has suggested that women's participation in politics is less than men's and that women's concerns and demands are a reflection of moral or familial commitments rather than an authentic political stance. For example, men are said to be concerned about pay and hours of work while women are more concerned with working conditions. However, they suggest that this literature has exaggerated the differences between men and women in political behaviour, and while suggesting that women's political behaviour is influenced by the private sphere it has discounted the influence of the private sphere on the political behaviour of men. In terms of voting behaviour, malestream researchers have claimed that women vote less than men, that women are more conservative than men, that women are more fickle than men, and that women are more influenced by personalities. However, a re-examination of the literature and research findings by feminists suggests that the evidence on which these conclusions are based is very flimsy indeed.

Susan Bourque and Jean Grosshaltz (1974) have argued that malestream researchers have often interpreted data and made assumptions that 'fit in' with their preconceived ideas of women's political behaviour. First, Bourque and Grosshaltz point to the 'fudging of the footnotes' which enables statements to be made about women's political orientations which are either unsupported by the references or misleading simplifications of the original. Second, they argue there is a tendency to assume that men (especially husbands) influence women's political opinions and behaviour, but not *vice versa* – especially in terms of voting. Third, there is the unquestioned assumption that the political attitudes, preferences and style of participation characteristic of men define mature political behaviour. Women's behaviour is seen as immature by definition, if it differs from this. Fourth, it is assumed that women's political concerns are located in their role as mothers, and this results in a constrained view of women's political potential. Similarly, Dowse and Hughes (1971) have shown that references to the fact that women are more conservative than men are often supported by data which in fact show at most very small differences.

Goot and Reid (1975) challenge the view that women's political participation demonstrates that women are less politically aware than men, or less interested. They argue that the evidence indicates the degree to which political parties, trade unions and the norms of political participation do not resonate with the concerns, needs and opportunities of many women. The timing of trade union and political party meetings often makes it difficult for women with domestic commitments to attend and participate. Women often find it difficult to participate in after-meeting drink sessions at the pub, where important business is discussed. Men often argue that issues of central concern to women are less important or somehow 'less political' than the issues which concern men. Indeed, some issues of critical concern to women are seen as tied in with their natural role and not something that should be on the political agenda at all. Political matters which have been interpreted in this light include workplace issues such as paid maternity leave, demands for the provision of workplace nurseries, school holiday play-schemes and paid time off from work to care for sick children. At a national level, 'the endowment of motherhood' – the idea that women should be paid to bring up children on behalf of the nation – has been viewed similarly, and it took a ruling by the European Commission for married women caring for a sick or disabled husband to be allowed to claim the invalidity care allowance (an allowance paid to someone who cares for a severely incapacitated adult or child). Women have had to fight to get issues such as abortion rights, contraception, equal pay and so on seen as important political issues. Given this, plus the fact that so few women are candidates in national or union elections, it is perhaps not surprising that women's political participation is not identical to men's.

However, careful research has suggested that gender differences are not a major factor in voting behaviour and that social class is a more important predictor. For example, it has been suggested that women are less likely to cast their vote than men, and this has been used to argue that women are less interested in politics. However, older people are less likely, statistically, to vote than younger people, and there are more old women than old men; when allowance is made for age, the apparent difference virtually disappears (Crewe 1979; R. Rose, 1976a). It is often argued that women are influenced in how they vote by the preferences of their husbands (see, e.g., Lazarsfeld *et al.*, 1968). However, the best conclusion from the evidence is that the influence is mutual (Maccoby *et al.*, 1954; Jennings and Niemi, 1974; Weiner, 1978; Prandy, 1986). Women are said to be more conservative than men – that is, more likely to vote for the Conservative Party. Goot and Reid (1975) have pointed out that gender differences in voting behaviour since 1945 have always been small. Indeed, in some general elections women have tended to prefer the Labour to the Conservative Party – in 1945, for instance (Durant, 1976) and in 1964 (Butler and King, 1965). Furthermore, in both the 1979 and the 1983 general elections more men than women voted Conservative.

Political scientists have not in general been much concerned with women's political behaviour, and it has generally been assumed that women are less interested in political issues because their main interest lies in the domestic sphere. However, this division between a public and a private or domestic sphere is itself a political issue, and to say that a concern with working conditions, the education of children, the availability of abortion and so on is the mark of a moral rather than a political concern is to make a definite and in many ways contemptuous value judgement (see Siltanen and Stanworth, 1984). It is indeed possible – likely, even – that women's experiences differ from men's and therefore determine their voting behaviour differently. Women may well be more affected than men by cuts in public expenditure in education, health and the implementation of community care, or at least more aware of the results of such policies. As Dorothy Smith (1979) has argued, women's lives are cast by their circumstances less in the 'abstract mode' of conceptual argument and more in the concrete reality in which such arguments are grounded; men may have theories on education or health care, but it is the women who take the children to school and to the doctor. Issues such as working hours, the provision of nurseries, ante-natal provision and the like may therefore loom larger for women than for men. They are political issues, however, and to ignore them or relegate them to domestic-sphere morality is to ignore the basis on which many women make their political choices. Finally, one may argue that if women were less interested in public politics than men – a proposition for which the empirical evidence is not strong – it would be because they felt, realistically, that they had little chance of influencing events because the political agenda and the processes of politics are dominated by men.

Thus some feminists have concluded that an emphasis on gender differences in political sociology is inappropriate. Such an emphasis would have a number of consequences:

1   By emphasizing the characteristics that are seen as 'male' or 'female', studies treat men and women as if they were homogeneous social groups, and the variations within each gender are played down. Thus, for example, the 'job model' – the view that a man's political attitudes and behaviour are determined by work experiences – is applied to men, and a 'gender model' to women.

2   Roles in the domestic sphere are seen as shaping women's and only

women's voting behaviour. It is suggested that women vote for candidates because of their personal qualities, though it has not been suggested that men voted for Mrs Thatcher because of her charms or wifely qualities.

3   The assumption that political parties, trade unions, etc. are gender-fair, and that women's lack of active participation is due to their lack of interest, ignores the male domination and control of such organisations. For example, Siltanen and Stanworth (1984) quote research that shows that many women are committed to the trade union movement but do not join, or leave having joined, because of disenchantment with the union's failure to deal with women's issues. Indeed, the difference in trade union membership between men and women has narrowed in recent years – mainly as a result of industrial restructuring and the concentration of women in unionised occupations such as teaching, nursing and social work (CSO, 1995).

Feminists have not been concerned, however, to argue that women's political action is identical to men's. They have argued that malestream research and male-dominated trade unions and political parties have a taken-for-granted definition of what is to count as political. However, this definition excludes much of women's expertise and political concerns. Feminists offer an alternative interpretation of women's relationship to public life. They demonstrate the extent to which the 'male as the norm' principle operates in political and social analysis – the way in which a demarcation between the 'political' and the 'social' or 'moral' is based on arbitrary but sex-linked criteria. For example, Greenstein (1965) found that girls scored more highly than boys on measures of 'citizen duty' and 'political efficacy' but relabel these attributes as moral rather than political. Feminists suggest that it is necessary to attribute new meanings to women's political activities. For example, refraining from voting may actually be a reflection of the low efficacy of voting. Given that women's political concerns are not reflected in politics, the question should be why women should vote rather than why they should not. Finally, it is argued that what are seen as women's skills need to be revalued and seen as of relevance to political life. It is suggested that the priorities, skills and issues that women bring with them from the domestic sphere are valuable additions to politics. Women's struggle to stay human in the workplace, by arguing for better conditions, might act as an example of this.

Defining feminist politics

Feminists have argued that women do engage in political activities as conventionally defined. As we have seen above, women's voting behaviour is very similar to men's. Women do belong to trade unions. There are women who are active members of trade unions and political parties, women local councillors, women members of Parliament, women general secretaries of trade unions, and so on. Women *are* active in politics, even if the number of women so engaged is much smaller than the number of men. Feminists have also suggested that women are often alienated from politics and excluded by the control and domination of organisations by men. However, feminists have also argued that women's political activities and concerns have been marginalised and 'hidden from history', as well as that politics and what is seen as political needs to be redefined. Thus they have maintained that feminism is itself political and is concerned with the struggle for women's liberation and emancipation. Feminists, for example, have had to rediscover the political activities of first wave feminists, a movement often portrayed as just a group of middle-class women fighting for the vote. The other activities they engaged in and the writings of nineteenth-century feminists are ignored or reinterpreted as concerned with moral/personal issues. However, the major argument of feminists has been that 'the personal is the political' – that is, that politics is concerned with the dynamics of power relationships in society and must therefore be concerned with the power relationships between men and women. Thus in the public sphere the power that men exercise over women is often ignored while their domination in the domestic sphere is even less often considered.

Kate Millett, in *Sexual Politics*, defines politics as 'power-structured relationships, arrangements whereby one group of persons is controlled by another' (1977, p. 23). The feminist definition of politics puts on the agenda not only power relationships between men and women at the personal level, but also the importance of patriarchal ideology in controlling women's lives. Thus the orthodox idea, for example, that women have a free choice in deciding whether to do housework is challenged. Furthermore, feminists argue that the very division between public and private is a patriarchal idea used to exclude women and women's concerns from politics. They argue that women have been excluded from participation in politics and public life and that the state has construed the family as private – as an institution outside state intervention. In this way, in the name of personal freedom and privacy, the arena in which women are most exploited and subordinated, in families, is exempted from political intervention. The separation between the public and the private has made possible the legislation of female equality in the former while ignoring the real differences that exist in the latter.

Furthermore, the public/private split makes it possible to keep women's values out of the public sphere. Some feminists, especially radical ones (see Chapter 2), argue that because of their roles as mothers women have a deeper sense of humility, caring and community, of belonging and selflessness, than men. Also, women are prevented from participating on equal terms with men in the public sphere because of the responsibilities they have or are attributed to have in the domestic sphere, and men are often prevented from taking on caring roles in the home.

Feminists have pointed out that this conceptual split between the public and the private does not even necessarily accord with the facts of social and political life. Indeed, it has been argued that the state has actually 'created' and sustained the family as an institution, and women's subordination within it (see Chapter 6). Legislation on matters such as social security and income maintenance has assumed that women do and should live with a man on whom they are financially dependent. On the other hand, matters arising in the public sphere are said to be private: for example, sexual harassment, legislation on contraception, and abortion, have all been said to be private/moral issues rather than political ones.

Feminist politics

The rediscovery of women's history has been a major achievement of feminist scholarship in recent years. As part of the reclaiming of 'herstory', first wave feminism as a political movement has been uncovered. However, contemporary feminists suggest that nineteenth-century (first wave) feminists fought for equal rights for women in the public sphere; late-twentieth-century feminists have sought to free women from subordination to men.

Women, and especially married women, had few rights in the nineteenth century, and throughout the century women struggled to achieve the same rights as men. Many of these women were middle-class and sought to have the same rights to education, to voting, to work, etc. as middle-class men, but few were concerned about the plight of working-class women, who were often forced to work long hours and had even fewer rights than their middle-class sisters. Nevertheless, working-class women were politically active, especially towards the end of the century, when women founded their own trade unions and participated in the suffrage movement.

The situation of Caroline Norton provides a graphic illustration of the lack of rights which married women experienced. She was married to a man who assaulted her physically and lived off her earnings as a writer. When she eventually decided she could take no more and left him, she found she had no right of access to her own children, no right to control her own property, including even her jewellery and clothing, and no right to her own earnings. It would have been impossible for her to remain separated from her husband if she had not had relatives who were prepared to keep her. In the nineteenth century women were a legally inferior caste; they were not regarded as persons under the law. Women did not gain the right to custody of infant children until 1839, nor to control their own property until 1882, nor to vote on the same basis as men until 1928, nor to get a divorce on the same grounds as men until 1934.

Juliet Mitchell (1986) traces the origins of the feminist movement to the concept of equality and equal rights that was first introduced during the English Revolution in the seventeenth century and was further developd in the eighteenth-century Enlightenment and the French Revolution. The first expressions of feminism were based on the concept of equality – that men and women should be treated equally. This was demanded by women who saw themselves as a social group completely excluded from the tenets and principles of the 'new' society that had developed after the English Revolution. Eighteenth-century feminists were middle-class women who argued their case in relation to the economic changes that were taking place. The emerging bourgeois class was seeking freedom and equality in society, and the feminists argued that these new freedoms and equalities should be extended to middle-class women as well as men. Writing on marriage in 1700, Mary Astell asked:

> If all men are born free, how is it that all women are born slaves? As they must be if their being subjected to the inconsistent, uncertain, unknown, arbitrary will of men be the perfect condition of slavery.
>
> (quoted in Mitchell, 1986, p. 71)

Eighteenth-century feminists rejected the view that women were naturally different from men. They argued against the social power of men and the ways in which men used that power to exclude women and prevent their being equal.

Arguably the main influence on first wave feminism, however, was Mary Wollstonecraft, who published *A Vindication of the Rights of Women* in 1792. She maintained that inequalities between men and women were not the outcome of natural (biological) differences but due to the influence of the environment, and especially the fact that women were excluded from education. She argued that both women and society in general were damaged by conditioning women into an inferior social status. What was necessary was both to educate women and to change society so that men and women were seen and treated as equal. Another major influence on the first wave feminist movement was *The Subjection of Women*, published in 1869 by John Stuart Mill and Harriet Taylor Mill. This was written at the height of the Victorian repression of women and put forward a coherent equal-rights argument – that men and women should have the same rights under the law.

Nineteenth-century feminism was mainly concerned with women having the same legal rights as men. The campaigns that were fought on issues connected with sexuality and sexual politics have been ignored or seen as right-wing because the women concerned were opposed to sexual liberation (Jeffreys, 1985). However, they argued that sexual liberation was for men and that it exploited women. They argued, for example, to raise the age of sexual consent from 13 to 16 for girls, which happened in 1885. Another issue that feminists campaigned around was the repeal of the Contagious Diseases Acts which were introduced in the 1860s in an attempt to reduce the spread of venereal diseases among men in the armed forces. The Acts, which applied to a number of garrison towns, enabled the police to stop any women they suspected of being a common prostitute and have her examined for venereal disease. If the women was found to have a venereal disease she was taken to a 'lock hospital' for compulsory treatment (Walkowitz, 1980).

During the nineteenth century it was believed that women had no interest in sex themselves and that sexual relations were purely for men's pleasure. Male homosexuality was against the law, but there was no law against lesbianism because it was not thought to exist. Women were seen as a moral force in the home and in society precisely because they were resistant to the pleasures of the body such as sexual relation, drinking and so on. The view of the early feminists was therefore to protect women from being exploited for men's pleasure.

> They were particularly outraged at the way in which the exercise of male sexuality created a division of women into 'the pure' and 'the fallen' and prevented the unity of 'sisterhood of women'. They insisted that men were responsible for prostitution and that the way to end such abuse of women was to curb the demand for prostitutes by enforcing chastity upon men rather than by punishing those who provided the supply. They employed the same arguments in their fight against other aspects of male sexual behaviour which they regarded as damaging to women, such as sexual abuse of children, incest, rape and sexual harassment in the street.
>
> (Jeffreys, 1985, p. 8)

They successfully campaigned against incest, legislation being passed in 1908, but were less successful in their attempt to get the law on 'rape in marriage' changed – the right of men to have sex with their wives was embodied in English Common Law. However, the Matrimonial Causes Act 1884 ended the power of husbands to imprison a wife who refused conjugal rights.

In other words, some feminists of the the late nineteenth and early twentieth century argued that men were able to exploit and abuse women sexually and that this was an abuse of power by adult men. Feminists in the late twentieth century, and especially radical feminists, have made very similar points and campaigned about the ways men use sexuality as a tool for controlling and subordinating women. In taking on these issues the early feminists exposed themselves to both ridicule and detestation. Sexuality was a 'taboo' subject and the feminists who campaigned around issues to do with sexuality destroyed their reputations by making public issues which were not discussed (Walkowitz, 1980).

While women did not achieve equality with men in the nineteenth century, or even the early twentieth century, most of the rights have been won with the passage of the Equal Opportunity and Equal Pay legislation implemented in 1975 (see Chapter 8). However, contemporary feminists have argued that the provision of formally equal rights is insufficient; while women are subordinated by men, while they remain dominated by the masculine ethic, they cannot be equal. Formally equal rights do not enable women to be equal with men. The demands of 'second wave' feminists have gone beyond those of the nineteenth century.

The contemporary feminist movement has been concerned to make women aware of the shared female condition that controls and constrains all women regardless of individual circumstances. A major element of the movement has been consciousness-raising – women meeting together in small groups to share their common experiences as women. The movement has rejected conventional political organisation and has sought to establish itself as a movement with no leaders, no spokespersons or privileged analysis – a key concept has been sisterhood. While the movement has been accused of being comprised predominantly of middle-class, young, educated, white women, it has nevertheless campaigned successfully and worked on a number of important issues, notably in relation to sexuality. The Women's Movement was primarily responsible for bringing to light the large number of women who are physically assaulted by their husbands, and the inadequacies of state services for these women. Women's groups have established hostels for abused women and their children around the country. Rape has been another issue about which women have campaigned. Not only has there been pressure for changes in attitudes and in the law, but also research that suggests that most women who are raped do not go to the police. Women's groups have also established confidential rape crisis lines to help women who have been raped or sexually abused. The Women's Movement has campaigned actively against sexual harassment at the workplace and raised awareness in trade unions and political organisations about the problems that women experience in relation to men. Women have also campaigned actively around contraception issues and abortion. Initially the Movement argued for free access to abortion on demand, but more recently it has argued for the woman's right to choose whether or not to have an abortion. The change came about as middle-class white women were made aware that some others, especially Black and working-class women, were pressured into having abortions. Also feminists are concerned that the choice should be made a realistic one – that is, women who choose to have the baby should have the financial and other necessary support to be able to provide for it adequately. Initially the fight was for abortion law reform, but more recently the fight has been to prevent the law being reformed so that women's access to abortions becomes very limited.

Women have been politically active, fighting for women and challenging laws and institutions that keep women in a subordinate role. The modern Movement has recognised that legislation is necessary but not sufficient for women's emancipation. The law has limited power to change attitudes and to transform an essentially masculine social order. As we saw in Chapter 2, feminists differ in their aims, but all feminists want to emancipate women from the power of men, whether this is seen as the power of individual men over individual women or structural power that maintains the dominance of patriarchal relations.

Gender politics

Sylvia Walby (1988a) has argued that we need to go beyond studies of women's political action and examine gender politics. She suggests that studies of women's political activity tend to portray it as exceptional rather than normal. Also, they focus on women rather than on the goal of gender politics, which is that women's activity is designed to change gender relations in the interests of women and men's to resist changes. Finally, they ask why so few women have participated in political activities rather than asking how men have managed so successfully to exclude women.

Thus in much feminist research, men as actors have been omitted, but Walby argues that patriarchal political practices are of vital significance in understanding gender politics. Women are not deviants in being concerned about gender politics, for men are equally concerned. In relation to women's struggle for the vote, she points out:

> Women (and a very few men) did not struggle for the vote against a vague non-gendered object. Rather, men (and a very few women) struggled against these feminist demands. Those opposing the demand for the vote for women were not passive, but rather active participants in a battle which raged for decades. They barred women from attending

political meetings (for fear they would ask the male politicians whether they would give votes to women), and they forcibly ejected women from these meetings. (Male) police arrested protesters; (male) magistrates convicted protesters; (male) members of Parliament passed Acts which regulated the imprisonment and temporary release of women suffragettes so that suffragettes would not have martyrs from the death of hunger strikers in prison; male by-standers beat up women attempting to present petitions to the Prime Minister.

(Walby, 1988a, p. 223)

She concludes by suggesting that:

we cannot understand the suffrage struggle unless we understand the nature and extent of the opposition to feminist demands by patriarchal forces.

(p. 223)

Walby also argues that most feminists have seriously underrated the radicalism of first wave feminism. She suggests that it was a large, many-faceted, long-lived and highly effective political movement. First wave feminism existed as an active political movement from about 1850 to 1930 and was involved in a variety of campaigns: examples would be access to training, education and employment for women, reform of the legal status of married women, equal right with men to divorce and legal separation, the vote for women, and issues surrounding sexuality.

A serious question, though, is why feminist political activity declined after the 1920s. To ask this question, however, Walby suggests, is to see feminism as normal, not exceptional. A number of answers to the question are probable: that women were successful in achieving what they wanted, that they were suppressed, that they had become incorporated in the trade unions and political parties; or that feminism merely *appeared* to disappear. Clearly more research is needed to make sense of what happened.

Walby concludes from her analysis:

1   that women are not as passive as is often assumed by both the malestream and some feminist literature;
2   that men resist women's political demands;
3   that the malestream view that politics is about class conflict may be challenged by the demonstration that it is also about gender conflict.

In the past, Walby suggests, gender politics has been marginalised and hidden; feminists need to uncover it. Walby concludes her arguments by suggesting

(p. 229) a number of key points that need to be taken into account in developing an analysis of gender politics:

1   Gender politics is an integral part of politics. Structural power relations between the interests of men and women are debated and fought over in political institutions.
2   Class politics and gender politics are both affected by gender politics.
3   Most political issues have a gender dimension; that is, they affect men and women differently even where this is not immediately obvious.
4   Gender politics is about the contestation between men and women, not just about women's political actions. Men resist women's demands. It is about the fight between feminists (generally women) and anti-feminists (generally men).
5   Not all women support feminist demands and not all men oppose them, but there is a high correlation between gender and political position.
6   Differences exist between feminists over the political demands to be made. There is not one feminist position. In this book we have made a distinction between a number of feminist positions (see Chapter 2). These categories, however, do not exhaust the different political positions adopted by feminists.
7   In the same way, there are varieties of patriarchal political position.
8   It is as important to ask why feminist politics appears to decline when it does as to ask why it arises when it does.

Walby is arguing, then, that if politics is about power struggles and contestation it is essential to analyse both parties to the struggle, both feminist and patriarchal political forces. We cannot understand women's political actions, nor women's participation in mainstream politics, unless we also examine the ways in which patriarchal forces resist women's demands and exclude women. So, for example, rather then asking why more women do not join political parties, stand for selection as candidates for parliamentary elections and so on, we need to ask why they were prevented from doing so.

Marxist feminists and socialist feminists would argue that it is necessary to articulate the analysis of gender politics with class politics, while many radical feminists would want to place more emphasis on the behaviour of individual men and on the politics of interpersonal relationships. Nevertheless, most feminists, we feel, would accept the main thrust of Sylvia Walby's arguments. If we are to understand women's political activities, we must analyse those with whom the women are in contestation. However, some marxist feminists would argue that this does not take account of the ways in which working-class men and women fight together on class issues, and Black feminists would argue that this does not recognise the ways in which racialised men and women fight as one to resist racism. (However, it is necessary to recognise that all women, racialised and working-class as well as white and middle-class, are subordinated by patriarchal relations.) Nor does Walby's argument take sufficient account of the ways in which the political activities of some women may be concerned with issues of relevance to them as, for example, middle-class women and totally ignore the problems confronting working-class or racialised women. This comes up clearly in the campaigns for access to abortion and contraception in the 1960s and early 1970s, and a similar point can be made about nineteenth-century middle-class women's demand to be allowed to take on paid employment while working-class women were forced to work long hours in the factories or mines. That is, while all women have in common their place in the sex–gender system, women's perceived interests and everyday experiences of patriarchal and class relations vary according to their own class and ethnic situation.

Women and the welfare state

Some feminists have argued that the state has played an important role in constructing and maintaining the bourgeois nuclear family and the ideologies that suggest that this type of family is normal and natural (e.g. Wilson, 1977; Abbott and Wallace 1992). They identify the 'welfare' aspect of the state as particularly instrumental in this respect. Here we are using 'the state' to refer to the government and all the other institutions involved in regulating society: the civil service, local government, the courts, the police and so on. The state is not just a set of institutions, but rather institutions that all exercise power and control in society and have the backing of physical force if necessary. In theory the power of the state is limitless, but in practice it is limited by ideas of non-intervention in civil society and in the domestic sphere. What we are arguing in this section is that the state does in fact play an important role in constructing and maintaining the private/domestic sphere and consequently the continuing subordination and exploitation of women. It is important to remember that women's role in the domestic sphere limits the role they can and are assumed to be able to play in the public sphere. As we suggested in Chapter 8, feminists have demonstrated the ways in which jobs are 'created' for married women and that women's employment opportunities are limited by assumptions about their future role as wives and mothers.

Women, family and caring

In Chapter 4 we saw that feminists have shown how an alliance between the male craft trade unions and the state resulted in the acceptance of the idea that a man should earn 'a family wage' – a wage sufficient to maintain a non-employed wife and children. This ideology was reinforced by protective legislation that limited the hours and types of work that women and children would be employed to do. This effectively resulted in wives becoming excluded from paid employment and the acceptance of the idea that women should care for their husbands and children in the domestic sphere. Similarly, compulsory schooling assumes that a parent (the mother) is available to take and collect children: school hours are not compatible with full-time employment for both parents. Similarly again, the lack of state provision of adequate nurseries, holiday child-care provision and the like makes it difficult for mothers to take on employment.

However, it is the interaction of ideologies about motherhood and the role of women, reinforced by state policies, that confines women to their domestic sphere or at least makes it difficult for women, and especially married women, to compete with men in the labour market and in political organisations. This is why legislation for equal opportunities has failed to result in women actually being able to compete on equal terms with men in the public sphere and why it has been equally difficult for men to take on responsibilities in the domestic sphere. The general assumption is that it is women's responsibility to care for their husbands and children, and men's to provide economic support for the family. Welfare state policies have been developed on the assumption that this is how people do and should live.

Abbott and Sapsford (1988) have examined how ideologies of the role of women as mothers, especially working-class women, developed in the late nineteenth century. The debates surrounding concern about the health of the working class at the time of the Boer War were used to reinforce the idea that women with children should not work but should care for them full-time in the home, that women (but not men) should be taught domestic skills, and that state intervention in the family was legitimate to ensure that mothers were adequately performing their role. (See also Sapsford, 1993, for a discussion of the later intrusion of psychologists into the control of mothers.)

Elizabeth Wilson (1977) draws attention to the way in which welfare as provided exercises control over its recipients and in which welfare provision is underpinned by ideologies that a particular family form is not just how people *do* live but how they *should* live – thus privileging one way of life and disadvantaging alternative patterns of social relationship. The welfare state legislation introduced in the 1940s clearly and explicitly made these assumptions in terms of providing, for example, for income maintenance during unemployment, sickness and old age with the assumption that women would be dependent on men and therefore did not need to pay full contributions in order to be entitled to these benefits.

In the 1970s and 1980s, partly as a result of pressure from the European Court of Human Rights, there have been some changes in welfare and taxation policies that remove the more gross aspects of discrimination. Most women, including married women, now pay full National Insurance contributions when in employment and can have contributions credited for periods when they are caring for dependent children or relatives. Married women are now entitled to claim the Care Allowance and are taxed separately from their husbands. However, few social policy measures have been implemented that would make it easier for married women to take paid employment – indeed, state provision for pre-school children has actually been reduced. The recently introduced Nursery Voucher Scheme by which parents can 'purchase' nursery places will not dramatically change the situation. The number of 'new' places that can be created will be limited, at least initially. Furthermore the voucher will not purchase a full-time place in a day nursery or even a nursery school and will therefore limit women's ability to take paid employment. Women who can secure well-paid employment will be assisted by the Scheme, others will not. Also, the ideological proposition that a woman's place is in the home caring for her children and husband continues to be a widely accepted and unquestioned one.

Pamela Abbott and Claire Wallace (1992) have argued that the New Right conservative government of Mrs Thatcher in Britain attempted in speeches and publications to reinforce the familial ideology that assumes the economic dependency of married women in the family. Policies such as community care (further emphasised in the 1990 National Health Service and Community Care Act) which assume that women are ready, able and willing to care for dependent and elderly relatives are an important aspect of this, assuming as they do that women are available to take on this burden and are naturally able to provide care. While the government has not repealed legislation passed in the 1970s that improved the position of women, nevertheless they have been concerned to argue that negligent mothers and mothers who work are a major cause of many contemporary social problems.

Women and poverty

State welfare policies and familial ideology also mean that women are more likely to be in poverty than men. An analysis of the groups most likely to be in poverty in modern Britain and of income distribution within households enables us to see that women are much more likely to be poor than men.

Analysis by household also conceals the ways in which women's low-paid employment can keep households out of poverty (Land, 1987) or mitigate against the full impact of poverty being felt by other members of a household (Graham, 1987b). The assumption that most women can depend on a man's wages to keep them out of poverty conceals the low pay among women workers and the low resources over which women have command, because some women are seen as financially dependent. Indeed, official statistics now talk about 'households on low incomes'.

The main groups in poverty in modern Britain are:

1   those on low wages;
2   the unemployed;
3   the long-term sick or disabled;
4   single parents; and
5   those over retirement age.

However, none of these factors is a cause of poverty. Most of these groups are dependent on state benefits; poverty ensues because state benefits are too low to lift the dependant above the poverty threshold. Governments have been explicit that benefits are designed as income maintenance, to provide a basic subsistence level. Women are over-represented in all the groups listed above. There are in addition two further reasons why women are likely to be in poverty:

6   as unpaid carers of sick, disabled or elderly relatives; or
7   as dependants of a male wage earner – either because that wage is at the poverty level or because the man does not share his resources equitably within the household.

Jane Millar and Caroline Glendinning (1987), in an analysis of the 1983 Family Expenditure Survey, found that two household types are the most likely to be poor (i.e. living on 140 per cent or less of the supplementary benefit level) – elderly women living alone (of whom 60 per cent were in poverty) and lone mothers (of whom 61 per cent were in poverty). Together the two types account for 32 per cent of households in poverty but constitute only 15 per cent of all households.

Feminists have argued that women's poverty has to be seen in the context of women's marginal position in the labour market and the assumed dependency of women on men for financial support. This latter assumption is employed both in the income support system (despite minor changes in recent years) and in the ideology of the 'family wage'. The assumption is not only that there is a sexual division of labour such that men are the economic providers and women the carers, but the ideology also carries over and influences the economic position of women who do not live with a man, whether because single, divorced or widowed. Women's position in the labour market means that they are less likely than men to earn a living wage and are concentrated in low-paid jobs (see Chapter 8). It is this assumed dependence of women on men that has been used, historically, to justify the higher pay of men (the 'family wage') and is reflected in welfare state legislation. The disadvantages that women in the labour market experience also contribute to the poverty of lone-parent mothers. Even when a woman bringing up children on her own feels that she can manage to take on paid employment as well, she may find that there is no economic advantage in doing so. The kind of low-paid work she is likely to be able to find, coupled with the expenses of work and childminding fees, mean that most lone mothers will not be better off than when drawing benefit.

Finally, women are expected to be primarily responsible for children, the elderly and other dependants, although if they take on these roles they will be in danger of falling into poverty. For many married women with children or other caring responsibilities, poverty will be the major problem.

Women's low pay, interrupted labour-market participation and tendency to take on part-time employment for a period of time also affects their entitlement to income maintenance when they are not economically active. Women are assumed to be dependent on the men with whom they live, whether married or not, and it is assumed that these men will make provision for income maintenance for themselves and their wives in old age. This assumption has been reflected in legislation, and while there have been some changes in social security legislation in recent years this has not markedly changed the situation. Under social security regulations current at the time of writing, a woman whose male friend stays more than three nights per week is deemed to be supported by him, and her benefit is cut. The case for this is particularly strong if she also does his washing or cooks him meals. It is clear that in social security regulations economic support should be provided in return for sexual and domestic services. While the 'cohabitation rule', as it is known, can also be applied to female visitors of men, this is very rare.

Women who are caring for children receive no income maintenance, although those caring for an adult dependant are entitled to a care allowance. However, this does not compensate for loss of wages, being paid in any case at a lower rate than contributory benefits such as unemployment or sick pay. Women who become unemployed are entitled to unemployment pay only if they have made sufficient contributions and can fulfil the criteria for registering as unemployed (i.e. available for work). Women may not be entitled to unemployment pay for a number of reasons: because they have not been working for long enough; because they were working too few hours to pay contributions; or because they elected to pay the 'married woman's rate' of contribution (before 1976). They may not be able to register because they cannot demonstrate satisfactorily their availability for full-time work (because they have young children) or because they will not state that they are prepared to travel anywhere in the country. Similarly, many married women are not entitled to claim contributory invalidity benefits, and the 'housework test' of the non-contributory benefit is extremely difficult to satisfy. Income support (the replacement for supplementary benefit) is paid to a household, and the principle of assessment is household need. While the female partner can claim it if she and her partner agree and she can demonstrate a commitment to the labour market, the assessment is based on household income. Feminists have also pointed out that household income is often not equally shared and that women can be in poverty even within a relatively affluent household if benefits and wages all go to the man (Graham 1984).

Feminists have therefore concluded that women's poverty can be understood only in the context of gender inequalities that persist throughout life. Ideologies of women's 'natural' abilities and 'natural' roles structure women's opportunities to take on paid work and the type of jobs that are offered to them. The realities of women's lives, structured by these ideologies and state policies, also limit their opportunities to take on employment and the range of types of employment they can take on. Furthermore, the assumption that men support their wives means that much female poverty is hidden. Women are expected to manage on the money, to be wise spenders and to make the money stretch. They are also likely to be the ones to have to refuse their children the treats, clothes, outings and activities that many children take for granted and to have continually to disappoint their children. Women also have to suffer the stress, the lack of opportunities for fulfilment and the feelings of insecurity that go with being poor. Also, women's health as well as their general well-being suffers as a result of being poor, especially if they lack an adequate diet because they put the needs of other family members before their own.

Conclusions

Thus the idea of the public and private and the exclusion of women from the public sphere have been created by political processes – government legislation and state policies. Familial ideologies that place women in the domestic sphere as wives and mothers are reinforced both by legislation and by the speeches and manifestos of political parties.

SUMMARY

1   Women have been stereotyped in conventional accounts of political behaviour as being uninterested in politics, politically conservative and influenced by their husbands. All these stereotypes have been shown not to hold.

2   Conventional politics reflects male concerns and has effectively excluded women. Hence women are under-represented in public political life.

3   The welfare state and welfare policies have constructed and reinforced women's traditional position as wives and mothers.

4   Feminists have struggled over issues affecting women – specifically their rights to property and custody of their children in the nineteenth century, and their rights to abortion, equal pay and nursery provision in the twentieth century. Furthermore, feminists have redefined the notion of politics around personal struggle as well as public campaign.

FURTHER READING

Abbott, P. A. and Wallace, C. (1992) *The Family and the New Right*, London: Pluto.

Banks, O. (1981) *Faces of Feminism*, Oxford: Martin Robertson.

Glendinning, C. and Millar, J. (eds) (1992) *Women and Poverty in Britain in the 1990s*, Hemel Hempstead: Harvester/Wheatsheaf.

Lovenduski, J. and Randall, V. (1993) *Contemporary Feminist Politics: women and power in Britain*, Oxford: Oxford University Press.

MacLean, M. and Groves, D. (eds) (1991) *Women's Issues in Social Policy*, London: Routledge.

Siltanen, J. and Stanworth, M. (eds) (1984) *Women and the Public Sphere: a critique of sociology and politics*, London: Hutchinson.

Chapter eleven

The production of feminist knowledges

A central argument of this book has been that sociology has ignored, distorted or marginalised women. We have also suggested that this is a result of the systematic biases and inadequacies in malestream theories, not just an omission of women from samples. Malestream theories do not ask questions or do research in areas of concern to women, and frequently women are excluded from the samples; when they are included they are viewed from a position that sees males as the norm. As we pointed out in Chapter 1, sociological theories have often taken for granted, rather than challenged, the view that the biological differences between men and women are sufficient to explain and justify the sexual division of labour. Feminist sociologists have argued that it is necessary to develop feminist theories: theories that explain the world from the position of women, theories that enable us to rethink the sexual division of labour and to conceptualise reality in a way that reflects women's interests and values, drawing on women's own interpretations of their own experiences. However, feminist theory has moved on from the work of the 1970s, when a few women were grappling with the malestream, to a position where sociology has begun, at least in part, to take the feminist challenge seriously and where there are debates between feminists, as women become more aware of their role in the production of knowledges.

Thus feminist theories criticise the abstraction and over-inclusiveness of male-generated categories that conceal women's oppression. They should enable us to make sense of our lives, to understand the ways in which we are oppressed and exploited by men, and to explain how and why men oppress women. Furthermore, they should enable us to relate our experiences to the ways in which the society in which we live is structured. Individual men may be the agents of oppression, but patriarchal relationships also exist in the institutions and social practices of society. Feminist theories must also enable us to understand how we come to see ourselves as individuals – how we come to accept that a woman's role is in the home, that women are capable only of certain jobs, that women are worse at mathematics and sciences than boys, that only women who have had and cared for children are fully developed women, and so on. They must enable us to understand how we become both subjects (housewives, nurses, secretaries) and subject to the idea that it is natural that women should take on these roles and therefore accept our subordinate position in society.

However, it is important to recognise that different women have different experiences of reality; the way in which they are subordinated is different. Feminist theory has tended to be developed by white, middle-class women who work in institutions of higher education. While all women share a subordinate position in our society, not all women experience it in the same way; theories developed by white middle-class women have been correctly criticised for marginalising the experiences of working-class and racialised women. To represent reality adequately from the standpoints of women, feminist theory must draw on a variety of women's experiences. To do this it is necessary to find ways in which all groups of women can participate in theory-building – to ensure that feminist theories adequately incorporate the experiences of working-class and Black women.

Feminist theories are also political: they set out not just to explain society but to transform it. Feminist theories are concerned to analyse how women can transform society so that they are no longer subordinated, by understanding how patriarchal relations control and constrict them. Consequently the adequacy of feminist theories is tested at least in part by their usefulness: that is, the extent to which they provide useful and usable knowledge for women. Feminist sociology is concerned, then, to build what Dorothy Smith (1987) has called a sociology for women – a sociology that relates to women, with which women can identify, in which women recognise themselves as the subject of what is being said, and which helps us to understand our everyday lives as well as the ways in which they are structured and established within a male-dominated society.

A sociology for women empowers women because knowledge is power. Women have inhabited a cultural, political and intellectual world from whose making they have been excluded and in which they have been recognised as of no more than marginal relevance. Malestream scientific knowledge, including sociology, has been used to justify the exclusion of women from positions of power and authority in cultural, political and intellectual institutions of society. Feminist knowledge, including sociology, challenges the objectivity and truth of that knowledge (which is presented as neutral) and seeks to replace it with more adequate knowledge – more adequate because it arises from the position of the oppressed and seeks to understand that oppression.

Some radical feminists would argue that we should not seek to develop new, feminist theories because the theoretical approach is an essentially masculine way of working. Theorising is seen as a task undertaken by an elite that devalues, or even ignores, the experiences of women not included in the elite. Feminist sociologists, they argue, are trying to replace one 'truth' by another 'truth' and in doing so fail to recognise the validity of the experience of all women. The feminist task, they suggest, is to use the experiences of all women in making sense of women's lives and fighting oppression.

However, we would argue that all explanation and research is an essentially theoretical activity, whether the theory is made explicit or remains implicit. 'Facts' – our experiences and our observations – do not speak for themselves; we have to explain them – that is, to theorise them. Feminist theories have enabled women to do this – to make sense of their lives and the cultural, political and intellectual worlds that they inhabit. Experience itself is a product of our theories; we *interpret* and *make sense of* what is happening in our lives. In the past women have had to use malestream theories; we need to replace them with more adequate feminist theories.

It could be argued that attempts to develop feminist sociology are themselves a contradiction (in much the same way as it has been argued that a marxist sociology is a contradiction): that the Women's Movement and feminism are themselves concerned with understanding women's lives and developing strategies that will enable women to liberate themselves from oppression. Feminists have sought to break down artificial – man-made – barriers between disciplines and to develop interdisciplinary studies that recognise that we cannot compartmentalise knowledge or women's lives into discrete areas. A Women's Studies syllabus would include, for example, women's literature, women's art, women's history and feminist biology as well as feminist social science. The subjects would not necessarily be taught as disciplines, but on a topic basis. We agree with this. Likewise, feminist theories are not bound by discipline. The theories that we have used in this book and the epistemological stances which we examine in more detail in this chapter are not restricted to sociology – they are not *sociological* theories and epistemological positions, but *feminist* ones. Nevertheless, feminists have been interested in many areas that concern sociologists, and many female sociologists would regard themselves and the work they do as feminist. Feminists have never claimed to be scientific observers of the world, however, and would argue that no knowledge is neutral; malestream knowledge has been used to control women, and feminist knowledge is an aid to the emancipation of women.

Collecting feminist evidence

Theories are world views that enable us to make sense of the world. They guide us in terms of what is important and relevant to question and how to interpret what is going on. However, to understand the world it is also necessary to collect evidence – to carry out research. Research methods are the means by which sociologists gather material about society. The main research methods used in sociology are usually divided into 'quantitative' methods – most notably the Survey and the statistical analysis of secondary-source data – and 'ethnographic' or 'qualitative' methods, most notably participant observation, in-depth interviewing and the qualitative analysis of secondary sources of data. One could argue that no research method is explicitly feminist or anti-feminist; it is the ways in which research is carried out and the theoretical framework within which the results are interpreted that determine if research is feminist or not. However, many feminists have rejected quantitative methods of data collection and analysis because they argue these assume a scientificity that sociology cannot and should not strive to attain, and because they treat people as objects, as natural scientists treat chemicals or rocks, rather than as human subjects.

Feminist research has been concerned to move away from the positivistic view of sociology as a science and to argue that research should involve a commitment to the emancipation of women. While some feminists have suggested that feminist research should be research by women, for women and with women, others have argued that it should include both men and women in its 'subject-matter', explicitly recognising and investigating the sex–gender system that exists in the society being researched.

Harding (1987b) has suggested that it is *not* the method of research that makes feminist research significantly different from malestream research, but:

1   the alternative origin of problems – raising problems and issues that are of concern to women rather than to men;
2   the alternative explanatory hypotheses that are developed and the evidence that is used;
3   the purpose of the enquiry – to facilitate an understanding of women's

views of the world and to play a role in female emancipation; and

4   the nature of the relationship between the researcher and the 'subjects' of her enquiry.

She points to the need to distinguish between methods, methodologies and epistemologies. Methods are techniques for gathering evidence. Methodologies are theories of how research should proceed. Epistemologies define what counts as an adequate theory and how research findings can be judged: what makes the findings of one piece of research more adequate than the findings of other research in the same area. The question of epistemology raises the issue of who the knower (researcher) can be, what tests of belief something must pass to count as legitimate knowledge, and what class of things can be known.

What is distinctive about feminist research is the methodology and epistemology that underlie it. However, feminists are not in total agreement; there are competing theories and arguments about the ways in which feminists should undertake research. There is, however, some measure of agreement about the reasons for rejecting malestream research:

1   In the name of science, malestream sociologists have helped to sustain an ideology that supports the continuing subordination of women.

2   Women, and women's concerns, have not been seen as a major aspect of the research project. When women are included in research they are seen as marginal and viewed from the perspective of men. There has also been a tendency to present man as norm, and when women do not conform to this norm to present them as deviant.

3   Those who have been researched have been treated as objects to be worked on. Researchers have also used those studied to serve the researchers' purposes rather than to meet the needs and aspirations of the researched. Feminists have referred to this as the 'research as rape' model. Shulamit Reinharz captures this criticism well:

> conducted on a rape model, the researchers take, hit and run. They intrude into their subjects' privacy, disrupt their perceptions, utilise false pretences, manipulate the relationships, and give little or nothing in return. When the needs of the researchers are satisfied, they break off contact with the subjects.
>
> (Reinharz, 1983, p. 80)

Feminists are concerned to develop research strategies to incorporate women and not to treat the researched as objects to be used by the researcher. There are differences among feminists as to how this is to be done – as to what exactly feminist research is and how to go about doing it. Initially much feminist scholarship and research was deconstructionalist – that is, concerned to expose the male-centred nature of existing sociological research, to point out that it was biased and ideological because it ignored the experiences and perceptions of women. The second stage was research on women by women. This research asked new questions and was concerned to provide knowledge from the perspective of women. It was recognised that it was necessary to develop theories to provide an understanding of women's experience. Many feminists see this as the main objective of feminist research – especially radical feminists. The third stage has been the development of the argument that feminists can develop a feminist sociology only if they research men as well as women, but with the proviso that the research is from the perspective of women, providing a fuller and more adequate knowledge.

The logic of the feminist position on research seems to demand non-individual co-research, where the researcher helps the women involved to undertake their own research, so that researcher and researched decide together on the object of the research, how the research is to be conducted and how the findings are to be used. In practice, few feminists have adopted this method. This is partly because it is not possible for the researcher to share her knowledge and expertise, and to imply that she is sharing them conceals a power relationship rather than overcoming it. Furthermore, most researchers are middle-class women with a university education, and many of those who are researched lack this privileged background.

Most feminists have argued, however, that feminist researchers in sociology must use qualitative methods, so that the women (and men) who are the subjects of research can be 'heard', so that it becomes possible to see and understand the world from the position of the research subjects. They have also rejected the view that feminist researchers can be objective in the sense of being uninvolved, because as researchers they are part of what is being researched. Involvement is seen as necessary and inevitable: necessary because the researcher must and does identify with the women she is researching, and inevitable because she is a part of what is being researched – she is involved. This means that reflexivity is essential – the researcher must be constantly aware of how her values, attitudes and perceptions are influencing the research process, from the formulation of the research questions, through the data-collection stage, to the ways in which the data are analysed and theoretically explained.

In practice, feminist sociologists have found it difficult to carry out research that lives up to the demands of the methodology that has been set out above. This is because of the sheer difficulty of doing research at all, because the training of most female researchers has taken place within malestream assumptions, because there are inevitably power relationships involved in research, because the funders of research have certain views about what constitutes 'good' research practice, and because feminist sociologists are part of a wider academic community to which they have to justify their research practices and findings. One of the main traps into which they fall is to take on a neutral stance, so that the research is on women, asks questions of interest to women and uses qualitative methods, but the researcher tries to stand back and remain detached from what is going on rather than being a part of the research process and making explicit her involvement as a woman. Ann Oakley (1982) suggests that she was often aware of how much of a danger this was when she was interviewing women about the events surrounding maternity and childbirth – a subject of central interest to the women being researched and to Oakley herself as a woman and mother.

Feminist sociologists also frequently use the research findings for publications that are as much for their career advancement as to help the women (and men) who were the subjects of research – although, of course, the publication of research findings can influence policy-makers and could result in changes in women's lives that meet their needs. The danger here is that the researcher does not have control over how others interpret and use the research findings.

Most feminists would argue against the view that the researcher/scientist is not responsible for how the findings of research are used, but once research is published the researcher has lost control. Janet Finch's research finding (1983b) that working-class mothers find it difficult to organise pre-school playgroups for their children could as easily be used to argue that this means that they are responsible for their children not having pre-school education as to argue that the state should organise and run pre-school facilities for working-class children. This does not mean that we reject feminist research or that we do not publish our findings. It means that we have to be constantly aware of the dangers of appearing to be a neutral scientist and of the ways in which research findings can be distorted by anti-feminist interpretation.

Feminist epistemologies

The problem for feminists in sociology is having their research findings taken seriously. On what basis are the findings better than, more true than, those of malestream sociologists? Indeed, why should we believe the findings of *any* sociological research? The claims for the truth or value of research are generally based on justificatory claims – referred to as epistemological stances. In the modern world the dominant basis for truth claims is that the research was scientific – that is, the researcher was objective and value-free and followed certain agreed procedures for carrying out the research – the

Scientific Method. This epistemology is generally referred to as 'positivism'. Although sociologists other than feminists have been critical of positivistic social science, feminists have made a significant contribution to the understanding of the connection between power and knowledge. In particular, they have pointed out that the recognition of knowledge claims is intrinsically tied to relations of domination and exclusion.

A major problem is that feminist research can be accused of being 'subjective' and therefore of no value. If it is seen as subjective then there is no way of showing how feminist conclusions are any better than those reached by anyone else and why the findings of feminist research are better than those of malestream research and should be taken seriously. There is a number of feminist epistemological stances which have been adopted to provide the basis for feminist truth claims, which we shall go on in this chapter to examine. However, we must be aware, as Liz Stanley and Sue Wise (1993) point out, that:

> Marking out the attributes of different although related feminist episte-mologies, such as feminist empiricism, feminist standpoint and feminist postmodernism, is useful as long as it is recognised that this produces *a model*, and is thus necessarily a simplified (not a literal/representational) account of the epistemological possibilities that exist.
>
> (p. 190)

They go on to argue that feminists typically encompass in their actual work elements of a number of epistemological stances. They suggest (p. 191) that five broad principles should be adopted in considering feminist epistemologies:

1   while there is a range of feminist epistemologies, in practice these shade into each other in people's research;
2   different feminist epistemological positions sometimes disagree over the basis of knowledge, who generates it and under what conditions;
3   feminist sociologists often combine elements of a number of epistemo-logical positions within their work, and this indicates not only that we can work within contradictions, but that either we do not think carefully through the basis of what we do and what we claim for it, or alternatively that we do think it through but choose to work with 'contradictory' elements because this is what social reality is like;
4   there is no 'true' feminist epistemology – each can be seen to be sensible and plausible given the purposes and project of those who hold it;
5   we can challenge and question other positions, but that we should have mutual respect for different feminisms and recognise the value of diversity.

Feminist empiricism

Feminist empiricists are critical of malestream research because it has been male-centred. They suggest that feminists are more likely to produce adequate knowledge because they include women and women's experiences in their research as central and normal rather than as marginal and deviant. The logical goal of this perspective is the development of non-sexist research. Magrit Eichler (1988) has produced guidelines for such research:

1   to avoid sexism in titles: titles should be explicit (for example, 'The Affluent Worker' study should be retitled 'The Male Affluent Worker' study);
2   sexism in language has to be eliminated: language should be used that makes it clear whether men or women or both are being addressed or referred to;
3   sexist concepts need to be eliminated (for example, defining class by reference to the occupation of the head of household);
4   sexism in research designs has to be overcome so that men and women are both included in the research where this is relevant;
5   sexism in methods has to be eliminated;
6   sexism in data interpretation has to be eliminated – the interpretation of data from the perspective just of men or just of women;
7   sexism in policy evaluation has to be eliminated, so that policies that serve the needs of both men and women are advocated.

Most feminists would agree with Eichler but argue that what she says is insufficient. They would reject the positivistic research stance that underlies her preoccupation with non-sexist methods, arguing that given the power relations that exist in society such research practices would continue to be male-dominated and meet the needs of men rather than of women. This is because such research does not challenge the underlying assumptions inherent in malestream research, which are presented as truths.

Liz Stanley and Sue Wise (1983) argue that research carried out in the traditional sociological framework, whether 'positivistic' or 'naturalistic', draws on a pre-chosen framework – the findings are abstracted from reality and presented as if given research logics had been followed. Material is organised for the reader, and information is not given about what happened, when it happened, how it happened and how the people involved (including the researchers) felt about it. They argue that it is essential to recognise that malestream sociological research is written up as if a formal pattern of procedures were carried out, but that in practice this is rarely what happens. We would argue that non-sexist research as advocated by Eichler would fall

291

into the same trap. This type of research account fails to examine the relationships between experience, consciousness and theory because it acts as if they are unimportant or do not exist. The researcher is presented as an objective, neutral and value-free technician who is following set procedures. All that Eichler does is to replace what she and feminists would agree are sexist practices with practices which attempt to overcome only the sexism. Most feminists would argue that following such a set of procedures would not produce feminist knowledge because they reject the view that the researcher can be neutral and value-free, that knowledge exists not only independently of the person(s) who produce it, but also that those who produce knowledge can do so without their values and attitudes influencing the knowledge they produce. That is, even if there is a reality independent of our understanding, we cannot reproduce that reality uncontaminated. However, it is important to keep in mind that while feminist empiricists do subscribe to the idea of an objective, knowable world, they are also committed to carrying out research for women and providing empirical knowledge to be used in feminist politics and campaigns (see, e.g., Riley, 1992).

'The feminist standpoint'

'Standpoint' feminists argue that they are concerned to produce socially relevant knowledge that is 'adequate' or 'good enough'; that is, they seek to justify their research findings as better, more adequate, than those produced by the malestream or other feminist researchers. The research findings should be both useful to and usable by women. It is a position taken mainly by academic feminists who want their work to be accepted as scholarship and to make a contribution to sociological knowledge as well as to produce research that will be of benefit to women. They are concerned that their research will advance the understanding of social life and to have a basis for claiming that those who do not share their starting position should be convinced by the conclusions. They are concerned to demonstrate why their research findings should be believed and why their research should be funded. It is a position most closely associated with dual-systems feminists and takes a realist stance – that is, it believes that there is an underlying material reality that structures the social world. Malestream theory, it is argued by women who take this position, has a distorted or partial view of this reality, but feminist research is able to provide a better, less partial account.

This position shares with positivism the assumption of a single and universal social as well as physical world and the view that trained experts have a greater degree of knowledge and understanding than others. However, people who adopt it recognise that the production of knowledge is a politically engaged activity. Malestream researchers have often refused to acknowledge this, but it is a problem which feminist researchers have confronted. They want to reject the view that all knowledge is equally valid (relativism) and to argue that it is essential to be able to justify some research findings and theoretical explanations as more adequate than others. If this is not possible then it is difficult to see why feminist research findings and explanations should be seen as better or more true than malestream ones. It is necessary to be able to demonstrate that some statements are better accounts of social reality than others, while recognising their inevitable partiality.

Researchers cannot avoid some selection and interpretation of their material, and it is essential that this is acknowledged. All knowledge is based on experience, and standpoint theorists claim their research is scientifically preferable because it originates in and is tested against a more complete and less distorted kind of experience than malestream research. Human activity, it is suggested, structures and sets limits to human understanding, and what we do shapes and constrains what we can know. However, human activity is structured for and experienced differently by men and women because the latter are subordinated; feminist sociologists have a privileged access to *real* social reality because the oppressed can see people and events as they really are. In the words of Dorothy Smith (1987), they have:

> a wider angle of view because they can see things from the perspective of not only the privileged (men) but also the oppressed women.
>
> (p. 99)

There is an important claim to power here – the power of knowledge and the power to claim true knowledge. Knowledge production is seen as a political process, with some knowledge claims certified as superior to others.

Standpoint theorists argue that men's knowledge can never be complete. It is not just that the oppressed can see more, but also that their knowledge emerges through their struggle against oppression – women's knowledge emerges from a struggle against men and the attempt to replace the distorted knowledge produced by men which is used to control and subordinate women. The feminist standpoint is an achievement – it is the portrayal of social life from the viewpoint of the activity which produces women's social experience, not from the partial and perverse perspective available from the 'ruling gender' experiences of men.

Standpoint feminists argue that their accounts of the social world are less partial and less distorted than malestream ones. Feminist science is better able to reflect the world as it is and is able to replace the distorted and distorting accounts produced by malestream sociology and consequently to advance sociological knowledge. It is based on the view that there is a real world, but that our accounts of it are always and inevitably partial, and that feminist accounts are less partial and less distorted than malestream ones. However, standpoint feminists have been criticised for ignoring differences *between* women and assuming an unproblematic commonality. The 'adding on' of difference – race, age, sexuality, etc. – is done in an unproblematic way that assumes that middle-class white feminist theory can be used to theorise the experience of non-white women. The same criticism can probably be made as of the inclusion of women as a category in malestream research – it does not take account of difference – difference that is the outcome of separate processes of racialism, ageism, heterosexism that result in super- and subordination.

Some Black feminists, for example Patricia Hill Collins, have argued that as a more oppressed group Black women's standpoint is not only different from but has a wider angle of vision than white women's standpoint. Subsequently (1990), however, she has questioned this earlier argument (1986) that the more oppressed you are the more correct your analysis of the social origins of oppression. Instead she has argued that Black women's accounts of the social world are different from but not necessarily better than white women's. Arguably this raises the question of how we choose the 'best' accounts of reality. Alternatively, it can be argued that all knowledge is partial and that accounts from different standpoints will add to our knowledge and understanding of social reality.

Feminist constructivism

Feminist constructivism challenges the foundationalism of both positivistic and standpoint epistemologies and argues for a social constructionist feminism. Foundationalism is the view that reality is singular and 'out there' independently of our understanding of it and available for experts to probe and discover – for example, that capitalism and patriarchy have an independent objective reality discoverable by experts. Constructivism argues that the social world is constructed and shaped by members of society – they reject the claim that there is a 'true' knowledge which certifies some feminist knowledge as better than, superior to, other feminist knowledges. However, in contrast to postmodern feminism, feminist constructivism retains the category 'woman', arguing that not to do so would be to dissolve into an ungendered deconstructionist position.

In rejecting the standpoint position, they argue that there cannot be a feminist science and that academic feminists who advocate the standpoint position are only trying to set up a new truth. These feminists are deeply sceptical about claims to universal knowledge and argue that there is no social world or set of social structures 'out there' waiting to be known, but only many subjective experiences. 'All that feminist (or indeed any) researchers can do is to uncover the many stories that different women tell and reveal the different knowledges that they have' (see Stanley and Wise, 1983, pp. 145–8). In a later book (1993), Liz Stanley and Sue Wise argue that all knowledge is a product of human social experience.

> Thus there is no way of moving outside of experience to validate theories 'objectively' – nothing exists other than social life, our place within it and our understandings of all this.
>
> (p. 193)

Feminists such as these are critical of malestream research because of its claims to objectivity, to reveal truth, and the claim that the researcher is not involved in the research process. They reject the view that the sociologist can be a dispassionate and uncritical 'scientific' observer and argue that the experiences and feelings of the subject should be at the centre of the production of all social knowledge. Also, they argue that it is only possible for women, because of their shared experiences of oppression, to do research on women. Stanley and Wise (1983), for example, argue that researchers in presenting accounts of their research 'do not tell it as it happened' but present a reconstructed account of how the research was undertaken that accords with textbook accounts. Not only are these accounts false, but they fail to reveal the ways in which the researcher was involved in the research process. Consequently they argue that feminist research must be genuinely reflexive – that is, the accounts of the research must make available to the reader the procedures which underlie the way the knowledge which is presented was produced out of the research and draw on the experience of 'being a researcher' and the experiences of being a feminist in any social situation – the 'intellectual autobiography' of the researchers. It is also essential not to deny one's experiences and feelings as a feminist, but to use them as part of the process of validating one's research rather than *vice versa* – that is, we should accept the validity of our own experiences as women. The adequacy of knowledge is based on the extent to which it enables us to understand better our situation as women and gives us the resources with which to emancipate ourselves.

This position rejects the idea of feminist grand theory but argues that women do have a unity of experience in the same way that racialised groups, lesbians, male homosexuals and heterosexuals do. These social/political constructions, it argues, are fundamental to the systematic assignment of positions of super- and subordination. However, it is also necessary for feminist theorisation to take account of the multiple fragmentation of women's experiences of oppression, based on age, sexuality, 'race', political persuasion, disability and so on. It argues for the valid existence of varieties of feminist epistemology, together with the

> acknowledgment of the contextual specificity of feminist as of other knowledge, the recognition that who a researcher is, in terms of their sex, race, class and sexuality, affects what they 'find' in research [and] is as true of feminists as any other researchers.
>
> (Stanley and Wise, 1993, p. 228)

The major problem with this position is its relativism. While we agree that researchers must be reflexive, that women must speak for themselves and that research findings should help the oppressed, we are sceptical of the view that all women's accounts are equally valid and that there is no way of selecting between them.

Postmodern feminist epistemology

Postmodernist epistemology totally rejects foundationalism – the attempt to provide knowledge with a firm foundation. As anti-foundationalists they reject the idea of a neutral world of 'facts' independent of theory. They argue that knowledge is rooted in the values and interests of particular social groups. They reject all truth claims – the production of knowledge, they would assert, is always a construction. Consequently, for them (unlike constructivist feminists) there can be no identity politics, because this assumes an active agent, a subject who exists prior to action. Nor can there be universal theories; the emphasis must be on difference and therefore there can be no category 'woman' about which feminist theory can be built.

A postmodernist epistemology is concerned with explaining the discursive procedures whereby human beings gain an understanding of their common world. By 'discourse' (and the adjectival form, 'discursive') we mean a conceptual framework which shows some current and historical consistency:

> Whenever, between objects, types of statement, concepts or thematic choices, one can define a regularity ... we will say, for the sake of convenience, that we are dealing with a *discursive formation*.
>
> (Foucault, 1969, p. 38)

Thus a discourse is a set of ideas. It is much more than this, however – it is the framework within which possible ideas can be set, and the conceptual sieve which passes some ideas as 'well formed' and rejects others as incoherent.

Furthermore the notion applies as much (or more, even) to practices which are conceptually governed as to the concepts themselves:

> the target of analysis [is] ... *practices* ... practices being understood here as places where what is said and what is done, rules imposed and reasons given, the planned and the taken for granted meet and interconnect ...
>
> (Foucault, 1980, p. 5)

Arguments happen within discourses. Discourses do not determine which shall win, in a clash of ideas, but they determine the way in which the debate must be held in order for it to make acceptable sense: they determine the rules of truth – what you have to do to win an argument – and, more importantly, the objects of analysis (what you may argue *about*, what there *is* about which to have ideas.) They therefore determine what may be thought and what may *not* be thought, in a given context, and thus what it makes sense to do and what makes no sense:

> ... programmes of conduct which had both prescriptive effects regarding what is to be done (effects of 'jurisdiction') and codifying effects regarding what is to be known (effects of 'verisdiction').
>
> (Foucault, 1980, p. 5)

A necessary consequence of thinking in terms of discourses is that the concept of 'truth' is greatly weakened; 'true' *means* 'what the discourse allows to be true'. Postmodern feminism accepts this consequence entirely, and it takes the position that there is not one truth (masculine/feminine) but many truths, none of which is privileged along gender lines. Thus it challenges the whole idea of an epistemological foundation for knowledge. Knowledge is not acquired by a subject studying an object, but knowledge, along with subject and object, is collectively constituted through discourse. There is nothing outside discourse – no objective reality or self. All knowledge is constituted discursively. The discourses that create knowledge also create the power that constitutes subjects and objects and the mechanisms by which subjects are subjugated. There is no way of stepping outside the discourse to check against an independent reality. For example, biological discourses construct 'male' and 'female', and the justification for the view that sex is biologically based and that women are inferior to men. Men's power over women is then justified by the knowledge. Knowledge and power are therefore inseparable. Knowledge is power to the extent that it is accepted as truth. There is, however, no final arbiter of truth.

Postmodernists therefore reject the 'will to truth' and the view that there can be true knowledge – that feminist knowledge is better than, truer than malestream knowledge. For this reason they argue that standpoint feminism which does not challenge the idea of a valid or universal truth cannot handle the concept of multiple realities or deconstructionist ideas.

In this view, then, all that feminist knowledge can do is to present alternative accounts, to question and to challenge.

> I want to attempt to analyse law in a way which recognises the power of law to disqualify or silence, yet does not seek to posit an alternative truth as the main strategy to resist legal discourse.
>
> (Smart, 1995, p. 78)

Using rape as the main example, Carol Smart goes on to suggest that:

> My point is that there may be other accounts of rape [than legal ones] which could become forms of resistance rather than sources of victimisation.
>
> (p. 86)

However, she refuses to privilege any account as more true, more accurate, and indeed parenthetically indicates that if women did take up an account that enabled them to resist the ways in which rape victims are characterised within legal discourse they might lose the existing protection from the law, We are left with the view that all sociology can do is 'construct subversive knowledge' (p. 230).

You will have realised from this account that we are not sympathetic to this position. We have been greatly influenced by it and take to heart its reminder that social reality is always more detailed and more specific than 'grand theory' would have one suppose; in the rest of the book you will have seen that we use post-structuralist ideas of discourse and discursive process extensively. Our major criticisms of it as a 'grand theory' in its own right would be:

1   The position is self-defeating in philosophical terms – it elevates the principle of 'no truth except within a discourse' to a general principle which is true outside of discourse (and, indeed, it is impossible to enunciate a general principle which others are to believe and not do so).
2   It abolishes both sociology and feminism as academic modes of research – if there are no general categories, then there can be no study of structured inequalities or power relations and no attempt to understand women's oppression. We sympathise with and are much influenced by postmodernism's insistence on the specific, the detailed and the

difference between elements which 'grand theory' may wish to combine. Nonetheless we still see the need for grand theory, however tentative it may have to be and however necessary it may be to remember that what is true of a collective does not necessarily explain the actions and experiences of any individual member of it. (See also Rattansi (1995), who makes the case for avoiding a polarisation into 'the postmodern' and 'the rest'.)

3   Postmodernism appears to abolish politics: if, for example, the category 'woman' is meaningless, then the notion of women fighting their oppressors is equally meaningless.

4   Finally, postmodernism strongly suggests that the very self is fragmented and that it makes little sense to talk about it as a coherent bounded whole which acts and takes decisions. Again we understand the force of this position. If taken to the extreme that some postmodernists adopt, however, it abolishes ethics, because there is no self to take responsibility for actions.

Conclusions

We are not suggesting that one feminist epistemology is correct and the others are wrong, in any simple 'black and white' way. (While attacking postmodernism as a 'grand epistemological stance', for example, we are nonetheless very much influenced by it.) We have tried to point out some of the inadequacies of epistemological positions, and we see this as constructive rather than destructive; it is by recognising what an epistemology cannot explain that we can develop more adequate ones. Our major contention in this book is that mainstream sociology is inadequate because it ignores or distorts or marginalises women. It is inadequate not only because it does not fully incorporate women, but because the knowledge it produces is at best partial because it does not take account of over half the population – women. Women have found that the knowledge provided by conventional sociology does not relate to their lives or their concerns.

Feminism does seek to speak to the experiences of women, to understand reality from the viewpoint of women, to ask questions that relate to women's lives and to uncover the systematic biases and distortions in malestream knowledge. In this book we have tried to show the ways in which feminist scholarship has made a contribution to sociology. We have argued that this does not mean that we can just add one more perspective to the list of sociological topics. What is necessary is a total rethinking of sociological knowledge and the ways in which that knowledge is produced. This is because it is not accidental or the result of an oversight that women have been ignored, marginalised or distorted in sociology, but the outcome of the theoretical underpinning of the discipline. Malestream sociology failed to confront the view that women are naturally determined and women's role the outcome of biological imperatives. Consequently the concepts developed to carry out sociological research, and the issues seen as there to be researched, ignored women. To produce adequate sociological knowledge it is necessary to reformulate these concepts and questions so that women become central to the concerns of the discipline.

A key question, however, is whether feminists have epistemological privilege – whether they can provide more adequate, better theoretical understanding than malestream theorists. Standpoint feminists such as Nancy Hartsock (1987) Alison Jaggar (1983) and Sandra Harding (1987a, 1991) argue that women as an oppressed group do provide more adequate, better accounts than malestream theorists. In other words, they are suggesting that feminist epistemology is privileged. In opposition to this, Liz Stanley and Sue Wise (1993) argue that feminist epistemologies provide a *different* view on what is taken for 'reality' and that it may indeed be a preferable view. Indeed, they suggest that it is an authentic position because it posits the oppressed as superior. However, they reject the view of the hierarchical relationship and indicate the problem of how we determine whose work to privilege as 'the oppressed', when we consider Black women, lesbians, Jewish women. They ask how claims to superior knowledge are to be adjudicated. Rejecting the argument that the category 'women' is oppressed and that suffering is used to calculate whose knowledge is to be privileged, they argue that there are:

> no foundational grounds for judging the *a priori* superiority of the epistemologies of the oppressed, nor of any one group of the oppressed, in the production of knowledge and the settling of its problems . . . there are, however, moral and political grounds for finding one of them *preferable* . . . the grounds of preference are . . . that it better fits with proponents' experiences of living or being or understanding.
>
> (p. 228)

A rather different perspective, but one that comes to a similar conclusion concerning the selection between competing theories, is indicated by Best and Kellner (1991). They argue that since there 'exists no one true, certain or obviously valid perspective, a critical social theory must be open to new theoretical discourses and perspectives' (p. 267). They suggest that 'to provide comprehensive perspectives on social phenomena it is useful to view events, institutions or practices from different subject perspectives' (p. 267). In other words, it is not that one is right and another wrong, but a question of the extent to which any given theory can illuminate, help make sense of, what is going on.

THE PRODUCTION OF FEMINIST KNOWLEDGES

For us the turn to feminist theory was to enable us to make sense of what was going on – something which malestream theories did not. However, we accept that feminist theories have themselves been partial and inadequate, were constructed from the point of view of white, middle-class, able-bodied, heterosexual women and therefore are seen as inadequate from the position of Black, lesbian, colonised, racialised, disabled women. Nevertheless we do believe that all women share the experience of being exploited and subordinated because of their sex and that this provides the basis for a shared set of experiences, while recognising that there are also differences between women. Furthermore, we see the construction of theory as dynamic, developing both in response to critique and to the complex task of explaining 'realities'. The relationship between theories and the 'realities' they are trying to make sense of is dynamic, not static. Theories are modified and changed as part of the continuing development of sociology as a discipline, and indeed – as we have indicated in the Introduction – sociology has begun to take account of feminist critiques, although the pace of change is slow and uneven.

SUMMARY

1   Research methods are not just 'tools of the trade': what gives meaning to the research is the underlying theory and epistemology used. The methods at the more quantified 'positivistic' end of the spectrum claim to be more scientific and neutral and for this reason feminists have attacked them, arguing that they in fact represent a malestream view of the world under the guise of science.

2   Feminists have tended to espouse qualitative methods as the better means for carrying out feminist research because they imply more equality between researcher and researched; they allow the viewpoint of the researched to be taken into account; and they do not turn the researched into fragmented objects.

3   Four feminist positions on epistemology have been described – empiricist, standpoint, constructivist and postmodern.

FURTHER READING

Hekman, S. J. (1990) *Gender and Knowledge: elements of a postmodern feminism*, Oxford: Polity.

Mitchell, J. and Oakley, A. (eds) (1986) *What is Feminism?*, Oxford: Blackwell.

Nelsen, J. M. (ed.) (1990) *Feminist Research Methods*, London: Westview.

Stanley, L. and Wise, S. (1993) *Breaking Out Again*, London: Routledge.

Tuana, N. and Tong, R. (eds) (1995) *Feminism and Philosophy*, Oxford: Westview.

References

Abbott, P. A. (1982) 'Towards a social theory of mental handicap', unpublished PhD thesis, Thames Polytechnic.

—— (1995) 'Conflict over the grey areas: district nurses and home helps providing community care', *Journal of Gender Studies* 3: 299–306.

—— (ed.) (1988) *Deprivation and Health Status in the Plymouth Health District*, Plymouth: Plymouth Polytechnic, Department of Social and Political Studies.

Abbott, P. A. and Ackers, L. (forthcoming) 'Women and employment', in T. Spybey (ed.) *op. cit.*

Abbott, P. A. and Giarchi, G. (forthcoming) 'Older people', in T. Spybey (ed.) *op. cit.*

Abbott, P. A. and Sapsford, R. J. (1987a) *Women and Social Class*, London: Tavistock.

—— (1987b) *'Community Care' for Mentally Handicapped Children: the origins and consequences of a social policy*, Milton Keynes: Open University Press.

—— (1988) *The Body Politic: health, family and society*, Unit 11 of Open University Course D211 *Social Problems and Social Welfare*, Milton Keynes: The Open University.

—— (1992) *Research into Practice: a reader for nurses and the caring professions*, Milton Keynes: The Open University.

Abbott, P. A. and Tyler, M. (1995) 'Ethnic variation in the female labour force: a research note', *British Journal of Sociology* 46: 339–53.

Abbott, P. A. and Wallace, C. (1989) 'The family', in P. Brown and R. Sparks (eds) *After Thatcher: social policy, politics and society*, Milton Keynes: Open University Press.

—— (1990) *An Introduction To Sociology: feminist perspectives*, London: Routledge.

—— (1992) *The Family and the New Right*, London: Pluto.

Abbott, P. A., Bernie, J., Payne, G. and Sapsford, R. J. (1992) 'Health and material deprivation in Plymouth', in P. A. Abbott and R. J. Sapsford (eds) *op. cit.*

Abbott, P. A., Lankshear, G. and Giarchi, G. (1992) 'Community Care: who cares?', paper presented at a conference on 'The Marginalisation of Elderly People', University of Liverpool.

Abel-Smith, B. (1960) *A History of the Nursing Profession*, London: Heinemann.

Abrahams, J. (1995) *Divide and School: gender and class dynamics in comprehensive education*, London: Falmer.

Acker, J. R. (1973) 'Women and social stratification', *American Journal of Sociology* 78: 2–48.

Acker, S. (1994) *Gendered Education*, Buckingham: Open University Press.

Ackers, L. and Abbott, P. A. (1996) *Social Policy for Nurses and the Caring Professions*, Buckingham: Open University Press.

Adkins, L. (1992) 'Sexual work and family production: a study of the gender division of labour in the contemporary British tourist industry', unpublished PhD thesis, University of Lancaster.

—— (1995) *Gendered Work: sexuality, family and the labour market*, Buckingham: Open University Press.

Adkins, L. and Lury, C. (1992) 'Gender and the labour market', in H. Hinds, A. Phoenix and J. Stacey (eds), *Working Out: new directions for Women's Studies*, London: Falmer.

Allen, H. (1987) *Justice Unbalanced*, Milton Keynes: Open University Press.

Allen, I. (1988) *Any Room at the Top? A study of doctors and their careers*, London: Policy Studies Institute.

Allen, S. (1982) 'Gender inequality and class formation', in A. Giddens and G. Mackenzie (eds) *Social Class and the Division of Labour*, Cambridge: Cambridge University Press.

Allen, S. and Walkowitz, C. (1987) *Homeworking: myths and realities*, London: Macmillan.

Amir, M. (1971) *Patterns in Forcible Rape*, Chicago, IL: University of Chicago Press.

Amos, V. and Parmar, P. (1981) 'Resistance and responses: the experiences of black girls in Britain', in A. McRobbie and T. McCabe (eds), *op. cit.*

Anthias, F. and Yuval Davis, N. (1993) *Racialised Boundaries*, London: Routledge.

Arber, S. (1990) 'Opening the "black box": inequalities in women's health', in P. Abbott and G. Payne (eds), *New Directions in the Sociology of Health*, Basingstoke: Falmer.

Arber, S. and Ginn, J. (1991) *Gender and Later Life: a sociological analysis of resources and constraints*, London: Sage.

Arber, S., Gilbert, N. and Dale, A. (1985) 'Paid employment and women's health: a benefit or a source of role strain?', *Sociology of Health and Illness* 7: 375–400.

Aries, P. (1962) *Centuries of Childhood*, London: Vintage Books.

Arnot, M. (1989) 'Crisis or challenge: equal opportunities and the National Curriculum', *NUT Education Review of Equal Opportunities in the New ERA* 3, Autumn.

ASE Educational Research Committee (1990) *Gender Issues in Science Education*, Hatfield: ASE.

Ashton, D. N. and Field, D. (1976) *Young Males*, London: Hutchinson.

Ashton, D. N. and Maguire, M. (1980) 'Young women in the labour market: stability and change' in R. Deem (ed.) *op. cit.*

Ashton, H. (1991) 'Psychotropic drug prescribing for women', *British Journal of Psychiatry* 158 (Supplement 10): 30–5.

Baldwin, S. and Twigg, J. (1991) 'Women and community care: reflections on a debate', in M. MacLean and D. Groves (eds) *op. cit.*

Ball, S. (1988) 'A comprehensive school in a pluralist world: division and inequalities', in B. O'Keeffe (ed.) *School for Tomorrow*, Lewes: Falmer Press.

Banks, O. (1981) *Faces of Feminism*, Oxford: Martin Robertson.

Barrett, M. (1980) *Women's Oppression Today*, London: Verso.

Barrett, M. and McIntosh, M. (1980a) *The Antisocial Family*, London: Verso.

Barrett, M. and McIntosh, M. (1980b) 'The family wage – some problems for socialists and feminists', *Capital and Class* 11: 51–72.

Barrett, R. D. and Phillips, A. (1992) *Destabilising Theory: contemporatry feminist debates*, Cambridge: Polity.

Bates, I. (1993) 'A job which is "right for me"?', in I. Bates and G. Risborough (eds) *op. cit.*

Bates, I. and Risborough, G. (eds) (1993a) *Youth and Inequality*, Buckingham: Open University Press.

Bates, I. and Risborough G. (1993b) 'Introduction: deepening divisions, fading solutions', in I. Bates and G. Risborough (eds) *op. cit.*

Baudrillard, J. (1988) *The Ecstasy of Communication*, New York: Semiotext.

Bayley, M. (1973) *Mental Handicap and Community Care*, London: Routledge and Kegan Paul.

Beechey, V. (1986) 'Familial ideology', in V. Beechey and J. Donald (eds) *Subjectivity and Social Relations*, Milton Keynes: Open University Press.

—— (1987) *Unequal Work*, London: Verso.

Beechey, V. and Perkins, T. (1982) 'Women's part-time employment in Coventry: a study in the sexual division of labour', report submitted to the Equal Opportunities Commission Social Science Research Council Joint Panel, May.

—— (1986) *A Matter of Hours: an investigation of women's part-time employment*, Cambridge: Polity.

Bell, C. and Roberts, H. (eds) (1984) *Social Researching: politics, problems, practice*, London: Routledge and Kegan Paul.

Benigni, L. (1989) 'Italian women in research: status, aims and family organisation', paper prepared for European Network for Women's Studies Seminar, 'The Interface of Work and Family', Brussels.

Bernard, J. (1973) *The Future of Marriage*, London: Souvenir Press.

Best, S. and Kellner, D. (1991) *Postmodern Theory: critical interrogations*, London: Macmillan.

Beveridge, W. (1942) *Social Insurance and Allied Services*, London: HMSO, Cmd 6404.

Beyres, T. J., Crow, B. and Wan Ho, M. (1983) *The Green Revolution in India*, Open University Course U204 *Third World Studies*, Milton Keynes: The Open University.

Bhavnani, K. (1993) 'Talking racism and the reality of Women's Studies', in D. Richardson and V. Robinson (eds) [1993].

Biggs, A. (1994) 'Gender and technology education', in F. Banks (ed.) *Teaching Technology*, London: Routledge.

Blackburn, C. (1991) *Poverty and Health: working with families*, Buckingham: Open University Press.

Black Report (1978) *A Report of a Royal Commission on Health Inequalities*, London: HMSO.

Blaxter, M. (1985) 'Self-definition of health status and consulting notes in primary care', *Quarterly Journal of Social Affairs* 1: 131–71.

—— (1990) *Health and Lifestyle*, London: Routledge.

Blumberg, R. L. (1981) 'Rural women in development', in N. Black and A. B. Cottrell (eds) *Women and World Change*, Beverly Hills, CA: Sage.

Bonney, N. (1988) 'Gender, household and social class', *British Journal of Sociology* 29: 28–46.

Bordo, S. (1990) 'Feminism, postmodernism and gender-scepticism', in L. J. Nicholson (ed.) *op. cit.*

Borkowski, M., Murch, M. and Walker, V. (1983) *Marital Violence: the community response*, London: Tavistock Press.

Boulton, M. (1983) *On Being a Mother*, London: Tavistock.

Bouquet, T. (1995) 'Rape trials: a second violation', *Readers' Digest*, May, 45–50.

Bourlet, A. (1990) *Police Intervention in Marital Violence*, Buckingham: Open University Press.

Bourque, S. and Grosshaltz, J. (1974) 'Politics and unnatural practice: political science looks at female participation', *Politics and Society* 4: 225–66.

Bowlby, J. (1963) *Child Care and the Growth of Love*, Harmondsworth: Penguin.

Bowles, S. and Gintis, H. (1976) *Schooling in Capitalist America: education reform and contradictions of economic life*, London: Routledge and Kegan Paul.

Box, S. (1971) *Deviance, Reality and Society*, London: Holt, Rinehart and Winston.

Box, S. and Hale, C. (1983) 'Liberation and female criminality in England and Wales', *British Journal of Criminology* 23: 35–49.

Bradshaw, J., Clegg, S. and Trayhorn, D. (1995) 'An investigation into gender bias in educational software used in English primary schools', *Gender and Education* 72: 167–74.

Brah, A. (1986) 'Unemployment and racism: Asian youth on the dole', in S. Allen *et al.* (eds), *The Experience of Unemployment*, London: Macmillan.

Braverman, H. (1974) *Labour and Monopoly Capital*, New York: Monthly Review Press.

Britten, N. and Heath, A. (1983) 'Women, men and social class', in E. Gamarnikow, D. Morgan, T. Purvis and D. Taylorson (eds) *Gender, Class and Work*, London: Heinemann.

Brod, H. (ed.) (1987) *The Making of Masculinities: the new Men's Studies*, London: Routledge.

Brown, C. (1985) *Black and White Britain*, Aldershot: Gower.

Brown, G. W. and Harris, T. C. (1978) *Social Origins of Depression: a study of psychiatric disorder in women*, London: Tavistock.

Brownmiller, S. (1976) *Against Our Will: men, women and rape*, Harmondsworth: Penguin.

Bruce, J. (1987) 'Users' perspectives on contraceptive technology and delivery systems: highlighting some feminist issues', *Technology in Society* 9: 359–83.

Bruegel, I. (1979) 'Women as a reserve army of labour: a note on recent British experience', *Feminist Review* 3: 12–23.

Bryan, B., Dadzie, S. and Scafe, S. (1985) *The Heart of the Race: black women's lives in Britain*, London: Virago.

Burgess, A. and Holmstrom, L. (1979) *Rape, Crisis and Recovery*, Bowie: Robert J. Brady.

Burgess, H. (1989) 'A sort of career: women in primary schools', in C. Skelton (ed.) *op. cit.*

—— (1990) 'Co-education – the disadvantages for schoolgirls', *Gender and Education* 2: 1.

Butler, D. E. and King, A. (1965) *The British General Election of 1964*, London: Macmillan.

Butler, J. (1990) *Gender Trouble*, London: Routledge.

Bynner, J. and Roberts, J. (1991) *Youth and Work*, London: Anglo-German Foundation.

Byrne, E. M. (1978) *Women and Education*, London: Tavistock.

Cain, M. (1973) *Society and the Policeman's Role*, London: Routledge and Kegan Paul.

—— (1987) 'Realist philosophy, social policy and feminism: on the reclamation of value-full knowledge', paper presented to the annual conference of the British Sociological Association in Leeds.

—— (1990) 'Realist philosophy and standpoint epistemologies, or feminist criminology as a successor science', in L. Gelsthorpe and A. Morris (eds) *Feminist Perspectives in Criminology*, Milton Keynes: Open University Press.

Campbell, A. (1984) *The Girls in the Gang*, Oxford: Blackwell.

Carby, H. V. (1982) 'White women listen! Black feminism and the boundaries of sisterhood', in Centre for Contemporary Cultural Studies, *op. cit.*

Carlen, P. (1983) *Women's Imprisonment*, London: Routledge and Kegan Paul.

Carlen, P. and Worrall, A. (eds) (1987) *Gender, Crime and Justice*, Milton Keynes: Open University Press

Carlen, P. *et al.* (1985) *Criminal Women*, Cambridge: Polity Press.

Cashmore, E. E. and Troyna, B. (1983) *Introduction to Race Relations*, London: Routledge.

Cavendish, R. (1982) *Women on the Line*, London: Routledge and Kegan Paul.

CEC (Commission of the European Community) (1993) *Employment in Europe*, Brussels: CEC.

Centre for Contemporary Cultural Studies (1982) *The Empire Strikes Back: race and racism in 70s Britain*, London: Heinemann.

Chaney, J. (1981) *Social Networks and Job Information: the situation of women who return to work*, report presented to the Equal Opportunities Commission – Social Studies Research Council Joint Panel.

Chapman, A. D. (1984) 'Patterns of mobility among men and women in Scotland, 1930–1970', unpublished PhD thesis, Plymouth Polytechnic.

—— (1990a) 'The mobility of women', in G. Payne and P. A. Abbott (eds) [1990b].

—— (1990b) 'The career mobility of women and men', in G. Payne and P. A. Abbott (eds) [1990b].

Chapman, D. (1968) *Sociology and the Stereotype of the Criminal*, London: Tavistock.

Clark, A. (1919) *Working Life of Women in the Seventeenth Century*, London: Routledge, 1982.

Clarke, L. and Lewis, D. (1977) *Rape: the price of coercive sexuality*, Toronto: The Women's Press.

Clarricoates, K. (1980) 'The Importance of Being Ernest – Emma..ture: reperception and categorisation of gender conformity and gender deviation in schools', in R. Deem (ed.) *op. cit.*

Cloward, R. and Ohlin, L. (1961) *Delinquency and Opportunity: a theory of delinquent gangs*, London: Routledge and Kegan Paul.

Coats, M. (1994) *Women's Education*, Buckingham: Open University Press.

Cockburn, C. (1983) *Brothers: male dominance and technological change*, London: Pluto Press.

—— (1987) *Two-Track Training: sex inequalities and the YTS*, London: Macmillan.

Cockburn, C. (1990) *In the Way of Women: men's resistance to sex equality in organisations*, London: Macmillan.

Coleman, J. C. (1980) *The Nature of Adolescence*, London: Methuen.

Comer, L. (1974) *Wedlocked Women*, New York: Feminist Books.

Commeyras, M. and Alvermann, D. (1996) 'Reading about women in world history textbooks from one feminist perspective', *Gender and Education* 8: 31–48.

Connel, R. W. (1987) *Gender and Power: society, the person and sexual politics*, Cambridge: Polity.

Cook, D. (1987) 'Women on welfare', in P. Carlen and A. Worrall (eds) *op. cit.*

Cooper, D. (1972) *The Death of the Family*, Harmondsworth: Penguin.

Cornwell, J. (1984) *Hard-Earned Lives*, London: Tavistock.

Coron, C. (1992) *Super Woman and the Double Burden*, London: Souvenir Press.

Cowie, C. and Lees, S. (1985) 'Slags and drags', *Feminist Review* 9.

Coyle, A. (1984) *Redundant Women*, London: The Women's Press.

Crewe, I. (1979) 'Who swung Tory?', *The Economist*, 12 May, 26–7.

Croft, S. (1986) 'Women, caring and the recasting of need: a feminist reappraisal', *Critical Social Policy* 6: 23–9.

Crompton, R. (1993) *Class and Stratification*, Oxford: Polity.

Crompton, R. and Jones, G. (1984) *White-Collar Proletariat: deskilling and gender in manual work*, London: Macmillan.

Crompton, R. and Mann, M. (eds) (1986) *Gender and Stratification*, Cambridge: Polity Press.

Crompton, R. and Sanderson, K. (1986) 'Credentials and careers: some implications of the increase in professional qualifications amongst women', *Sociology* 20: 24–42.

—— (1990) 'Credentials and careers', in G. Payne and P. A. Abbott (eds) [1990b].

CSO (Central Statistical Office) (1988) *Social Trends 18*, London: HMSO.

—— (1995) *Social Trends 25*, London: HMSO.

Dale, A., Gilbert, N. and Arber, S. (1983) *Alternative Approaches to the Measurement of Social Class for Women and Families*, report to the Equal Opportunities Commission.

Dalley, G. (1983) 'Ideologies of care in a feminist contribution to the debate', *Critical Social Policy* 8: 72–82.

—— (1988) *Ideologies of Caring: rethinking community and collectivism*, London: Macmillan.

Dalton, K. (1961) 'Menstruation and crime', *British Medical Journal* 2: 1972.

Daly, M. (1978) *Gyn/Ecology: the metaethics of radical feminism*, Boston, MA: Beacon Press.

Darwin, C. (1871) *The Descent of Man and Selection in Relation to Sex*, London: John Money.

David, M. (1985) 'Motherhood and social policy – a matter of education?', *Critical Social Policy* 12: 28–43.

Davidoff, L., L'Esperance, J. and Newby, H. (1976) 'Landscape with figures: home and community in English society', in J. Mitchell and A. Oakley (eds) [1976].

Davies, L. (1984) *Pupil Power: deviance and gender in schools*, Brighton: Falmer Press.

Davies, M. (1979) 'Women's place is at the typewriter: the feminisation of the clerical labour force', in Z. R. Eisenstein (ed.) *Capitalist Patriarchy*, New York: Monthly Review Press.

Davies, M. L. (1915) *Maternity: letters of working women*, London: Bell.

Davin, A. (1979) 'Mind that you do as you are told: reading books for Board School girls 1870–1902', *Feminist Review* 3: 89–98.

de Beauvoir, S. (1977) *Old Age*, Harmondsworth: Penguin.

Deem, R. (1987) *Women and Leisure*, Milton Keynes: Open University Press.

—— (ed.) (1980) *Schooling for Women's Work*, London: Routledge and Kegan Paul.

Delphy, C. (1977) *The Main Enemy*, London: Women's Research and Resource Centre.

—— (1981) 'Women in stratification studies', in H. Roberts (ed.) *Doing Feminist Research*, London: Routledge and Kegan Paul.

—— (1984) *Close to Home: a materialist analysis of women's oppression*, London: Hutchinson.

Deshormes LaValle, F. (ed.) (1987) *Women and Men of Europe*, Women of Europe Supplements No. 26, Brussels: Commission of the European Communities.

DES (Department of Education and Science) (1990) *Statistics of Education*, London: HMSO.

Dex, S. (1985) *The Sexual Division of Work*, Brighton: Wheatsheaf.

—— (1987) *Women's Occupational Mobility*, London: Macmillan.

Dobash, R. E. and Dobash, R. P. (1992) *Women, Violence and Social Change*, London: Routledge.

Dobash, R. P. and Dobash, R. E. (1980) *Violence against Wives: a case against the patriarchy*, Shepton Mallet: Open Books.

Dobash, R. P., Dobash, R. E. and Gutteridge, S. (1986) *The Imprisonment of Women*, Oxford: Blackwell.

Downing, H. (1981) 'They call me a life-size Meccano set: super-secretary or super-slave?', in A. McRobbie and T. McCabe (eds) *op. cit.*

Dowse, R. and Hughes, J. (1971) 'Girls, boys and politics', *British Journal of Sociology* 22: 53–67.

Doyal, L. (1987) 'Women and the National Health Service: the carers and the careless', in E. Lewin and V. Olsen (eds) *op. cit.*

—— (1995) *What Makes Women Sick*, London: Macmillan.

Doyal, L., Hunt, G. and Mellor, J. (1981) 'Your life in their hands: immigrant workers in the National Health Service', *Critical Social Policy* 1: 54–71.

Dreifus, C. (ed.) (1978) *Seizing our Bodies*, New York: Vintage Books.

Durant, H. (1966) 'Voting behaviour in Britain', in R. Rose (ed.) [1976b].

Durkheim, E. (1897) *Suicide: a study in sociology*, London: Routledge and Kegan Paul, 1952.

Dyhouse, C. (1981) *Girls Growing Up in Late Victorian and Edwardian England*, London: Routledge and Kegan Paul.

EC (European Commission) (1990) *Mothers, Fathers and Employment*, Brussels: Commission of the European Communities, European Commission Childcare Network.

—— (1994) *Bulletin on Women and Employment in the EU No. 5*, Brussels: European Commission Directorate-General for Employment, Industrial Relations and Social Affairs.

Edgell, S. (1980) *Middle-Class Couples*, London: Allen and Unwin.

Edwards, S. (1984) *Women on Trial*, Manchester: Manchester University Press.

—— (1987) 'Prostitutes: victims of law, social policy and organised crime', in J. Carlen and A. Worrall (eds) *op. cit.*

—— (1989) *Policing Domestic Violence*, London: Sage.

Ehrenreich, B. and English, D. (1979) *For Her Own Good: 100 years of the experts' advice to women*, London: Pluto Press.

Eichler, M. (1988) *Non-Sexist Research Methods*, London: Allen and Unwin.

Einhorn, B. (1993) *Cinderella Goes to Market*, London: Verso.

Eisner, M. W. C. (1986) 'A feminist approach to general practice', in C. Webb (ed.) *op. cit.*

Elston, M. A. (1980) 'Medicine', in R. Silverstone and A. Ward (eds) *op. cit.*

Engels, F. (1884) *Der Ursprung der Familie, des Privateigentum and des Staat*, Zurich: Hattingen. English edn: *The Origin of the Family, Private Property and the State*, Harmondsworth: Penguin, 1986.

Erikson, R. (1984) 'The social class of men, women and families', *Sociology* 18: 500–14.

Evetts, J. (1990) *Women in Primary Teaching*, London; Unwin Hyman.

—— (ed.) (1994) *Women and Career: themes and issues in advanced industrial societies*, London: Longman.

Eysenck, H. J. (1971) *The IQ Argument: race, intelligence and education*, New York: Library Press.

Family Policy Studies Centre (1988) 'Fact sheet 1', London: FPSC.

Finch, J. (1983a) *Married to the Job: wives' incorporation in men's work*, London: Allen and Unwin.

—— (1983b) 'Dividing the rough and the respectable: working-class women and pre-school play-groups', in E. Gamarnikow, D. Morgan, T. Purvis and D. Taylorson *The Public and the Private*, London: Heinemann.

—— (1984) 'Community care: developing non-sexist alternatives', *Critical Social Policy* 3: 6–19.

Finch, J. and Groves, D. (1980) 'Community Care and the family: a case for equal opportunities?', *Journal of Social Policy* 9: 437–51.

Firestone, S. (1974) *The Dialectic of Sex: the case for feminist revolution*, New York: Morrow.

Flitcraft, A. H., Hadley, S. M., Hendricks-Mathews, M. K., McLeer, S. W. and Warshaw, C. (1992) 'American Medical Association diagnostic and treatment guidelines on domestic violence', *Archive of Family Medicine* 1: 39–47.

Ford, J. (1969) *Social Class and the Comprehensive School*, London: Routledge and Kegan Paul.

Foster, P. (1995) *Women and the Health Care Industry*, Buckingham: Open University Press.

Foucault, M. (1969) *The Archaeology of Knowledge*, London: Tavistock, 1972.

—— (1980) 'Questions of method', *Ideology and Consciousness* 8 (1981): 3–14.

Friedan, B. (1963) *The Feminine Mystique*, New York: Norton.

Fuller, M. (1980) 'Black girls in a London comprehensive school', in R. Deem (ed.) *op. cit.*

Gamarnikow, E. (1978) 'Sexual division of labour: the case of nursing', in A. Kuhn and A.-M. Wolpe (eds) *Feminism and Materialism*, London: Routledge and Kegan Paul.

Garber, L. (ed.) (1994) *Tilting the Tower*, London: Routledge.

Garnsey, E. (1978) 'Women's work and theories of class stratification', *Sociology* 12: 223–43.

Gavron, H. (1966) *The Captive Wife: conflicts of housebound wives*, Harmondsworth: Penguin.

Gender and Society (1989) (special issue) vol. xx. Beverly Hills, CA: Sage.

Giarchi, G. G. (forthcoming) *'Aging' in Europe: bleak winter or second spring?*, London: Longman.

Giddens, A. (1993) *Sociology* (2nd edn), Oxford: Polity.

Gillborn, D. (1995) *Racism and Antiracism in Real Schools*, Buckingham: Open University Press.

Gittens, D. (1985) *The Family in Question: changing households and familial ideologies*, London: Macmillan.

—— (1992) 'What is the family? Is it universal?', in L. McDowell and R. Pringle (eds) *op. cit.*

Glasner, A. (1992) 'Gender and Europe: cultural and structural impediments to change', in J. Bailey (ed.) *Social Europe*, London: Longman.

Glass, D. V. (ed.) (1954) *Social Mobility in Britain*, London: Routledge and Kegan Paul.

Glendinning, C. and Millar, J. (eds) (1987) *Women and Poverty in Britain*, Brighton: Wheatsheaf.

—— (eds) (1992) *Women and Poverty in Britain in the 1990s*, Hemel Hempstead: Harvester/Wheatsheaf.

Goddard-Spear, M. (1989) 'Differences between the written work of boys and girls', *British Educational Research Journal* 15: 271–7.

Goffee, R. and Scase, R. (1985) *Women in Charge: the experiences of female entrepreneurs*, London: Allen and Unwin.

Gold, K. (1990) 'Get thee to a laboratory', *New Scientist*, 14 April, 42–6.

Goldthorpe, J. H. (1983) 'Women and class analysis: in defence of the conventional view', *Sociology* 17: 465–88.

—— (1984) 'Women and class analysis: a reply to the replies', *Sociology* 18: 491–9.

Goldthorpe, J. H. and Payne, C. (1986) 'On the class mobility of women: results from different approaches to the analysis of recent British data', *Sociology* 20: 531–55.

Goldthorpe, J. H., Llewlyn, C. and Payne, C. (1980) *Social Mobility and Class Structure in Modern Britain*, Oxford: Oxford University Press.

Goldthorpe, J. H., Lockwood, D., Bechhofer, F. and Platt, J. (1969) *The Affluent Worker in the Class Structure*, Oxford: Oxford University Press.

Goot, M. and Reid, E. (1975) *Women and Voting Studies: mindless matrons or sexist scientism?*, London: Sage.

Graham, H. (1984) *Women, Health and the Family*, Brighton: Wheatsheaf.

—— (1987a) 'Providers, negotiators and mediators: women as hidden carers', in E. Lewin and V. Olsen (eds) *op. cit.*

—— (1987b) 'Women's poverty and caring', in C. Glendinning and J. Millar (eds) [1987].

—— (1991) 'The concept of care in feminist research: the case of domestic service', *Sociology* 25: 61–78.

—— (1993) *Hardship and Health in Women's Lives*, Hemel Hempstead: Harvester/Wheatsheaf.

Graham, H. and Oakley, A. (1981) 'Competing ideologies of reproduction: medical and maternal perspectives on pregnancy', in H. Roberts (ed.) *op. cit.*

Greed, C. (1994) 'Women surveyors: constructing careers', in J. Evetts (ed.) *op. cit.*

311

Greenstein, F. (1965) *Children and Politics*, New Haven, CT: Yale University Press.

Gregory, J. (1986) 'Sex, class and crime: towards a non-sexist criminology', in R. Matthews and J. Young (eds) *op. cit.*

Griffin, C. (1985) *Typical Girls?*, London: Routledge and Kegan Paul.

Groves, D. (1991) 'Women and financial provision for old age', in M. MacLean and D. Groves (eds) *op. cit.*

—— (1992) 'Occupational pension provision and women's poverty in old age', in C. Glendinning and J. Millar (eds) [1992].

Guillaumin, C. (ed.) (1995) *Racism, Sexism, Power and Ideology*, London: Routledge.

Guillebaud, J. and Low, B. (1987) 'Contraception', in A. McPherson (ed.) *Women's Problems in General Practice*, Oxford: Oxford University Press.

Hakim, C. (1979) *Occupational Segregation: a comparative study of the degree and patterns of differentiation between men's and women's work in Britain, the United States and other countries*, London: Department of Employment, Research Paper No. 9.

Hall, R. (1985) *Ask Any Woman*, Bristol: Falling Wall Press.

Hall, S. (1982) 'Managing conflict, producing consensus', in *Conformity, Consensus and Conflict*, Block 5 of Open University Course D102 *Social Sciences: a foundation course*, Milton Keynes: The Open University.

—— (1992) 'Introduction', in S. Hall, D. Held and T. McGrew (eds) *Modernity and its Futures*, Cambridge: Polity.

Hall, S. and Jefferson, T. (1976) *Resistance through Ritual*, London: Hutchinson.

Halson, J. (1989) 'The sexual harassment of young women', in L. Holly (ed.) *Sex in Schools*, Milton Keynes: Open University Press.

—— (1991) 'Young women: sexual harassment and mixed-sex schooling', in P. A. Abbott and C. Wallace (eds) *Gender, Power and Sexuality*, London: Macmillan.

Hanmer, J. (1990) 'Men, power and the exploitation of women', in J. Hearn and D. Morgan (eds) *op. cit.*

Hanmer, J. and Leonard, D. (1984) 'Negotiating the problem: the DHSS and research on violence in marriage', in C. Bell and H. Roberts (eds) *op. cit.*

Hanmer, J. and Maynard, M. (eds) (1987) *Women, Violence and Social Control*, London: Macmillan.

Hanmer, J. and Saunders, S. (1984) *Well-Founded Fear*, London: Hutchinson.

Hansard Society (1990) *Report of the Hansard Society Commission on Women at the Top*, London: Hansard Society.

Harding, J. (1980) 'Sex differences in performance in science examinations', in R. Deem (ed.) *op. cit.*

Harding, S. (1987a) 'Introduction: is there a feminist method?', in S. Harding (ed.) *op. cit.*

—— (ed.) (1987b) *Feminism and Methodology*, Milton Keynes: Open University Press.

—— (1991) *Whose Science? Whose Knowledge?*, Ithaca, NY: Cornell University Press.

Hargreaves, A. (1996) Contribution to Review Symposium of J. Abraham (1995) *Divide and school: gender and class dynamics in comprehensive education*, London: Falmer, *British Journal of Sociology of Education* 17(1): 95–7.

Hartmann, H. (1978) 'The unhappy marriage of marxism and feminism: towards a more progressive union', *Capital and Class* 8: 1–33.

Hartsock, N. C. M. (1987) 'The feminist standpoint', in S. Harding (ed.) [1987b].

Haste, H. (1992) 'Spitting images: sex and science', *New Scientist*, 15 February, 32–4.

Haugh, M. R. (1973) 'Class measurement and women's occupational roles', *Social Forces* 52: 85–97.

Hawkes, G. (1985) 'Responsibility and irresponsibility: young women and family planning', *Sociology* 29: 257–74.

Hearn, J. (1982) 'Notes on patriarchy, professionalisation and the semi-professions', *Sociology* 26: 184–202.

Hearn, J. and Morgan, D. (eds) (1990) *Men, Masculinities and Social Theory*, London: Unwin Hyman.

Hearn, J. and Parkin, P. W. (1988) *Sex at Work: the power and paradox of organisational sexuality*, Brighton: Wheatsheaf.

Heath, A. (1980) *Social Mobility*, Edinburgh: Fontana.

Heath, A. and Britten, N. (1984) 'Women's jobs do make a difference', *Sociology* 18: 475–90.

Heidensohn, F. (1986) *Women and Crime*, London: Macmillan.

Hekman, S. J. (1990) *Gender and Knowledge: elements of a postmodern feminism*, Oxford: Polity.

Hill Collins, P. (1986) 'Learning from the outsider within: the sociological significance of Black Feminist thought', *Social Problems* 33: 14–32.

—— (1990) *Black Feminist Thought*, London: HarperCollins.

Himmelweit, S. (1988) *In the Beginning*, Unit 1 of Open University Course D211 *Social Problems and Social Welfare*, Milton Keynes: The Open University.

Hochschild, A. R. (1983) *The Managed Heart*, Berkeley, CA: University of California Press.

Hockey, J. (1993) 'Women and Health', in D. Richardson and V. Robinson (eds) *op. cit.*

Hockey, J. and James, A. (1993) *Growing Up and Growing Old: aging and dependency in the life course*, London: Sage.

Hoff, L. A. (1990) *Battered Women as Survivors*, London: Routledge.

Home Office (1987) *Criminal Statistics, England and Wales 1986*, London: HMSO.

—— (1994) *Criminal Statistics England and Wales 1993*, London: HMSO, Cm 2680.

Homer, M., Leonard, A. and Taylor, P. (1984) *Private Violence and Public Shame*, Middlesbrough: Cleveland Refuge and Aid for Women and Children.

hooks, b. (1982) *Ain't I a Woman? Black Women and Feminism*, Boston, MA: South Park Press.

House of Commons, Social Security Committee (1991) *Low Income Statistics: households below average income – tables 1988*, London: HMSO, HC 401.

Humphries, J. (1977) 'Class struggle and the persistence of the working class family', *Cambridge Journal of Economics* 1: 241–58.

Hunt, A. (1975) *Management Attitudes and Practices towards Women at Work*, London: Office of Population Census Surveys.

Hunt, P. (1980) *Gender and Class Consciousness*, London: Macmillan.

Jackson, P. and Salisbury, J. (1996) 'Why should secondary schools take working with boys seriously?' *Gender and Education* 8: 103–16.

Jaggar, A. (1983) *Feminist Politics and Human Nature*, Brighton: Wheatsheaf.

Jeffreys, S. (1985) *The Spinster and her Enemies: feminism and sexuality 1880–1930*, London: Pandora.

Jennings, M. K. and Niemi, R. G. (1974) *The Political Character of Adolescence: the influence of families and schools*, Princeton, NJ: Harvard University Press.

Jensen, A. R. (1973) *Educability and Group Differences*, New York: Harper and Row.

Jezierski, M. (1992) 'Guidelines for interventions by ER nurses in cases of domestic abuse', *Journal of Emergency Nursing* 18: 298–300.

Johnson, N. (1995) 'Domestic violence: an overview', in P. Kingston and B. Penhale (eds) *op. cit.*

—— (ed.) (1985) *Marital Violence*, London: Routledge and Kegan Paul.

Johnson, P. and Webb, S. (1990) *Poverty in Official Statistics: two reports*, London: Institute for Fiscal Studies.

Johnson, T. (1972) *Professions and Power*, London: Macmillan.

Jones, A. (1993) 'Becoming a "girl": post-structuralist suggestions for educational research', *Gender and Education* 5: 157–66.

Jordan, E. (1995) 'Fighting boys and fantasy play: the construction of masculinity in the early years of school', *Gender and Education* 7: 69–96.

Joseph, G. (1981) 'Black mothers and daughters: their roles and functions in American society', in G. Joseph and J. Lewis (eds) *In Common Differences*, Garden City, NY: Anchor.

Joshi, H. and Davies, H. (1994) 'Mothers' forgone earnings and child care: some cross-national assessments', in L. Hantrais and S. Mangen (eds) *Family Policy and the Welfare State*, Loughborough: University of Loughborough, Cross-National Research Paper No. 3.

Journal of the American Medical Association (1990) 'Domestic violence begets other problems of which physicians must be aware to be effective' (Medical News and Perspectives Section) 264, No. 8, 943–4.

Jowell, R., Curtice, J., Brooks, L. and Ahrendt, D. (1991) *British Social Attitudes: the 7th report*, Aldershot: Dartmouth.

Kahn, A. and Holt, L. H. (1989) *Menopause*, London: Bloomsbury.

Kane, P. (1991) *Women's Health: from womb to tomb*, London: Macmillan.

Kelly, A. (1982) 'Gender roles at home and school', *British Journal of Sociology of Education* 3: 281–96.

—— (1985) 'The construction of masculine science', *British Journal of Sociology of Education* 6: 133–54.

—— (1987) *Science for Girls*, Milton Keynes: Open University Press.

—— (ed.) (1981) *The Missing Half: girls and science education*, Manchester: Manchester University Press.

Kelly, E. (1988) *Surviving Sexual Violence*, Cambridge: Polity.

Kelsall, R. K. (1980) 'Teaching', in R. Silverstone and A. Ward (eds) *op. cit.*

Khotkina, Z. (1994) 'Women in the labour market', in A. Posadskaya (ed.) *op. cit.*

Kiel, T. and Newton, P. (1980) 'Into work: continuity and change', in R. Deem (ed.) *op. cit.*

Kingston, P. and Benhale, P. (eds) (1995) *Family Violence and the Caring Professions*, London: Macmillan.

Koblinsky, M., Campbell, O. and Harlow, S. (1993) 'Mother and more: a broader perspective on women's health', in M. Koblinsky, T. Timyan and J. Gray (eds) *The Health of Women: a global perspective*, Boulder, CO: Westview Press.

Land, H. (1978) 'Who cares for the family?', *Journal of Social Policy* 7(3): 357–84.

—— (1980) *The Family Wage*, Liverpool: Liverpool Free Press.

—— (1987) 'Social policies and women in the labour market', in F. Ashton and G. Whitting (eds), *Feminist Theory and Practical Policies*, Bristol: School of Advanced Urban Studies.

Langberg, K. (1994) *Housework and Childcare – from Doing to Sharing: a Danish example of how work in the family has changed*, Graz, Austria: Graz University of Technology, Working Paper.

Larkin, G. (1983) *Occupational Monopoly and Modern Medicine*, London: Tavistock.

Latter, P. (1991) *Getting Social: feminist research and pedagogy with/in the post-modern*, London: Routledge.

Lawrence, B. (1987) 'The fifth dimension: gender and general practice', in A. Spencer and D. Podmore (eds) *op. cit.*

Lazarsfeld, P. F., Berelson, B. and Gaudet, H. (1968), *The People's Choice* (2nd edn), Chicago, IL: University of Chicago Press.

Lazzaro, M. V. and McFarlane, J. (1991) 'Establishing a screening program for abused women', *Journal of Nursing Administration* 21: 24–9.

Leach, E. (1967) *A Runaway World?*, London: BBC Publications.

Lee, D. (1990) 'Chatterbox', *Child Education* 67: 267.

Lees, S. (1986) *Losing Out: sexuality and adolescent girls*, London: Hutchinson.

—— (1989) 'Naggers, whores and Libbers: provoking men to violence', paper presented to the annual conference of the British Sociological Association, Plymouth.

—— (1993) *Sugar and Spice: sexuality and adolescent girls*, Harmondsworth: Penguin.

Leeson, J. and Gray, J. (1978) *Women and Health*, London: Tavistock.

Lee-Treweek, G. (1994) 'Discourse, care and control: an ethnography of residential and nursing-home elder care work', unpublished PhD thesis, University of Plymouth.

LeGrand, J. (1982) *The Strategy of Equality*, London: Allen and Unwin.

Leila, H. and Elliott, P. (1987) *Infertility and In Vitro Fertilisation*, London: BMA Family Doctors Publications.

Leiulfsrud, J. and Woodward, K. (1987) 'Women at class crossroads: repudiating conventional theories of family class', *Sociology* 21: 393–412.

Leonard, E. B. (1978) *Women, Crime and Society*, London: Longman.

Lewin, E. and Olsen, V. (eds) (1987) *Women, Health and Healing: towards a new perspective*, London: Tavistock.

Lewis, J. (1980) *The Politics of Motherhood: child and maternal welfare in England 1900–1939*, London: Croom Helm.

—— (ed.) (1993) *Women and Social Policies in Europe: work, family and the state*, Aldershot: Edward Elgar.

Lincoln, R. and Kaeser, L. (1988) 'Whatever happened to the contraceptive revolution?', *Family Planning Perspectives* 20: 20–4.

Lindroos, M. (1995) 'The production of "girls" in an educational setting', *Gender and Education* 7: 175–84.

Llewelyn Davies, M. (1915) *Letters from Working Women Collected by the Women's Cooperative Guild*, republished London: Virago, 1981.

Lobban, G. (1975) 'Sex roles in reading schemes', *Forum* 16: 57–60.

Locker, D. (1981) *Symptoms and Illness*, London: Tavistock.

Lockwood, D. (1958) *The Black-Coated Worker*, London: Allen and Unwin.

Lockwood, D. (1986) 'Class, status and gender', in R. Crompton and M. Mann (eds) *op. cit.*

Loudon, N. (ed.) (1991) *Handbook of Family Planning*, Edinburgh: Churchill Livingstone.

Lovenduski, J. and Randall, V. (1993) *Contemporary Feminist Politics: women and power*, Oxford: Oxford University Press.

Mac an Ghaill, M. (1994) *The Making of Men: masculinist sexualities and schooling*, Buckingham: Open University Press.

Maccoby, E., Matthews, R. and Morbin, A. S. (1954) 'Youth and political change', *Public Opinion Quarterly* 18: 23–9.

MacDowell, L. and Pringle, R.C. (eds) (1992) *Defining Women: social institutions and gender divisions*, Cambridge: Polity.

MacEwan Scott, A. (1994) *Gender Segregation and Social Change*, Oxford: Oxford University Press.

MacIntyre, S. (1977) *Single and Pregnant*, Beckenham: Croom Helm.

Mackie, L. and Pattullo, P. (1977) *Women at Work*, London: Tavistock.

Mackinnon, C. (1987) *Feminism Unmodified: disocurses on life and law*, Cambridge MA: Harvard University Press.

MacLean, M. and Groves, D. (1991) *Women's Issues in Social Policy*, London: Routledge.

McRobbie, A. and Garber, P. (1977) 'Girls and subcultures: an exploration', in S. Hall and T. Jefferson (eds) *op. cit.*

McRobbie, A. and McCabe, T. (eds) (1981) *Feminism for Girls: an adventure story*, London: Routledge and Kegan Paul.

Maguire, J. (1980) 'Nursing', in R. Silverstone and A. Ward (eds), *op. cit.*

Maguire, S. (1988) 'Sorry love – violence against women in the home and the state response', *Critical Social Policy* 23: 34–46.

Mama, A. (1989) 'Violence against black women: gender, race and state responses', *Feminist Review* 28: 16–55.

Mandaraka-Sheppard, K. (1986) *The Dynamics of Aggression in Women's Prisons in England*, London: Gower.

Marshall, G., Rose, D., Newby, H. and Vogler, C. (1988) *Social Class in Modern Britain*, London: Unwin Hyman.

Marshall, G., Roberts, S., Burgoyne, C., Swift, A. and Routh, D. (1995) 'Class, gender and the asymmetry hypothesis', *European Sociological Review* 11: 1–15.

Marsland, D. (1988) *The Seeds of Bankruptcy*, London: Claridge Press.

Martin, E. (1987) *The Woman in the Body*, Milton Keynes: Open University Press.

Martin, J. and Roberts, C. (1984) *Women and Employment: a lifetime perspective*, London: HMSO.

Maruani, M. (1992) *The Position of Women in the Labour Market: trends and developments in the twelve member states of the European Community 1983–1990*, Brussels: Commission of the European Communities.

Massey, D. (1983) 'The shape of things to come', *Marxism Today*, April, 18–27.

Matthews, R. and Young, J. (eds) (1986) *Confronting Crime*, Beverly Hills, CA: Sage.

Mawby, R. (1980) 'Sex and crime: the results of a self-report study', *British Journal of Sociology* 31: 525.

Mead, M. (1943) *Coming of Age in Samoa: a study of adolescence and sex in primitive societies*, Harmondsworth: Penguin.

Measor, L. and Sikes, P. (1992) *Gender and Schools*, London: Cassell.

Mickelson, R. A. (1992) 'Why does Jane read and write so well? The anomaly of women's achievement', in J. Wrigley, (ed.) [1992b].

Miles, S. and Middleton, C. (1990) 'Girls' education in the balance: the ERA and inequality', in M. Hammer (ed.) *The Education Reform Act 1988: its origins and implications*, Lewes: Falmer Press.

Milkman, R. (1976) 'Women's work and economic crises', *Review of Radical Political Economy* 9: 29–36.

Mill, J. S. and Mill, H. T. (1869) *The Subjection of Women*, London. Reprinted 1929, London: Everyman.

Millar, J. and Glendinning, C. (1987) 'Invisible women, invisible poverty', in C. Glendinning and J. Millar (eds) [1987].

Miller, R. and Hayes, B. (1990) 'Gender and intergenerational mobility', in G. Payne and P. A. Abbott (eds) [1990b].

Millett, K. (1977) *Sexual Politics*, London: Virago.

Mills, C. W. (1954) *The Sociological Imagination*, Harmondsworth: Penguin

Mirza, H. (1992) *Young, Female and Black*, London: Routledge.

Mitchell, J. (1986) 'Women and equality', in J. Donald and S. Hall (eds) *Politics and Ideology*, Milton Keynes: Open University Press.

Mitchell, J. and Oakley, A. (eds) (1976) *The Rights and Wrongs of Women*, Harmondsworth: Penguin.

—— (eds) (1986) *What is Feminism?*, Oxford: Blackwell.

Moore, H. (1995) *A Passion for Difference*, Oxford: Polity.

Morris, A. (1987) *Women, Crime and Criminal Justice*, Oxford: Blackwell.

Muncie, J. (1984) *The Trouble with Kids Today: youth culture and post-war Britain*, London: Hutchinson.

Murphy, R. (1984) 'The structure of closure: a critique and development of the theories of Weber, Collins and Parkin', *British Journal of Sociology* 35: 574–602.

Nairne, K. and Smith, G. (1984) *Dealing with Depression*, London: Women's Press.

Nelsen, J. M. (ed.) (1990) *Feminist Research Methods*, London: Westview.

Newsom Report (1963) *Half our Future*, London: HMSO.

Nicholson, L. J. (ed.) (1990) *Feminism/Postmodernism*, London: Routledge.

Nissel, M. and Bonnerjea, L. (1982) *Family Care of the Handicapped Elderly: who pays?*, London: Policy Studies Institute.

NUT (National Union of Teachers) (1980) *Promotion and the Woman Teacher*, London and Manchester: National Union of Teachers/Equal Opportunities Commission.

Nuttall, P. (1983) 'Male takeover or female giveaway?', *Nursing Times*, 12, January, 10–11.

Oakley, A. (1972) *Sex, Gender and Society*, London: Temple Smith.

—— (1974a) *Housewife*, London: Allen Lane.

—— (1974b) *The Sociology of Housework*, London: Martin Robertson.

—— (1980) *Women Confined: towards a sociology of childbirth*, Oxford: Martin Robertson.

—— (1982) *Subject Women*, London: Fontana.

—— (1984a) *The Captured Womb*, Oxford: Blackwell.

—— (1984b) 'The importance of being a nurse', *Nursing Times*, 12, December, 24–7.

—— (1986) *Taking it Like a Woman*, London: Flamingo.

—— (1987) 'From walking wombs to test-tube babies', in M. Stanworth (ed.) [1987b].

—— (1993) *Essays on Women, Medicine and Health*, Edinburgh: Edinburgh University Press.

Oakley, A. and Oakley, R. (1979) 'Sexism in official statistics', in J. Irvine, Ian Miles and Jeff Evans (eds) *Demystifying Social Statistics*, London: Pluto Press.

Obbso, C. (1980) *African Women: their struggle for economic independence*, London: Zed Press.

Olsen, V. and Lewin, E. (1985) 'Women, health and healing: a theoretical introduction', in E. Lewin and V. Olsen (eds) *op. cit.*

OPCS (Office of Population Censuses and Surveys) (1982) *Labour Force Survey 1981*,
London: HMSO.

—— (1984) *Census 1981: Economic Activity – Great Britain*, London: HMSO.

—— (1986) *Occupational Mortality: December Supplement, England and Wales,
1979–1980*, London: HMSO.

—— (1993a) *Census 1991: report for Great Britain*, London: HMSO.

—— (1993b) *Census 1991: ethnic group and country of birth*, London: HMSO.

—— (1995) *Social Trends*, London: HMSO.

Orr, J. (1992) 'Working with women's health groups', in P. A. Abbott and R. J.
Sapsford (eds) *op. cit.*

Osborne, A. F. and Morris, T. C. (1979) 'The rationale for a composite index of social
class and its evaluation', *British Journal of Sociology* 30: 39–60.

Oudshoorn, N. (1994) *Beyond the Natural Body: an archaeology of sex hormones*,
London: Routledge.

Page, H. (1989) 'Calculating the effectiveness of in vitro fertilisation: a review', *British
Journal of Obstetrics and Gynaecology* 96: 334–9.

Pagelow, M. (1985) 'Violent husbands and abused wives: a longitudinal study', in
J. Pahl (ed.) *op. cit.*

Pahl, J. (1980) 'Patterns of money management within marriage', *Journal of Social
Policy* 19: 313–35.

—— (1983) 'The allocation of money and the structuring of inequality within
marriage', *Sociological Review* 31: 237–62.

—— (1995) 'Health professionals and violence against women', in P. Kingston and B.
Penhale (eds) *op. cit.*

—— (ed.) (1985) *Private Violence and Public Policy*, London: Routledge and Kegan
Paul.

Pahl, R. and Wallace, C. (1985) 'Household work strategies in economic recession',
in E. Mingione and N. Redclift (eds) *Beyond Employment*, Oxford:
Blackwell.

Parkin, F. (1979) *Marxism and Class Theory: a bourgeois critique*, London: Tavistock.

Parton, N. (1985) *The Politics of Child Abuse*, London: Macmillan.

Payne, G. (1987a) *Employment and Opportunity*, London: Macmillan.

—— (1987b) *Mobility and Change in Modern Britain*, London: Macmillan.

Payne, G. and Abbott, P. A. (1990a) 'Beyond male mobility models', in G. Payne and
P. A. Abbott (eds) [1990b].

—— (eds) (1990b) *The Social Mobility of Women: beyond male mobility models*,
Basingstoke: Falmer.

Payne, G., Ford, G. and Ulas, M. (1981) 'Occupational and social mobility in Scotland',
in M. Gaskin (ed.) *The Political Economy of Tolerable Survival*, Beckenham:
Croom Helm.

Payne, S. (1991) *Women, Health and Poverty: an introduction*, Brighton: Harvester
Wheatsheaf.

Pearson, R. (1992) 'Looking both ways: extending the debate on women and citizenship in Europe', in A. Ward, J. Gregory and N. Yuval Davis (eds) *Women and
Citizenship in Europe*, Stoke on Trent: Trentham Booles.

Penfold, P. S. and Walker, G. A. (1984) *Women and the Psychiatric Paradox*, Milton
Keynes: Open University Press.

Petchesky, R. P. (1987) 'Foetal images: the power of visual culture in the politics of reproduction', in M. Stanworth (ed.) [1987b].

Peterson, P. B. and Lach, M. A. (1990) 'Gender stereotypes in children's books: their prevalence and influence in cognitive and effective development', *Gender and Education* 2: 185–97.

Phillips, A. and Taylor, B. (1980) 'Sex and skill: notes towards a feminist economics', *Feminist Review* 6: 79–88.

Phizacklea, A. (1983a) 'In the front line', in A. Phizacklea (ed.) [1983b].

—— (ed.) (1983b) *One Way Ticket: migration and female labour*, London: Routledge and Kegan Paul.

Phoenix, A. (1992) 'Narrow definitions of culture: the case of early motherhood', in L. McDowell and R. Pringle (eds) *op. cit.*

Pill, D. and Stott, N. (1986) 'Concepts of illness causation and responsibility: some preliminary data from a sample of working-class mothers', in C. Currer and M. Stacey (eds) *Concepts of Health, Illness and Disease: a comparative perspective*, Leamington Spa: Berg.

Pinchbeck, I. (1977) *Women Workers and the Industrial Revolution 1750–1850*, London: Cassells.

Pinchbeck, I. and Hewitt, M. (1993) *Children in English Society*, London: Routledge and Kegan Paul.

Pollack, O. (1950) *The Criminality of Women*, Philadelphia, PA: University of Pennsylvania Press.

Pollack, S. (1985) 'Sex and the contraceptive act', in H. Holmans (ed.) *The Sexual Politics of Reproduction*, Aldershot: Gower.

Pollert, A. (1981) *Girls, Wives, Factory Lives*, London: Macmillan.

Popay, J. and Jones, J. (1990) 'Patterns of wealth and illness among lone parents', *Journal of Social Policy* 19: 499–534.

Posadskaya, A. (ed.) (1994) *Women in Russia*, London: Verso.

Prandy, K. (1986) 'Similarities of life-style and occupations of women', in R. Crompton and M. Mann (eds) *op. cit.*

Pratt, J. *et al.* (1984) *Option Choice: a question of equal opportunity*, Windsor: National Foundation for Educational Research/Nelson.

Pringle, R. (1989) *Secretaries Talk: sexuality, power and work*, London: Verso.

Radford, J. (1987) 'Policing male violence – policing women', in J. Hanmer and M. Maynard (eds) [1987].

Ramazanoglu, C. (1987) 'Sex and violence in academic life, or you can keep a good woman down', in J. Hanmer and M. Maynard (eds) *op. cit.*

Rapaport, R. and Rapaport, R. N. (1969) 'The dual-career family: a variant pattern and social change', *Human Relations* 22: 3–30.

Rattansi, A. (1995) 'Forget postmodernism? Notes from de Bunker', *Sociology* 29: 339–50.

Reid, K. (1985) 'Choice of method', in N. Loudon (ed.) *op. cit.*

Reinharz, S. (1983) 'Experiential analysis: a contribution to feminist research', in G. Bowles and R. D. Klein (eds) *Theories of Women's Studies*, London: Routledge and Kegan Paul.

Richardson, D. and Robinson, V. (1994) 'Theorising Women's Studies, Gender Studies and masculinity: the politics of naming', *European Journal of Women's Studies* 1: 11–27.

—— (eds) (1993) *Introducing Women's Studies: feminist theory and practice*, London: Macmillan.

Riley, D. (1992) 'A short history of some preoccupations', in J. Butler and J. Scott (eds) *Feminists Theorise the Political*, London: Routledge.

Roberts, E. (1982) 'Working class wives and their families', in J. Barker and M. Drake (eds) *Population and Society in Britain 1850–1980*, London: Batsford.

Roberts, H. (1985) *The Patient Patients: women and their doctors*, London: Pandora.

—— (1987) *Women and Social Classification*, Brighton: Wheatsheaf.

—— (ed.) (1981) *Women, Health and Reproduction*, London: Routledge and Kegan Paul.

Roberts, K. (1993) 'Career trajectories and the mirage of increased social mobility', in I. Bates and G. Risborough (eds) *op. cit.*

Roll, J. (1992) *Lone Parent Families in the European Community*, Luxembourg: Statistical Office of the European Communities.

Rose, H. (1976) 'Women's work: women's knowledge', in J. Mitchell and A. Oakley (eds) [1976].

Rose, N. (1986) *The Psychological Complex: psychology, politics and society in England 1869–1939*, London: Routledge and Kegan Paul.

Rose, R. (1976a) 'Social structure and party differences', in R. Rose (ed.) [1976b].

—— (ed.) (1976b) *Studies in British Politics*, London: Macmillan.

Royal College of General Practitioners (1974) *Oral Contraceptives and Health*, London: Pitman Medical.

—— (1990) *Mortality Statistics from General Practice 1981–82: third national study*, London: HMSO.

Rutter, M., Graham, P., Chadwick, O. and Yuk, O. (1970) 'Adolescent turmoil: fact or fiction?', *Journal of Child Psychology and Psychiatry* 17: 35–56.

Sahgal, G. (1989) 'Fundamentalism and the multiculturalist fallacy', in Southall Black Sisters (eds) *Against the Grain: Southall Black Sisters 1979–1989*, Southall: Southall Black Sisters.

Sapsford, R. J. (1993) 'Understanding people: the growth of an expertise', in J. Clarke (ed.) *A Crisis in Care? Challenges to social work*, London: Sage.

Sarsby, J. (1983) *Romantic Love and Society*, Harmondsworth: Penguin.

Sassetti, M. R. (1993) 'Domestic violence', in B. A. Elliott, M. D. Halverson and M. Hendricks-Mathews (guest eds) *Primary Care* 20 (2): 289–306.

Savage, W. (1986) *A Savage Enquiry*, London: Virago.

Sayers, J. (1986) *Sexual Contradictions: psychology, psychoanalysis and feminism*, London: Tavistock.

Scambler, G. and Scambler, A. (1984) 'The illness iceberg and aspects of consulting behaviour', in R. Fitzpatrick, T. Hilton, S. Newman, G. Scambler and T. Thompson (eds) *The Experience of Illness*, London: Tavistock.

Scott, J. (1995) *Sociological Theory: contemporary debates*, Aldershot: Edward Elgar.

Scully, D. and Bart, P. (1978) 'A funny thing happened on the way to the orifice: women in gynaecology textbooks', in J. Ehrenreich (ed.) *Cultural Crisis of Modern Medicine*, New York: Monthly Review Press.

Seager, J. and Olsen, A. (1986) *Women in the World: an international atlas*, London: Pluto Press.

Sears, J. (1992) 'Uptake of science 'A' levels: an ICI and BP sponsored project for ASE', *Education in Science* 149: 30.

Segal, L. (1987) *Is the Future Female?*, London: Virago.

Seidler, V. J. (1989) *Rediscovering Masculinity: reason, language and sexuality*, London: Routledge.

—— (1994) *Unreasonable Men*, London: Routledge.

Shaklady Smith, L. (1978) 'Sexist assumptions and female delinquency', in C. Smart and B. Smart (eds) *op. cit.*

Shapiro, R. (1987) *Contraception: a practical and political guide*, London: Virago.

Sharpe, S. (1976) *Just Like a Girl*, Harmondsworth: Penguin.

—— (1984) *Double Identity: the lives of working mothers*, Harmondsworth: Penguin.

—— (1995) *Just Like a Girl*, 2nd edn, Harmondsworth: Penguin.

Shaw, J. (1976) 'Finishing school: some implications of sex-segregated education', in D. Barker and S. Allen (eds) *Sexual Divisions and Society: process and change*, London: Tavistock.

Shelley, V. and Whaley, P. (1994) 'Women in science: access, experience and progression', in B. R. Singh (ed.) *Improving Gender and Ethnic Relations*, London: Cassell.

Siim, B. (1987) 'The Scandinavian welfare states: towards sexual equality or a new kind of dominance?', *Acta Sociologica* 30: 255–70.

Siltanen, J. and Stanworth, M. (1984) *Women and the Public Sphere: a critique of sociology and politics*, London: Hutchinson.

Silverstone, R. and Ward, A. (eds) (1980) *Careers of Professional Women*, Beckenham: Croom Helm.

Skeggs, B. (1995) 'Introduction', in B. Skeggs (ed.) *Feminist Cultural Theory: process and production*, Manchester: Manchester University Press.

Skelton, C. (1993) 'Women and education', in D. Richardson and V. Robinson (eds) *op. cit.*

—— (ed.) (1989) *Whatever Happens to Little Women?*, Milton Keynes: Open University Press.

Smart, C. (1976) *Women, Crime and Criminology*, London: Routledge and Kegan Paul.

—— (1995) *Law, Crime and Sexuality*, London: Sage.

Smart, C. and Smart, B. (eds) (1978) *Women, Sexuality and Social Control*, London: Routledge and Kegan Paul.

Smith, D. E. (1979) 'A peculiar eclipse: women's exclusion from men's culture', *Women's Studies International Quarterly* 1: 281–95.

—— (1987) *The Everyday World as Problematic: a feminist sociology*, Milton Keynes: Open University Press.

Smith, L. J. F. (1989) *Domestic Violence: an overview of the literature*, London: HMSO, Home Office Research Study No. 107.

Spencer, A. and Podmore, D. (eds) (1987) *In a Man's World*, London: Tavistock.

Spencer, H. R. (1927) *The History of British Midwifery from 1650 to 1800*. London.

Spender, D. (1982) *Invisible Women: the schooling scandal*, London: Writers' and Readers' Publishing Co-operative.

Springhall, J. (1983) 'The origins of adolescence', *Youth and Policy* 2.

Spring-Rice, M. (1939) *Working-Class Wives: their health and conditions*, London: Virago, 1981.

Spybey, T. (ed.) (forthcoming) *Britain in Europe*, London: Routledge.

Stanko, E. (1988) 'Keeping women in and out of line: sexual harassment and occupational segregation', in S. Walby (ed.) *Gender Segregation and Work*, Milton Keynes: Open University Press.

Stanley, L. (1984) 'Why men oppress women, or how experiences of sexism can tell us interesting and useful things about women's oppression and women's liberation', in S. Webb and C. Pearson (eds) *Looking Back: some papers from the BSA Gender and Society Conference*, Manchester: Manchester University Department of Sociology, Studies in Sexual Politics.

Stanley, L. and Wise, S. (1983) *Breaking Out*, London: Routledge and Kegan Paul.

—— (1993) *Breaking Out Again*, London: Routledge.

Stanworth, M. (1983) *Gender and Schooling: a study of sexual divisions in the classroom*, London: Hutchinson.

—— (1984) 'Women and social class analysis: a reply to Goldthorpe', *Sociology* 18: 159–70.

—— (1987a) 'Reproductive technologies and the reconstruction of motherhood', in M. Stanworth (ed.) *op. cit.*

—— (ed.) (1987b) *Reproductive Technologies: gender, motherhood and medicine*, Cambridge: Polity.

Stark, E. D, and Flitcraft, A. (1988) 'Violence among intimates: an epidemiological review', in V. B. Hasselt *et al.* (eds) *Handbook of Family Violence*, New York: Plenum.

Stone, K. (1983) 'Motherhood and waged work: West Indian, Asian and white mothers compared', in A. Phizacklea (ed.) [1983b].

Storey-Gibson, M. J. (1985) *Older Women around the World*, Washington: Washington International Federation on Aging.

Strauss, M. A. (1980) 'Victims and aggressors in marital violence', *American Behavioural Scientist* 23: 681–704.

Strauss, M. A. and Gelles, R. (1986) 'Societal change and change in family violence 1975–1985 as revealed in two national surveys', *Journal of Marriage and the Family* 48: 465–79.

Strauss, M. A., Gelles, R. and Stinmetry, R. (1980) *Behind Closed Doors: violence in the American family*, Garden City, NY: Anchor.

Sutherland, E. and Cressey, D. (1966) *Principles of Criminology*, Philadelphia, PA: J. P. Lippincott.

Taylor, I., Walton, P. and Young, J. (1975) *The New Criminology: for a social theory of deviance*, London: Routledge and Kegan Paul.

Taylor, P. J. and Johnstone, R. J. (1979) *The Geography of Elections*, Harmondsworth: Penguin.

Thomas, K. (1990) *Gender and Subject in Higher Education*, Buckingham: Open University Press.

Thorne, B. (1982) *Feminist Rethinking of the Family: an overview*, New York: Longman.

Tiano, S. (1987) 'Gender, work and world capitalism: Third World women's role in development', in B. B. Hess and M. M. Ferree (eds) *Analysing Gender: a handbook of social science research*, Beverly Hills, CA: Sage.

Tindall, V. R. (1987) *Jeffcoate's Principles of Gynaecology* (5th edn), London: Butterworth.

Toner, B. (1977) *The Facts of Rape*, London: Hutchinson.

Townsend, P., Phillimore, A. and Beattie, A. (1987) *Health and Deprivation: inequality and the North*, Beckenham: Croom Helm.

Tuana, N. and Tong, R. (ed.) (1995) *Feminism and Philosophy*, Oxford: Westview.

Tyler, M. and Abbott, P. A. (1994) 'The commodification of sexuality: sexualised labour markets', paper presented at a conference on 'Work Employment and Society', University of Kent, Canterbury.

United Nations (1989) *Violence against Women in the Family*, Vienna: United Nations, Centre for Social Development and Humanitarian Affairs.

Ussher, J. (1989) *The Psychology of the Female Body*, London: Routledge.

Versey, J. (1990) 'Taking action on gender issues in science education', *School Science Review* 71: 256.

Verslusyen, M. C. (1980) 'Old wives' tales? Women healers in English history', in C. Davies (ed.) *Rewriting Nursing History*, London: Croom Helm.

—— (1981) 'Midwives, medical men and "poor women labouring of child": lying-in hospitals in eighteenth-century London', in H. Roberts (ed.) *op. cit.*

Victor, C. (1991) *Health and Health Care in Later Life*, Milton Keynes: Open University Press.

Volman, M. and Van Ecke, E. (1995) 'Girls in science and technology: the development of a discourse', *Gender and Education* 7: 283–92.

Voronina, O. (1994) 'The mythology of women's emancipation in the USSR as the foundation for a policy of discrimination', in A. Posadskaya (ed.) *op. cit.*

Wajcman, J. (1994) 'Technology as masculine culture', in *The Polity Reader in Gender Studies*, Cambridge: Polity.

Walby, S. (1986) *Patriarchy at Work*, Cambridge: Polity.

—— (1988a) 'Gender, politics and social theory', *Sociology* 22: 215–32.

—— (1988b) 'The historical periodization of patriarchy', paper presented to the annual conference of the British Sociological Association, Edinburgh.

—— (1990) *Theorising Patriarchy*, Oxford: Blackwell.

Walker, A. (1992) 'The poor relation: poverty among old women', in C. Glendinning and J. Millar (eds) [1992].

Walkerdine, V. (1990) *Schoolgirl Fictions*, London: Verso.

Walkowitz, J. (1980) *Prostitution and Victorian Society: women, class and the state*, Cambridge: Cambridge University Press.

Wallace, C. (1987) *For Richer for Poorer: growing up in and out of work*, London: Tavistock.

—— (1989) 'Youth', in R. Burgess (ed.) *Investigating Society*, London: Longman.

Wallace, G. (1996) 'Personal communication', based on the findings of *Making Your Way Through Secondary School* research project.

Webb, C. (ed.) (1986) *Feminist Practice in Women's Health Care*, Chichester: Wiley.

Weiner, G. (1986) 'Feminist education and equal opportunities: unity or discord?', *British Journal of Sociology of Education* 7: 265–74.

—— (1994) *Feminisms in Education*, Buckingham: Open University Press.

Weiner, T. S. (1978) 'Homogeneity of political party preferences between spouses', *Journal of Politics* 40: 208–11.

West, J. (ed.) (1982) *Work, Women and the Labour Market*, London: Routledge and Kegan Paul.

Westwood, S. (1984) *All Day Every Day: factory and family in the making of women's lives*, London: Pluto Press.

Westwood, S. and Bhachu, P. (1988) *Enterprising Women: ethnicity, economy and gender relations*, London: Routledge.

Whitehead, M. (1987) *The Health Divide*, London: Health Education Council.

Williams, A. (1987) 'Making sense of feminist contributions to women's health', in J. Orr (ed.) *Women's Health in the Community*, Chichester: Wiley.

Williams, W. M. (ed.) (1974) *Occupational Choice*, London: Allen and Unwin.

Willmott, P. and Young, M. (1957) *Family and Kinship in East London*, Harmondsworth: Penguin.

Willis, P. (1977) *Learning to Labour*, Farnborough: Saxon House.

Wilson, E. (1977) *Women and the Welfare State*, London: Tavistock.

Wilson, E. S. (1985) 'Ingestible contraceptives', in N. Loudon (ed.) *op. cit.*

Wittig, M. (1979) 'One is not born a woman', in *Proceedings of the Second Sex Conference*, New York: Institute for the Humanities.

Witz, A. (1985) 'Patriarchy and the labour market: occupational control strategies and the medical division of labour', in D. Knights and M. Willmott (eds) *The Gendered Labour Process*, Aldershot: Gower.

Wollstonecraft, M. (1792) *A Vindication of the Rights of Women*, London.

Wolpe, A.-M. (1977) *Some Processes in Education*, Birmingham: Women's Research and Resource Centre, Explorations in Feminism 1.

—— (1988) *Within School Walls: the role of discipline, sexuality and the curriculum*, London: Routledge and Kegan Paul.

Women's National Commission (1985) *Violence against Women: report of an ad hoc working group*, London: Cabinet Office.

Wrigley, J. (1992a) 'Gender and education in the welfare state', in J. Wrigley (ed.) [1992b]

Wrigley, J. (ed.) (1992b) *Education and Gender Inequality*, Basingstoke: Falmer.

Yeandle, S. (1984) *Women's Working Lives: patterns and strategies*, London: Tavistock.

Young, M. and Willmott, P. (1973) *The Symmetrical Family*, London: Routledge and Kegan Paul.

Young, S. (1981) 'A woman in medicine: reflections from the inside', in H. Roberts (ed.) *op. cit.*

Youthaid (1981) *A Study of the Transition from School to Working Life* (vols 1–3), London: Youthaid.

Author index

Abbott, P. A. 27, 57, 58, 59, 61,
  63, 66, 68, 111, 139, 150, 151, 165, 166,
  189, 195, 198, 202, 203, 204, 205, 210,
  213, 214, 218, 220, 221, 276, 277, 278,
  282; *see also* Payne, G.,
  Sapsford, R. J.
Abel Smith, B. 187
Abrahams, J. 92, 96
Acker, J. 57
Acker, S. 93, 94, 95, 115
Ackers, L. 162: *see also* Abbott, P. A.
Adkins, L. 222, 223
Ahrendt, D.: *see* Jowell, R.
Allen, H. 235
Allen, I. 216
Allen, S. 57, 72, 210
Alvermann, D.: *see* Commeyres, M.
Amir, M. 252
Amos, V. 106
Anthias, F. 43, 45, 72, 75
Arber, S. 129, 131, 133, 136, 175, 182,
  198
Aries, P. 118
Arnot, M. 93
Ashton, D. N. 110, 111
Ashton, H. 166
Association for Science Education 98,
  99

Baldwin, S. 203
Ball, S. 92

Banks, O. 282
Barrett, M. 37–8, 52, 103, 105, 144, 160
Bart, P.: *see* Scully, D.
Bates, I. 84, 87, 105, 110, 111, 114, 115
Baudrillard, J. 44
Bayley, M. 202
Beattie, A.: *see* Townsend, P.
Beechey, V. 147, 195, 209, 222, 224
Benigni, L. 198
Bernard, J. 145, 162, 175
Best, S. 300
Beyres, T. J. 79
Bhachu, P.: *see* Westwood, S.
Bhavnani, K. 70, 71
Black Report 134, 165
Blackburn, C. 162
Blaxter, M. 166, 170
Blumberg, R. L. 79
Bonnerjea, L.: *see* Nissel, M.
Bonney, N. 69
Bordo, S. 11
Borkowski, M. 181
Boulton, M. 156
Bouquet, T. 250, 251
Bourlet, A. 253, 256
Bourque, S. 264
Bowlby, J. 156
Bowles, S. 104
Box, S. 229, 233, 235
Brah, A. 75
Brannen, J. 151

Subject index

Abortion 44, 157, 173–4, 179, 273
Adolescence 110–14, 117, 122–7
Age as socially constructed 117–19, 120,
  121, 122–3, 124–5, 126–7

'Bedroom culture': *see* Culture of
  femininity
Biological determinism 7–8, 10–11, 21,
  27–8, 39–40, 43, 45, 46, 70–1, 72, 117,
  121, 123, 128, 130, 147, 167, 176–7,
  199, 214, 228, 235, 249, 283
Black women and employment: *see*
  Ethnicity

Cervical cancer 166
Child abuse 156, 228, 247
Childbirth: *see* Pregnancy and childbirth
Child care 156, 210, 217
Class:
  Class and education 83, 84, 85, 90–1,
    93, 104–5, 106, 107
  Class, measures of:
    dominance principle 67
    Hope–Goldthorpe Scale 55, 56,
      62
    joint household measures 67, 69
    Registrar General's scale 55, 56
  Class position, derived 56–7, 58, 67,
    68
  Class theories, malestream: 53–6, 59,
    60–2

Marxist 53–4, 73
  Weberian 53, 55, 75
Class, women as a: *see* Feminism,
  materialist
Class, women's perceptions of 69
see also Feminism, Marxist;
  Feminism, materialist
Clerical work: *see* Women's occupations
Cohabitation 148–50
Community care 131, 161–2, 201–4, 214
Consciousness-raising 262
Constructivism: *see* Feminist
  epistemologies
Contraception 147, 154, 156–7, 161–4,
  167, 262–3
Co-research 288–9
Crime:
  biological theories 227–8, 235–6
  differential association 238, 239
  disorganisation theory 238–9
  environment and 228
  labelling theory 238, 240–2
  left realism 229
  new criminology 228–9
  radical feminism and 244
  social control 242–4
  statistics 229–34
Critical criminology 228–9, 232–5,
  239–40
Cross-class marriages 58, 67
Culture of femininity 115–16